MACEDONIA AND THE MACEDONIANS

STUDIES OF NATIONALITIES

Wayne S. Vucinich, founding General Editor of series

The Crimean Tatars
Alan Fisher

The Volga Tatars: A Profile in National Resilience
Azade-Ayşe Rorlich

The Making of the Georgian Nation
Ronald Grigor Suny
(copublished with Indiana University Press)

The Modern Uzbeks: From the Fourteenth Century to the Present; A Cultural History
Edward A. Allworth

Estonia and the Estonians, updated second edition
Toivo U. Raun

The Azerbaijani Turks: Power and Identity under Russian Rule
Audrey L. Altstadt

The Kazakhs, second edition
Martha Brill Olcott

The Latvians: A Short History
Andrejs Plakans

The Moldovans: Romania, Russia, and the Politics of Culture
Charles King

Slovakia: From Samo to Dzurinda
Peter A. Toma and Dušan Kováč

The Czechs and the Lands of the Bohemian Crown
Hugh LeCaine Agnew

Macedonia and the Macedonians: A History
Andrew Rossos

MACEDONIA AND THE MACEDONIANS

A History

Andrew Rossos

HOOVER INSTITUTION PRESS
Stanford University
Stanford, California

With its eminent scholars and world-renowned library and archives, the Hoover Institution seeks to improve the human condition by advancing ideas that promote economic opportunity and prosperity, while securing and safeguarding peace for America and all mankind. The views expressed in its publications are entirely those of the authors and do not necessarily reflect the views of the staff, officers, or Board of Overseers of the Hoover Institution.

hoover.org

Hoover Institution Press Publication No. 561

Hoover Institution at Leland Stanford Junior University,
Stanford, California, 94305-6003

First printing 2008
27 26 25 24 23 22 21 8 7 6 5 4 3 2

Library of Congress Cataloging-in-Publication Data
Rossos, Andrew, 1941–
Macedonia and the Macedonians : a history / by Andrew Rossos.
p. cm.—(Hoover Institution Press publication ; no. 561)
(Studies of nationalities)
Includes bibliographical references and index.
ISBN-13: 978-0-8179-4881-8 (cloth : alk. paper)
ISBN-13: 978-0-8179-4882-5 (pbk. : alk. paper)
1. Macedonia–History. I. Title. II. Series: Hoover Institution Publication ; 561. III. Series.
DR2185.R34 2008
949.5'6–dc22. 2007033666

ISBN 978-0-8179-4881-8 (cloth)
ISBN 978-0-8179-4882-5 (pbk)
ISBN 978-0-8179-4883-2 (epub)
ISBN 978-0-8179-4887-0 (mobi)
ISBN 978-0-8179-4888-7 (ePDF)

To the memory
of my grandparents
dedo DIČO *& baba* SOFA

Contents

Abbreviations

ARM	Army of the Republic of Macedonia
ASNOM	Anti-Fascist Assembly of National Liberation of Macedonia
AVNOJ	Anti-Fascist Council for the National Liberation of Yugoslavia
BAN	Bulgarian Academy of Sciences
BKF	Balkan Communist Federation
BKP	Bulgarian Communist Party
DA	Democratic Alternative
DPA	Democratic Party of Albanians
DPT	Democratic Party of Turks
DSE	Democratic Army of Greece
DUI	Democratic Union for Integration
EAM	National Liberation Front (Greece)
EC	European Community
EKS	Emigrant Communist Union
ELAS	National Popular Liberation Army (Greece)
EU	European Union
FYROM	Former Yugoslav Republic of Macedonia

ICG	International Crisis Group
INI	Institute of National History
JNA	Yugoslav National Army
KKE	Communist Party of Greece
KPJ	Communist Party of Yugoslavia
KPM	Communist Party of Macedonia
LP	Liberal Party
MAAK	Movement for All-Macedonian Action
MANU	Macedonian Academy of Sciences and Arts
MEFO	Macedonian Émigré Federalist Organization
MFRO	Macedonian Federalist Revolutionary Organization
MLK	Macedonian Literary Circle
MNK	Macedonian National Committee of the Macedonian Brotherhoods
MPC	Macedonian Orthodox Church
MPD	Macedonian Progressive Movement
MPO	Macedonian Political, Patriotic, after the Second World War, Organization of the United States and Canada
NATO	North Atlantic Treaty Organization
NDP	People's Democratic Party
NF	Popular Front
NFRJ	People's Federal Republic of Yugoslavia
NOB	National Liberation War
NOF	National Liberation Front
NOV i POM	National Liberation Army and Partisan Detachments of Macedonia
NRM	People's Republic of Macedonia
OF	Fatherland Front
OSCE	Organization for Security and Cooperation in Europe
OZNa	Department for the Protection of the People
PASOK	Panhellenic Socialist Movement
PDP	Party for Democratic Prosperity
PK na KPJM	Regional Committee of the Communist Party of Yugoslavia for Macedonia
PP or PPBOVMRO	Provisional Representation of the Former United Internal Macedonian Revolutionary Organization

RM	Republic of Macedonia
SDSM	Social Democratic Union of Macedonia
SFRJ	Socialist Federal Republic of Yugoslavia
SKJ	League of Communists of Yugoslavia
SKM	League of Communists of Macedonia
SKZ	Serbian Literary Society
SNOF	Slav-Macedonian National Liberation Front
SNOV	Slav-Macedonian National Liberation Army
SPC	Serbian Orthodox Church
SRM	Socialist Republic of Macedonia
SSRNJ	Socialist Alliance of Working People of Yugoslavia
UDBa	Administration of State Security
UN	United Nations
VMRO	Internal Macedonian Revolutionary Organization
VMRO (ob.[edineta])	Internal Macedonian Revolutionary Organization (United)
VMRO-DPMNE	Internal Macedonian Revolutionary Organization–Democratic Party of Macedonian National Unity

Maps

Preface

Macedonia is an ancient land in the central part, the heart, of the Balkan Peninsula. It controls the great north–south corridor route from central Europe to the Mediterranean along the Morava-Vardar valleys. It also possesses fertile agricultural lands in its many river valleys and plains, as well as the great port of Salonika (Thessaloniki). Both its strategic function and its economic value help account for its turbulent history.

Throughout the centuries, every power that aspired to dominate the Balkans, this crucial crossroads between Europe, Asia, and Africa, found it necessary and thus sought to control Macedonia. After the destruction of the remnants of the ancient Macedonian kingdom, successive invaders—Roman, Gothic, Hun, Slav, Ottoman—passed through or subjugated the area and incorporated it into their respective dynastic or territorial empires. The last, the Ottoman Turks, ruled Macedonia for over five hundred years, until the Balkan Wars of 1912–13.

More recently, in the age of imperialism and nationalism in the nineteenth and twentieth centuries, Macedonia became the peninsula's "bone of contention," its "apple of discord." After the Congress of Berlin in 1878, the so-called Macedonian question dominated Balkan politics, the central issue dividing the new and ambitious Bulgaria, Greece, and Serbia and their respective patrons among the great European powers.

Balkan nationalists—Bulgarian, Greek, and Serbian—who had already achieved independent or autonomous statehood from the Ottoman empire with aid from one or more great powers, chose to deny the existence of a separate Macedonian identity; indeed, each group claimed Macedonia and the Macedonians as its own. They fought over the territory, which remained under Ottoman sovereignty, with propaganda and armed force and against each other and the nascent Macedonian nationalists. The prolonged struggle culminated in 1913 with the forceful partition of Macedonia and the Macedonians after the Second Balkan, or Inter-Allied War between Bulgaria and allied Greece and Serbia. However, even after partition, the Macedonian question remained, and it continued to dominate Balkan politics and peoples until the Second World War and its revolutionary aftermath—and even to the present day.

Although Macedonia figured prominently in history, it remained a little-known land, virtual *terra incognita*, until the nineteenth century. To be sure, the battles and conquests of Alexander the Great of Macedonia had become legendary, but after the Romans conquered the last parts of ancient Macedonia in 168 BC the Macedonian name disappeared from the historical stage and consciousness. It became merely a geographical expression describing a disputed territory of indeterminate boundaries, which passed under the sovereignty of ambitious medieval Balkan dynastic and territorial states—especially Bulgaria, Byzantium, and Serbia. Briefly in the early eleventh century, Macedonia became the center of the most dominant Balkan state. However, Tsar Samuil, the native ruler of this "Macedonian kingdom" (George Ostrogorsky's label for it) and its ruling elite continued, for reasons of legitimacy, to call the state 'Bulgaria.' During centuries of Ottoman rule, authorities never used the Macedonian name even for administrative purposes.

A state took the appellation only in the mid-1940s, when Vardar (Serbian/Yugoslav) Macedonia—as the People's Republic of Macedonia (and later the Socialist Republic of Macedonia)—became a constituent of the Communist Yugoslav federation. After the collapse of federal Yugoslavia in 1991, it declared its complete sovereignty and independence as the republic of Macedonia.

Moreover, even less known was Macedonia's ethnically mixed population, especially its Slav-speakers or Slav Macedonians who, in the age of nationalism, became simply Macedonians. For almost thirteen hundred years, until ethnic cleansing and forced ethnic-national assimilation began early in the twentieth century, they comprised the largest ethno-linguistic group and the majority of the population on the territory of Macedonia. About mid–nineteenth century, their spokesmen began to adopt the land's name as their national name and symbol and embarked on the daunting process of building a nation.

The struggle for Macedonia—an irreconcilable competition for Macedonians' "hearts and minds" by Bulgarian, Greek, and Serbian nationalisms—did not increase the knowledge about and understanding of the land and its people. It only made a bad situation worse: it transformed ignorance into confusion. By denying Macedonian identity or by claiming the Macedonians, the Bulgarians, Greeks, and Serbs created two false but lasting perceptions: first, that the Macedonians were Bulgarians or Greeks or Serbs and, second, that Macedonia was a hopeless ethnic mix, a *mélange*.

Undoubtedly, through the centuries the population of Macedonia was ethnically mixed. However, in the age of nationalism the Macedonian Slavs, the largest ethnic group, began forming a national identity on the basis of their own ethnic (linguistic, cultural, and historical) attributes, their mythology, and their political, social, and economic interests, just as the Bulgarians, Greeks, and Serbs had recently done. Once one accepts and factors in this historical reality—the existence of the Macedonian Slavs, the Macedonians—their land no longer appears a "hopeless" ethnic mixture, as the neighbors' irredentist propaganda has claimed. Indeed, other areas in the Balkans, eastern Europe more generally, and Europe as a whole were just as mixed ethnically as parts of Macedonia.

This volume surveys the history of Macedonia from antiquity to the present day. As the title implies, and without in the least questioning or denying the existence and identity of many other ethnic groups in Macedonia—Albanians, Greeks, Roma, Vlachs, Turks, Jews, and so on—it focuses on the Slav-speaking Macedonians. The latter comprised the largest ethno-cultural group, the only one to adopt the land's name as its own in the age of nationalism, and the only one to seek to build a Macedonian nation.

Macedonia since the mid–nineteenth century has consisted roughly of the three Ottoman *vilayets* of Salonika, Monastir (Bitola), and Kosovo—approximately the ancient Macedonian kingdom. This has been the general geographic definition of Macedonia in Europe, in the Balkans, and among the spokesmen for the Macedonian national and revolutionary movements.

In accordance with the general aim of this Hoover Institution series on the histories of the peoples of east central Europe, my work stresses the modern era. As is evident from the table of contents, three-quarters of the volume relates to the age of nationalism and imperialism since about 1800.

This study represents a summation of my long-standing interest in Macedonia and the Macedonians. Their history, especially of the modern era, has preoccupied me for well over thirty years. During this lengthy period, I searched for sources in major research libraries in North America as well as in western and eastern Europe: the Hoover Institution on War, Revolution and Peace, Stanford, California; the New York Public Library; the Library of Congress; the University of Toronto libraries; the British Museum Library; the V. I. Lenin Library and the Fundamental Library of the Social Sciences of the Academy of Sciences of the USSR, both in Moscow; the Library of the Institute of National History, Skopje; the Library of the Institute for Balkan Studies, Salonika (Thessaloniki); the Slavonic Library, Prague; and the national and/or university libraries in Prague, Vienna, Belgrade, Sofia, Athens, Rome, and Skopje.

The largest relevant holdings are in various archives in Bulgaria and Greece. However, obtaining access there has been virtually impossible for scholars such as I who do not subscribe to the official Bulgarian and/or Greek position on Macedonian matters, which denies the formation and existence of the Macedonian national identity in all parts of Macedonia. Although I sought it, I did not obtain access to the archives in Greece. In the early 1980s, the Central Administration of the State Archives in Bulgaria gave me permission for research on the period before 1914 in the Manuscript Division of the National Library, the Archive of the Bulgarian Academy of Sciences, and the State (Diplomatic) Archives. Unfortunately, after my three weeks of strictly controlled research, it withdrew its consent—or, as a visibly embarrassed supervisor of the reading room in the State Archives informed me regretfully: "Your permission has been lifted."

Fortunately, however, on many occasions and for prolonged periods I was able to work elsewhere freely and in congenial surroundings. I am grateful to staff members at several institutions for generous assistance over the years: the Archive of Serbia and the Archive of Yugoslavia in Belgrade; the Archive of the Republic of Macedonia and the Archive of the Macedonian Academy of Sciences and Arts in Skopje; the Public Records Office in London and Kew Gardens; the National Archive and Records Service in Washington, D.C.; and the Archive of the Ministry of Foreign Affairs in Rome.

I would like to record in particular my gratitude to the late W. S. Vucinich, "Uncle Wayne," my mentor at Stanford University, and to the late Peter Brock, for many years my senior colleague at the University of Toronto, for their thoughtful advice and long-standing and sincere interest in my work. The late Elisabeth Barker, Hugh Seton-Watson, and L. S. Stavrianos, as well as my Macedonian colleagues Blaže Ristovski, Stojan Kiselinovski, and Jovan Donev, encouraged me constantly, especially when the unavoidable problems and complexities in studying the Macedonians' history almost overwhelmed me.

I would like to thank Victoria University in the University of Toronto for a Senate Grant to complete the preparation of the manuscript, John Parry for his editorial assistance, and the Cartography Office, Department of Geography, University of Toronto, for producing the maps.

Finally and most important, I wish to thank profoundly and with great affection my wife, Cecilia, and our daughters, Monica and Veronica, for their patience, understanding, and love. They seemed never to tire of hearing about Macedonia and the Macedonians.

MACEDONIA AND THE MACEDONIANS

1 Land and People at the Crossroads

Land

Macedonia is in the central part of the Balkan Peninsula. Its geographical boundaries have varied with time, but since the nineteenth century, when the "thorny" Macedonian question began to obsess the new Balkan states, Greece, Serbia, and Bulgaria, and the chancelleries of the great powers of Europe, they have been clear and have received general recognition.

Geographic Macedonia's border consists of the mountains of Šar Planina, Skopska Crna Gora, Kozjak, Osogovo, and Rila to the north; the western slopes of Rhodope upland and the lower Mesta (Nestos) River to the east; the Aegean Sea and the Aliakmon (Bistrica) River to the south; and the Gramos massif, Lake Prespa, and Lake Ohrid, and the Korab and Jablonica range, to the west, toward Albania. Macedonia covers about 67,741 square kilometers, or about 15 percent of the Balkan Peninsula.

Throughout recorded history, Macedonia has been a strategic and economic crossroads. The Vardar-Morava valley forms the most direct and most natural highway and corridor-route from central Europe to the Mediterranean and to the Near East and the Suez Canal. Macedonia also controls the best approaches to the Drin valley routes leading to the Adriatic Sea. The Via Egnatia—the shortest Roman-era cross-Balkan route from Durrës (Durazzo, Drač) on the Adriatic to the Bosphorus—passed through Ohrid, Bitola (Monastir), and Salonika (Thessaloniki) on the way to Constantinople (Istanbul). Finally, the imperial powers in Constantinople/Istanbul could reach their possessions further afield in Greece, Albania, Serbia, Bosnia, and elsewhere only through Macedonia.

The Balkan Wars of 1912–13, particularly the Second Balkan, or Inter-Allied War, led to the first violation of Macedonia's territorial integrity since dynastic states fought each other in the medieval Balkans and the Ottoman empire conquered the region in the late fourteenth and early fifteenth centuries. In 1913, force of arms partitioned Macedonia between the kingdom of Bulgaria and the allied kingdoms of Greece and Serbia. This arrangement, with minor modifications, survives to this day.

Serbia—"Yugoslavia" after the Great War—took Vardar Macedonia, about 25,775 square kilometers. After 1945, as the People's Federal Republic of Macedonia and, after 1971, as the Socialist Federal Republic of Macedonia, that region formed one of six republics of the Communist-led federal Yugoslavia. Following the violent collapse of the federation, it proclaimed its complete sovereignty and independence as the republic of Macedonia in 1991.

In 1913, Greece acquired Aegean Macedonia, at about 34,000 square kilometers the largest piece of Macedonian territory. Bulgaria took the smallest part, Pirin Macedonia, with about 6,778 square kilometers. Albania, a state that the great powers created in 1912, received the relatively small areas of Mala Prespa and Golo Brdo. Albania, Bulgaria, and Greece have completely absorbed their portions, not recognizing them even as distinctive, let alone autonomous.

In geographic Macedonia, large and high mountain ranges give way to wide, flat valleys and plains. Deep ravines and lakes—Ohrid, Prespa, Dojran, Besik, and Lagodin—interconnect the valleys. Vardar Macedonia is largely a plateau lying from 2,000 feet to 8,000 feet (610 meters to 915 meters) above sea level, with mountains (Jakupica) reaching 8,331 feet (2,541 meters). The main valleys are those of the Vardar, the lower Bregalnica, and the lower Crna rivers. The Kožuf and the Nidže ranges, with Mt Kajmakčalan as the highest peak (8,271 feet, or 2,526 meters), divide Vardar from its southern neighbor, Aegean Macedonia. In the latter, the coastal belt lies along the Aegean Sea, as do the flat and extensive plain of Salonika and the plains of the lower Sruma (Strymon) River and of Kavala. The border between Aegean and Pirin Macedonia consists of two valleys—of the Sruma (Strymon) and the Mesta rivers—that cut the Belasica (Oros Kerkni) range, whose peak (Radomir) reaches 6,655 feet (2,230 meters). Between these two river valleys to the south rises the wild and, in Macedonian folklore, legendary Pirin massif. To the west, the Maleševski and the Osogovski ranges separate Pirin and Vardar Macedonia, with the Strumica valley connecting the two.

Macedonia lies almost entirely between latitudes 40 and 42 degrees north. It is a transitional climatic zone. The climate in the south and the great river valleys is Mediterranean; in the north, continental. Summers are hot and dry; rainfall is relatively low: about 700 millimeters (27.56 inches) annually in the west, 500 millimeters (19.69 inches) in the east and along the sea coast, and only 450 millimeters (17.72 inches) in the middle, Vardar region.

The climatic, soil, and moisture conditions principally determine the variety of vegetation and crops. There are olive groves in the extreme south; deciduous trees, such as oak, chestnut, and beech, further to the north; and conifers in the high ranges of the Rhodopes and Pelister. Pasturelands occur both in the lowlands and in higher altitudes, and raising of sheep and cattle is common and valuable throughout. The chief crops are wheat, barley, maize, potatoes, and central European fruits; Mediterranean products, such as rice, grapes, olives, and figs; and industrial cultures such as tobacco, cotton, and opium poppies. The lakes and rivers provide rich fishing, and the mountains and forests, hunting grounds.

Mineral resources abound. Lead and zinc underlie the Kratovo-Zletovo massif and the Chalcidice Peninsula; iron ore, Kičevo and the Demir Hisar basin; lime and manganese ore, the mountains near Kičevo; and antimony and arsenic ores, the Mariovo and Meglen districts. There are also deposits of talc, magnesite, asbestos, mica, quartz, gravel, quartzite, and silex and large quantities of granite, basalt, travertine, and marble.[1]

People

There are few pre-1800 statistics on Macedonians' ethnicity. And the existing Ottoman estimates for the nineteenth century reflect the em-

Map 1 Macedonia in East Central Europe

pire's *millet* system of organization, which focused on religious affiliation, not on ethnic belonging. For example, before the establishment of the separate Bulgarian exarchate in 1870, the Orthodox *millet* included all of the sultan's Orthodox subjects, regardless of ethnicity.

Post-1850, pre-1913 sources on the ethnic composition of Macedonia—the Ottoman *vilayets* (provinces) of Salonika, Monastir, and Kosovo—are notoriously unreliable and confusing. Mostly Bulgarian, Greek, or Serbian, they reflect those countries' claims on Macedonia's Slavic-speaking inhabitants. Nonetheless, all but the Greek sources find the Slavic speakers, the Macedonians, the majority of the population before 1913. On the basis of "a fairly reliable estimate in 1912," the British Foreign Office cited the following figures, with Slavic-speaking Macedonians by far the largest group and about half of the total: Macedonian Slavs 1,150,000, Turks 400,000, Greeks 300,000, Vlachs 200,000, Albanians 120,000, Jews 100,000, and Gypsies (Roma) 10,000.[2]

Because the Bulgarians, Greeks, and Serbs did not recognize Macedonians as a separate ethnic group or nationality, gauging ethnographic structure became virtually impossible after partition. The Bulgarians continued to claim all Macedonians as Bulgarians. The Greeks and Serbs moderated their claims; the former claimed only the Macedonians of Aegean Macedonia as Greeks, or Slavophone Greeks, and the latter only those of Vardar Macedonia as Serbs, or South Serbs. Consequently, the interwar censuses could not include a Macedonian category but treated Macedonians as Bulgarian, Greek, and Serbian nationals, respectively.

All pre-1913, non-Greek statistics find Macedonians the largest single group in Aegean Macedonia. The figures range from 329,371, or 45.3 percent, to 382,084, or 68.9 percent, of non-Turks, and from 339,369, or 31.3 percent, to 370,371, or 35.2 percent, of the total population of approximately 1,052,227 inhabitants.

The region's number of Macedonians began to decline in both absolute and relative terms during the Balkan Wars. The process accelerated after 1918 under Greek plans to transform the region's ethnic structure. Policies included colonization, internal transfers of Macedonians, and "voluntary" (with Bulgaria) and compulsory (with Turkey) exchanges of populations, or what we now call "ethnic cleansing." By the mid-1920s, removal of 127,384 Macedonians and settlement of 618,199 Greeks (most of them refugees from Asia Minor) had completely changed the ethnography of Aegean Macedonia. Macedonians had become an unrecognized minority in their own land.

Greece's census of 1928, and its successors, presented the kingdom as ethnically homogeneous. It classified Macedonians as "Slavophone" Greeks and cited only 81,984 of them—a figure far too low in the light of all the non-Greek, pre-1913 statistics.[3] The 1951 census, the first after the Civil War (1947–49), by which time the Greek state had become even more oppressive and repressive vis-à-vis Macedonians, recorded only 47,000 Slavophones—an equally unreliable and misleading figure. Today, some Macedonians in the region, in the diaspora, and even in the

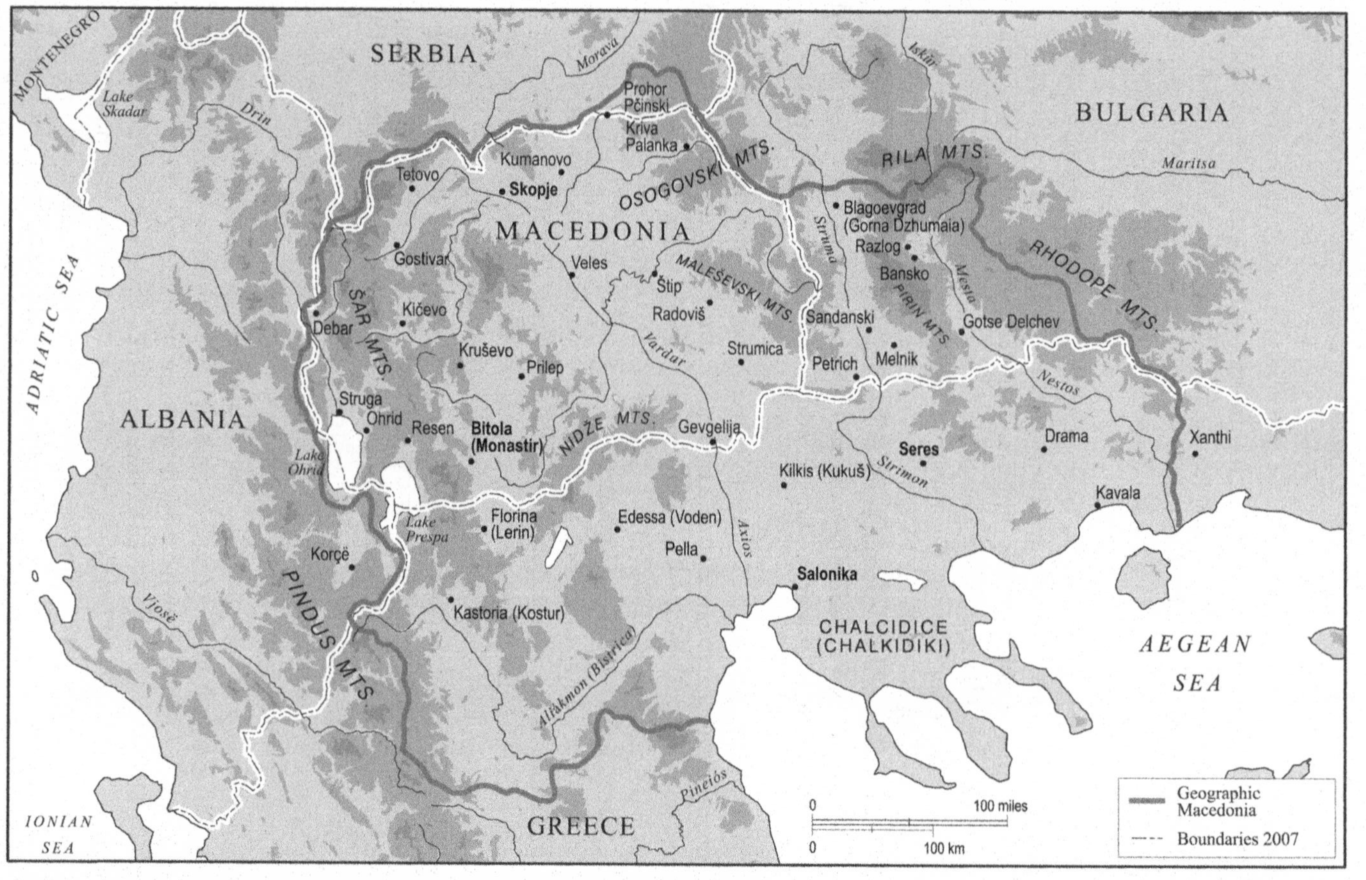

Map 2 Geographic Macedonia

republic of Macedonia claim some half-million Macedonians in Aegean Macedonia. More-reasonable estimates suggest 350,000 or even as few as 150,000–200,000, but even these are educated speculation at best.[4]

Clearly, long-standing denial, repression, and forced assimilation have affected numbers. Yet, despite these policies and against overwhelming odds, the Aegean-Macedonian minority has survived. And since Greece's return to democracy in the mid-1970s, and especially the country's accession to the European Community (now Union) in 1981, its members have formed semi-legal or illegal cultural associations and political organizations. However, their numbers will remain unfathomable unless and until Athens officially recognizes this minority's existence and ends its repressive and discriminatory policies.

Macedonians in the other three parts of their divided homeland also experienced discrimination, repression, and forced de-nationalization and assimilation, but not the mass-scale ethnic "engineering" of their Aegean counterparts. They constituted majorities in their regions between the wars and may do so even today.

In 1945, Bulgaria's new Communist-led government renounced the royalists' position and recognized a Macedonian nation. The 1946 census allowed Macedonians in Pirin Macedonia and in Bulgaria as a whole to declare their nationality as such. Authorities did not publish figures for these people, but Macedonian sources say that 252,908 respondents claimed such nationality. (In 1991, the Bulgarian embassy in London reported to Hugh Poulton that "169,544 people registered themselves as Macedonians in 1946.") In the census of 1956, 178,862 people declared themselves Macedonian—63.7 percent of Pirin Macedonia's 281,015 inhabitants.

Communist Bulgaria maintained recognition of Macedonians officially until Stalin and Tito split in 1948 and unofficially until 1956. However, in April 1956 the Communist Party abandoned that stance and returned to the country's prewar policy of negation. The census of 1965 showed only 8,750 self-declared Macedonians; later censuses did not mention that nationality.[5] After the collapse of Communism in Bulgaria in 1989–90, Macedonian activists formed illegal and semi-legal cultural and political associations and organizations demanding national and civil rights. However, as in Aegean Macedonia, so in Bulgaria, credible estimates of Macedonians' numbers remain unachievable as long as the state denies their existence and continues its policies.

Until very recently, we knew little about the Macedonians in Mala Prespa and Golo Brdo in Albania. In the interwar years, the Albanian authorities showed very little interest in them but did not deny their existence. Apparently only the Internal Macedonian Revolutionary Organization (Vnatrešna Makedonska Revolucionerna Organizacija, or VMRO) paid any attention to them. Communist Albania recognized these Macedonians and allowed the teaching of their language in their area, but purposely underestimated their numbers. Official census statistics claimed only 4,235 of them in 1960, 4,097 in 1979, and 4,697 in 1989. Yugoslav and/or Macedonian sources are equally inaccurate for the region, citing figures between 55,000 or 60,000 and 140,000.[6] An internationally organized, financed, and monitored census in Albania might provide an accurate estimate of the Macedonian minority and of the country's ethnic composition.

As long as Vardar Macedonia was a republic in the Communist-led federal Yugoslavia (i.e., 1944–91), the regime recognized all ethnic groups, and the country's ethnic composition was a matter of record. Censuses may not have been perfect, but the international community generally accepted and respected them. Through those years, ethnic Macedonians comprised consistently about two-thirds of the total population of Vardar Macedonia.

According to the newly independent republic's 1994 census, which involved international monitors and has received extensive analysis and general acceptance, Macedonia had 2,075,196 inhabitants. Ethnic Macedonians numbered 1,288,330 (66.5 percent), Albanians 442,732 (22.9 percent), Turks 77,252 (4 percent), Roma 43,732 (2.3 percent), Serbs 30,260 (2 percent), and Vlachs 8,467 (0.04 percent). The remainder consisted of small minorities, which included Croatians, Bosnians, and Bulgarians.[7]

Despite official Bulgarian and Greek denials, in addition to the Macedonians in the republic of Macedonia, there are Macedonian minorities in Aegean Macedonia, Pirin Macedonia, and Mala Prespa. However, the number of Macedonians in geographic Macedonia remains a mystery as long as Bulgaria and Greece deny their existence and they, and Albania, do not carry out fair, internationally monitored censuses.[8]

PART ONE

FROM ARGEAD KINGDOM TO OTTOMAN VILAYETS (c. 600 BC–c. AD 1800)

Chapter 2 looks at Macedonia's ancient history in terms of four periods: the kingdom's early years (c. 600–359 BC); expansion and empire under Philip II and Alexander IV, the Great (359–323 BC); the division and decline of Alexander's vast empire (323–168 BC); and rule by Rome and from AD 395 its successor, Byzantium, and the Goth and Hun invasions (168 BC–c. AD 600).

The rest of part I considers Macedonian history to about 1800. In chapter 3, after the Slavs penetrated the Balkans between the third and the sixth centuries, challenging Byzantine hegemony, they began settling in Macedonia after about AD 600. At various times over the next eight centuries, Macedonia experienced both independence and domination by neighbors—Bulgaria, Byzantium, and Serbia.

Next, another rising regional power—the Ottoman empire, Muslim successor to Byzantium—conquered the Balkan Peninsula; it took Macedonia about 1400, and in 1453 it finally won Byzantium/Constantinople, which it renamed Istanbul. Chapter 4 examines four centuries of Ottoman rule, to about 1800.

2 From Argeads to Huns (c. 600 BC–c. AD 600)

The territory of geographic Macedonia has had inhabitants since the early Neolithic era (c. 6000 BC). The scanty archaeological evidence indicates two powerful influences shaping its development: the Aegean-Anatolian and the central European and internal Balkan. By the late Neolithic (c. 4000–c. 2800 BC), central and western Macedonia had sizeable populations, and the Early Iron Age (c. 1050–c. 650 BC) "probably saw the establishment of the basic ethnic pool from which the historical Macedonians and their neighbors were derived."[1] The first inhabitants about whom information exists were Illyrian and Thracian tribes.

Historians still debate the origin of the Macedonians. Most recent archaeological, linguistic, toponomic, and written evidence indicates gradual formation of the Macedonian tribes and a distinct Macedonian identity through the intermingling, amalgamation, and assimilation of various ethnic elements. The Macedonians invaded the autochthonous peoples of the lower Danube—Illyrians, Thracians, and later Greek ethnic elements. Thracians probably dominated the ethno-genesis of Macedonian identity.[2]

The Macedonians developed into a distinct ethnic people with a language or dialects, about which we know very little, and customs of their own. They were different from the Illyrians to the north and northwest, the Thracians to the east and northeast, and the culturally more advanced Greeks to the south, in the city-states. By the fourth century BC, official communication took place in Greek; court and elite gradually became Hellenistic by embracing aspects of Greek culture. However, the Macedonians remained themselves: "they were generally perceived in their own time *by Greeks and themselves not to be Greeks*."[3]

Insofar as the Macedonians embraced and used philhellenism, they did so to enhance their own interests.[4] Indeed, "many [members of the] Macedonian elite may have talked like Greeks, dressed like Greeks, but they lived and acted like Macedonians, a people whose political and social system was alien to what most Greeks believed, wrote about, and practiced."[5]

In any event, as E. Borza has pointed out, "the bloodlines of ancient people are notoriously difficult to trace. Besides, determining the exact ethnic make-up of the ancient Macedonians is not historically significant. However, . . . they made their mark [on world history] not as a tribe of Greeks or any other Balkan peoples, but as Macedonians."[6]

The Early Kingdom (c. 600–359 BC)

Historians know little about the early history of the first Macedonian state. Many assume that it formed gradually from the early seventh century BC on. Its establishment started about 700 BC when Macedonian tribes under King Perdiccas I (founder of the Argead dynasty) began their migration from western and northwestern 'Upper' Macedonia to the central area of the plain of 'Lower' Macedonia.

The core of this Macedonian state was and remained the region between the rivers Ludias and Axius (Vardar), which included its first and later capitals—Aegae, Edessa (Voden), and Pella. From there, the kingdom expanded in all directions. In the process, it subjugated the Macedonian mountain tribes to the west and north and conquered, assimilated, or expelled the Thracian, Greek, and other indigenous peoples to the north and east. Under Philip II (359–336 BC), it reached its maximal extent, covering virtually all of geographical Macedonia—almost all of what today is Aegean (Greek) Macedonia and most of Vardar Macedonia (now the republic of Macedonia) and Pirin (Bulgarian) Macedonia.[7]

Evidence about Perdiccas's successors until about 500 BC is extremely scarce. State formation and expansion apparently led these rulers to war constantly with neighboring tribes. The Illyrians seem to have been their most determined opponents, especially during the reigns of Argaeus (c. 654–645 BC) and Philip I (644–640 BC). In the second half of the sixth century BC, Macedonia fell under Persian rule, and the dynasty's sixth ruler became and remained a Persian vassal.

Under his son and successor, Alexander I (c. 498–454 BC), Macedonia became much more active in the political life of the eastern Mediterranean. His byname, the "philhellene," shows his appreciation of the culture of the Greek city-states, and he began the Hellenization of Macedonian court and elite.

Until the battle of Plataea (479 BC), when Macedonia regained independence from Persia, Alexander I played up to both sides in the Persian Wars to further his dynasty and state. He took advantage of the fighting to subdue the independently minded princes of Upper Macedonia. Moreover, he captured the Greek colony of Lydua and pushed his eastern frontiers to the lower Strymon (Struma) River, an area with rich mineral—particularly silver—deposits. Athens's long-standing ambition to control the entire Thracian coastal area inevitably clashed with Macedonia's pursuit of an exit to the sea.[8]

In the second half of the fifth century BC, Macedonia's political and economic development seemed vulnerable to Athens's growing power as head of the Delian confederation and the leading Greek power and to its Thracian allies. However, Alexander I's son and successor, the politically astute and skillful Perdiccas II (454–413 BC), ably used to Macedonia's advantage the intensified antagonism and struggle for hegemony among the Greek city-states, especially between the two chief rivals, Athens and Sparta. He allied himself early on with Athens; next with the old Greek and Thracian cities along the Aegean coast in the north against Athens; then with Brasidas, the famous Spartan leader; and still later with Athens again. In short, he became master at playing off the Greek rivals against each other to safeguard his kingdom's power and economic influence.

The Peloponnesian Wars (431–404 BC), which exhausted the Greek city-states, especially Athens, without resolving any of their problems, created a more stable environment for further Macedonian consolidation. Archelaus I (c. 418 or 413–399 BC), son and successor to Perdiccas II, implemented reforms to enhance the court's power and the state's unity. He transferred the capital to Pella, almost on the sea, near the estuary of the Axius (Vardar) River and with far greater political and economic growth. Greek architects designed the court, to which the ruler invited leading Greek artists and writers; it became a center for the spread of Greek cultural influence. Archelaus built roads and fortresses, reformed the army, and modernized its equipment. In foreign policy he maintained friendly relations with Athens and established a solid basis for Macedonian influence in Thessaly, the gateway to the Greek world.

However, his reign ended in 399 BC and gave way to almost four decades of instability, internal anarchy, and foreign interventions. Macedonia experienced three rulers in the 390s and six more before Philip II became king in 359 BC. During this time, Macedonia faced threats from the Illyrians in the north and the Chalcidic League in the east. Amyntas III (c. 390–370 BC), the era's only ruler of any stature, allied himself with the Spartans and with their aid defeated and dissolved the League. His son, Alexander III (c. 369–368 BC), however, oversaw defeat of the Macedonians and their expulsion from Thessaly by the forces of its Chalcidic League ally, Thebes. The period of weakness ended with the death of his brother Perdiccas III (365–359 BC) fighting the Illyrians.

Expansion and Empire (359–323 BC)

Philip II (359–336 BC), their younger brother, launched the kingdom's most glorious era. He transformed the country from a weak and fragmented land to Balkan dominance.[9] He weakened the clan aristocracy and centralized administration. His financial reforms, including introduction of a gold coin, spurred growth of trade and commerce and made Macedonia a political and economic factor in the eastern Mediterranean. He reorganized the army; modernized its training, tactics, and weaponry; and harnessed it for territorial expansion.

In the late 350s BC, he fought the Paionians and the Illyrians, expanded to Lake Lychnida (Ohrid) in the northwest, and secured access to the sea by capturing trading centers on the Macedonian and Thracian littoral. Although he thereby threatened the interests of Greek city-states, particularly Athens, the latter could not retaliate. As before the ruinous Peloponnesian Wars, deep rivalries divided the Greek city-states, with alliances frequently changing and wars too common.

The long-lasting crisis in the Greek world and the existence of its pro-Macedonian factions helped Philip establish hegemony there. Between 356 and 338 BC, he conquered Thessaly, Chalcidice, and then Thrace. At the decisive battle at Chaecronea in 338 BC, he crushed the combined Greek forces, under Athens and Thebes, and subjugated all of the peninsula. In the Congress of Corinth, which Philip soon summoned, the city-states recognized the hegemony of Macedonia.[10]

Philip planned to turn next to the east and fight the common enemy, the Persian empire. His untimely assassination in 336 BC thrust that task onto his able 20-year-old son and successor, Alexander IV, the Great (336–323 BC). Alexander led his armies on an extraordinary march eastward. In three major battles between 334 and 331 BC, he destroyed the might of the Persians. By 331 BC, after his victory at Gaugamela, he was master of the Near and Middle East. He had fulfilled his father's plans and ambitions.

Alexander's motivations and intentions after this victory (and the murder of Darius III the following year) are difficult to determine, and historians still debate them. Alexander proclaimed himself successor of the Persian "King of Kings" and marched his wary and discontented troops further and further east through Central Asia. By the time his rebellious troops balked at going any further, he had conquered a vast empire stretching from the western Balkans east to India and from the Danube and the Black Sea south to Egypt, Libya, and Cyrenaica. His death of fever at Babylon in 323 BC, on his painful return journey, ended his triumphal march and launched the collapse of his virtually ungovernable empire.[11]

Division and Decline (323–168 BC)

Alexander's successors long struggled for the spoils, from 323 until 281–277 BC. By then, Macedonian rulers governed three Hellenistic states in Alexander's former empire: the Seleucids in the former Persian empire in Asia, the Ptolemies in Egypt, and the Antigonids in Macedonia, including mainland Greece. This cultural fusion of Greek, Egyptian, and Persian elements dominated the eastern Mediterranean and embodied the Hellenistic Age, lasting until the Roman conquest in 168 BC.

Alexander's campaigns and the posthumous struggles greatly weakened Macedonia, which lacked political authority and stability, had exhausted its human resources, and lost its economic strength. In the third century BC, the Antigonids oversaw recovery and consolidation. Antigonus II Gonatas (277–239BC) restored the monarchy's authority. His successors Demetrius II (239–229 BC) and Antigonus III Doson (229–221 BC) fought rebellious Greek city-states and the Achaean and Aetolian Leagues and reimposed uneasy control. When Philip V (221–179 BC) became king, Macedonia again dominated the Balkans and was the strongest factor in the eastern Mediterranean.[12]

By then, however, Macedonia's real competitor for Balkan hegemony was no longer its weak and divided neighbors or the Greek city-states, but powerful Rome. The Romans, already in control of the western Mediterranean, wanted to expand eastward and openly courted Macedonia's neighbors and opponents.

The unavoidable struggle between these two great powers terminated in the so-called Macedonian Wars, which took place over almost half a century. In the first conflict (215–205 BC), Philip V, who sought access to the Adriatic, attacked the Roman client state in Illyria and fought a coalition of Greek and neighboring states. Philip secured relatively favorable peace terms, but the war changed little: Rome was not a direct participant in the war but in the long run benefited the most. Philip's inability to assist his ally Hannibal completely isolated the Carthaginian, with whom Rome was waging a mortal struggle.

In the second Macedonian War (200–197 BC), the Romans invaded the Balkans to support the anti-Macedonian coalition there. Philip's army did well until a disastrous defeat at Cymoscephalae in Thessaly in 197 BC. The humiliating peace treaty forced Macedonia to recognize the independence of the Greek city-states. Macedonia's hegemony over the Balkans and its dominance in the eastern Mediterranean were over.

During the third Macedonian War (168 BC), Persius (179–168 BC), Philip V's successor and the last Macedonian ruler, sought to create an effective coalition before the final confrontation with the Romans. Despite Balkan weariness with Rome's overwhelming influence and presence, he failed to bring these states together, winning over only the kings of the Illyrians and Odrisians. In the war's only and decisive encounter, the powerful Roman army, under Consul Lucius Aemilius Paulus, crushed the Macedonians. The battle, near Pydna on 22 June 168 BC, ended Macedonian independence and launched Roman rule, which was to last under Rome and its successor, Byzantium, until the Slavic incursions of the sixth century AD.[13]

Roman and Byzantine Rule, Goths, and Huns (168 BC–c. 600 AD)

Applying the rule *divide et impera*, Rome split Macedonia into four weak, autonomous republics, or Meridiams. It denied them the right to links of any kind and rendered them totally dependent on Rome, which exploited them. Oppression provoked a massive mid-century revolt under Andriscus, a son of Persius's. Disgruntled Thracian tribes joined the Andriscus Rebellion. After its suppression in 148 BC, Rome deprived Macedonia even of its nominal autonomy and transformed it into a Roman province; a Roman administrator governed it, with the four sections as administrative units. As Rome's first province in the Balkans, it became a center for the empire to project its strategic interests in the eastern Mediterranean.

During the many centuries of Roman rule, the geographic-ethnic conception of Macedonia changed frequently as administrative units shifted. The province originally included parts of Illyria, Thessaly, and Epirus. Late in the republic (first century BC), it extended to the Rhodope Mountains in the east, stretched almost to the Danube in the north, and included Illyria in the west. After Augustus created two types of provinces (senatorial and imperial) in 27 BC, Macedonia became a much smaller, senatorial province. The reform of Emperor Diocletian (AD 285–305) saw incorporation of Macedonia into the diocese of Moesia; and under Constantine (AD 306–337) it became part of the prefecture of Illyria. By the late fourth century AD, sources refer to two provinces: Macedonia Prima and Macedonia Salutaris. Late in the fifth century AD, Macedonia Prima had Salonika as its capital, and Macedonia Seconda, Stobi. After the division of the Roman Empire in 395 AD, Macedonia, like most of the Balkans, became part of the Eastern, or Byzantine empire.[14]

The frequent changes in the geographic and administrative definition of Macedonia between 168 BC and the sixth century AD went hand in hand with shifting ethnic structure. Under Alexander the Great, and as a result of his eastern campaigns, the Macedonian element in the population declined. After his death, the Antigonids' migration and resettlement policies strengthened the Greek segment.

The upper strata of Macedonians, Thracians, and Illyrians were culturally Hellenizing. Conquest led many Roman officials and colonists to settle in Macedonia, and Romanization began. In the empire's last centuries, Macedonia experienced the effects of the Barbarian migrations and invasions. In the third–fifth centuries AD, Goths invaded and devastated Macedonia; in the fourth and fifth, the highly mobile Huns did the same.

In the sixth century, Slavic tribes began to invade and settle in large and growing numbers. Unlike the Goths and Huns, however, they planned to stay. They gradually assimilated the older inhabitants and altered permanently the ethnic structure of Macedonia. Available sources and evidence indicate that until the early twentieth century these Macedonian Slavs comprised the largest ethno-linguistic group in geographical Macedonia.[15]

3 Medieval, Slavic Macedonia (c. 600–c. 1400)

The Byzantine Commonwealth

The Slav invasions of the Balkans in the sixth and seventh centuries AD launched a new phase in Macedonia's history. The Slavs settled throughout geographic Macedonia in huge numbers, largely absorbed the indigenous local inhabitants, and, most important, imposed on them their Slavic speech. Until well into the twentieth century, the Slavic speakers—the Slav Macedonians, or, in the age of nationalism, the Macedonians—comprised the largest linguistic-ethnic group.

Throughout the medieval period, until the Ottoman conquest at the end of the fourteenth century, Macedonia and its Slavs were integral components of Obolensky's "Byzantine Commonwealth."[1] The neighboring Slav tribes to the north and northeast fell in the late seventh and early eighth centuries to the Bulgars—a Finno-Tatar horde of warrior horsemen. The more numerous Slavs, however, assimilated their conquerors but took their name. The Bulgarians also belonged to the multiethnic, multilingual Christian Orthodox Commonwealth, as did the Slav tribes to the north and northwest—the future Serbs. However, unlike the Bulgarians and the Serbs, the Macedonian Slavs did not form a medieval dynastic or territorial state carrying their name.

True, the powerful, but short-lived empire of Tsar Samuil (969–1018) centered in Macedonia under a largely domestic ruling elite. This

"Macedonian kingdom," as the great Byzantologist Ostrogorsky refers to it, "was essentially different from the former kingdom of the Bulgars. In composition and character, it represented a new and distinctive phenomenon. The balance had shifted toward the west and south, and Macedonia, a peripheral region in the old Bulgarian kingdom, was its real center." However, for reasons of political and ecclesiastical legitimacy, crucial in the Middle Ages, Samuil and the Byzantines thought it part of the Bulgarian empire, and so it carried the Bulgarian name.[2]

Consequently, in almost all of the Middle Ages Macedonia and its Slavic inhabitants belonged to one or another of three dynastic or territorial states of the Byzantine Commonwealth—Bulgaria, Byzantium, and Serbia.[3] That the medieval Macedonian Slavs, like many other European peoples, did not establish a long-lasting, independent, eponymous political entity became significant much later, in the age of nationalism and national mythologies. In the nineteenth and twentieth centuries, such romantic ideologies sought to explain—to legitimize or to deny—national identities, aims, and programs by linking present and past. Bulgarian, Greek, and Serbian nationalists justified their modern nations' existence and their imperialistic ambitions—including their claims to Macedonia—by identifying their small, ethnically based states with the territorial, dynastic empires of the Middle Ages.

By the same token, they denied the existence or the right to exist of a separate Macedonian identity and people. They seemed to argue that the absence of a medieval state bearing that name meant that a Macedonian identity and nation did not and could not exist, and each claimed the Slav Macedonians as its own. That was the essence of the three nations' struggle for Macedonia and for its people's hearts and minds—the so-called Macedonian question—in the age of nationalism (see chapters 5–6).

Contrary to romantic nationalists' claims, however, the medieval Balkan states were not national in the modern sense, and any connection between them and the ethnically based modern states is tenuous at best. As Jean W. Sedlar points out: "The abstraction which in modern times is called a 'state'—namely a territory and people under a common government—was a concept foreign to the Middle Ages. The medieval mind was accustomed to thinking in the more human and concrete framework of loyalty to the person of the monarch. . . . The dynastic idea was an important component of power throughout all of medieval East Central Europe."[4] Or, as Barbara Jelavich writes: "The government represented

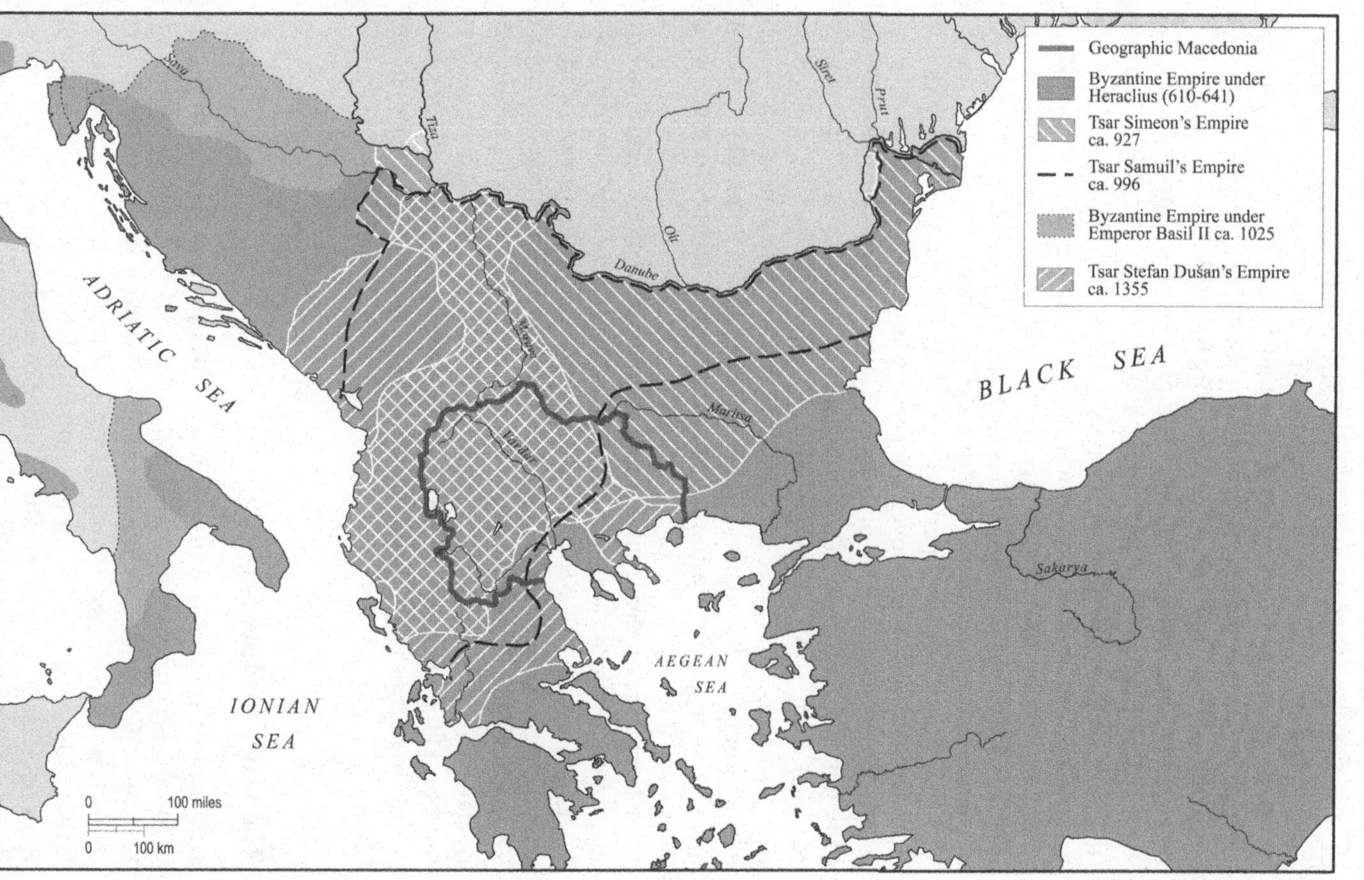

Map 3 Medieval Political Boundaries in Macedonia

primarily alliances of strong nobles around a central leader. . . . Feudal loyalties rested on the mutual interest of the most powerful men in the state in the protection and extension of its frontiers."[5]

Attachment to religion, family, and place played a much greater role in medieval Europe than did ethnic identity. Even the word "nation" (the Latin *nation)* referred not to people of similar language and cultural heritage, but to a group possessing certain legal privileges.[6] The masses of the population identified themselves not by nationality, but rather by family, religion, and locality. They considered religion, not nationality, as the primary source of any group's identification.

Even more important perhaps was political loyalty—"most often an expression of fidelity to a sovereign person, not an emotional attachment to a cultural or linguistic community. Governments were the creations of reigning dynasties and their associated nobilities, not the product of national feeling. Medieval monarchies typically assumed a supranational attitude, since their allegiance belonged to the dynasty, not to the ethnic group."[7] "Sovereigns happily annexed lands inhabited by people alien in language and custom both to themselves and to the majority of their own subjects."[8]

Clearly, the modern, small, ethnically bound Balkan states had little in common with the large territorial or dynastic medieval empires.

In any event, irrespective of shifting political affiliations, the Macedonian Slavs shared in the fortunes of the Byzantine Commonwealth. They contributed to the common Orthodox civilization and, more particularly, to the common south Slav Orthodox cultural heritage, and they benefited from both. Like all peoples whose ancestors belonged to the Byzantine Commonwealth, they can claim it as their common heritage.

The Slavic Invasions

Between the third and sixth centuries, Slavs from northeastern Europe gradually penetrated and settled the Balkans, challenging Byzantine supremacy. We know little about the Slavs' history before then. Any records begin rather late, with the works of Jordanes and Procopius, the leading historians of the sixth century. Indeed, sources on the Middle Ages, especially for the Balkan south Slav societies, are rather scarce, mostly of Byzantine origin, and religious in nature.

Most scholars believe that the Indo-European-speaking Slavs originated north of the Carpathians, between the river Vistula in the west and the river Dnieper in the east, in lands today in (west to east) eastern Poland, northwestern Ukraine, and southwestern Belarus. During the first century AD, the slow spread began of these numerous, closely related, often-feuding tribes, with no central organization but a shared worship of nature and a common language or closely related dialects.

The Slavs moved in three directions and evolved into the three groupings (western, eastern, and southern) of the Slav world. Some migrated westward (today's Czechs, Poles, Slovaks, and the remaining Slavs of eastern Germany), some eastward (Russians, Ukrainians, and Belorussians), and still others, southward to the Balkans (Slovenes, Croatians, Serbians, Montenegrins, Bosnians, Macedonians, and Bulgarians).

It appears that the Slavs heading south crossed the Carpathians and approached the basins of the Danube and the Sava in the second century. They moved slowly, however, and in small groups and, unlike previous nomadic, transitory invaders, were looking for land to occupy and settle. For a time, the Visigoths ruled them, and then the Huns, who destroyed the state of the Visigoths in 375. Late in the fifth century, the Slav invaders reached and began to occupy the banks of the mid- and lower Danube, the frontier of eastern Roman, or Byzantine Europe.

Throughout the sixth century, they repeatedly crossed the Danube and roamed, ravaged, and plundered Byzantine possessions from the Adriatic to the Black Sea. In the second half of the century, taking the lead from their overlords, the Avars—a Mongolian, or Turco-Tatar tribe that had established a powerful state in the area—they extended their raids and plunder further to the south. They penetrated as far as the Peloponnesus, reached even the island of Crete, and threatened the walls of Constantinople. On numerous occasions in 584 and 586 and four more times in the following century (616, 618, 674, and 677), they unsuccessfully attacked Salonika, the empire's second largest, most important, and wealthiest center.

The Byzantine rulers, struggling with Persia in the east, could not block the gradual, but massive and continuous Slav infiltration of their Balkan possessions. They could not destroy the Slav danger in battle and resorted to various defensive measures. They set up garrisons in the towns and cities and, during the brilliant reign of Justinian I (527–65), built a series of fortresses and watchtowers along the Danube and strengthened urban defenses. Such policies undoubtedly slowed the Slavs' southward movement.

By the end of the sixth century, large numbers of Slavs were settling throughout the Balkans. Finally, in 629 Emperor Heraclius (610–64) accepted the inevitable and irreversible and permitted them to settle in certain areas, frequently close to existing Slavic settlements. For their part, the new arrivals, under the rule of their chiefs, acknowledged Byzantine sovereignty and agreed to pay tribute and perform certain military tasks.

During the seventh century, the Slavs colonized virtually the entire peninsula, except for some of the larger cities and most of the Mediterranean coast, which retained a Greek character. The Slav tribes that penetrated farthest south, into Greece proper, came under its culture, and the more numerous Greeks gradually absorbed them. However, the Slavs controlled the Adriatic coast and its hinterland and became dominant in the central Balkans, between the Aegean, the Danube, and the Black Sea.

Slav colonization changed the region's ethnic character. The original inhabitants suffered losses in battle and absorption and assimilation by Slavs, who displaced them and forced them into smaller, safer areas. Illyrians escaped or were forced south, into the remote areas of present-day Albania. Latinized Thracians and Dacians had to retreat and found safety in the mountains. Their descendants emerged centuries later and survive today in mountainous regions of Albania, Greece, Macedonia, and Bulgaria as Vlachs (Kutsovlachs, Tsintsars, and so on), speaking a Latin language akin to modern Romanian.[9]

The rest of this chapter looks at five phases of Macedonia's medieval history. First, by the early seventh century, Macedonian Slavs occupied most of the land and absorbed the native inhabitants; by the early ninth century, Byzantium reasserted control. Second, in the mid–ninth century, Macedonia became part of the Bulgarian empire. Third, about 971, Tsar Samuil created a Macedonian empire, though with traditional Bulgarian titles, and it lasted until 1018. Fourth, Macedonian Slavs adopted Christianity, and their culture became a cradle of Slav Orthodoxy. Fifth, in the four centuries or so after 1018, a number of powers ruled Macedonia: Byzantium again to the 1070s, and thereafter variously Bulgaria, Epirus, the Normans, Serbia, and others, until the Ottoman conquest about 1400.

Macedonia (c. 600–c. 850)

Macedonia was one of the peninsula's first areas where Slavs settled. Except for major cities such as Salonika, Seres, Edessa (Voden), and Veroia (Ber), numerous Slav tribes had colonized all of Macedonia by the 610s. The Berziti settled northwestern Macedonia, around the upper Vardar River; to their east, along the middle and lower Struma River, lived the Strumjani. Further east, along the Mesta River and the Thracian-Macedonian border, were the Smoljani; to the southwest, along the Aegean and in the Chalcidice Peninsula east of Salonika, the Rinhini; and around that city, the Sagudati. The area west of Salonika and along the Aliakmon (Bistrica) River toward Veroia (Ber) and northwest toward Pelagonia became home to the Dragoviti. Southern Macedonia, bordering on Thessaly, was territory of the Velegeziti.

By the second half of the sixth century, Byzantine writers referred to these Slavic-settled areas in Macedonia as Sklavinii (Sklavinias) and often identified a Sklavinia with a particular tribe—for example, the Sklavinia of the Dragoviti, or the Dragovitia. The Sklavinii had tribal chieftains or elders to whom Byzantine sources ascribed Byzantine titles such as *archon* and *exarch*. Their Slav titles remain unknown.

The relationship between the Sklavinii and the Byzantine empire was in flux. Until the mid–seventh century, the Sklavinii recognized the nominal sovereignty of the Byzantine emperors but in effect governed themselves and, as their attacks on Salonika showed, frequently fought their overlords. In 658, Emperor Constantine II (641–68) decisively defeated the Sklavinii besieging Salonika and forced them to acknowledge the real authority of the Byzantine state.

However, the struggle for control of the Sklavinii continued. At the end of the seventh century, it became part of the wider struggle in the peninsula, when the new Bulgarian state in the northeast began to challenge Byzantium for control not only of the Macedonian Sklavinii but also of Constantinople itself. In the war with Byzantium from 809 to 811, the Bulgarian ruler, Khan Krum, with Avar and Sklavinii support, defeated the army of Emperor Nikiforus I (802–11). In 814, the Sklavinii joined Krum's army that marched on Constantinople. Krum's unexpected death ended the advance and allowed Byzantium to establish its real sovereignty and rule over the Sklavinii in Macedonia.

During the next forty or so years, the empire extended its *theme* administrative and military system into all of Macedonia, consolidating its direct control there for the first time since the Slav invasions and settlement. The new dispensation eliminated the Sklavinii; the last Byzantine reference to a Sklavinia relates to events in 836–37.[10]

For Byzantium, Macedonia's complete reintegration into the empire's administrative and military structure was crucial. Macedonia controlled its communication between the Adriatic and Constantinople (i.e., between its western and eastern halves) as well as the main route to the north, into central Europe. Moreover, unlike some of the empire's outlying Slav-settled areas, Macedonia and its Sklavinii were close to Byzantium and could challenge its stability and security. Their very proximity also made it easier for the imperial authorities to establish and maintain real control over them. Their strategic location may also help explain why the Macedonian Sklavinii did not develop a more advanced politics or state.

Bulgarian Rule (864–971)

As we saw above, early in the ninth century the growing power of the Bulgar rulers was challenging Byzantium's authority in Macedonia and throughout the Balkans. The Bulgars, a Finno-Tatar horde of mounted warriors, had crossed the lower Danube in 679. They conquered the lands north of the Balkan mountains—the province of Moesia—which had been home to Slavic tribes, and founded a state of their own. Emperor Constantine IV recognized it in 681. Although militarily powerful, the Bulgar conquerors were few, and by the ninth century the far more numerous and culturally more advanced Slavs absorbed and assimilated them.

From the very outset, the Bulgar rulers of the new state sought to expand south and southwest at the expense of the Byzantine empire. We saw above Khan Krum's military campaigns (802–14) in Macedonia and Thrace and his march on Constantinople. The Bulgarian offensive against Byzantium resumed and continued with even greater vigor under Khan Presian (836–52) and Khan Boris (852–89). Taking advantage of Byzantium's wars with the Arabs, Presian invaded the lands of the Smoljani, and he conquered much of northern Macedonia.

Boris continued the expansion, taking over the upper Struma valley as well as the Bregalnica valley and extending his state across the Vardar into western Macedonia. His peace treaty with Byzantium in 864 kept him a large part of Macedonia. In return, he swore to accept Christianity from Constantinople rather than from Rome, with Orthodox Christianity his state's official church and religion.

This medieval territorial state, or the first Bulgarian empire, reached its zenith under Tsar Simeon (893–927), Boris's second son. Simeon, who had had a superb education in Byzantium and admired its culture, harbored great ambitions and aspired to the imperial throne in Constantinople. He extended his frontiers in every direction: to the Sava and Drina rivers, into Serbian lands in the northwest, to the Adriatic in the west, into Macedonian and Albanian lands in the southwest, and into Thrace in the southeast. He assumed the title "Tsar of the Bulgars and Autocrat of the Romans [Greeks]"[11] and became master of the northern Balkans and probably the most powerful ruler in eastern Europe. However, his numerous campaigns against Constantinople failed; he could not seize the imperial crown. When he died in 927, he left his vast, multiethnic empire in a state of exhaustion and rife with internal dissension.

According to the peace agreement with Byzantium that Simeon's son and successor, Tsar Peter (927–69), concluded in 927, Bulgaria returned some Byzantine lands, and Constantinople recognized Peter as "Tsar of the Bulgarians." However, Bulgaria did not return the Macedonian lands that Presian, Boris, and Simeon had conquered, and Byzantium acknowledged them as Bulgarian possessions. And Byzantium began to refer to and treat the Macedonian Slavs as Bulgarian subjects, and Byzantine historians and chroniclers soon followed suit.[12]

The Macedonian lands became part of the Bulgarian military-administrative system of provinces, which Boris and Simeon had devised and in which the state chose the governors. Similarly, Bulgaria introduced its methods of administering the church and religious institutions. This centralization of secular and religious authority in Macedonia, which Byzantium started and the Bulgarians continued, gradually broke down the self-governing tribal and later territorial communal system of the Macedonian Sklavinii. It also launched a feudal system, with power in the hands of a wealthy land-holding administrative-military ruling elite and rich land-holding religious institutions, at the cost of the vast peasant majority's descent into poverty and servility.

During Tsar Peter's reign, political divisions within the ruling elite and a potent combination of religious heresy and mass popular unrest and discontent—Bogomilism—weakened the empire; Bogomilism in fact threatened the foundations of both state and church. It started in Macedonia, and its founder was a priest *(pop)*, Bogomil (Theophilus, or Dear to God). It mixed primitive, Old Testament Christianity and dualistic teachings that the Paulicians imported from the Near East. Its adherents believed in the eternal struggle between good, or the human soul that God creates, and evil, or the body and the material world, the work of Satan. They rejected the rituals, doctrines, and organization of the established church and denounced the ecclesiastical hierarchy.

In a medieval society, such beliefs and teachings had dangerous political, social, and economic implications; indeed, the movement was also a revolt against the secular feudal order. As Presbyter Cosmas, its most determined enemy, wrote: "They teach their own people not to obey their lords, condemn the *boyars*, regard as vile in the sight of God those who serve the tsar, and forbid every servant to work for his master." And, as Obolensky stressed: "The Bogomils were not only in revolt against the authorities of the church and the hierarchical structure of Bulgarian society but, by preaching civil disobedience, urged the people to rebel against the established political order."[13]

Church and state persecuted the Bogomils ruthlessly and violently, but the heresy spread to many areas of the Byzantine world and survived in the Balkans—in Macedonia, Serbia, and particularly Bosnia—until the Ottoman conquest in the late fifteenth century. In the second half of the twelfth century, it also influenced heretical movements in western Europe, such as the Albigensians in Italy and France.

Late in Tsar Peter's reign, the empire faced external threats from the military might of Byzantium in the southeast and of Prince Sviatoslav of Kievan Rus in the northeast. In July 971, the Byzantine emperor and military leader John I Tzimisces (969–76) routed the forces of Sviatoslav, Byzantium's former ally, at Silistria on the Danube. Thus the emperor saved Bulgaria from the Rus threat, but Bulgaria paid dearly. John I Tzimisces soon dethroned Tsar Peter's son and nominal successor, Boris II (969–71), annexed Bulgaria and Raška (the Serbian lands), and in effect shut down the Bulgarian empire of Simeon and Peter.

Tsar Samuil's Macedonian Empire (971–1018)

After the death of Tsar Peter and the collapse of central authority in Bulgaria, four brothers seized power in the Macedonian lands. David,

Moses, Aaron, and Samuil, or the so-called *cometopuli* (young counts, or princes), were the sons of *Comes* (count or prince) Nikola, governor of a Macedonian province and an influential official in Tsar Peter's state.[14] Historians know little about the rule of the cometopuli during the reign of John I Tzimisces in Byzantium. The brothers controlled the Macedonian lands, or the southwestern territories of the former Bulgarian empire, but exact boundaries are not clear. Sources say almost nothing about relations between them and Byzantium or the emperor. The emperor seems to have left them in peace after taking over the other former Bulgarian lands.

When John I Tzimisces died in 976, his throne went to Basil II (976–1025).[15] The same year, the four cometopuli organized a revolt against Byzantium in Macedonia. Soon "the rising took on serious proportions and became a war of liberation, which spread over the whole of Macedonia and sought to remove the greater part of the Balkans from Byzantine rule." At first the brothers ruled jointly, but after the two oldest, David and Moses, were killed, Aaron and Samuil fought for power. In the end, "the heroic Samuil," younger but more able politically and militarily, eliminated his brother. "Samuil became the founder of a powerful empire which had its center first at Prespa and later at Ochrida" (Ohrid) in Macedonia.[16]

A man of enormous vigor, determination, and ambition, Samuil took advantage of Byzantium's weak state, its internal strife, and its preoccupation with the Arabs in the east and struck first in a southerly direction. He attacked Seres and Salonika, launched repeated incursions into Thessaly, and plundered Greek lands as far south as the Bay of Corinth. His first major success was the capture of Larissa in 985 or early 986, after a siege of several years. Basil II's counter-offensive in Bulgaria ended in disaster; Samuil devastated the retreating Byzantine cavalry and infantry at the so-called Trojan's Gate (today's Ihtiman) on 17 August 986.

In the following decades, while Basil II had to concentrate on the renewed and more intense civil war in Byzantium, Samuil extended his rule throughout the Balkans, from the Adriatic to the Black Sea. He consolidated his position in Bulgaria and secured part of Albania and Epirus. He captured Durrës (Dyrachium, Durazzo), marched into Dalmatia, plundered and laid waste to the coast as far north as Zadar, and annexed Dioclea (Montenegro) and Raška (Rascia). And even though in 997, on his return from an invasion of Greece, his army suffered defeat in central Greece at the hands of the outstanding Byzantine general Nicephorus Uranius, and he himself narrowly escaped death, in the late 990s Samuil had attained the pinnacle of his power. He was master of most of the Balkans: "gradually [he] built a kingdom . . . which by the end of the century comprised most of the former Bulgarian lands between the Black Sea and the Adriatic, with the addition of Serbia up to the lower Sava, Albania, Southern Macedonia, Thessaly and Epirus."[17]

This large territorial empire centered in Macedonia; its capital was first on an island in Lake Prespa and later in Ohrid, and it had an ethnically diverse population. In addition to the Macedonian Slavs and the Slavs of Greece, it included Bulgarians, Serbs, Croats, Greeks (Byzantines), Albanians, and Vlachs. There were also Romans (Italians) on the Adriatic coast and Vardariot Turks and Armenians, whom Samuil settled in Polagonia, Prespa, and Ohrid.

Samuil proclaimed himself tsar of the multi-ethnic "Samuil's State,"[18] or "Macedonian Kingdom."[19] A representative of Pope Gregory V (996–99) probably crowned him. And since a great and powerful state had to have its own church, he established the archbishopric of Ohrid, and Rome probably invested the first incumbent. As Ostrogorsky, Obolensky, and others stressed, this "Macedonian kingdom was essentially different from the former kingdom of the Bulgars." However, since "apart from Byzantium, only Bulgaria at that time possessed a tradition of empire with a patriarchate of its own," for reasons of legitimacy Samuil sought recognition and acceptance as a direct successor of the empire of Simeon and Peter. Hence the title "Tsar of the Bulgars" for Samuil, 'Servant of God'; his empire and the Ohrid archbishopric bore Bulgarian names.[20] These names had no real or symbolic ethnic, let alone national, significance but acquired importance in the nineteenth century, in Bulgarian and Greek romantic nationalist, anti-Macedonian political discourse and historiography (see chapters 5–6).

Samuil's Macedonian kingdom, or empire, survived relatively briefly. His opponent, Basil II, an exceptional ruler in charge of the enormous resources and great tradition of the Byzantine state, was eager to destroy him and reconquer his lands. After AD 1000, with internal order and stability in the empire and peace with the Arabs, Basil began to implement his carefully prepared military plan for an all-out offensive. In a series of campaigns he forced Samuil's armies to retreat, gradually conquered the non-Macedonian lands, and finally struck at the heartland. He moved first into Bulgaria; his armies captured the old Bulgarian capitals Pliska and Great and Little Preslav and occupied Danubian Bulgaria. Then, in 1001, his forces marched through Salonika toward Veroia (Ber) and seized Thessaly.

Next he turned north, toward Macedonia, and, following a difficult struggle, captured the strategic and naturally well-fortified city of Edessa (Voden). In 1002, he prepared to invade Macedonia from the north. After an eight-month siege, he captured Vidin, the strategic fortress on the Danube, and his troops advanced south toward Skopje. When they reached the Vardar, Samuil had set up camp on the other side, not far from Skopje. He was confident that the Byzantine forces would not be able to cross the swollen river. However, they did; Samuil's surprised troops fled in disarray without resistance, and Basil secured Skopje's surrender. By 1005, when Byzantium took Dyrachium (Durazzo, Durrës), Samuil found himself besieged in his shrinking heartland. "The Byzantine state, backed by centuries-old tradition, had once again shown its superiority. The valiant tsar could not match the skillful military leadership, organization and technical resources of the old empire."[21]

Historians know little about the two warlords' clashes in the next decade. However, a detailed record survives of their final battle for control of the Balkans, on 29 July 1014. Ostrogorsky recounted it well and succinctly: "Samuil's army was surrounded in a narrow pass of the Belasica mountain, the so-called Kleidion, in the region of the upper Struma; it is true that the tsar managed to escape to Prilep, but a large number of his army were killed and still more were taken prisoner. Basil the Bulgaroctonus celebrated his victory in a terrible fashion. The captives—allegedly numbering fourteen thousand—were blinded, and were then dispatched in batches of a hundred men, each group having a one-eyed man as a guide, to their tsar in Prilep. When Samuil beheld the approach of this gruesome cavalcade, he fell senseless to the ground. Two days later [6 October 1014] the gallant tsar was dead."[22]

Samuil's family and empire soon crumbled. His son and successor, Gabriel Radomir, perished less than a year later at the hands of his first cousin John (Jovan) Vladislav—Aaron's son—who also killed Gabriel's wife and his brother-in-law John (Jovan) Vladimir of Deoclea (Montenegro). John Vladislav continued resisting until his own death in February 1018, during the siege of Dyrachium (Durrës, Durazzo). In the following months, Basil II received the submission of the tsar's widow, other members of the royal family, and most of the nobles and crushed the resistance of some of Samuil's commanders.

By the summer of 1018, when Basil entered Samuil's capital, Ohrid, the four-decades-long struggle was over. Samuil's Macedonian kingdom was no more; Macedonia would remain under direct Byzantine rule for two centuries. The Byzantine empire was master of the Balkans for the first time since the Slav occupation.

Macedonia: Cradle of Slav Orthodox Culture

The last two hundred years of the first millennium profoundly shaped the historical evolution of east, west, and south Slavs. The Slavs experienced active contact with the more advanced Christian world. They officially adopted its religion, either from Rome or Constantinople, along with its culture and civilization. From then on, western Roman Catholicism or eastern Orthodoxy shaped their historical development.

Early on, Macedonia became a major religious and cultural center and as such played a role in the cultural beginnings of all the Slavs. And it made a special contribution to the common cultural heritage of the Slavs of the Orthodox Byzantine Commonwealth during what Dvornik calls the "Golden Age of Greco-Slavonic civilization."[23]

Christianity arrived in Macedonia during the Roman era. St. Paul engaged in missionary activity in the area, and Macedonian urban centers were among the first in the Mediterranean region to embrace the faith. By the fourth century, Christianity was flourishing all over Macedonia. The invasion and settlement of pagan Slavs in the area over the next few centuries altered the situation, but only temporarily. The papacy began missionary work among them in the seventh century, and the patriarchate of Constantinople continued such efforts.

Macedonia probably became the focal point of Byzantine proselytizing. Its extremely high concentration of Slav settlers lived very close to Constantinople and Salonika, the empire's major political and religious cities, and it controlled the routes linking Byzantium with its western territories. Its Christianization almost guaranteed imperial power in the area. The Slavs of southern Macedonia, closest to the Byzantine centers, became Christian well before the mid–ninth century; those in the north followed suit later in the century, after conquest by the new Bulgar state.

Macedonia became a cradle of Slav Orthodox culture. There must have been efforts to convey Christian teachings to the Slavs in their own language during this period. Constantine (monastic name: Cyril) and Methodius—two brothers from Salonika, the 'Apostles of the Slavs' and later saints—represented the pinnacle of this process. These linguists were sons of the military deputy commander of the Salonika region and received an excellent education. Cyril was librarian to the patriarch of Constantinople and taught philosophy at the palace school or university in the city. Methodius was a high-ranking administrator and diplomat. They must have learned the speech of the Macedonian Slavs in their childhood. Their native Salonika "was in the ninth century a bilingual city," with many Slavic inhabitants and Slav communities all around. According to one source, even the emperor believed that "all Thessalonians speak pure Slav."[24]

In 862, at the request of the Moravian prince Rostislav (reigned 846–70), Byzantine emperor Michael III (842–67) named the two brothers to lead a Slavic-language mission to take the Christian faith to the Moravians. Before departing, Cyril invented the so-called Glagolithic alphabet and adapted it to the speech of the Salonika-area Macedonian Slavs. Cyrillic script emerged later, probably in Bulgaria, from disciples of Methodius. It was simpler than the Glagolithic and more resembled the Greek alphabet. All Orthodox Slavs still use Cyrillic.

In the ninth century, Slav dialects were very similar, and so the Moravians and all the other Slavs could understand the Macedonian dialect. Cyril, Methodius, and their disciples then translated the Holy Scriptures and liturgical books into this Slavic language. "The dialect of the Macedonian Slavs was thus promoted to be a literary language and was adapted to the needs of the Slavs first in Great Moravia and later in other regions."[25]

The Moravian mission did not succeed. Rome's German bishops and missionaries, influential in central Europe, prevailed in Great Moravia. In 870, Prince Svatopluk, an ally of the pro-German party, overthrew his uncle Prince Rostislav and sealed the mission's fate. Cyril had died of a broken heart in 869 in Rome. Methodius, whom the German bishops had imprisoned for nearly three years, continued the struggle, but after his death in 885 Moravia drove out his disciples.

However, the brothers' linguistic and literary work and legacy transformed the Slavic world. From the Macedonian Slav dialect and a Greek model, they created a new literary language, Old Church Slavonic, "the literary language of all Slavs in the oldest period of their cultural evolution."[26] Moreover, as Obolensky writes, that tongue "became the third international language of European people . . . who gained entry into the Byzantine commonwealth." Cyril and Methodius established the foundations of a "composite Graeco-Slav culture," which served as "a channel for the transmission of Byzantine civilization to the medieval peoples of Eastern Europe."[27] Or, as Ostrogorsky stresses: "For the southern and eastern Slavs this achievement was of undying significance. These people are, indeed, indebted to the brothers from Thessalonika, 'the Apostles of the Slavs', for their alphabet and for the beginnings of their national literature and culture."[28]

After leaving Moravia, many of the brothers' most prominent disciples returned to the Balkans. Tsar Boris welcomed them to his newly Christian, rapidly expanding Bulgarian state, where they helped spread the new faith and Byzantine culture. The most outstanding among them were Kliment (died 916) and Naum (died 910), later saints. About 886, Kliment went to Ohrid, in southwestern Macedonia, as a teacher; in 893, Tsar Simeon made him bishop. Kliment's life-long friend and collaborator Naum succeeded him.

Under their leadership and direction, Ohrid and its district became the cradle of Slavic liturgy, literature, and culture, long before Tsar Samuil made the city his capital and an archbishopric. They founded the famous Ohrid Literary School, which continued the endeavors of Cyril and Methodius in spreading Byzantine Christianity and civilization among the Slavs. Unlike in Preslav, the Bulgarian capital, where Cyrillic became the official alphabet in 893, the Glagolithic survived co-equal "in the geographically remote and culturally more conservative Macedonian school founded by Clement."[29]

Under Kliment and Naum's guidance, the Ohrid Literary School trained about 3,500 teachers and priests. It also continued translating religious texts from Greek into Old Church Slavonic and maintained the Salonika brothers' high literary standards. Indeed, "few, if any, of the subsequent translations into that language equaled those of Cyril and Methodius and their immediate disciples, carried out in Constantinople, Moravia and Macedonia."[30] Kliment himself wrote many sermons, prayers, hymns, and songs of praise to God, Christ, the Mother of God, and so on. Finally, both Kliment and Naum helped build many churches and monasteries. They introduced Byzantine architecture, decorative arts, and music to Orthodox Slavs.

The quality of work from the Ohrid Literary School declined after the deaths of Naum (910) and Kliment (916). Nevertheless, the institution remained a cultural center of the southern Slavs through the twelfth century and, to a lesser extent, until the abolition of the Ohrid archbishopric in 1767 by the Ottoman sultan and the patriarch of Constantinople.

At its height, under Kliment and Naum and their immediate disciples, however, the Ohrid Literary School helped disseminate Byzantine civilization among the Orthodox Slavs. Indeed, it played a role in creating the common Byzantine-Slavic culture, which all Orthodox south Slavs shared throughout the Middle Ages, whoever their rulers.

Byzantine Rule and Chaos (1018–c. 1400)

Basil II's policy after 1018 toward his new Balkan conquests was rather conciliatory. He divided Samuil's empire into *themes* and integrated them into his imperial military administration. Much of Macedonia, the heart of Samuil's state, now formed the *theme* Bulgaria, with its capital at Skopje. Paradoxically, Bulgaria proper, along the lower Danube, became the *theme* of Paristrion, or Paradunovon. The other major *theme* in Macedonia was Salonika, and Macedonian lands also joined the *theme* of Durrës (Dyrrachium), the major Byzantine stronghold in the Adriatic. Macedonia's smaller *themes* included Ohrid, Pelagonia, Prespa, Kastoria (Kostur), Vardar, Strumica, and Seres.

Although he disempowered the old ruling elite, Basil sought to conciliate the local feudal landlords, allowing them to retain or even expand their landed estates and rewarding them with favors and titles. He respected local customs and traditions and sought to ease the financial burdens on land that had experienced almost forty years of continuous warfare.

Most noteworthy in this respect was Basil's enlightened treatment of the patriarchate of Ohrid—if it was ever a patriarchate. Although he reduced it to an archbishopric, he ensured its special status within the Byzantine Orthodox church. It enjoyed many privileges as well as control of all the bishoprics of Samuil's empire. Most important, it was autocephalous, "Subject not to the Patriarch of Constantinople but to the will of the Emperor, who reserved for himself the right of appointment to the see. This arrangement—a masterstroke of imperial policy—secured for Byzantium control over the churches of the south Slavs, but avoided any further extension of the already vast share of jurisdiction of the Patriarch of Constantinople, and at the same time properly emphasized the special claims as an ecclesiastical center of Ohrid, whose autocephalous archbishops occupied in the hierarchy of the Greek Church a significantly higher place than other princes of the church who were subordinated to the Patriarchate of Constantinople."[31]

Basil's conciliatory policies expired after his death in 1025. His weaker successors appeared anti-Slav and helped alienate the Slav majority of Macedonia's population. Hellenizing measures included appointment of Greeks to the higher positions in the Ohrid archdiocese, including the archbishop and bishops; attempts to exclude Old Church Slavonic from worship; settlement of non-Slavs among Macedonian Slavs; and resettlement of some of the latter in Thrace and Asia Minor.

At the same time, the empire sent many lay officials—administrators, military personnel, tax collectors—to Macedonia to fill positions that local feudal lords had valued. These interlopers—and ecclesiastical dignitaries, churches, and the growing number of monasteries—received generous grants of lands or control over the remaining free peasant villages. These policies virtually completed the long process of disbanding the once-free peasant communities, just as financial and economic obligations on the lower classes were increasing rapidly.

Both Hellenization and mounting hardship provoked unrest, opposition, and even organized rebellions. Leaders of the two largest uprisings had close family ties to Tsar Samuil and claimed to be his legitimate successors. The first rebellion broke out in 1040 around Belgrade under Petar Deljan, Gabriel Radomir's son and Tsar Samuil's grandson. The rebel army proclaimed him tsar, marched south toward Niš, and took over Skopje, before the imperial authorities grasped the situation and responded.

The initial encounters proved disastrous for the imperial armies. The rebels then moved in all directions: they took the *theme* of Durrës (Dyrrachium), advanced into Epirus and Thessaly in the south, and moved toward Sofia (Serdica) in the east. Thus, before the end of the year, the rebellion had spread over a huge area stretching from the Danube to central Greece and from the Albanian coast to Bulgaria, and the rebel army was ready to attack Salonika. From the very outset, however, dissension among rebel leaders had threatened unity and success. A dangerous rivalry erupted between Petar Deljan and his blood relative Alusian, the second son of John (Jovan) Vladislav. Alusian had defected from the imperial service and joined the rebellion; when his large army suffered a disastrous defeat near Salonika, he turned against Deljan, blinded him, and rejoined the imperial camp. In the spring or summer of 1041, Emperor Michael IV (1034–41) routed the rebel forces at Lake Vegoritis (Ostrovo), captured the blinded Petar Deljan, and defeated the rebellion in the region of Prilep.[32]

The second uprising broke out in 1072 at Skopje under a local notable, Georgi Vojtech. With support from local feudal landlords, he appealed for help to Michael (Mihailo), ruler (1052–81) of Zeta (Montenegro), who had connections to Tsar Samuil's dynasty. He dispatched his son Konstantin Bodin with a contingent of armed men to Prizren, where the rebel leaders proclaimed him tsar.

This revolt lasted almost as long as, but did not attain the dimension or the success of, Deljan's. The rebels took control of the Skopje-Prizren region and then split. One group, under Bodin, moved north toward Niš (Nissus); the other, under his trusted commander Petrilo, marched southwest and, virtually without a serious fight, gained control of the Ohrid region. The Byzantine army had withdrawn in an orderly fashion and reestablished its positions further south, in the fortified lake town of Kastoria (Kostur). There, it outmaneuvered and crushed Petrilo's forces.

The defeat at Kastoria sealed the uprising's fate. A united Byzantine army marched on Skopje, the center of the uprising, which surrendered without a fight, and then intercepted and defeated Bodin's retreating army in Kosovo Polje. It captured Bodin and sent him, together with the already imprisoned Vojtech, to Constantinople. Vojtech did not survive the journey; Bodin eventually found his way back to Zeta (Montenegro).[33]

Byzantium's difficulties in suppressing the rather localized uprisings in Macedonia reveal its gradual weakening. The empire's decline, which began in the decades after the death of Basil II in 1025, speeded up after the 1060s. In 1071, Byzantium suffered a catastrophic military defeat at the hands of the Seljuk Turks at Manzikert in Armenia, and within a decade it lost its rich possessions in Anatolia. Also in 1071, another costly setback occurred; the Normans captured Bari, the last Byzantine outpost in southern Italy, and turned their attention to the Balkans.

These defeats brought into question Constantinople's ability to stop the empire's decline, let alone to revitalize it. This in turn launched a long and many-sided struggle for domination of the Balkans and ultimately for the Byzantine inheritance.

During the more than three centuries of uncertainty that followed, which ended with Ottoman victory, control over Macedonia and its people—the heart of the Byzantine possessions in Europe—shifted rapidly. Between 1081 and 1083, the Normans roamed through and devastated most of Macedonia. Rulers of Zeta and Raška, early states of the Serbs, took advantage of the chaos and occupied the regions of Ohrid and Skopje, respectively. In the 1090s, the First Crusade ravaged and pillaged everything in sight as its forces traveled east along the Via Egnatia. In 1107 and 1108, Normans again laid waste to western Macedonia. Byzantium then reestablished its nominal authority. The imperial government was too weak, and local or regional feudal lords usurped real authority. And after the death of Emperor Manuel II Comnemus (1143–80), imperial authority in most of Macedonia disappeared almost completely.

In 1185, the Normans again landed in Durrës (Dyrrachium, Durazzo) and marched east. In August they entered and looted Salonika and then moved on to Seres. Moreover, chaos in the imperial domains encouraged Macedonia's neighbors to challenge Byzantine rule. In 1185, Bulgaria declared its independence, and, under the Asen dynasty, the second Bulgarian empire sought to dominate the Balkans. The Serbs, now united under the native Nemanja dynasty, had similar hopes. Ambitious feudal lords in Macedonia followed the Bulgarian and Serbian examples and declared their own independence from Constantinople. Dobromir Hrs for almost two decades (1185–1202) ruled his domain, which centered on Strumica and Prosek, north and northeast of Salonika, respectively, in eastern Macedonia.

The disintegration of Byzantium was complete on 13 April 1204, when the Fourth Crusade, against the infidel in Egypt, captured and looted Constantinople. The victorious Latins, who held the imperial capital only until 1261, abolished the Orthodox Byzantine empire and set up their own feudal states, with the most important being the Latin empire at Constantinople and the Latin kingdom in Salonika. Various states competed for the Byzantine tradition and inheritance: the empire of Nicaea, across the Straits; the despotate of Epirus, on the Adriatic; and the kingdom of Serbia and the empire of Bulgaria, which controlled the northern Balkans.

Throughout Latin rule in Constantinople, control of Macedonia and/or its parts shifted from one power to another. At the beginning, one area was under the kingdom of Salonika, while the regions of Skopje and Ohrid became parts (1204–7) of the Bulgarian empire under Tsar Kaloian (1197–1207), the third Asen monarch. After Kaloian died while besieging Salonika, most of his Macedonian possessions—from Prosek northeast of Salonika to Ohrid in the west—went, with Serbian aid, to the enigmatic aristocrat Strez, his relative. After the latter's unexpected death in 1214, part of Macedonia, which included Skopje and Ohrid, fell to the despotate of Epirus.

In the 1220s, especially after 1224, when it conquered the Latin kingdom of Salonika, Epirus appeared the rising power in the Balkans and successor to Byzantium. However, in 1230, at the battle of Klokonitsa, Ivan Asen II (1218–41), that dynasty's greatest ruler, defeated the Epiriotes and eliminated Epirus from the succession struggle. Bulgaria annexed Thrace, most of Macedonia, and part of Albania.

After Ivan Asen II died, internal power struggles weakened Bulgaria, and Mongols threatened it from outside; when the Asens expired in 1280, the country descended into complete feudal anarchy. The Nicaean empire challenged Bulgaria's dominance in Macedonia and the Balkans and began to expand its influence on the European side of the Straits. Its armies moved into eastern Macedonia and threw Epirus out of Salonika in 1246. Nicaea, Epirus, Bulgaria, and Serbia struggled over the rest of Macedonia until the Nicaeans forced the Latins out of Constantinople and reestablished the Byzantine empire. Byzantium once again and for the last time was master of all of Macedonia.[34]

However, merely two decades later, the Serbian king Milutin (1282–1321) began to challenge Byzantium's position. In the first months of his reign, he invaded northern Macedonia and occupied Skopje, Tetovo, and Ovče Pole. Before peace came in 1299, his army had advanced to the walls of Strumica in the east, to Ohrid in the west, and to Prilep in the south.

His son and successor, Stephen (Stefan) Dečanski (1322–31), continued the expansion to the south along the upper Bregalnica and the middle Vardar, taking towns such as Štip and Veles. Serbia was thus acquiring control of the approaches to Salonika and threatened to cut off Byzantium from its western provinces. In order to stop Serbia's advance and growing power, Byzantium allied with Bulgaria, but after the latter's decisive defeat on 28 July 1330 at Velbuzlid (Kiustendil), where its tsar, Michael (Mikhail) Shishman, perished, Emperor Andronicus III (1328–41) abandoned the campaign.

Serbia completed its conquest of Macedonia under Stephen (Stefan)

Dušan (1331–55), the empire's greatest medieval ruler. In 1334, his forces captured Ohrid, Prilep, and Strumica; a decade later, Kastoria (Kostur), Florina (Lerin), and Edessa (Voden) further south. The occupation of Seres in 1345 consolidated Serbian control of Macedonia except Salonika, and Stephen assumed the title "Tsar of the Serbs and Greeks." The following year, he made the Serbian archbishopric a patriarchate, and on Easter Sunday his new patriarch, Joannakie, crowned him at Skopje.

During the next decade, Stephen pushed his empire's boundaries west and south. He occupied Albania, Epirus, and Thessaly and reached the Gulf of Corinth. Like his illustrious predecessors—Simeon, Samuil, and Ivan Asen II—he ruled a vast, multi-ethnic, territorial empire, dominated the Balkans, and dreamed of taking Constantinople, the imperial prize. And, as with his predecessors, the impressive edifice that he created did not long survive him.

Already at the beginning of the reign of his son and successor, Tsar Stephen (Stefan) Uroš (1355–71), central authority was on the decline and power was passing to regional feudal lords. Ten such potentates controlled Macedonia. The most powerful were two brothers: Vukašin (1366–71) declared himself king and lorded over the Prizen-Skopje-Prilep area; Ugleša ruled the southeast. Ugleša's domains faced the advancing Ottoman forces, and he persuaded his brother to launch a joint military campaign to stop them in the Maritsa valley. Hostilities culminated at Chernomen, between Philippopolis and Adrianople, on 26 September 1371. In a surprise dawn attack, the Ottoman forces won decisively. The Christians suffered extremely heavy losses, including the two ruling brothers. Vukašin's son and successor, Marko Kraljević, a popular subject of Serbian, Macedonian, and Bulgarian folklore, became an Ottoman vassal.[35]

The battle of Chernomen marked the beginning of the Ottoman conquest of Macedonia. Before 1400, the Ottoman empire ruled all Macedonia except Salonika, which it occupied temporarily in 1387 but would not conquer until 1430. Macedonia would remain under Ottoman domination for well over five hundred years, until the Balkan Wars of 1912–13.

4 Ottoman Rule (c. 1400–c. 1800)

Macedonia was among the first Balkan lands that the Ottoman empire conquered and integrated into its rapidly expanding realm.[1] Ottoman conquests in the Balkans continued through the last quarter of the fourteenth and the first half of the fifteenth centuries, culminating with capture of the Byzantine imperial capital, Constantinople (Istanbul), at the very end of May 1453.

Before the end of his great reign, Mohammed II, the Conqueror (1451–81), ruled virtually all of the Balkans—in fact, the entire area from the Black Sea to the Adriatic and from the Carpathian Mountains to the Mediterranean coast of Greece. The only exceptions were Slovenia and Croatia (Catholic provinces under the Habsburgs and the Hungarians, respectively), the principality of Montenegro, the city republic of Dubrovnik (Ragusa), a number of ports in Dalmatia, Albania, and Greece, and a few islands in the eastern Mediterranean.

Mohammed's grandson Selim I (1512–20) turned to the east and across the Mediterranean to North Africa. He captured Syria, extended his empire into Mesopotamia in the east, and established control over Egypt and the Nile valley. His son Suleiman I, the Magnificent (1520–66), secured virtually the entire coast of North Africa and the approaches to the Persian Gulf. He also won the northern shore of the Black Sea and pushed his frontiers into central Europe with conquests in Hungary and several unsuccessful sieges of Vienna.

During Suleiman's long, successful reign, the empire reached its height, as the dominant power on three continents. After his death, however, it began a gradual and, as it turned out, irreversible decline, as a result of a combination of factors, external and internal. Outside the empire, western Europe was going through a transformation that began with the Renaissance, the Protestant Reformation, and the scientific and commercial revolutions. It was leaving behind feudal particularism and church domination and moving toward capitalism and centralized, secular, absolutist, monarchial states, which created the basis for the rise of nations and nation-states.

Within the Ottoman empire, however, these revolutionary changes had little impact. Its system of government, which rested largely on the Sacred Law of Islam, proved unable to introduce change, to reform and modernize itself. It could not keep up with the times, did not progress, and stagnated. Indeed, because of degeneration and corruption at the top, the once-efficient centralized administration gradually disintegrated into a stagnant feudal anarchy. The empire of the sultans fell from dominance in Europe under Suleiman the Magnificent to "sick man of Europe" by the late eighteenth century.

Needless to say, the empire's decline had far-reaching repercussions. The rising powers of Europe—first the Habsburgs and then the Romanovs—took advantage of its weakness. By the late seventeenth century, the Ottoman empire was experiencing not military victories and territorial expansion, but defeats and contraction. Equally significant, the weakening of the center and the prevailing anarchy worsened the plight of Balkan Christians. By the late eighteenth century, they felt total alienation vis-à-vis the Muslim-dominated state and lost any vested interest in its survival.

The four-century flow and ebb of Ottoman fortunes, especially in the Balkans, and their impact on Macedonia form the central topics of this chapter. First, we consider the Ottoman administration and the Orthodox *millet* that it created in the Balkans. Second, we look at the empire's roughly two hundred years of expansion and the following two centuries or so of gradual decline. Third, we examine the breakdown of Ottoman rule in the Balkans between about 1600 and 1800. Fourth, we look at Ottoman Macedonia: its changing ethnic composition, its longstanding resistance to imperial rule, its anarchy in the eighteenth century, and the stagnation of its Slavic culture.

The Ottoman Administration and the Orthodox Millet

In the Balkan lands south of the Danube, the Ottoman conquerors destroyed the former states of the Byzantine Orthodox Commonwealth, their dynasties, their secular ruling elites, and, except for converts to Islam, their land-owning classes. The new rulers integrated all this territory into the Ottoman administrative system and ruled most of it directly from Istanbul (Constantinople).[2]

They also established a distinctive system of government. Their empire was highly centralized and autocratic and centered on the High Porte (or exalted gate, from the Turkish name for the imperial court) in Istanbul. All power resided with the sultan, who was the secular and religious head of state. He was an absolute, divine-right ruler of all his lands and peoples. Even a constitution—which consisted of the Sacred Law of Islam; the Sheri, based on the Koran, the word of God; and the Hadith, the sayings of the Prophet, Mohammed—left the sultan's administrative authority almost complete and without restriction.

The sultan exercised this authority through the governing class, or "ruling institution,"[3] the administration; and the standing army, which consisted of janissaris (infantrymen) and spahis of the Porte (cavalrymen). All the administrators and soldiers were converts to Islam and slaves of the sultan, who obtained them variously through purchase, taking prisoners in war, and, most notably, the *devshirme* ("to collect") system—a periodic levy of unmarried Orthodox Christian males between eight and twenty. "[The] sultan had the power of life and death"[4] over this powerful, privileged, slave-manned ruling elite.

The sultan's highest official—his first deputy—was the grand vizier. Assisting this person was the divan (imperial council), which consisted of the highest officials of both the ruling institution and the Muslim institution, or Ulema—leaders of Muslim law, religion, and education. The divan supervised a vast bureaucracy that ran the central and provincial administrations.

The highly centralized system of provincial government functioned for its first two centuries effectively and efficiently. After 1400 or so, the Balkans, or Rumelia, formed one of the empire's two large administrative units, along with Anatolia, or the Asiatic part. A *baylerbey*, or lord of lords, headed each. As the empire expanded, Istanbul divided it into sections, which it termed variously *vilayets*, *eyalests*, or *pashaliks*. By about 1600, these units numbered about twenty-five, and each consisted of lower and smaller jurisdictions, *sanjaks* or *livas*. Heading vilayets were *velis*, and sanjaks, *sanjakbeys*; assisting these officials were administrative staffs. Making up the sanjaks were *kazas*, which consisted of *nahiyes*. The judiciary and the treasury, or tax collection, had separate, territorial organization.

Local authorities cooperated with spahis (cavalrymen), to whom the sultan granted large fiefs (*ziams*) or small fiefs (*timars*) in return for wartime military service. Spahis had clearly defined rights vis-à-vis the Christian peasants, or *rayas*, who worked their lands, as well as duties and obligations toward them and the state.

The autocratic empire was also a theocratic state. It did not recognize or value ethnic, linguistic, racial, and other differences, but emphasized religious divisions. It divided and organized its polyglot population not by ethnic group or previous territorial division, but by religious community, or *millet*. This principle applied to all accepted religious groups. Islam was the dominant religion, and the Muslim millet the dominant community. However, the empire had also a Gregorian Armenian, a Jewish, a Christian Orthodox, a Protestant, and a Roman Catholic millet. The Orthodox Christian was the largest millet in the Balkans.

The system presupposed distinctive and exclusive Muslim and non-Muslim religions. It did not assume equality; it held Islam to be superior. The Muslim faith enjoyed special status and privileges; non-Muslims faced discriminatory political, social, economic, and cultural obligations and restrictions. However, the system tolerated these other religions to a degree that Europe did not. Religious persecution and forced large-scale conversions were rare. Furthermore, the millets enjoyed considerable self-government and autonomy in both temporal and secular affairs.

As we saw above, the Ottoman conquest cost the Balkan peoples their secular ruling elites. Most of the sultan's Christian Orthodox subjects were peasants. Whether Slavs or non-Slavs, and whatever their ethnic group or language, they all belonged to the Orthodox millet. The millet's secular and spiritual head was the patriarch of Constantinople. Mohammed the Conqueror captured Constantinople in 1453, and the next year he chose as patriarch George Scholarios, who as a monk took the name Genadius. The sultan's *berat* to him conferred far greater ecclesiastical and secular powers than the Orthodox Byzantine emperors had ever offered his predecessors. The patriarch became religious head of the Orthodox church and millet (a *millet bashi*) and secular ruler of all the Orthodox (the *ethnarch*).

The patriarch of Constantinople clearly overshadowed the four other eastern patriarchs, and with the disappearance in 1393 of Tsar Simeon's Bulgarian patriarchate and in 1459 of Tsar Dušan's Serbian patriarchate, his jurisdiction extended even over the Slavic-populated areas. True, the archbishopric of Ohrid, in Macedonia, retained some autonomy and continued as an ecclesiastical center of the Balkan Slavs. And after 1557, when Serbian-born Grand Vizier Mohammed Sokoli (Sokolović) set up the Serbian patriarchate of Peć (Ipek), it took on a parallel role vis-à-vis the Serbs. However, neither the archbishopric of Ohrid nor the patriarchate of Peć was, or claimed to be, equal to Constantinople. Long before 1700 they became powerless, and the patriarchate of Constantinople, effectively in the hands of phanariots (Greek officials in Istanbul) and other wealthy Greek elements, saw to their abolition: Peć in 1766, and Ohrid in 1767.

Constantinople's patriarch was also a high Ottoman official—a vizier and the Orthodox Christians' highest representative in the imperial administration. He controlled all matters of doctrine and the hierarchy of the clergy, all Orthodox churches and their properties, the levying and collection of taxes in the Orthodox millet, and judicial power over the Orthodox in marriage, divorce, and inheritance—indeed, in most civil disputes and in criminal cases that did not involve Muslims.

Most important, however, the Greek-dominated patriarchate had exclusive control over and was responsible for education and cultural and intellectual life in the Orthodox millet in general. The level of education, learning, and intellectual life remained low. The few teachers were priests; the only writings were modest theological works. As L. S. Stavrianos observes: "In place of several Balkan literatures there existed only one Orthodox ecclesiastical literature, written either in a debased classical Greek incomprehensible to most Greeks, or in an archaic Church Slavonic incomprehensible to most Slavs."[5]

Ottoman Expansion and Decline

During the first two centuries of Ottoman rule in the Balkans—the empire's golden age—the autocratic and theocratic system worked extremely well. The sultans had devised it to fight successful wars against the infidel (the Christian west), to extend Islam, to expand the state, and to enrich its coffers. Everyone—Muslim and non-Muslim—had to assist, with special tasks and obligations. Under the all-embracing and all-powerful central government, they did just that, and the empire prospered.

The Balkan Christian peasants, the *rayas*, were a major, perhaps the largest source of revenue for the constant military campaigns. Their situation was not enviable, but not intolerable either. Despite their inferior status, they were much better off and far more secure than their ancestors had been under rapacious, native, landed aristocrats or than their counterparts in Christian Europe.

They might dwell in undivided mountainous areas; on land that belonged to spahis, higher administrative officers, members of the imperial family, or the sultan himself; or on *vakf*—land that supported Muslim religious, educational, and charitable causes. No matter where their homes were, they bore a lighter tax burden than peasants in Christian Europe. Despite regional variations and exceptions, Balkan peasants paid a light head tax to the imperial government; a *tithe*, or a tenth of their produce, to the fief holder or the vakf; and some additional, minor levies. They enjoyed hereditary use of their land, which they considered their own.

Furthermore, unlike western European feudal landlords, their Ottoman counterparts could not legally impose feudal services and obligations on peasants and had no legal jurisdiction over them. They could not force them off the land; peasants at least theoretically enjoyed freedom of movement. The clearly defined rights and obligations of the rayas received respect and protection as long as the empire waged victorious wars, the central government was strong and in control, and the administration functioned according to established laws, rules, and practices.

However, no imperial power could expand forever; even Ottoman expansion eventually slowed and stopped, before reversing itself. Suleiman I's failure to capture Vienna, his forces' defeat there in 1529, and his long, inconclusive struggle with the Habsburgs revealed a loss of military preponderance in Europe. While for over a century after Suleiman's death in 1566 the Ottoman empire suffered no major defeats, it did not undertake any additional campaigns, and its European expansion ended.

In the late seventeenth century, Europe began to take advantage of the weakened and declining Ottoman empire and went on the offensive.

The Habsburg-led Holy League—an anti-Ottoman coalition of Christian powers, which included the papacy, Venice, Poland-Lithuania, and Russia—defeated the empire's armies in Hungary, Dalmatia, and the Peloponnesus. The historic Treaty of Karlowitz (Sremski Karlovci) of 26 January 1699 ended the wars of the Holy League. The Ottoman empire ceded to Austria Transylvania, Croatia, Slavonia, and most of Hungary; to Venice, the Peloponnesus and most of Dalmatia; and to Poland, the province of Podolia; it also made concessions to Russia in the Crimea. The Ottoman frontier moved south to the Drava, Sava, and Danube rivers.

Less than three-quarters of a century later, Catherine the Great took the initiative and leadership against the Ottoman forces. Russia won two wars against the Ottoman empire, to many observers the "sick man of Europe." In the first (1768–74), the Russians scored impressive victories at sea in the Aegean islands off the coast of Asia Minor and on land in Moldavia, Bessarabia, Dobruja, and Bulgaria.

The resulting Treaty of Kuchuk Kainarji, on 16 July 1774, represented a massive change for the Balkan peoples. The High Porte made strategic territorial concessions to Russia around the Black Sea, ceded to it the great estuary that the Dnieper and the Bug rivers create, gave it a say in the government and administration of the Danubian principalities Wallachia and Moldavia, allowed it to appoint consuls in the Ottoman lands, and gave its subjects the right to navigate freely in the Black Sea and to trade in the Ottoman empire. As well, the Ottoman empire surrendered for a new, independent state the territories of the Crimean Khan. Most important, it had to recognize Russia as protector of Ottoman Christians, with the right to intervene in Constantinople on their behalf; this principle permitted Russia's all-too-frequent interventions in the Balkans in the following century.

In Catherine's second Ottoman war (1787–92), her army defeated Ottoman forces in the Danubian principalities and near the mouth of the Danube. The Treaty of Jassy, 9 January 1792, consolidated Russia's gains of 1774. The High Porte recognized Russia's 1783 annexation of the Crimea and gave it the Black Sea shore as far west as the Dniester River. Russia now dominated the Black Sea and became a great power in the Near East.[6]

The Ottoman empire was now weak and in full decline. It lagged behind the European powers politically and militarily and depended on them economically. It little resembled the imperial power of Suleiman I.

Its stagnation and decline, which, as we saw above, had commenced with his death in 1566, resulted from external and internal factors.

Externally, since the Renaissance, the European powers had been advancing, progressing, modernizing; they surpassed and left the Ottoman empire far behind in every respect. Internally, the empire's tradition-bound Muslim ruling elite could not adapt to match the European advances. The empire's military defeats and territorial contraction threw its war machine into disarray. As L. S. Stavrianos points out: "The only way out was a basic reorganization of the imperial institutions, but this proved incapable of realization. The failure of the Ottoman Empire was, in the broadest terms, a failure of adjustment, a failure to respond to the challenge of the new dynamic West."[7]

Internally, the empire stagnated, and by 1700 the once-enviably efficient and effective administration was breaking down. Weak and ineffectual rulers emerged following changes in the succession about 1600. A clique consisting of favorites of the puppet sultan now controlled the administration and exploited the empire for their own benefit or that of the Muslim interests that they represented. The slave system, which underlay the ruling institution, the administration and the military, rested and based itself on training, merit, and service to the faith and sultan, but widespread and unbridled corruption weakened it. Administrative and military posts went no longer to dedicated and deserving converts, slaves of the sultan, but rather to well-connected born Muslims and some Christians who bought offices and exploited them for private profit. In short, the system became corrupt and staffed itself with people who bribed their way into office and sought only personal gain.[8]

Ottoman Decline and the Balkans (c. 1600–c. 1800)

In the seventeenth and eighteenth centuries, the decline of the Ottoman empire, the weakening of the central government, and the degeneration of the administration hurt many people, especially non-Muslim, predominantly Orthodox Christian peasants.

The breakdown of the *timar* landholding system, which began with the conquest, hit them hard. As we saw above, this system allowed Istanbul to control the spahis—the service-bound Muslim fief holders—and determined the obligations and protected the rights of the rayas. It provided the latter with security of tenure and some protection from undue exploitation. By 1600, the system began to break down. The empire was no longer expanding but suffering costly military defeats and, by the late seventeenth century, territorial losses.

Facing financial difficulties, the central government brought some timar land under its own control and taxing powers; courtiers and high officials received land grants as gifts. Furthermore, the shrinkage of the timar lands and the decline in central power and control allowed the spahi fief holders to transform state land into private and heritable property, or *chifliks*. The new owners could do with the land whatever they wished and treat the rayas as they pleased. The result was much harsher tenancy terms, including the landlords' right to evict the rayas and to restrict their movement. This change had no legal or official sanction, but it spread rapidly and by the eighteenth century had become standard.

The Orthodox peasants' worsening economic situation and their harsher treatment by corrupt administrators and fief holders had political repercussions. Some peasants ran away and joined the growing number of bands of outlaws (*klephts* in Greek, *khaiduts* in Bulgarian, *haiduks* in Serbian, and *ajduts* in Macedonian). This movement, which became a feature of the declining empire, increased instability and insecurity throughout the Balkans, especially along major trade routes and around commercial and administrative cities. Peasant rebellions and unrest in general became more frequent; whenever armies of the great powers crossed the Danube or the Pruth rivers and penetrated into the Balkans, peasants supported or even joined them in their fight against their overlords. By the eighteenth century, they began to view Austrian and Russian forces, and during the Napoleonic Wars the French, as armies of liberation.

The conversion of landholding was partly a response to western Europe's growing demand for products such as cotton and corn that grew in the Ottoman empire. Landowners could see financial benefits from exports. Balkan trade with Europe and Russia, largely through Christian merchants, increased after Austria's successes against the Ottoman empire and Russia's expansion to the Black Sea.

This growing commerce stimulated Balkan handcrafts and small-scale industry and the rise of a native middle class, consisting of well-to-do artisans, craftspeople, merchants, and mariners. After 1750, this expanding social element became politically relevant. Its members knew about western Europe's progress and increasingly resented their own

Map 4 Macedonia in the Ottoman Empire in Europe

society's backwardness and lawlessness. They absorbed secular and democratic western European ideas and would soon join the peninsula's growing opposition to misrule and oppression.[9]

The system's degeneration and corruption also hurt the patriarchate of Constantinople and the Orthodox church. Simony began to determine the choice of patriarchs and the highest church officials, and bribery permeated the millet's operations. By 1700, Phanariotes—"Greeks who entered the Ottoman service and gained great power and wealth as administrators, tax farmers, merchants and contractors"[10]—controlled the patriarchate and through it the millet.

The Greek ethnic element, always a leader in the church and millet hierarchy, gradually assumed complete control; Greek displaced Church Slavonic and became the church's exclusive language in the empire. This development slowed the spread even of limited education and culture to the vast non-Greek majority of Slavs, Romanians, and Albanians under the partriarch's jurisdiction. Hellenization culminated in the abolition of the patriarchate of Peć in 1766 and the archbishopric of Ohrid in 1767. Even the pretense that the patriarch of Constantinople represented all the sultan's Orthodox subjects disappeared. And Hellenization provoked a strong reaction against all Greek influences during the national awakenings that soon followed.[11]

Macedonia: Ethnic Transformation, Resistance, Anarchy, and Cultural Stagnation

After Macedonia's conquest, the Ottoman empire made its entire territory part of the *beylerbeylik* of Rumelia and subdivided it into *sanjaks*. For a long time, the largest part of Macedonia belonged to one of the oldest and largest Balkan sanjaks, the so-called Pasha sanjak. Imperial authorities considered this their most crucial sanjak strategically, and the *beylerbey* of Rumelia administered it personally and directly. In the fifteenth and sixteenth centuries, new sanjaks incorporated Macedonian lands: the Kiustendil, areas of eastern Macedonia, and the Ohrid, parts of the west. In the mid–sixteenth century, the empire set up Skopje (Üsküb) sanjak exclusively on Macedonian lands; the slightly older Salonika sanjak embraced southern Macedonia.

As we saw above, nahias made up the sanjaks and constituted the smallest territorial administrative units. In Macedonia, they normally corresponded to pre-Ottoman *župas*. In parallel with the administrative-territorial division, there were judicial-territorial units, or *kazas*. Each kaza was under the jurisdiction of a *kadi*, a representative of the Ottoman legal system. There were kazas in all areas containing Muslims, and their size depended on the number of Muslims there; frequently they covered several nahias.[12]

The Ottoman conquest and centuries-long rule transformed ethnic composition and distribution in Macedonia. Some areas, especially those on major strategic routes or where military clashes took place, lost people during the conquest. Many Slav Macedonians there died in battle or became prisoners, some left to escape the onslaught, and others underwent deportation to Albania, Asia Minor, or elsewhere. At the same time, the new rulers forced or encouraged Turks from Asia Minor to settle in Macedonia: along important routes, in fertile river valleys, and in the fertile Aegean plain. Nomads from Anatolia set up a belt of small settlements of livestock breeders near Salonika and in the districts of Nevrokop, Strumica, Radoviš, Kočani, and Ovეč Pole in eastern Macedonia.

Conversions augmented Muslim numbers. While the Ottoman empire was generally rather tolerant of other religions, Islamization, sometimes on a large scale, did take place. Some landholding nobles converted soon after the conquest to safeguard or even expand their holdings. Later, during the empire's decline, deteriorating economic conditions led to many conversions in a large number of rayas—even entire villages or districts—in the most eastern and western regions, as well as by some urban dwellers. In towns, conversion often meant linguistic and cultural assimilation as well. New rural Muslims, however, normally preserved their language and many folk and religious customs. Slav-Macedonian converts in the east became "Pomaks," and those in the west, "Torbeši." Both groups survive to the present day.[13]

Even more notable was the fifteenth-century colonization of urban places. Towns became administrative, military, and judicial centers of the new order. They also provided more comfort and safety and attracted a steadily growing number of Muslims. Evidence suggests that until the mid– or late sixteenth century, the Muslim population in larger towns was increasing, and the Orthodox Christian, stagnating or declining. In 1455, Skopje had 511 Muslim and 339 Orthodox households, and in 1519, 717 Muslim and 302 Orthodox. About 1460, Veles had 9 Muslim and 222 Orthodox households, and in 1519, 42 and 247, respectively; in 1476, Kičevo had 31 Muslim and 186 Orthodox households, and in 1519, 111 and 145; and about 1460, Bitola (Monastir) had 295 Muslim and 185 Orthodox households, and in 1519, 750 and 330.[14]

As a result of the Inquisition in western Europe, after the late fifteenth century many Jews fled Spain and Portugal and settled in the more tolerant Ottoman empire. Jewish colonies emerged in all major

Macedonian towns—Salonika, Bitola, Skopje, Verroia (Ber), Seres, Kastoria (Kostur), Štip, Kratovo, and Strumica. Salonika's became one of the empire's largest and most influential: about mid–sixteenth century, the city had 3,000 Jewish households, the renowned Talmud Torah academy, and a Jewish printing house (1515). Bitola, with 87 Jewish households in 1544, had a Talmudic school as well. In the seventeenth century, Skopje's Jewish quarter boasted two synagogues and schools.[15]

Opposition against the new Ottoman overlords, who held total power but were completely alien in language and religion, was present from the beginning. During the empire's zenith, it was passive: individual peasants and entire villages resisted Islamization, and some villages enlarged or built new churches without the requisite approval. Peasants found creative ways to lessen their tax burden or avoided paying taxes altogether. They also discovered methods to beat the "blood tax"—the devshirme—and saved their young sons from the sultan's slave system.

The conversion of timar landholding into chiflik, as well as the impoverishment of the rayas during the empire's long decline in the seventeeth and eighteenth centuries, intensified opposition and provoked armed resistance. As elsewhere in the Balkans, a bandit movement surfaced and grew. Desperate peasants abandoned their fields and fled to the mountains, where they led the lives of outlaws. Macedonians called them "ajduts" and their movement "ajdutstvo." The movement became especially widespread in times of war, epidemic, famine, and anarchy, when entire villages joined up. It reached its high point in Macedonia during the seventeenth century.

The ajduts usually consisted of bands (*družinas*) of twenty to thirty members, but some bands numbered as many as two or even three hundred. Each band elected a leader—a *vojvoda*, or *arambaša*—for his or her experience, courage, loyalty, and fairness. The bands usually assembled about St. George's Day (23 April on the old calendar / 6 May, new calendar) and disbanded about St. Demetrius's Day (26 October / 8 November). A few ajduts or bands operated through the winter.

Most ajduts were peasants, but some were priests and monks. Moreover, although Slav Macedonians were the most numerous group, there were other people from Macedonia, such as Albanians, Vlachs, and Greeks. Most bands were ethnically homogeneous, but some were mixed. There were women ajduts as well; they usually joined a band together with a husband or a brother, and some became well-known ajdut leaders.

The ajduts attacked and robbed the estates and properties of Ottoman lords and ambushed tax collectors and trade caravans; but they did not spare rich Christian oligarchs and wealthy monasteries. Larger bands also attacked targets in urban centers. For example, they looted the marketplace in Bitola in 1646 and 1661; and records reveal successful incursions into towns such as Florina (Lerin), Resen, and Ohrid. Although the authorities did all they could to eradicate the ajduts, they failed. The ajduts enjoyed the sympathy and, at times, even the protection of Christians at large. The peasants viewed them and romanticized them in Macedonian folk songs, tales, and tradition, as fighters against foreign exploitation and for social justice.[16]

The ajduts also influenced and provided leaders for peasant unrest and rebellions, as in the largest and most significant peasant uprising in Macedonia before 1800. The revolt broke out in mid-October 1689 in the northeast, between Kiustendil and Skopje, under a well-known ajdut vojvoda, Karpoš, and took his name. The immediate cause was the Holy League's success in wars against the Ottoman empire. The Habsburg armies marched southward, penetrated deep into Serbia, reached western Macedonia, and on 25 October 1689 entered Skopje. The complete collapse of the Ottoman administration and the presence of the Austrian army enabled the rebels to take control of the region. They established headquarters in nearby Kriva Palanka, which had been the area's strongest Ottoman fortified position.

Late in the month, Ottoman leaders stabilized their positions and counter-attacked the rebels and the stretched-out Austrian forces with help from seasoned Tartar units of their ally, Selim Girei, khan of the Crimea. They forced the rebels to retreat toward Kumanovo and on the town's outskirts defeated them, capturing Karpoš and many of his fighters and taking them to Skopje. There, in early December and in the presence of Selim Girei, authorities impaled Karpoš by the Stone Bridge (Kamen most) and later threw his body into the Vardar. His death marked the end of the rebellion.[17]

After this victory, a combined Ottoman-Tartar offensive pushed the Austrian forces north, beyond the Danube and Sava rivers. Many Macedonian Christians fled with the Austrians to escape the devastation and Ottoman retribution. Some ended up in southern Russia, where they, like other Balkan refugees, set up military colonies, including a "Macedonian Regiment" (Makedonski polk), in the regular Russian army. Muslim Albanian settlers took their place in northwestern Macedonia, changing the region's ethnographic composition.

The eighteenth century was disastrous for the Ottoman empire and created a multifaceted vacuum in Macedonia. Serious military defeats and territorial losses to European powers occurred as the central government weakened internally and virtual anarchy emerged in the Balkans as local feudal potentates with their own private mercenary armies usurped imperial power. These new overlords terrorized their domains in opposition to the sultan's government.

In Macedonia, Mahmud Pasha Bushatliya, for example, ran the districts of Ohrid, Debar (Dibra), and Skopje; Ali Pasha Tepelen of Yanina, the southwest; the family of Abdul Aga Shabanderoglou, the Dojran, Petrich, Melnik, and Demir Hisar areas; and the clans of Ali Aga and Ismail Bey, the Seres region. They used their private armies as well as organized units of bandits—four hundred to five hundred men strong and consisting of Albanians and Turks—to terrorize Christians in the countryside and in the towns. Even the *martolozi*, well-paid Christian recruits in groups of twenty to one hundred, hired to seek and destroy the ajduts, exploited the very villages they were paid to protect.

In the last quarter of the eighteenth century, during the Russian-Ottoman wars, the feared bands of *krdžali* made their bases in the mountains, the Rhodopes, and the Šar, but especially in the Pljačkovica and Ogražden mountains. Their large groups, some numbering two thousand members, consisted of villagers, army deserters, and men and women of various ethnic and religious backgrounds. They rode horses, had ample arms, and in well-planned, rapid attacks on urban centers robbed both wealthy Muslims and Christians.[18]

The prevailing anarchy affected most of all the Christian peasants. As in other Balkan lands, many peasants in Macedonia left their villages in search of greater security. Some went into the mountains and joined ajdut bands. Others sought safety in the towns and thus helped gradually to re-Christianize and re-Slavicize the urban centers. There they worked as servants and laborers, practiced various crafts and trades, or engaged in commerce and even finance. They were joining and taking over the direction of some guilds.

Some Slav Macedonians did well, acquired certain wealth, and began the gradual formation of a native middle class in places where

Turks, Greeks, Jews, Vlachs, and, in some cases, Armenians had previously dominated crafts, trades, and especially commerce and internal and foreign trade. Slav Macedonians owned trading houses in Salonika, Kastoria (Kostur), Bansko, Seres, Edessa (Voden), and Ohrid, with representation in Budapest, Vienna, Bucharest, Venice, Odessa, and Moscow. They would assist in the cultural and national awakening of Macedonian Slavs in the following century.[19]

During the centuries of Ottoman rule, Orthodox culture virtually froze in Macedonia and throughout the Balkans. Ottoman Muslim culture, in contrast, flourished; its most visible achievements—architectural masterpieces in the form of mosques, bridges, and hans—still delight visitors, especially in Vardar Macedonia, now the republic of Macedonia.

The Ottoman state had no interest in or influence on the culture of its non-Muslim subjects. The Orthodox rayas were distinct from the dominant Muslims not only in language, religion, and social customs but, virtually until the eighteenth century, also in geography. The Turks resided mostly in towns, which acquired an oriental character, while the mostly peasant Orthodox were overwhelmingly rural. Moreover, except for folk culture in the numerous vernaculars, which people passed on orally, the Orthodox church was the source of all culture. And ecclesiastical culture—teaching, learning, writing, in both the debased classical Greek and the archaic Church Slavonic—was at a very low level; Orthodox intellectual life was stagnant.

Furthermore, throughout the centuries of Ottoman rule, Greeks dominated the Orthodox church. The Bulgarian patriarchate ceased to exist in 1393; the Serbian, in 1459. The autocephalous archbishopric of Ohrid, which Basil II reduced from a patriarchate, continued, and in 1557 Grand Vizier Mohammed Sokoli (Sokolović) saw to establishment of the Serbian patriarchate of Peć (Ipek).

However, neither of these Slavic churches could question, let alone challenge, the Greek-dominated patriarchate of Constantinople. Greeks held the church's highest offices and thus administered the Orthodox millet and helped to run the Ottoman state. Greek influence was predominant, and "Greek became increasingly the language of the Orthodox Church and also of education, which was closely associated with it. There thus developed a type of Greek ecclesiastical imperialism which operated to the detriment of the native elements in the Slavic and Romanian lands."[20]

Greek control over church and education became total after the abolition of the Serbian patriarchate of Peć in 1766 and the archbishopric of Ohrid in 1767. "The Constantinople patriarchate once more reigned supreme in the peninsula. It continued to do so as long as the Balkan peoples remained subject to Ottoman authority."[21] And Macedonia and the Macedonians were, as we see in Part Two, to remain under the domination of both longer than any other Balkan land or people.

Macedonia's most significant religious and thus cultural institution was the Ohrid archbishopric. After the Ottoman capture of Ohrid, the authorities permitted this autocephalous church to continue. They did so partly or largely because of traditional animosities that marred its relations with the Constantinople patriarchate and represented to them opposition to Byzantium. Until about 1500, Ohrid expanded its authority in all directions. It took over the Sofia and Vidin eparchies in Bulgaria about 1400 and Walachia, Moldavia, and parts of the former Peć patriarchate, including Peć, at mid-century. For a period, it also held sway over the Orthodox communities in Italy (Apulia, Calabria, Sicily), Venice, and Dalmatia.

However, Ohrid's territorial jurisdiction began to shrink after 1500, when it lost the metropolitanate of Walachia to Constantinople. In the second quarter of the century, it gave up the metropolitanates of Smederovo in Serbia and Kastoria (Kostur) in Macedonia. After establishment of the Peć patriarchate in 1557, Tetovo, Skopje, Štip, and Gorna Dzhumaia, in a belt across northern Macedonia, broke away from Ohrid and accepted Peć's jurisdiction. In 1575, the Orthodox of Dalmatia and Venice came under Constantinople, and after 1600 Ohrid lost the eparchies in southern Italy. Thereafter the archbishopric remained stable until its abolition in 1767.[22]

Eight monasteries generated or sponsored most of Macedonia's limited cultural activity (in the environs of the urban centers in parentheses): Leskovo (near Kratovo), Matejče and St Prohor Pčinski (Kumanovo), Slepče (Demir Hisar), Treskavets (Prilep), Prečiste (Kičevo), Jovan Bigorski (Debar), and Prolog (Tikveš). These monasteries possessed many Church Slavonic manuscripts and continued "copying and reproducing liturgical, philosophical, didactic and other ecclesiastical documents." Late in the sixteenth century, but more so in the seventeenth and eighteenth centuries, they produced the so-called damascenes, containing translations of various miscellanies from Greek into—and this was new—the Slav-Macedonian vernacular.[23]

In the fifteenth and sixteenth centuries, the monasteries also maintained the only schools in Macedonia, which trained clerics. In the seventeenth and eighteenth, they sponsored some elementary Slav-language education outside their establishments. Monks opened schools in some towns, usually near a church, to teach literacy to a small number of boys there. Such monastic (*keljini*) schools existed in Veles, Prilep, Skopje, and some other towns in Macedonia.

Yet Greek schools were emerging much more quickly, with the patronage of Greek or Hellenized metropolitans and bishops. These schools enjoyed the support of the Constantinople patriarchate and of well-to-do Greek and Vlach urban merchants and developed into an extensive network, especially in southern Macedonia. They offered a more up-to-date, advanced, secular education; their example helped spur eventual modernization of the rather archaic monastic Slav schools. More important, they represented and symbolized Greek control of Macedonia's slight educational and cultural life on the eve of the age of nationalism.[24]

PART TWO

NATIONAL AWAKENING (c. 1800–1913)

At the beginning of the nineteenth century, the Ottoman empire was still a great power. Its territorial possessions presented an imposing façade. It controlled most of North Africa, Asia Minor, and the Middle East and all of the Balkans south of the Danube and west of the Pruth river. Behind the façade, however, lay the "sick man of Europe": an empire that had been in decline for a couple of centuries and was falling further and further behind the great powers of Europe politically, economically, and militarily. The central government in Istanbul had lost effective control over large parts of its territory to ambitious individuals who acted as independent rulers. Internally, the theocratic state lacked any semblance of modernity: it remained a conglomeration of diverse religious communities (*millets*), of a range of ethnic, linguistic, and religious groupings, which lacked a centralized and efficient bureaucracy, a common state ideology and legitimizing doctrines, common interests, and a vision of a common future to hold them together.

During the nineteenth century, enlightened statesmen—sultans or high imperial officials who admired the example of the West—moved to the fore. They became conscious of the empire's problems and sought far-reaching reform to modernize it and reverse its decline. All the attempts at reform—most important, those of the Tanzimat period (1839–80)—however, failed because of the determined opposition of the Muslim ruling elite, which was suspicious of the West and had vested interests in the antiquated system. Consequently, the empire continued to decline until its final collapse and partition after the Great War.

The empire's continued decline complemented the rise of nationalism among its Christian peoples. Democratic, liberal, and nationalist ideas began to filter into the Balkans from the west in the late eighteenth century. Members of the still-small but growing middle class and the emerging intelligentsias of the Balkan peoples felt alienation from the Ottoman status quo and rejected it. Ottoman backwardness and decline provided fertile ground especially for the spread of nationalist ideas, whose acceptance further undermined Ottoman rule and legitimacy in the Balkans.

In the nineteenth century, nascent national movements in the region claimed to represent their respective people. In all cases, the ultimate aim was struggles for liberation and establishment of independent national states. And, largely as a result of interventions by the great powers, they were successful. An autonomous Serbian principality came into existence in 1815, an independent Greek kingdom in 1830, an independent principality of Montenegro in 1857, and an autonomous Romanian principality in 1861.

The Congress of Berlin of 1878 declared Serbia, Montenegro, and Romania independent kingdoms. It also sanctioned establishment of an autonomous Bulgarian principality, which in 1885 annexed Eastern Rumelia and in 1908 declared its complete independence and received recognition as a kingdom. The conclave in Berlin also authorized Austria-Hungary to garrison the sanjak of Novi Pazar separating Serbia and Montenegro and to occupy, but not to annex, Bosnia and Herzegovina. The provinces' formal annexation took place 30 years later, in 1908. The Berlin gathering disregarded Greece's territorial claims, but in 1881, at a conference in Constantinople/Istanbul, the great powers and the Ottoman government agreed to award Greece nearly the whole of Thessaly and the district of Arta in Epirus.

Consequently, in the aftermath of the 1878 congress, the Ottoman empire retained sovereignty in the Balkans only over the center of the peninsula, between newly formed Greece, Montenegro, Novi Pazar, Serbia, and Bulgaria—lands that stretched from the Adriatic in the west to the Sea of Marmara and the Black Sea in the east. The area included Epirus, Albania, and Kosovo in the west, Macedonia in the center, and Thrace in the east.

Bordering Bulgaria, Greece, and Serbia, the Macedonian lands were the most important and desirable. All three neighbors chose to claim them and their people, and already by 1870 competition for the hearts and minds of the Slavic-speaking majority there was under way. The struggle, which began as a war of propagandas, of educational, cultural, and religious institutions, became before 1900 a war of armed bands and, during the Balkan Wars of 1912–13, a war of standing armies. Its main victims were the Macedonians themselves, and its inescapable outcome was conquest and partition of their land by force of arms in the Interallied, or so-called Second Balkan War in 1913.

For various reasons, which I discuss in chapter 6, the national awakening of Macedonia's Slav-speaking majority, who adopted their land's name as a national name and symbol, lagged behind that of their neighbors. The first, or Slav phase in the Macedonian awakening began in the first quarter of the nineteenth century. And by the 1860s, there was clear evidence of the formation of a distinct Macedonian consciousness and identity, of Macedonian nationalism. As I mentioned above, however, by then the neighboring states were competing for Macedonia and the hearts and minds of its people, and that struggle affected the future growth of Macedonian consciousness.

Unlike other nationalisms in the Balkans or in central and eastern Europe more generally, Macedonian nationalism developed without the aid of legal, political, church, educational, or cultural institutions. Macedonian movements not only lacked any legal infrastructure, they also lacked the international sympathy, cultural aid, and, most important, benefits of open and direct diplomatic and military support accorded other Balkan nationalisms. Indeed, the nascent Macedonian nationalism, illegal at home in the theocratic Ottoman empire, and illegitimate internationally, waged a precarious struggle for survival against overwhelming odds: in appearance against the Ottoman empire, but in fact against the three expansionist Balkan states and their respective patrons among the great powers.

The development of Macedonian nationalism under Ottoman rule reached its high point with the ill-fated Ilinden Uprising (2 August, St. Elias's Day) of 1903, which became and remains the focal point, the most cherished source, of national mythology and pride. A decade after its bloody suppression, Macedonian patriotism and nationalism suffered their most devastating blow: partition of the land and its people, which Macedonian patriots and nationalists sought so desperately to prevent, and from which they would never entirely recover.

5 Ottoman Reform and Decline (c. 1800–1908)

This chapter charts Ottoman reform and catastrophic decline in the nineteenth century, improvements in Macedonians' lives up to mid-century and troubles thereafter, and Bulgaria, Greece, and Serbia's fierce competition for their loyalty in the Balkan vacuum that began to emerge following the Congress and Treaty of Berlin in 1878.

In 1800, all of geographic Macedonia formed an integral part of the large Ottoman eyalet of Rumelia, with its administrative center in Sofia. For political and strategic reasons, Istanbul later in the century moved its capital to Bitola (Monastir), and this former seat of a kaza began to emerge as a major Ottoman administrative and military center.

Until the 1830s, individual Turkish *pashas* (governors) usurped power and transformed their *pashaliks* virtually into semi-independent private possessions. Such was the case with the pashas of Salonika, Bitola, Skopje, Seres, and Tetovo. The best known, the most powerful and wealthy, in the European part of the empire was Ismail Bey of Seres. His authority extended all the way to Sofia in the north, Štip in the west, and the Salonika area in the south. He maintained a regular force of two thousand armed men and, if necessary, could raise the number to fifteen thousand or twenty thousand.

By the early 1840s, the sultan was able to destroy the pashas' power and bring the pashaliks back under central officials. From then on, Macedonia consisted of six legal-administrative units, the sanjaks of Salonika, Bitola, Skopje, Seres, Ohrid, and Kiustendil. The Ohrid sanjak embraced some Albanian lands, and the Kiustendil, some Bulgarian.

There are no reliable statistics on Macedonia's ethnic composition between 1800 and 1850. According to one French source of 1807, all of Macedonia but the most northerly districts had 968,500 inhabitants. Three-quarters, or 724,000, of them were Orthodox Christians, and one-quarter, or 204,000, Muslims.[1]

Serbian revolts in 1804 and 1815 and creation of the autonomous principality of Serbia in 1815, and particularly the inability of the Ottoman military to crush the rebellious Greeks and the establishment of the small independent kingdom of Greece in 1830, forced the Ottoman empire on the path of reform. The first Western-influenced, reforming sultan, Selim III (1789–1808), lost his throne in May 1808, and he died three months later at the hands of traditionalist opponents of reform, the janissaries and their patrons and allies. Mahmud II (1808–39), his nephew and a pupil, who soon took the throne with help from Selim's friends, became the first successful Ottoman reformer. "He stands out as one of the great reforming sultans of his dynasty. Mahmud was convinced that his empire must reform or perish, and he was aware that the Janissaries were the principal obstacle to reform."[2]

Mahmud turned his attention to imperial disintegration and used all means at his disposal. Before any meaningful reform could occur, he had to deal with the janissaries, by then a useless fighting force but an adamantine defender of the untenable status quo. Mahmud carefully prepared for the decisive confrontation. He surrounded himself with trusted and dependable ministers, advisers, and officials; won the support of the ulema with promotions, bribes, and favors; and when the time came acted with great dispatch and determination.

After Mahmud presented his plan for western European–style military modernization, on the night of 14 June 1826 the janissaries in Istanbul were ready to revolt. However, Mahmud was ready. Reliable troops and artillerymen crossed the Bosphorus to Istanbul, and within a matter of hours, after an intense bombardment of their barracks, the once-feared janissaries were no more. Those who survived went into exile in outlying provinces in Asia.

Mahmud could now focus on reform. He introduced western European dress and styles at court and appeared in public frequently; sent young men to study abroad, in western Europe and North America; and saw increasing political and economic contacts steadily increase the numbers of Europeans in the Ottoman capital. He built roads and bridges, opened the Danube to steamer navigation, and introduced a new tariff system in order to stimulate trade and commerce. He sought to recruit more capable officials, emphasized merit, raised salaries, and so forth.

However, as Stavrianos writes: "So far as the Balkan people were concerned, Mahmud's reforms were less significant than might be expected. His great success was in asserting imperial authority by destroying the Janissaries and such semi-independent local potentates as Ali Pasha of Albania. But this did not appreciably alter everyday life in the Balkans. The Ottoman officials remained, and they were inefficient and corrupt as before. Appointments to prominent posts still were dependent on favoritism and bribery, and salaries still were discouragingly low. Nevertheless, Mahmud's assertion of central authority made possible further reforms in the following decades."[3]

During the 1830s, Mahmud's attention turned to the Near Eastern crisis, which the expansionist ambitions of his vassal Pasha Mehmet Ali of Egypt provoked. After Mahmud's death in 1839, further and more far-reaching changes continued under Sultan Abdul Mejid (1839–61). The new ruler was only sixteen but from the outset embraced reform. On 8 November 1839, he issued a decree—the Hatti Sherif of Gulhané. It launched the reform movement Tanzimat,[4] which continued until Sultan Abdul Hamid took power in 1880.

The architect of and driving force behind the Gulhané decree and reform was Reshid Mustafa Pasha, the greatest enlightened Ottoman statesman and bureaucrat. The decree proclaimed certain basic aims: security of life, honor, and material possessions; a modern system of assessing and levying taxes; and up-to-date methods of military recruitment and service. The changes were to institutionalize the rule of law and ensure equal rights to all Ottoman subjects regardless of religious affiliation.

Throughout the 1840s, Reshid Mustafa Pasha formulated and issued complementary edicts that set up fixed salaries for governors of provinces, cities, and towns and merit-based promotions; a new penal code that assumed equality for all citizens; educational reforms, with minimum salaries, better schoolbooks, and European-style colleges to train civil servants and military officers; and a commercial code, which included mixed tribunals of Turkish and European representatives to decide commercial cases involving Ottoman subjects and foreigners.

These measures changed the empire's atmosphere. Most remained on paper only; the rest underwent only partial implementation because of determined opposition from traditionalists. Nonetheless, life and property became more secure, and officials who committed gross criminal offenses faced trial and punishment. Arbitrary confiscation of property was still taking place, but it was no longer the rule or common practice. Equality before the law gained acceptance at least in theory.

Simultaneous steps to improve provincial administration and ease Christians' plight, which attracted Europe's attention, proved even less effectual. Sending commissioners to inspect provinces and calling delegates thence to report to imperial representatives did not produce any useful results. The setting up of subjects' advisory councils, or *mejliss*, for each provincial governor produced little. Most of the Christian representatives were wealthy and defended local vested interests, as did their Muslim counterparts. The councils tended to be more conservative than the governors.[5]

The intensive reform halted with the Crimean War of 1854–56, which pitted Russia against the Ottoman empire, Britain, France, Sardinia, and Russia's traditional ally Austria. Russia's defeat at Sebastopol and Austria's threat to intervene convinced Russia to accept a ceasefire and eventually the humiliating Treaty of Paris of 30 March 1856. Reforming activities resumed, along with efforts to improve the conditions of Balkan Christians.

In order to satisfy his partners, especially Britain, the sultan on 18 February 1856, before conclusion of the Treaty of Paris, issued the Hatti-Humayun, the second Tanzimat, or reform decree. It made far-reaching promises to non-Muslims: equality in taxation, justice, military service, education, and the public service, as well as social respect and freedom of thought and religion. It seemed to anticipate reorganization of the administration, the judiciary, and the tax system.

However, very little happened. Failure resulted from inefficiency and corruption, but also from flaws in the millet system, with its virtually autonomous, largely self-governing religious communities under their respective ecclesiastical leaders. Most Balkan Christians belonged to the Orthodox millet, and, according to most accounts, their own corrupt leaders misruled and exploited them as much as the Ottoman ruling elite did. Consequently, even imperial reform would not have aided them, except with overhaul of the millet system. In fact, "reform decrees in Constantinople would have meant little for the Christian peoples as long as their relations with their own ruling class remained unchanged."[6] The Hatti-Humayun had anticipated this obstacle and called for reorganization of the millets.

Calls for reform of the millets, and specifically the Orthodox one, came both from the central government and from lay elements in the millet itself. However, reforming or reorganizing the Orthodox millet was not a simple matter. For all practical purposes, five metropolitans, who elected the patriarch of Constantinople, controlled it. Between 1860 and 1862, changes called for lay participation in election of the patriarch and in millet affairs. They did not improve the situation; the lay representatives were influential Greeks who wanted to preserve the status quo, as did the ecclesiastical dignitaries. If anything, relations between the church and millet's Greek ruling elite and the Slavic-speaking majority worsened.

The Hatti-Humayun also proposed reorganization of provincial administration, and the *vilayet* law of 1864 divided the empire into new vilayets, or provinces, and set up six in the empire's European part. The vilayets consisted of *sanjaks* containing smaller administrative units. Parts of geographic Macedonia lay in three vilayets, which also comprised some non-Macedonian areas. Northern Macedonia was part of the Kosovo vilayet and later of the Skopje; the south was in the Salonika vilayet. Further reorganization created the Bitola (Monastir) vilayet for central Macedonia. This administrative division lasted until the Balkan Wars of 1912–13.

The new system was to decentralize the empire and make local self-administration more representative. Provincial governors took on greater powers, as did officials in the lower administrative units. Partly appointed, partly elected councils, or *mejlisses*, were to represent the local population and interests.

Provincial reform proved no more effective than changes to millets. They created the semblance of a European-style administration but failed because the Ottoman empire lacked a modern public service: enlightened, educated, dedicated, patriotic, and honest. And the advisory bodies came under the thumb of wealthy notables who had no interest in or conception of progress or the larger public good.[7]

In any event, by 1871, when instigator Ali Pasha died, reform activities had ended. The unbalanced Sultan Abdul Aziz (1861–76) could finally establish his own personal regime and misrule until he lost the throne in late May 1876, in a coup under Midhat Pasha, another statesman. The mentally unstable Murad V ruled until Midhat Pasha replaced him three months later with a younger brother, Abdul Hamid II (1876–1908). On 23 December, Midhat forced Abdul Hamid to promulgate a rather liberal constitution, which promised a constitutional monarchy. The sultan soon dismissed Midhat Pasha but allowed the elected parliament to meet on 9 March 1877 and to deliberate until the start of war with Russia in late April provided him with a pretext to adjourn that body, which sat next after the revolution of 1908.[8]

Throughout the 1870s, serious problems pushed reform into the background. Devastating drought and famine hit Asia Minor, and financial difficulties and deficits pushed the state to the brink of bankruptcy. Furthermore, the eventful Balkan crisis of 1875–78 shook the empire. It included a revolt by Christian peasants in Bosnia-Herzegovina in 1875, a Bulgarian revolt in May 1876, Serbia and then Montenegro's declaration of war and invasion of Bosnia-Herzegovina in late June 1876, the great powers' unsuccessful diplomatic intervention and mediation, and war with Russia in 1877–78. The Ottoman empire had to accept the humiliating Treaty of San Stefano of 3 March 1878, but Britain and Austria-Hungary insisted on the document's revision. The more palatable Treaty of Berlin of 13 July 1878 ended this latest Balkan crisis.[9]

The accession of Abdul Hamid II and his indefinite adjournment of the first Ottoman parliament—in effect, the defeat of the constitutional experiment—launched the "Hamidian" reaction and autocracy. Most important, they terminated the era of Tanzimat reform and its failure to improve the circumstances of Balkan Christians and to inspire in them loyalty and allegiance to the empire. As L. S. Stavrianos observes: "The essential failure of Ottoman reform efforts in the Balkans meant that the imperial *status quo* could have no attraction to counteract the centrifugal force of Balkan nationalism. Neither millet reform nor vilayet reorganization had succeeded in inducing among the subject Balkan peoples a sense of loyalty to Constantinople strong enough to neutralize their growing feeling of national consciousness."[10]

Macedonian Growth and Decline (1800–1870)

Imperial weakness and anarchy in the provinces speeded up the transformation prior to 1850 of the timar-ziam into the chiflik system of landholding. Individual spahis and other people in positions of authority turned land from peasants, communes, and the state into privately owned chifliks, which they could expand through additional purchases or put up for sale. The largest owners were the semi-independent potentates, most infamously the ruthless and wealthy Ali Pasha of Yanina. At his death, he owned about thirty-five sizeable properties in Macedonia and about nine hundred throughout the area that he ruled.

By mid-century, the transformation of landholding was complete. After 1834, the Ottoman state was calling for liquidation of the timars. The spahis, long useless militarily, had to turn over their timars to a state land bank. Those who could prove rightful possession obtained financial compensation; those who could not received none. In any case, 30 percent of the spahis escaped the process and changed their timars into chifliks before the reform. The state turned some of the lands that it expropriated over to village tenants and sold the rest at low prices to well-to-do individuals or local notables.

The triumph and legalization of chiflik landholding imposed on peasants higher payments in cash or in kind and in obligatory services and labor, as well as restricting their freedom of movement. It also brought growing insecurity for the now-captive rural population in the form of constant warfare among the semi-independent pashas. The central government and its local representatives lacked means to curb the growing anarchy and insecurity. The situation only worsened with uprisings in Serbia, in 1804 and 1815, and the Greek revolution and war of independence, 1821–30.

As in the past, many peasants fled to more secure regions or into mountainous areas, where they founded new settlements. Many others, however, found greater security in urban centers and, with expanding trade and commerce, better opportunities to make a living. The urban migration, which began before 1800, continued throughout the century and helped expand the Orthodox Macedonian population in towns and cities. According to a French source from 1807, Salonika had 60,000 inhabitants, one-third of them Muslim and two-thirds Christian and Jewish; Seres, 25,000, one-third Muslim and two-thirds Orthodox;

Kastoria (Kostur), 6,000, 500 Muslim, 500 Jewish, and the rest Orthodox; Melnik, 6,000 Orthodox and 100 Muslim; Edessa (Voden), 3,000 Orthodox; and Ohrid, 3,000, half of them Muslim.

Three decades later, according to Ami Bue, who traveled in Macedonia three times between 1836 and 1838, the population of Salonika and Seres remained the same. However, that of Bitola (Monastir) and Štip increased more than three times to 40,000 and 15,000–20,000, respectively; that of Ohrid doubled to 6,000, and that of Edessa (Voden) more than doubled to 7,000–8,000. He also noted other towns with 3,000–10,000 inhabitants: Skopje (10,000), Prilep (6,000–7,000), Kratavo (5,000–6,000), Tetovo (4,000–5,000), Debar (4,200), Dzhumaia (3,000–4,000), and Kavardarci (2,000–3,000).[11]

The migration of Macedonians into towns, which had been predominantly Turkish, or rather Muslim, altered their ethnic composition. It also made Macedonians increasingly important in urban economic life. The newcomers worked in the craft industries and in commerce or established their own operations, which expanded throughout the first half of the nineteenth century. Some of these industries—fur, leather, textiles—were producing to supply growing demand in the rest of the empire and beyond. According to Ami Bue, in 1827 Bitola had 1,380 shops, the majority of which were handicraft workshops; a decade later, he reported 2,150 shops. In the first half of the century, Skopje was a manufacturing center, with sixty craft industries. Salonika attracted artisans and craftspeople from all over Macedonia, and many other artisans and craftspeople sought employment in Istanbul, Smyrna, Sofia, and the autonomous principality of Serbia.[12]

The handicraft industries grew as trade and commerce expanded in Macedonia, with neighboring lands, and even with central Europe and Russia. The focal points of increasing economic activity were annual fairs *(panagjuri)* throughout Macedonia, especially in Seres, Prilep, Struga, Ohrid, Dojran, Giannitsa (Enidže Vardar), Petrich, and Nevrokop. The number of Macedonian merchants grew as well; some established good contacts with Serbia and Bosnia as well as with Albanian, Bulgarian, and Greek towns and cities. A few carried trading activities to Austria, Germany, France, and Russia. Among the most notable, Giorgi Drandar of Veles in 1836 received a special *berat* from the sultan for unhindered travel abroad. The Robev brothers of Ohrid had business establishments in Bitola, Vienna, and Leipzig and offices in Belgrade and Trieste; merchant families in Bansko exported large quantities of cotton from the Seres region to central and western Europe and brought back luxury goods and industrial products. All in all, however, while Macedonian artisans and craftsmen were gaining urban dominance, Vlach, Jewish, and Greek merchants still controlled trade and commerce.[13]

After the Crimean War (1854–56), the European powers involved themselves more in Ottoman economic life. They financed improvement of the empire's communication and transportation to further their economic domination and their exploitation of its natural resources. In the 1860s, a new road system connected major towns and cities in Macedonia. At the same time, the first telegraph lines connected Skopje with Priština and, through Belgrade, with Europe and, through Bitola, with Elbasan in Albania. In 1869, foreign companies began tracing the first railway lines in Macedonia; the track, from Salonika to Skopje and on to Kosovska Mitrovica, went into operation in 1873. It connected Salonika with its natural Macedonian and Balkan hinterland and with central Europe and helped make it Macedonia's political and economic center.

Modest improvements in Balkan communication and transportation continued until the end of Ottoman rule. However, in the short run, after 1850 European commercial interests benefited from the changes much more than the Ottoman lands themselves did. The empire could not compete economically with the rest of Europe, on which it depended financially, and it became a virtual economic colony, a source of raw materials, and a dumping ground for agricultural surpluses and cheaper manufactured goods. In Macedonia, evidence suggests that economic growth slowed, stagnated, even declined.

Macedonia's agrarian sector was too backward and inefficient to withstand the foreign challenge. After the American Civil War ended in 1865, Macedonia could not compete with cheaper and better U.S. and Indian cotton and grain. The Ottoman state did nothing either to improve crops or to stimulate production. Indeed, burdensome, unfair, and arbitrary taxation and corrupt "farming" of tax collection held the sector back. Peasants had no incentives to produce more: they were turning to subsistence farming and worked only enough land to feed their own families. There was no tax on uncultivated lands, and so only one-fifth of Macedonia's arable land was under cultivation—the rest was pasture.

Small-scale manufacturing, crafts, and trades, which grew rapidly before 1850, suffered even more. After the 1860s, Europe and even the United States sent large quantities of factory-made finished and semifinished goods, which were cheaper and better than local products.

Small-scale domestic manufacturing, particularly in towns and villages, could not compete, and it stagnated and in some instances declined. [14]

Growing political insecurity and instability hurt the economy too. Organized armed bands continued widespread pillaging, and after 1870 the emergence of the so-called Macedonian question—a struggle by Bulgaria, Greece, and Serbia for control and possession of Macedonia—made instability chronic.[15]

Propaganda War for Macedonia (1870–1900)

The history of Macedonia and the Macedonians, especially in the second half of the nineteenth century, responded to political and socioeconomic developments in the Ottoman empire and particularly to Balkan nationalism. For various geographical, historical, and contemporary reasons, which we examine in the next chapter, the Greek, Serbian, and Bulgarian national awakenings developed earlier and more rapidly than the Macedonian.

A small, autonomous Serbian state emerged after the second Serbian uprising in 1815, and by the 1860s it was virtually independent. The Congress of Berlin in 1878 recognized it as an independent kingdom. The Greeks rebelled against their Ottoman rulers in 1821, and, after a nine-year struggle that involved all the great powers, a small kingdom of Greece came into being in 1830. By the 1840s, the Bulgarian national movement could challenge Greek domination of religious and cultural life. With the aid of Russian diplomacy, the Bulgarians triumphed and in 1870 secured their own national church, the exarchate.

The Treaty of San Stefano of 1878 proposed a large, autonomous principality, a Great Bulgaria, with an elected prince. This land was to stretch from the Black Sea almost to the Adriatic and from the Danube to the Aegean and to include virtually all of Macedonia. The treaty, which Russia imposed on the defeated Ottoman empire, met with determined opposition from the great powers, especially Britain and Austria-Hungary, as well as from Serbia and Greece.

The powers met in Berlin in July and revised and replaced the document with the historic Treaty of Berlin. The new agreement divided San Stefano's Bulgaria into three parts: an autonomous Bulgaria, north of the Balkan Mountains, with its own elected prince, but under Ottoman sovereignty; Eastern Rumelia, south of the Balkan Mountains, an Ottoman province, under a Christian governor whom the High Porte appointed and the powers approved; and, Macedonia, under direct Ottoman administration.[16]

In 1885, Bulgaria annexed Eastern Rumelia; in 1908, during the European crisis that followed Austro-Hungarian annexation of Bosnia-Herzegovina, Bulgaria declared its complete independence and received recognition as a kingdom.

Already by the 1840s, a struggle for Macedonia between Bulgaria, Greece, and Serbia was clearly in the offing, and it divided them through the nineteenth and twentieth centuries. The main cause "is the strategic and economic value of the area." As we saw at the start of the book, Macedonia "commands the great corridor route that leads from central Europe to the Mediterranean along the Morava and Vardar valleys . . . Macedonia is also desirable because it includes the great port of Salonika as well as the fertile plains much coveted in the mountainous Balkan Peninsula."[17] Indeed, whoever would acquire Macedonia would dominate the Balkans.

Consequently, all three nationalisms and states created complex justifications—historical, ethnic-religious, and ethno-linguistic—for their imperial ambitions toward Macedonia and its people. They claimed both land and people on historic grounds. At one time or another, long before the age of nationalism, and before the Ottoman conquest, in the distant medieval Balkans, Macedonia was part of various dynastic or territorial empires in several centuries: Tsar Simeon's Bulgarian empire in the tenth, Byzantium in the eleventh and twelfth, and Stefan Dušan's Serbian empire in the fourteenth. Modern nationalist leaders conveniently overlooked the fact that these were territorial states that at times controlled each other's lands as well.

In the second half of the nineteenth century, the three competing states also claimed the Macedonians on ethnic grounds, purposely confusing church affiliation with ethno-linguistic belonging. All three had recognized "national" Orthodox churches and hence millets in the theocratic Ottoman state. These national churches could operate freely in Ottoman Macedonia: establish parishes and schools and, especially after 1870, serve as instruments of their respective nationalist drives and propaganda there. The Macedonians did not and could not set up their own church and therefore could not organize and conduct legally any religious and educational activities under their national name.

The Greeks claimed as "Greek" all Macedonians who attended Patriarchist (Greek) churches and schools; the Bulgarians, as "Bulgarian" all those who belonged to Exarchist (Bulgarian) churches and schools; and Serbians, as "Serbian" all who went to "their" churches and schools. In towns and in larger villages where two or all three churches operated, many families would divide or split in religion. For various reasons—social prestige and particularly economic or financial motives or inducements—three brothers could end up at three churches; each nationalist movement would claim one for its own "nation."

Finally, all three neighboring states claimed Macedonia and Macedonians or justified these assertions on ethnic-linguistic grounds. "The Serbians pointed to certain characteristics of their grammar and to their 'slava' festival as proof of their Serbian origin. The Bulgarians argued that physiologically the Macedonians were closer to them than to the Serbs and that the Macedonian language was in reality a Bulgarian dialect. And the Greeks claimed that many Macedonians considered themselves to be Greeks and therefore they referred to them as Slavophone Greeks."[18]

The Crimean War, which pushed the Eastern Question to the fore, also renewed interest in the future of the "sick man of Europe." The great powers paid close attention, and the Balkan national states and movements began to organize and work more systematically in the empire's Orthodox areas, which centered on Macedonia—the ultimate spoil of unavoidable partition.

The Greek presence and influence in Macedonia had been solid for a long time. Greek or Hellenized clerics occupied the higher ecclesiastical posts. They controlled churches and schools, and the language of both—liturgy and education—was Greek. With the spread of Serbian and Bulgarian influence in Macedonia, especially after the establishment of the Bulgarian exarchate in 1870, Greek propaganda became much better organized and more systematic. And, after the Russo–Ottoman War in 1877–78 and the emergence of the autonomous Bulgarian principality, the Greek state, through its consulates in Macedonia, took over direction of the Greek campaign for Macedonia from the prelates of the Constantinople patriarchate.

With the support of the Greek state and under its direction, Greek propaganda intensified and scored notable success. Greece opened numerous new schools and founded cultural organizations to spread Greek national consciousness among Macedonians and some other ethnic groups. It was very successful among the Vlachs, who tended to educate their children in Greek schools.

From Athens, the Society for the Propagation of Greek Literacy directed the nationalist effort, with the help of the Ministry of Foreign Affairs through its diplomatic representation and its consulates in Salonika, Bitola (Monastir), Seres, and Skopje. In 1879, the organization was allocating 189,000 drachmas per year for schools and the Hellenization of the Macedonians; by 1885, the sum rose to 536,000 drachmas. Its aim was always the same: propagation of the Greek language, culture, and national consciousness. By 1886, Greek propaganda organs and institutions maintained and controlled 836 schools in Macedonia. The institutions included three teacher-training colleges, two middle schools in the south, a boys and girls gymnasium (high school) in Bitola, and theological seminaries. They enrolled 45,000 students. In addition, the society had organized and was running various cultural, gymnastic, musical, and theatrical societies and a printing press.[19]

Serbian propaganda in Macedonia began later. Its ideological foundations appear in a memorandum of 1844 by the Serbian statesman Ilija Garašanin. In this illuminating document on foreign policy, Garašanin argues that the small principality could not survive within its existing borders and should aim and strive to annex all the surrounding Serbian-inhabited lands, including Macedonia. In 1868, Serbian "outreach" began when Belgrade created the Educational Council (Prosvetni odbor) to set up schools in Old Serbia and Macedonia and to provide them with Serbian teachers and schoolbooks. The Eastern Crisis of the 1870s interrupted the council's work, but it resumed its activities with greater determination after the Congress of Berlin and the secret Serbian-Austro-Hungarian Convention of 1881.

Until Austria's occupation of Bosnia-Herzegovina in 1878, Serbia sought primarily northward expansion. The Dual Monarchy later encouraged the Serbs to look south and promised to help them expand into Old Serbia and Macedonia. However, Bulgaria's military defeat of the Serbs and its annexation of Eastern Rumelia raised the ghost of San Stefano Bulgaria and provoked the Serbians into a more systematic and aggressive campaign for Macedonia. Belgrade set up the Society of Saint Sava (Društvo Sveti Sava), under first the Ministry of Education, and later Foreign Affairs, to set up schools, train teachers, print books, and organize propaganda in Macedonia. A new convention with the High

Porte permitted it to establish consulates in Macedonia, which it did, in Salonika and Skopje in 1887 and in Bitola in 1888.[20]

Because the Serbians lagged behind the Greeks, and fell behind the Bulgarians in propaganda, they devised a novel approach—collaboration with Macedonian patriots. In 1888, Stojan Novaković, the Serbian envoy in Constantinople, went to members of the Secret Macedonian Committee in Sofia with a proposal for cooperation. In Belgrade, the two sides agreed on a four-point program: to seek reestablishment of the Ohrid archbishopric, under the Constantinople patriarchate, and thus win the right to organize Macedonian church-school communities; to strive for publication in Constantinople of a newspaper titled *Makedinski glas* (Macedonian Voice) in Macedonian; to open schools in Macedonia and to appoint teachers who would teach in Macedonian; and to print schoolbooks and other publications in Macedonian.

This strange and short-lived experiment assumed what we call "mutual exploitation." Novaković and the Serbs had three goals: to make the Macedonians dependent on Serbia, to draw them over to its cause, and to use them to further its influence and interests in Macedonia. The plan could not reconcile the two parties' conflicting interests. It benefited Macedonianism more than Serbianism, and the Serbs soon abandoned it in favor of more traditional tactics.[21]

After persistent efforts, in the early 1890s the Serbs won the consent of the patriarch of Constantinople, who feared growing Bulgarian influence in Macedonia, to appoint a bishop in Skopje and to organize church-school communities in Macedonia. The headquarters and leadership of Serbian propaganda in Macedonia moved from Constantinople to Skopje, the supporting budget rose from 200,000 dinars in 1890 to 300,000 in 1891, and Serbian consular officials participated in church-school communities. As a result, Serbian propaganda scored some successes: church-school communities in Bitola, Prilep, and Poreče in 1890, in Kičevo in 1891, and in Galičnik, Debar, and Kruševo in 1892. Between 1890 and 1892, many such communities emerged in the Skopje vilajet in Kumanovo, Kočani, Kratovo, Gostivar, Kriva Palanko, Štip, and so on. By 1900, there were 217 such schools, with 9,179 students.[22]

The Bulgarians, however, raised the first successful challenge to Greek hegemony in Macedonia. Unlike the Serbs, the Macedonians and the Bulgarians shared experiences of foreign domination. Until 1878, both peoples were subjects of the sultan and oppressed Christians in a Muslim empire; until 1870, the Greek-dominated Patriarchist church sought to exploit and Hellenize them. Moreover, as fellow Slavs, going through an initial, very similar Slav phase in their national awakening, they both opposed the empire politically and the Greeks culturally. The Bulgarian national movement was more mature and stronger and led this common struggle. Thus, even before the exarchate became a Bulgarian national church in the empire, Bulgaria's nationalism and its national movement had made inroads in Macedonia.

The exarchate (1870), however, was the most notable Bulgarian national achievement until then. It not only furthered Bulgarian nationalism, but also spread Bulgarian influence and Bulgarianism in Macedonia. Its founding Ottoman *firman* ended the patriarchate of Constantinople's jurisdiction over the eparchies in the Bulgarian lands between the Danube and the Balkan Mountains, as well as those of Niš and Pirot (Serbia) and Veles (Macedonia), and placed religious-educational affairs there under control of the exarchate and a synod.

The firman's article 10 stipulated that other eparchies might join the Exarchist church if two-thirds of the inhabitants voted in favor.[23] The eparchies of Skopje and Ohrid soon did just that. By 1912, seven bishoprics in Macedonia were under the exarchate's control. Macedonians opted for the exarchate not because they felt themselves Bulgarian, but rather because they were Slavs who opposed Greek domination. Nonetheless, "the fact remains that the expanding Exarchate provided an instrument for Bulgarian propaganda in Macedonia just as the Patriarchate earlier had served as a means for Greek propaganda."[24]

After creation of the autonomous principality of Bulgaria in 1878, its propaganda became the most powerful and best organized in Macedonia. The new state and the exarchate worked as one in Macedonia. The government determined the aims and strategies of national propaganda and provided the resources, and the exarchate, with headquarters in Constantinople, dutifully carried them out in Macedonia. Financial support increased from 100,000 levas in 1881 to 574,874 in 1885 and, according to one Serbian report, to 5.5 million French francs in 1890.

With such generous backing, the exarchate was able to reopen many church-school communities whose work had ceased during the Russo-Ottoman war of 1877–78 and to establish more elsewhere in Macedonia. Most notable were the new boys and girls boarding gymnasia in Salonika and teacher-training colleges in Skopje and Seres and attached to the Salonika and Bitola gymnasia. In 1886, the exarchate operated

306 schools in Macedonia; by 1888/89, over 800, with 25,000–30,000 students.[25]

In addition to Greek, Serbian, and Bulgarian propaganda, which aimed to proselytize Macedonians, there was other, sectarian propaganda in Macedonia. It operated on a smaller scale and dealt mainly with religious conversion. The Catholic activities were the purview of emissaries of the Vatican. In 1886, 3,950 households, or about 20,000 inhabitants of Macedonia, recognized the pope's authority. British and American Protestant missionaries' activities took hold in eastern Macedonia, in Razlog and Nevrokop districts, and in the Struma valley. Both nationalities established and maintained schools and published mostly Bulgarian-language schoolbooks and religious pamphlets.[26]

Needless to say, the constant interference of outsiders, particularly the institutionalized nationalist interventions by Greece, Serbia, and Bulgaria, was destabilizing Macedonia and damaging its interests. It divided the small educated elite as well as the population at large into opposing camps. And this more than any other factor weakened the Macedonian movement. That movement rejected foreign propaganda and nationalist ideologies, sought Macedonian national consciousness and national identity, and called for unity behind a domestic national program defending Macedonia and its people.

6 National Awakening and National Identity (1814–1913)

Historiography

The national awakening and the formation of the Macedonian national identity formed a complex and turbulent process. They covered more time than those of most, if not all, the other "small," "young" nations in Europe and continued until the mid–twentieth century. They also engendered far greater controversies and debates than most, if not all, other nationalisms in eastern Europe, and they continue still in both politics and scholarship.

The protracted and violent struggle over Macedonia and the intense hatreds and antagonisms that it generated influenced and came to dominate the writings of both scholars and publicists in and outside the Balkan Peninsula. Hence, most of the literature on the Macedonian question, though vast, tends to be biased and tendentious, and even the scholarly works are of uneven and dubious quality and value. Moreover, the latter are of little use for the study of Macedonian nationalism. Many treat the Macedonian question as solely a European or Balkan diplomatic issue; bourgeois historians and publicists who concentrate on the question's internal aspects view it in the light of the competing states' interests and claims and define it as strictly a Bulgarian, Greek, or Serbian problem.

These scholars reflect closely the views of their respective ruling elites and thus their official nationalist ideologies. Since these in turn deny the existence of a distinct Macedonian ethnic entity, nationality, or nation, such writings cannot acknowledge, let alone consider, any expression of authentic Macedonian identity, and thus they do not study Macedonian nationalism or nationalisms in Macedonia. Rather, they look uncritically at the propaganda and armed activities of their respective Balkan nationalisms struggling for the hearts and minds of the Macedonian population. At best, they rationalize their respective national interventions and ambitions in Macedonia; at worst, they justify Balkan nationalist irredentism and imperialism.[1]

Needless to say, some writings challenged the neighbors' nationalist ambitions. The Austrian Karl Hron[2] and the Bessarabian Bulgarian Petar Draganov,[3] among others, argued before 1900 that the Macedonians constituted a distinct Slav ethnic group with all the necessary cultural attributes for nationality. Before 1914, many left-wing publicists in Balkan Social Democratic parties grasped the reality of Macedonian political consciousness and asserted Macedonians' right to self-determination. Between the wars, their successors, the Balkan Communist parties, recognized the existence of an ethnic Macedonian nation as well.[4] All in all, however, such views could not compete with the nationalist ideologies emanating from Balkan capitals.

Finally, there were Macedonians—a few scholars and many publicists and spokespeople for the national and revolutionary movements—who attempted to present and interpret their people's past and present on a Macedonian basis. However, their task was difficult: they lacked material means, and Ottoman authorities pursued and prosecuted them (until 1912), as did nationalist proponents and defenders in the neighboring Balkan states. Consequently, many of their writings never surfaced. Their publications often provoked denunciation or quick suppression; their newspapers and periodicals usually had short lives. Their writings constitute superb historical sources and are invaluable for the student of Macedonian nationalism and history. Very little of this work, however, represents scholarly investigation of either field.[5]

The systematic and scholarly study of the history of the Macedonian people began more recently, with creation of the Macedonian republic in the Yugoslav federation in 1944. The Macedonian Marxist historiography in Yugoslavia accomplished a great deal but focused on socialist and revolutionary traditions and on social and economic conditions in

Macedonia. The study of nationalism—the national awakening, the development of Macedonian thought, and the formation of Macedonian identity—did not attract much serious attention until the 1960s.[6] This was only partly the result of the federation's ideological, political, and national considerations and sensitivities. A serious practical difficulty confronts the student of Macedonian national history: scarcity of sources.

A vast amount of the requisite material is in archives, collections of manuscripts and rare books, and libraries outside the republic of Macedonia: in capitals of the former and present great powers of Europe, especially Russia, and, most important, in Balkan capitals, especially Sofia. Western archives, as well as those of Serbia/Yugoslavia, are almost completely open for research on Macedonia. The Greek archives and those of the patriarchate in Constantinople remain almost totally inaccessible for such investigation.

The Bulgarian archives and libraries, with by far the richest collections on the development of Macedonian nationalism, became and remained open while Bulgaria recognized (1944–early 1950s) the existence of the Macedonian nation. They were readily available until Yugoslavia's expulsion from the Communist bloc in 1948 and somewhat so during the "thaw" in Yugoslav–Soviet bloc relations in the late 1950s and early 1960s. After 1948, the Bulgarian Communist Party gradually shifted from recognition to negation and closed the archives and other major institutions to Yugoslav researchers, though keeping them open somewhat to others.

The Soviet archives—the richest non-Balkan source on Macedonia—became easily accessible to Yugoslav historians after 1956 and up to the late 1960s. Thereafter, cooling Yugoslav-Soviet relations and possibly Bulgarian pressure led to severe restrictions on research relating to Macedonia.[7] More recently, since the fall of Communism in 1990–91, Bulgaria and particularly Russia seem to have been relaxing such policies.

This chapter presents what historians now know about the emergence of Macedonian nationalism between about 1814 and about 1870, and it outlines the major paths to Macedonian nationhood that developed and attracted Macedonians between 1870 and 1903—the year of the Ilinden Uprising—and beyond.

Early Macedonian Nationalism (to 1870)

The examination of Macedonian nationalism is still in its early stages. Nonetheless, work to date makes it possible to survey and appraise its development and to relate it to Balkan nationalism and the Slav awakening and to the historical experiences of the other "small," "young" eastern European nations.

The national development of the Macedonians started later and trailed behind that of the Greeks, Serbs, and Bulgarians. The explanation lies substantially in Macedonia's geographic location. Macedonia did not have any direct land contact or common border with any western European land, and the Aegean littoral had mostly Greek inhabitants. Nationalist ideas reached the Macedonians mainly through Greece, Serbia, and Bulgaria.

As well, Macedonia was strategically crucial to the Ottoman empire and close to its center of power. The imperial authorities maintained a strong military presence there and, in case of unrest, could easily dispatch reinforcements to restore order. For the same reason, they settled many Turks and other Muslims in Macedonia, controlled the towns, and relegated Macedonians to isolated rural areas far more than they did people in other, more distant and strategically less important Balkan lands.

Otherwise, Macedonian national development generally resembled the process in neighboring Balkan nations. And it was almost identical to that in the other "small," "young" nations of eastern and even western Europe. The Macedonians shared, especially with the latter, certain attributes, certain "disadvantages," at the time they first experienced the force of nationalism: they all lacked a continuous historical state, a distinct church, a continuous and distinct literature, a cultural or political elite, and clearly defined historical boundaries and ethnic territory. Finally, and most important, they possessed no distinct ethnic name that would have clearly distinguished, dissociated, them from peoples with which they had in the distant past shared common experiences and traditions, which the others in the modern period appropriated. The Greeks put forth exclusive claims to the heritage of Byzantium; the Bulgarians, to that of their first and second empires and even of Samuil's "Macedonian kingdom"; and the Serbs, to that of Stephen Dušan's empire.

Needless to say, the Macedonian case also exhibited many particularities. Most of these, however, were the result of its specific circumstances and environment. The other Balkan peoples, though the Albanians less so than the rest, emerged as nations with the aid of their own state, church, and educational and cultural institutions and organizations. They frequently helped each other's cause and derived cultural aid and benefited from some or all of the great powers' open and direct diplomatic and military intervention. The Macedonian movement, in contrast, developed without a formal institutional base or infrastructure and without external aid and support. Indeed, the Macedonians had to fight for survival not only against the Ottoman empire, but also, and much more difficult, against their Balkan neighbors and their great-power patrons.

The first stage in the Macedonian awakening, from about 1814 to 1870, shows no dominant tendency or prevailing national consciousness. From the appearance of Joakim Krčovski's work, the first known printed book in the Macedonian language in 1814,[8] up to about the Crimean War (1854–56), Slav consciousness was on the rise, and we could label the era a "Slav phase." It expressed itself in scattered stirrings of the native population against the Patriarchist church and against the total domination of the Greek language in local schools and churches under its control. Macedonians worked for local community schools and churches and the introduction of the local speech *(naroden jazik)* in both. Since there were few schoolbooks in that language, and producing the writings of Joakim Krčovski, Kiril Pejčinović, and Teodosij Sinaitski was prohibitively expensive, most books for the new schools, as well as many teachers, came at first from Serbia and, after the mid-1840s, from Bulgaria, which had formed its own literary language by then.

The first generation of the Slav-Macedonian intelligentsia led these unorganized and uncoordinated stirrings of Slav consciousness. The most outstanding figures were Jordan Hadži Konstantinov-Džinot, the brothers Dimitar and Konstantin Miladinov, Kiril Prličev, and Rajko Žinzifov. All of them studied in Greek schools, but later had contact with the Slav world of Serbia, Bulgaria, or Russia and de-Hellenized themselves. Their writings, together with those of some of their predecessors, laid the foundations of a Slav-Macedonian literary tradition.[9]

However, neither they nor the population at large yet had a clearly defined national or territorial consciousness or a sense of belonging. While travelling through Macedonia in 1854, Hadži Konstantinov-Džinot reported to *Tsargradskii vesnik*, the leading Bulgarian newspaper, that he arrived in the "Bulgarian-Serbian city Skopje in Albanian Macedonia, where [they] speak the Slav (Bulgarian-Serbian) language."[10] And on 8 January 1861, K. Miladinov wrote to the Bulgarian awakener G. Rakovski to explain his use of the term "Bulgarian" in the title of his and his brother's collection of Macedonian folk songs: "In the announcement I called Macedonia West Bulgaria (as it should be called) because in Vienna the Greeks treat us like sheep. They consider Macedonia a Greek land and cannot understand that [Macedonia] is not Greek."[11] Miladinov and other educated Macedonians worried that use of the Macedonian name would imply attachment to or identification with the Greek nation.

The Macedonians referred to themselves by a confusing and changing mixture of names. To the extent that they transcended local, regional labels (Bitolčani, Kosturčani, Prilepčani, and so on), people identified themselves as Orthodox Christians and Slavs. Another popular term was *giaur* (infidel), the demeaning name that the Ottoman authorities applied to them. But they sometimes used the names of the neighboring peoples whose medieval dynastic states ruled Macedonia.

The label "Greek," more or less the official one for Orthodox Ottoman subjects, came from the Greek-controlled Patriarchist church. Until the mid–nineteenth century, most affluent Macedonians tended to regard themselves, especially abroad, as Hellenes, for reasons of both prestige and material gain and well-being.

With the Slav awakening in Macedonia, however, "Greek" began to lose some of its glamour and went into a gradual but continuous decline. "Serbian" was common among individuals and small groups in certain regions. Until adoption of "Macedonian" as a national name and symbol in mid-century, "Bulgarian" seemed to predominate, especially in religious and monastic institutions. According to Krste P. Misirkov, the ideologue of Macedonian nationalism about 1900, "Bulgarian" was a "historical relic";[12] Byzantine Greeks first applied the term to them, the Ohrid archbishopric preserved it, and Macedonians adopted it to differentiate themselves from Greeks. It did not imply unity or community with the real Bulgarians: between the 1820s and the 1840s, the Macedonians had very little contact with them, knew even less about them, and called them "Šopi." In any event, except for "Slav" (a national name, self-identification, and self-ascription), these labels came from other people, had no roots in popular tradition, and did not denote and carry any sense of national consciousness.[13]

As we saw above, the Crimean War, which reactivated the Eastern Question, also renewed interest in the future of the "sick man of Europe." This was true of the great powers, but even more so of the Balkan peoples, who, to prepare for partition of the Ottoman empire, began to organize and to work more systematically in the empire's Orthodox areas, which centered on Macedonia. The long-standing and solid Greek presence was now facing a vacillating challenge from Serbia and a much more determined approach by the Bulgarian national movement. The latter was becoming confident and strong at home, as well as in Constantinople, Romania, and Russia, and had the backing of Russia's diplomacy.

The intensified general interest—no longer just educational in Macedonía—put educated Macedonians in closer contact especially with their Slav neighbors and awakened their interest in themselves and concern for their future. Since they knew of the weak Slav awakening in Macedonia, they tended to join forces, as junior partners, with the Bulgarians in a common struggle against well-entrenched Hellenism. Such a united effort seemed only natural: the two peoples shared linguistic affinity, some historical traditions, and Greek cultural domination, and they were the only Orthodox Christians still under Ottoman rule. As a result of this situation, the Bulgarian national idea made major inroads in Macedonia. Many formerly Greek positions went to Bulgarian patriots or to Macedonians who studied in Bulgarian schools in the Ottoman empire or in Russia. There was an influx into Macedonia of Bulgarian schoolbooks, newspapers, and teachers, and use of the Bulgarian language started in schools and churches.

These activities, which aimed to entrench the Bulgarian national idea in Macedonia, provoked a considerable reaction in the 1860s. Educated Macedonians embraced the name of their land as a national name and symbol and rose in defense of Macedonian interests. They argued—and the Bulgarian press condemned them—that "a Bulgarian and a Bulgarian language was one thing and a Macedonian and a Macedonian language something else." They insisted that it was necessary "to protect the Macedonian youth," who "should be taught and should develop exclusively in the Macedonian speech." Indeed, some of these "Makedonisti," as the Bulgarian press called them, went much further. They claimed to be the "purest Slavs" and "descendants of the ancient Macedonians" of Philip and Alexander. They were in effect asking: "We broke away from the Greeks, should we now fall under others?"[14]

Although we know little about the Makedonisti, available evidence suggests reasonable, extensive, coordinated activity. By the late 1860s, they had apparently become a significant movement that alarmed the Bulgarians. The most reliable and enlightening information about them comes from the outstanding Bulgarian awakener, publicist, and poet Petko R. Slaveikov. He helped direct the Bulgarian drive in Macedonia and grasped the situation there. In "The Macedonian Question," an article for *Makedoniia* (Constantinople) early in 1871, he revealed the existence of the Macedonian movement and question. He explained that the problem was not new, that it had been around for well over a decade, and that the Bulgarians had not taken it seriously; as late as 1870, he himself had tended to underestimate the force of the ideas of the Makedonisti. However, more recent contacts with Macedonians "showed to us that we are dealing not merely with empty words, but rather with an idea that many wish to turn into life."[15]

Three years later, the exarch sent Slaveikov to Macedonia to inquire about growing sentiment against his church. In February 1874, Slaveikov reported from Salonika that the Macedonians believed that answers to the Macedonian question favored only the Bulgarians; they insisted that they were not Bulgarian, wanted their own, separate church, and resisted the "east" Bulgarian language in their literature. He stressed the trend of thought that sought elevation of Macedonian to a literary language and creation of a Macedonian hierarchy through reestablishment of the Ohrid archbishopric. He concluded: "If steps are not taken from a place of authority, there is danger that this [tendency] would grow into common thinking. Then the consequences will be much more serious."

Two days later, in another letter from Salonika, Slaveikov told the exarch: "Even in the language of communication of the Macedonian activists there is talk of a 'Macedonian movement,' which should be understood as independent national and religious emancipation . . . the separatism is spreading from a religious to wider national foundation."[16]

The clash between Bulgarianism and Macedonianism, which began about mid-century, involved crucial questions for any people: language, historical and religious traditions, ethnicity, national identity, local patriotism, and so on. It produced a clear distinction between the interests of the well-established Bulgarian national movement and the Macedonians. More important, it aided the national awakening of the Macedonians and the shaping of their separate national identity. In the long run, it gave rise to two distinct national conceptions—Bulgarian and Macedonian—for the future of Slavs still under Ottoman rule.

Paths to Nationhood (1870–1913)

In this section, we look at the Macedonians' reactions to the nationalist claims of the neighboring Balkan states, which we examine first. Their responses coalesced into three national trends, which also represented paths to Macedonian nationhood: the masses' Macedonianism, or *naši-zam* (nativism), and the intelligentsia's two competing trends, Macedono-Bulgarianism and Macedonianism. In setting the context for the last two trends, we look also at the "philisms" of a number of intellectuals vis-à-vis Bulgaria, Greece, and Serbia.

The establishment of a Bulgarian national church, the exarchate, in 1870 represented a turning point for both the Bulgarians and the Macedonians. For the former, it was the most notable triumph of their national movement until then; for the latter, the greatest stumbling block and challenge to the continued development of their national consciousness and identity. The Ottoman government set it up as an Ottoman institution—in effect a (Slav) Orthodox millet, in addition to the (Greek) Orthodox one under the Patriarchist church. As a legal institution, the exarchate received all the rights and privileges that the patriarchate enjoyed: to establish, direct, and control the cultural, the social, and, to a lesser extent, the economic and political life of those communities or regions that it was able to win over to its jurisdiction.

As the Ottoman empire's only legal and free Slav church, the exarchate became influential among the empire's Slav masses and soon was leading the anti-Patriarchist, or anti-Greek movement in its remaining Slavic-populated areas, in Bulgaria and Macedonia. The exarchate participated in this struggle, along with its other activities, not in the name of Slavdom, but rather for the Bulgarian national cause.

From its inception, the exarchate became the guiding force behind Bulgarian nationalism and the most effective instrument for spreading the Bulgarian national idea, especially in Macedonia. In the theocratic Ottoman state, the central administration took virtually no interest in non-Muslim cultural and social life, leaving the field wide open for the exarchate. With the state's consent, it gradually became influential among the Macedonians. After 1878, the new principality of Bulgaria placed its power and resources at the disposal of the national church in its struggle with the Patriarchists.[17]

Growing Bulgarian influence in Macedonia provoked challenges. As we saw in the previous chapter, the Patriarchist church was determined to preserve its traditional dominance. After 1870, it worked even harder, and supportive Greece matched every Bulgarian move. Furthermore, Serbia, whose interest in Macedonia had long been rather cursory, entered the fray in serious fashion after 1878, and particularly following its crushing military defeat by Bulgaria in 1885.

Thus by the 1880s a vicious three-way struggle for Macedonia was under way. As we saw above, the antagonists sought control of Macedonia's cultural and spiritual life through domination of schools, churches, the press, and communal organizations. They fought first with propaganda, political pressure, and enormous financial expenditures. Over time, however, and especially after Macedonia's Ilinden Uprising of 1903, they resorted to armed force. All three antagonists sought to terrorize the others and their followers and to win over the Macedonian population, or rather terrorize it into submission. They aimed variously to annex the entire territory (Bulgaria's plan) or to partition it (Greece and Serbia's later hope).

The Ottoman administration tolerated and tacitly encouraged the competition, in total accord with the basic principle of its statecraft: divide and rule in order to survive. In such circumstances, Macedonian national consciousness could hardly continue to awaken and grow. With strong pressure from every side—state authority and the other Balkan nationalisms—the young and weak Macedonian movement could barely function and lacked material means and institutional foundations. Even the new but impoverished middle class was vulnerable to the foreign propaganda. As well, the opposition was overwhelmingly strong. Consequently, Macedonian movements could operate only illegally and underground and, until the revolutionary organization emerged in the 1890s, in isolation from its population.

In this post-1870 situation, the ethnically homogeneous, Orthodox Slavic Macedonians experienced an artificial division into three "faiths," attending variously a Bulgarian (Exarchist), Greek (Patriarchist), or Serbian church. And such church affiliation split them into Bulgarian, Greek, and Serbian "nations," or rather "parties." This situation, of course, did not necessarily represent assimilation, the acquisition of a particular national consciousness. It only reflected Macedonia's peculiar political reality.

Most Macedonians attended religious services in a language they did not understand; as well, in the 1880s most were illiterate or semiliterate, and into the interwar years many Macedonians would remain so. The vast majority of students at foreign (propaganda) schools received only one to three years of elementary schooling—insufficient even to grasp Bulgarian and Serbian, let alone Greek. Macedonian dialects remained the language of home and everyday life for Macedonians, who continued to identify with them and with the rich folklore and the traditional ways of Macedonia.

Populist Macedonianism, or našizam, was to become a powerful force among the Macedonians. If the masses of the population had any political awareness, it was certainly *not* a developed Bulgarian, Greek, or Serbian national consciousness, as we can see from reports by Balkan diplomatic and religious representatives in the Ottoman empire, as well as by foreign officials in Macedonia.[18] Their protonational consciousness was largely a response to such factors as language, folklore, customs, traditions, and local interests—symbols that they now identified with Macedonia and which differentiated them from their neighbors and others.

In August–September 1907, M. Petraiev, a Russian consular official and keen Balkan observer, accompanied Hilmi Pasha, inspector general for Macedonia, and an Austro-Hungarian representative on a tour of Macedonia. Afterward, he reported to his Ministry of Foreign Affairs: "In the Kastoria kaza, delegations from the villages came to see us and declared that they wanted neither Greek nor Bulgarian teachers and priests; rather, they insisted that they be Macedonians. When questioned about their nationality, they replied that they are Macedonians. These declarations, which are far from being isolated, demonstrate that the Christian population of Macedonia is fed-up with the oppression of the various propagandas, and that in them is beginning to awaken a national consciousness different from those being imposed on them from the outside."[19]

Macedonians' sense of belonging, of togetherness, colored their perceptions of themselves and others, and they normally expressed it with the dichotomy *nie–tie* (we–they), *naš–vaš* (ours–yours), or *naš–čuž* (our–foreign, strange). Already in the first two decades of the 1800s, Kiril

Pejčinović, one of the first writers of Macedonian vernacular, referred to his people as *našinski* (our).[20] And *naš* is by far the most common self-ascription in the brothers Miladinov's famous 1861 collection of folk songs.[21] This prevalent attitude—a peasant conception, or ideology, of našizam—prevented entrenchment of foreign national ideas. This form of incipient, or latent national consciousness survived in the three parts of divided Macedonia well into the 1930s and is still common among Aegean Macedonians and their compatriots in Canada, the United States, and Australia.

Našizam was evident to Captain P. H. Evans, a British officer with the Special Operations Executive (SOE) who was dropped in western Aegean Macedonia in September 1943 and spent almost a year there as a British liaison officer (BLO) and station commander. He dwelled and moved freely among the Macedonians, "who accepted and trusted him." He described them as "temperamental and distrustful creatures." Living under so many masters, they had developed "a perfect duplicity" of character, and "this makes them difficult to know. . . . It is hard to find out what they are thinking." "The ordinary Macedonian villager," Evans continues, "is curiously neutral, he adopts a protective coloring and, like the chameleon, can change it when necessary." However, he emphasizes:

> It is also important to emphasize that the inhabitants, just as they are not *Greeks*, are also not *Bulgarians* or *Serbs* or *Croats*. They are *Macedonians*. . . . The Greeks always call them *Bulgars* and damn them accordingly. . . . If they were *Bulgars*, how is it that while they are spread over part of four countries, one of which is *Bulgaria*, they consider themselves a single entity and for the most part describe themselves as *Macedonians*? . . .
>
> The *Macedonians* are actuated by strong but mixed feelings of patriotism . . . , a thriving and at times fervent local patriotism; and a feeling hard to assess because rarely uttered before a stranger . . . for *Macedonia* as such, regardless of present frontier-lines, which are looked upon as usurpation. . . .
>
> The same tenacity comes out in *Macedonian* songs, the traditional ones as well as those which have been made expressly in the present war. It is true that the songs usually mention *Macedonia* and not one particular place in *Macedonia*, but the feeling, which runs through them, is a simple and direct love of country, not an intellectual enthusiasm for a political idea. . . . Passing through them all is the *Macedonian*'s love of the place he lives in. . . .
>
> *Macedonian* patriotism is not artificial; it is natural, a spontaneous

> and deep-rooted feeling which begins in childhood, like everyone else's patriotism.[22]

Radically different conditions after 1870, however, affected the small intelligentsia, some of whose members had profound attachments—"philisms"—toward Bulgaria, Greece, and Serbia, which feelings began to wane in the face of Macedono-Bulgarianism and Macedonianism, which we consider below.

Those youths whose families had private means or benefited from the great generosity of the propaganda spreaders could continue studies in Athens, Belgrade, Sofia, or the famous Exarchist gymnasium in Salonika. There young Macedonians mastered the host state's language and became familiar with its national ideology and culture. Some embraced the new teaching, for all practical purposes assimilating themselves into what seemed a superior culture and moving toward "philism." The others rejected this road partially or totally and assumed leadership in both the Macedonian national and revolutionary movements.

Cleavages within the Macedonian intelligentsia had been discernible and found expression in pre-1870 debates. After 1870, or rather in the last quarter of the century, however, they intensified and coalesced into three major orientations: philisms (Bulgarian, Greek, and Serbian), Macedono-Bulgarianism, and Macedonianism. These survived in modified forms and in varying strength well into the twentieth century.

The actively philist section of the intelligentsia had few adherents but tended to represent more affluent elements in the small middle class. Though initially strongest, Grecophilism continued its downward slide; Serbophilism, while it attracted a following, never spread widely. Both Grecophiles and Serbophiles tended to total assimilation and absorption by the two respective nations. Except for the minority among them whose lingering patriotism led them to seek Macedonian territorial autonomy or independence as the only practical resolution of the Macedonian question, they did not help develop Macedonian national consciousness.

Bulgarophilism, in contrast, was increasing not so much in Macedonia as among Macedonians in Bulgaria proper. Many Macedonians sought refuge there from Ottoman oppression, and their numbers grew greatly after the unsuccessful uprisings of 1878 and 1903 and after the two Balkan Wars and the First World War. The Bulgarophiles experienced cultural assimilation and considered themselves Bulgarian. But unlike Grecophiles and Serbophiles, or at least far more than those two groups, they maintained their Macedonian connection, continued to identify with Macedonia, and called themselves "Macedonian Bulgarians" (Makedonski būlgari). They accepted the Bulgarian national cause wholeheartedly and dreamt of a Great Bulgaria in which Macedonia was to take a central place.

They welcomed the exarchate as the first and most significant victory and, after creation of the Bulgarian principality in 1878, advocated annexation of Macedonia as one people in a common territorial state. The Bulgarophiles were behind the founding in 1895, in Sofia, of the Supreme Macedonian-Adrianople Committee (Vūrkhoven Makedonsko-odrinski komitet)—a rival to the Internal Macedonian Revolutionary Organization (Vnatrešna Makedonska Revolucionerna Organizacija, or VMRO) of 1893—to carry on the struggle.

By 1901, the government and court in Sofia, which continued to seek a Great (San Stefano) Bulgaria, brought it under their control, and the *vrhovisti* and their ideology, *vrhovism*, identified themselves totally with the interests of the Bulgarian state in Macedonia.

Bulgarophilism, like Greco- and Serbophilism, did not further Macedonian national consciousness and in fact strongly harmed its evolution. By using the Macedonian name and through its influence among the Macedonian émigrés in Bulgaria and its connections with the Bulgarian establishment, it sought and often was able to manipulate and divert authentic expressions of Macedonian patriotism and nationalism in the interests of Bulgarian expansionism.[23]

In contrast to the philisms of some intellectuals, the two major national trends within the intelligentsia—Macedono-Bulgarianism and Macedonianism—constituted a fateful duality as parallel and somewhat separate developments of Macedonian national consciousness. The former represented a political and territorial sensibility, and the latter, ethnic and cultural as well.

Macedono-Bulgarianism initially attempted a compromise between Macedonianism and Bulgarianism, as its members of the intelligentsia sought to reconcile lack of a Slav-Macedonian state and church with the existence of distinct Macedonian cultural traits and political and socioeconomic interests.

The group's study of the past, though incomplete, uncovered a medieval Slav state in Macedonia—Tsar Samuil's "Macedonian kingdom," which carried the Bulgarian name—and a church, the Ohrid archbishopric, which identified with it. The group's adherents took the name "Macedono-Bulgarians," but they felt themselves different from the "upper Bulgarians" *(gorni Būgari)*, the 'Šopi' of the earlier period. Their debates with the Bulgarians centered on language. They rejected the Bulgarian literary language, which derived from the most easterly Bulgarian dialects; they insisted on use of Macedonian *(narečje)* in elementary schooling, and schoolbooks in that language came from Partenija Zografski, Kuzman Šapkarev, Venijamin Mačukovski, Dimitar Makedonski, Dimitar Uzunov, and particularly Ǵorǵija Pulevski.

Furthermore, they sought a common, compromise literary language, which would not only factor in Macedonian but would come from it, since, they argued, it was the direct successor of the old language of SS Cyril and Methodius. Zografski, Šapkarev, and Mačukovski even worked on "Bulgarian grammars of the Macedonian speech," which attempts jolted the Bulgarian establishment.[24]

Their efforts, however, went nowhere. The victorious and confident Bulgarian national movement was in no mood for compromise. More important, the three-way struggle for Macedonia and the land's relative weakness forced the Macedono-Bulgarians to adjust to current conditions. Soon after 1870, they abandoned the demand for an autonomous church and thus accepted the new exarchate's jurisdiction, and they also acquiesced to use of Bulgarian in schools.

Over time, however, they intensified their defense of the political interests of Macedonia and its people. They denounced all foreign interference, propagated full political separation of the Macedonians from the Bulgarians, and began a long struggle for an autonomous or independent Macedonia.

Although they expected sympathy and support from the Bulgarians, the latter consistently condemned the movement as "political separatism." In fact it was much more: it represented authentic Macedonian patriotism, indeed, political nationalism. Macedono-Bulgarianism manifested itself in at least three ways between 1870 and 1890: in a widespread movement (early 1870s) for an autonomous Macedonian church through reestablishment of the Ohrid archbishopric or creation of a Uniate or a Protestant church for Macedonia; in uprisings at Razlog (1876) and Kresna (1878); and in a spontaneous mass social-political movement (late 1880s) against the Exarchist church and its growing interference in Macedonian life, especially in towns and cities.

In the 1890s, these stirrings of discontent and expressions of Macedonian consciousness coalesced into a powerful movement under the new Internal Macedonian Revolutionary Organization (Vnatrešna Makedonska Revolucionerna Organizacija, or VMRO). The VMRO, which Misirkov believes represented "a landmark in our [Macedonian] history,"[25] raised the slogan "Macedonia for the Macedonians" and provided leadership and organization in the struggle for liberation of Macedonia from Ottoman rule.

Even though many of its leaders were Macedono-Bulgarians, its proclamations, statutes, and programs addressed all Slav Macedonians, regardless of church or "party," as well as non-Slav minorities, Turks, Vlachs, Greeks, and Jews. Its ultimate aims were autonomy, independence, and eventually a place in a Slav or a wider Balkan federation. From the outset, it prized its own freedom of action. While welcoming aid, it rejected all outside interference; it stressed repeatedly that the struggle was the task exclusively of Macedonians, who alone should liberate their homeland.

From its launch, the VMRO and the national movement as a whole focused on political liberation. The VMRO downplayed questions about the ethnic identity of the (Slav) Macedonians, which seemed potentially explosive and divisive at a time when unity was essential. The movement often appeared to outsiders to be leaning to or even being under the sway of Bulgaria; most of its leaders had studied in Bulgaria or in Exarchist schools, and the Exarchist side tolerated and sometimes aided their activities. However, the VMRO condemned the interference of all the neighboring states and blamed them for the artificial divisions among the (Slav) Macedonians.

There was not total internal unity on this issue; there were differences even among the VMRO leaders. The body's right wing had many adherents among Macedonians living in Bulgaria and was openly Bulgarophilic in its cultural and national orientation. The left wing, which included the most outstanding leaders (Delčev, Gruev, Sandanski, Petrov, Hadžidimov, Poparsov, and Tošev), operated in Macedonia, was in closer touch with the našizam of the masses, leaned toward socialism, and usually played down or ignored the ethnic question. Thus political, ideological, tactical, and practical considerations encouraged these leaders to postpone consideration of this issue for Macedonians to resolve on their own after liberation.[26]

As long as the left wing directed and controlled the VMRO, until after the Ilinden Uprising of 1903, the organization emphasized the Macedonian people *(narod)*, patriotism, political consciousness, and total equality of all ethnic groups and religions in Macedonia. After Ilinden, the right wing took over the organization, along with Bulgarophiles and *vrhovisti* (Supremists), and its orientation changed substantially.

Macedonianism (Makedonizam), the second major post-1870 trend (along with Macedono-Bulgarianism), represented a clear and authentic expression of national consciousness and identity. Its roots appear in that section of the Macedonian intelligentsia of the 1860s that took the name of the land as a national name and proclaimed the Macedonians direct descendants of the ancient eponymous people and a distinct and separate Slav nation. Most of its advocates hailed from the lower classes, village and petty-bourgeois intellectuals and craftspeople.

The "Makedonisti" differed from the "philes" and the right-wing Macedono-Bulgarians in their early education. The "philes" had studied in the schools of only one propaganda or in one of the respective Balkan states; the Macedono-Bulgarians, almost exclusively in Exarchist schools or in Bulgaria. Many leading figures of Macedonianism, like some left-wingers in the VMRO, had attended schools of two or all three of the proselytizers, and a few, just Serbian schools in Macedonia or in Belgrade.

It appears that such varied exposure strengthened their conviction, which they derived from našizam, that Macedonians were not Bulgarian, Serbian, or Greek and that Macedonian constituted a separate Slav language somewhere between Bulgarian and Serbian. They therefore denounced all three forms of propaganda operating in Macedonia and their efforts to divide Slavic Macedonians. As a result they ended up facing pursuit and persecution by all three and having to work mostly in secret, with no aid and no institutional base or organizational network in Macedonia.

Consequently, Macedonianism, which seemed promising in the 1860s, could evolve after 1870, but only in a rather haphazard and unsystematic fashion. It found expression in the works of individuals such as Ǵ. Pulevski, a self-taught philologist, poet, and historian, or in the activities of the Exarchist metropolitan of Skopje, Teodosija Gologanov, who split with the exarchate in the hope of reestablishing the Ohrid archbishopric as a Macedonian church and of founding Macedonian schools. Spontaneous mass outbreaks occurred, mainly against the exarchate, demanding a Macedonian church and use of Macedonian in schools; many people tried to prepare Macedonian grammars, dictionaries, and schoolbooks and to secure publication of newspapers in the language.

In the late 1880s, the breeding ground for Macedonianism was numerous secret and legal circles and societies. Some emerged in Macedonia, but most of them abroad, in Belgrade, Sofia, and Russia, some with their own, short-lived publications. More than twenty existed before the Balkan Wars—most notably, the Young Macedonian Literary Group (Sofia, 1892), with its journal, *Loza* (Grapevine); the Vardar Student Society (Belgrade, 1893); the Macedonian Club, with its reading room and *Balkanski glasnik* (Balkan Herald) (Belgrade, 1902); and the Macedonian Scientific-Literary Society (Makedonsko naučno-literaturno drugarstvo) (St. Petersburg, 1902), which served until 1917 as a Macedonian *matica*. Through its many activities and publications, including the monthly *Makedonskii golos (Makedonski glas)* (Macedonian Voice) in 1913 and 1914, the St. Petersburg society presented a Macedonian point of view and the interests of Macedonia and the Macedonians.

Memberships in these organizations, which included also major left-wing leaders of the VMRO, frequently overlapped. Circumstances forced many individuals to keep moving until many found safe haven in the Russian capital. These bodies contributed some of the best-known ideologues and activists of Macedonianism, such as K. P. Misirkov, D. Čupovski, N. Dimov, Dr. G. Konstantinović, Stefan Dedov, and D. T. Mišajkov. And in that context, a clear national program crystallized, which the Bulgarians dubbed "national separatism." Its principal points received public expression in 1902 in the newspaper *Balkanski glasnik* and on 12 November of that year in a lengthy memorandum from the Macedonian Scientific-Literary Society to the council of the St. Petersburg Slavic Benevolent Society and to the Russian government. However, Krste P. Misirkov's Macedonian-language *Za makedonckite raboti*, which he wrote during the Ilinden Uprising and published in Sofia in December 1903, gave its fullest elaboration.[27]

The principal aims of Macedonianism were recognition of the Macedonians as a distinct Slav nation; acceptance of Macedonian as a literary language and its introduction in schools and administration; reestablishment of the Ohrid archbishopric as a Macedonian autocepha-

> lous church and termination of all foreign propaganda; and autonomy within the Ottoman empire, which would guarantee unity and normal national development of the people.
>
> Thus, unlike the VMRO, the "political separatists," Makedonisti, or "national separatists," sought above all free and unhindered national cultural development through expulsion of foreign propaganda organizations. For this reason, they opposed a revolutionary struggle against the Ottoman empire, which they viewed as a potential ally in the confrontation with Bulgaria, Greece, and Serbia. Only evolution and cooperation with the Ottoman empire, and perhaps help from some great powers, could free Macedonia from the pretenders and prepare its people for an independent national and political life.[28]

Such parallel and somewhat separate development of Macedono-Bulgarianism and Macedonianism as expressions of Macedonian consciousness and identity weakened the movement for national liberation. In the final analysis, however, the divisions appeared as an unavoidable consequence of the hazy historical tradition; they resulted above all from the complex contemporary reality of Macedonia and the Macedonians.

The three major strands—the intelligentsia's Macedono-Bulgarianism and Macedonianism and popular Macedonianism (našizam)—would come together only in the 1930s, under entirely different circumstances.

7 The VMRO and Ilinden (1893–1903)

The Internal Macedonian Revolutionary Organization (Vnatrešna Makedonska Revolucionerna Organizacija, or VMRO) and the Ilinden (St. Elias's Day) Uprising on 2 August 1903 occupy a sacred place in Macedonian history and in the imagination of patriotic Macedonians everywhere.[1]

The VMRO organized the 1903 uprising in Ilinden and aimed to establish an autonomous or an independent Macedonian state, or a "free Macedonia" *(slobodna Makedonija)*. The VMRO and the revolt help explain the subsequent history of Macedonia and the Macedonians. The VMRO, in one or another of its variants, became a permanent fixture in Macedonian history and survives today.

Ilinden became synonymous with the Macedonian national struggle. The push for national recognition and statehood during the Second World War and the achievement of both within Tito's Communist-led Yugoslav national liberation movement before war's end earn the term "second Ilinden." And the proclamation of independence by the republic of Macedonia in 1991, in the wake of Yugoslavia's bloody disintegration, is often the "third Ilinden."

The leaders of the original VMRO, in the Ilinden period, and the failed uprising itself have become icons in the Macedonian pantheon and mythology. They have served as sources of pride and inspiration for generations of Macedonians in their efforts for national recognition and freedom.

Two sections make up this chapter. First, the VMRO emerged in 1893 and grew over the following decade. Second, the VMRO's Ilinden Uprising started 2 August 1903 and ended with its bloody suppression in the autumn.

The VMRO (1893–1903)

On the eve of the twentieth century, Macedonia was a backward, unstable, and neglected region of the Ottoman empire. The lot of the mass of its inhabitants was difficult and deteriorating; this was particularly true of the Macedonians, the majority of the multi-ethnic population. The empire's economic stagnation was clearly evident in Macedonia, with a general decline in economic life. The small-scale manufacturing that had made a promising beginning in the first half of the century was not growing. Some new small enterprises were emerging, but in cities such as Salonika and Bitola (Monastir) and usually under the control of foreigners or members of the other ethnicities in Macedonia: Greeks, Jews, Vlachs.

The basis of the economy remained agriculture: 80 percent of the population was rural and worked in farming, as did half of the urban inhabitants. However, the agrarian sector, like the economy as a whole, was suffering. There was shortage of cultivated land, and by 1900 the oppressive chiflik landholding system embraced all the fertile areas of Macedonia. Muslim lords, or *beys*, were the de facto owners of virtually all the fertile arable land; 552 chifliks controlled half of it.[2] Most of the other chifliks were breaking down into small and unprofitable estates. The entire sector was backward and primitive in operation and working methods.

There were some 180,000 agricultural households in Macedonia in 1900; only 15,000 possessed large or medium holdings, and 10,000, small holdings. About 70 percent owned no land or a totally inadequate amount. They worked under unbearable conditions on chiflik lands, which usually belonged to Turkish or Albanian beys. Most residents of chiflik villages and exploited workers on chiflik lands were Macedonian. In fact, four-fifths of those villages were home to Macedonians, and the rest of the agrarian population eked out an almost equally miserable existence tilling the poor soil surrounding their mountainous villages.[3]

The taxation system had become corrupt, unjust, and oppressive to the Christian peasants. Tax collectors bought their posts from the government at high prices and enriched themselves at the expense of the poor tax-paying raya. The latter had to make numerous payments to the government—a military head-tax, an education tax, a tax for the upkeep of roads and bridges, and so on—and received nothing in return. However, "The most onerous tax imposed on Christian peasants was the *ösür*, 10 percent levy on their total income, crops and produce. Tax collectors, acting as officers of the state, overtaxed peasants in order to turn a profit, sometimes demanding five or six times the *ösür*, arrived at by overestimating the market value of the crops. There were instances when peasants were left with virtually nothing after the visit of a tax collector, and sometimes the *raya* simply destroyed their crops rather than pay the exorbitant rates, since the deficit was no greater than if they had paid the taxes."[4]

Political conditions were even worse. The imperial officials sent to peripheral provinces such as Macedonia were corrupt, inefficient, and ineffective. The administrative apparatus guaranteed Muslim predominance; it could not ensure law and order or provide minimal security of life and property to Christians. According to one estimate, in 1895 alone there were 150 Muslim armed bands terrorizing Macedonian villages, committing murder, rape, and extortion.[5]

The neighboring states' continuing and intensifying struggle for Macedonia further complicated the political situation. A church-sponsored drive for control of Macedonians' spiritual and cultural life via propaganda, threats, and enormous funding had by the 1890s become state-sponsored and -supported campaigns of increasing violence. By 1900, use of force was almost standard, with armed bands terrorizing Macedonians.

The Greek drive in Macedonia was now under the leadership of the National Society (Ethniki Hetairia)—a secret organization that started in Athens in 1894—and had support from the Greek government, army officers, and wealthy and influential citizens. In place of the St. Sava Society, Belgrade created the Political Education Department (Političko prosvetno odelenie) to direct Serbia's efforts in Macedonia. The great successes of the exarchate and Bulgarian diplomacy in Macedonia inspired creation in Sofia of the Macedonian Supreme Committee (Makedonski vūrkhoven komitet) in 1895. The new body "ostensibly represented the Macedonian immigrants in Bulgaria," but in reality "it was organized under the auspices of the Bulgarian crown and was essentially a Bulgarian instrument."[6]

All the antagonists sought to browbeat each other and each other's "parties" in Macedonia and to win the support of its people—or rather to terrorize them into submission. Their ultimate goal was to prepare conditions either for the land's annexation (Bulgaria's objective) or for its partition, which gradually became acceptable to Greece and Serbia.

It was Macedonia's unenviable and untenable situation—economic backwardness and exploitation, political instability, insecurity, oppression, and the real threat of annexation or partition—that drove patriotic intellectuals to start organizing to defend the interests of their land and people. As we saw in the previous chapter, in the 1880s and early 1890s they formed various groups and circles in towns in Macedonia, as well as in Bulgaria, Serbia, and outside the Balkans. Many of them, however, wanted a body that would unite them and organize and coordinate the efforts of all patriots.

The foundations of such an association, which became the Internal Macedonian Revolutionary Organization (Vnatrešna Makedonska Revolucionerna Organizacija, or VMRO),[7] were the work of young men who met in Salonika on 23 October (O.S.) / 3 November (N.S.) 1893. The founders were five Exarchist schoolteachers, Hristo Bataldžiev (1868–1913), Andon Dimitrov (1867–1933), Damian (Dame) Gruev (1871–1906), Ivan Hadžinikolov (1872–1903), and Petar Poparsov (1868–1941), and a physician, Dr. Hristo Tatarčev (1869–1952), who had studied in Zurich and Berlin.

In 1894, schoolteacher Giorgi (Goce) Delčev (1872–1903) joined them; the military academy in Sofia had recently expelled him for revolutionary activities. He soon emerged as the movement's outstanding leader but died in the spring of 1903 in a highly suspicious ambush by Ottoman troops. His death deprived the VMRO of its most charismatic, selfless, devoted leader and its guiding spirit shortly before the Ilinden Uprising, which he sought to forestall.

Others who joined in the mid-1890s and left their imprint were Jane Sandanski (1872–1915), a shoemaker who emerged as a post-Ilinden leader of the VMRO's left wing, and Dimo Hadžidimov (1875–1924) and Ǵorče Petrov (1864–1921), both teachers, writers, intellectuals, and ideologists of the movement's left.

The body that these well-educated young men[8] founded was not a modern political party with a particular ideology. It was rather a movement for national liberation comprising different ideological orientations, ranging from conservatism and clericalism on the right to socialism and anarchism on the extreme left. Its outstanding leaders were in effect populists within a not clearly defined left. They came together not through a common political ideology but rather because of their shared love for Macedonia and its people *(narod)*, their common patriotism, and their common national-political consciousness.

Their and the VMRO's main, if not sole, common aim was the liberation of Macedonia and its people and the establishment of an autonomous and eventually an independent homeland or an equal partnership in some sort of Balkan federation. Such a state would liberate the Macedonians from Ottoman domination, which they equated with political oppression, economic exploitation, and cultural backwardness. It would also free them from the devastating foreign—Bulgarian, Greek, Serbian—propaganda, intervention, and terror, which split the Slav Macedonians in family, village, town, and homeland into antagonistic "parties," or camps, and threatened annexation or partition. Macedonians were to free their land for the Macedonians.[9]

The VMRO's founders and most of its pre-Ilinden leaders sincerely believed in autonomy and had a clear idea about territorial boundaries—to include all of geographic Macedonia[10]—but not about terms such as "Macedonian people" (Makedonski narod) and "Macedonians" (Makedonci). They knew about the many religions—Orthodox Christians, Muslims, Jews, and so on—and that Orthodox Christians consisted of Exarchists, Patriarchists, and adherents of the Serbian church. They were equally aware of the many ethnic groups: Turks, Greeks, Jews, Albanians, Vlachs, Roma (gypsies), and so forth. But the VMRO's pronouncements and the writings of its leaders and spokesmen suggest less-clear thinking about the ethnic belonging and identity of their own people—the majority Macedonians, or Macedonian Slavs, the Makedonski narod—which they claimed to represent and on whose behalf they launched a life-or-death struggle.

As we saw in chapter 6, the Makedonisti in the movement identified themselves and all Slav Macedonians, irrespective of church affiliation, as Macedonians, as a distinct ethnic entity related to, but different and separate from, the Bulgarian and Serbian. At the other extreme, the Bulgarophiles considered themselves and all Slav Macedonians Bulgarian.

However, the views of many, if not most, top leaders were not so clear-cut or easily discernible. They had studied in Exarchist (Bulgarian) schools and worked in Exarchist (Bulgarian) institutions or organizations. They referred to themselves and to Exarchist Macedonians as Macedonian Bulgarians (Makedonski Būlgari).

Yet their patriotism and national identity were Macedonian, not Bulgarian. Did they consider themselves and all the other Exarchist Macedonians ethnically the same as the Bulgarians of Bulgaria proper, or different (i.e., Macedonian Bulgarians)? If either was the case, then what was the ethnic identity, or belonging, of their cousins or even siblings who may have affiliated themselves with the Greek (Patriarchist) or the Serbian (Orthodox) "party"? Did members of such divided families belong to the different ethnicities and nations fighting for Macedonia? It seems strange and paradoxical that, at a time when ethnic-linguistic identity obsessed politicians and intellectuals and grounded nation and state building in the Balkans and elsewhere in eastern Europe, the VMRO's leaders did not pay greater attention to this critical issue.

There is no simple answer to this paradox, and one must speculate. Perhaps, unlike the Makedonisti and bourgeois politicians and intellectuals in general, the VMRO's left-leaning leaders consciously avoided or side-tracked the issue. Since they belonged to the political left and were populist or even socialist, the inclusive concept *narod* (people) may have been more important and appealing to them than the narrower and exclusive *nacija* (ethnic nation). However, practical considerations must also have played a role. Because their sole aim was a united, free Macedonian state, they may have deliberately set aside that issue until liberation came. Slav Macedonians' ethnicity was a highly divisive subject; foreign propagandists had already divided them into antagonistic sectarian camps. Raising this matter would have only exacerbated these divisions at the time when unity and cooperation were indispensable.

Furthermore, the leaders had attended Exarchist schools or studied in Bulgaria and felt greater affinity to that country. They could not afford to alienate the Bulgarians, because most of them worked at Exarchist schools or in Exarchist-controlled institutions or organizations in Macedonia or in Bulgaria. Finally, they needed international aid, funds, supplies, arms, and political and diplomatic support. Greece and Serbia were openly antagonistic and were doing all they could to undermine and defeat their movement. Bulgaria's paternalistic attitudes and policies appeared to them more acceptable and promising.

The VMRO statutes, which Delčev and Petrov had prepared early in 1897, after the Salonika Congress of 1896, and which Delčev revised in 1902, called on all discontented elements in Macedonia and the Adrianople area to unite "to win full political autonomy for these two provinces through revolution." They appealed for an end to "propaganda and national dissensions which divide and weaken the population . . . in the struggle against the common foe."[11]

However, for reasons we considered above, others saw the movement as pro-Bulgarian; except for Exarchist Vlachs, most members of other ethnicities ignored the VMRO's call. Even Macedonians belonging to the Partiarchist (Greek) or the Serbian "party" showed little enthusiasm. Hence, the VMRO had and maintained its base only among Exarchists—its greatest weakness as an all-encompassing national movement.

The VMRO's immediate task was to prepare the restless masses for revolution, and so it set up a secret, hierarchical network of committees to that end. The organization was to be sovereign and independent and free of foreign influences and interference. A central committee was, in name at least, the highest decision-making organ.

The VMRO set up regional, district, and local organizations. It divided Macedonia into revolutionary regions, each with a regional committee in charge. At the outset the following were such regions: Salonika, Bitola, Skopje, Štip, Strumica, Gorna Dzhumaia, and Veles-Tikveš. Within each region were districts with revolutionary committees, whose chiefs, the *vojvoda(i),* enjoyed great power. Local cells reported to local committees. The three levels of committees organized and had at their disposal armed units, *četa(i),* consisting of *komita(i)* and with a *vojvoda* (chief), which comprised the VMRO's standing paramilitary arm. The četi performed police and security duties for the organization and, most important, readied the vilayets for rebellion.

Activists at all levels recruited new adherents, and membership slowly grew. At first, most newcomers were teachers, students, and priests, but soon craftspeople, tradespeople, and merchants joined as well. Before Ilinden, the VMRO had won active support from some peasants and passive acceptance and sympathy from the vast majority. By 1903, the VMRO was in virtual control of some areas of Macedonia, where it administered its own postal service, tax collection, and justice system. It was becoming a state within a state in Ottoman Macedonia.

Despite considerable organizational accomplishments, the VMRO was far from ready for the planned popular revolt. It did not gather the financial resources to procure the arms and train the masses, the army of the revolution. The conservative and practical peasants were hesitant to risk joining the struggle unarmed and defenseless.

Moreover, the VMRO had no political or diplomatic allies, and it was extremely weak and vulnerable. As we saw above, Greece and Serbia were openly hostile to it and its aims. Official Bulgaria, while occasionally sympathetic, disliked its aims and sought to undermine its independence. Help from Bulgaria appeared more and more unlikely. The great powers, especially Russia and Austria-Hungary, which had strong interest in the area, had massive internal problems, and they did not want to see unrest and disorder in the remaining Ottoman possessions in the Balkans. About 1900, Russia and Austria-Hungary were seeking to preserve the territorial and political status quo there; an 1897 agreement between their foreign ministers, Count Muraviev and Count Goluchowski, respectively, aimed "to keep the Balkans on ice."[12]

Events swept the VMRO along against its better judgment. In the first years of the new century, its founders thought conditions unfavorable for a successful insurrection and feared the resulting disaster. However, by default, or more probably by design, open or concealed opponents of it and its national aims called for a revolution.

The Supreme Revolutionary Committee (Sofia, 1895) and its members, Supremists, sought to achieve Bulgarian aims: direct annexation of Macedonia or nominal autonomy. From the outset it competed with the VMRO, sought to take it over, and, when it failed, became a determined opponent. It tried to discredit the organization among the people, betrayed or physically eliminated some of its leaders, and hindered its activities and sabotaged its development with armed raids and premature and doomed uprisings, such as that in Gorna Dzhumaia in the autumn of 1902.

Ilinden

In January 1902, Ottoman authorities in Salonika arrested a VMRO activist and former Supremist, who, under pressure and torture, revealed the names of VMRO members. As a result of this—the so-called Salonika Affair—close to two hundred people went to jail, including virtually all the members of the central committee. When Ivan Hadžinikolov, the only exception, learned that the police wanted him, he turned over to

Ivan Garvanov, leader of the Salonika regional committee, the VMRO's symbols of authority and secret and sensitive information about the organization, membership, and so forth. Then Garvanov allegedly betrayed Hadžinikolov, whom the Ottoman police arrested as well.

Ivan Garvanov, a Bulgarian-born physics teacher in the Salonika Boy's Gymnasium, was a former leader of the anti-VMRO Revolutionary Brotherhood, which had close links to the Supreme Revolutionary Committee. Hadžinikolov had thus unwittingly passed de facto control of the VMRO to an opponent in the service of the Supreme Revoloutionary Committee. As Perry writes: "Garvanov, who was in the right place at the right time[,] stepped into the leadership void created by the arrests of the legally constituted Central Committee members. Thus what he was unable to achieve by force and coercion, Garvanov accomplished thanks to a twist of fate, possibly augmented by a bit of duplicity, though this is unsubstantiated."[13]

With the VMRO's reins in his hands, Garvanov abandoned its policy of patient, careful, systematic preparation and called for an immediate uprising. He argued that the failed Gorna Dzhumaia revolt, which the Supremists organized in 1902, had created a desperate situation, that events were moving fast, and that the VMRO had to act soon. At the end of December 1902, he announced a VMRO congress in Salonika in early January 1903 to decide whether to launch the uprising in the spring. The unconstitutional and unrepresentative congress, which met on 15 January (N.S.) / 26 January (O.S.), attracted 17 delegates of less importance, and Garvanov appears to have chosen most of them himself.

The gathering debated whether to aim for spring. Even the carefully selected delegates divided on the issue. At the outset only one supported the proposal unreservedly. However, after lengthy and at times acrimonious discussions, during which Garvanov applied every possible pressure tactic, including unfounded promises that the Bulgarian army was ready to aid the insurgents, Garvanov had his way. In the end, the opponents backed down for the sake of unity, and the participants agreed unanimously to call for a revolt in the spring.

The decision divided the VMRO leadership at all levels. Some of its best-known figures, such as Delčev, Petrov, and Sandanski, rejected it. In fact, Petrov denounced it as Supremist inspired and destructive. Delčev was the top-ranking leader who could have mounted a successful opposition campaign. Evidence suggests that he was planning to do that at a congress of regional leaders, near Seres on St. George's Day (6 May 1903).

When he was on his way there, Ottoman troops attacked him and his četa in the village of Banica. Delčev suffered serious wounds and died on 4 May. There are no satisfactory explanations of the ambush. It is possible that an Ottoman spy discovered Delčev's plans or that Garvanov betrayed them to the authorities. In any case, the "MRO [Macedonian Revolutionary Organization] lost its most charismatic figure, a man who had come to symbolize the spirit and aspirations of the organization. Delčev's death removed from the revolutionary movement its most popular and effective leader and the most potent and influential opponent of Garvanov."[14]

During the spring of 1903, the atmosphere in Macedonia grew more tense and violent. In late April, violence by the Gemidžii in Salonika rattled Europe. This group of revolutionaries and anarchists resorted to terrorism to bring Macedonia's plight to the attention of the great powers. On 28 April, they sank the *Guadalquivir*, a French-owned ship, in Salonika harbor; on the same day, members threw three bombs at the Constantinople Express as it pulled into Salonika railway station.

On the night of 29–30 April, explosions shook many parts of the city: bombs devastated popular cafés, blew up the city's gas supply, and hit the Ottoman Bank, the post office, and the German school. The Ottoman authorities responded by mass arrests, detaining more than five hundred people. The great powers sent ships to Salonika, and Russia and Austria-Hungary pressed on the High Porte a reform program to enhance Christians' security in Macedonia.

In this extremely tense atmosphere, a rational discussion, let alone reversal, of the decision of the Salonika congress was not possible, and planning continued. A congress of the Bitola (Monastir) revolutionary region met from 2 to 7 May in the mountain village of Smilevo. The leaders there acted for the VMRO as a whole and represented the most important revolutionary districts—eight of them, stretching from Ohrid and Kičevo in the west to Kastoria (Kostur) in the south, Demir Hisar in the east, and Prilep in the north. The vast majority of the region's inhabitants were Macedonians and Vlachs, Exarchists, and VMRO supporters. Its mountainous terrain seemed ideal for guerrilla warfare, and its population appeared willing and ready to join the uprising because Ottoman abuses in the vilayet were particularly severe.

Dame Gruev, who also represented the VMRO's central committee, chaired the gathering. Some delegates strongly opposed the Salonika decision, and even Gruev expressed reservations, but, as he had told Delčev at their last meeting, it was too late to turn back. The majority agreed with him and resolved to launch the revolution after the harvest. It also selected a three-member general staff—Gruev, Boris Sarafov, and Anastas Lozančev—to determine the exact date. In late July, the general staff felt the situation ripe for revolution, and on 28 July it issued a circular, which set the date as 2 August, St. Elias's Day. It also called on the people of Macedonia to join the struggle. A memorandum to the great powers declared that failure to introduce reforms had driven the exploited and oppressed Christian masses of Macedonia and the Adrianople region to armed struggle. It also expressed the hope that the great powers would at least ensure introduction of real reforms.

The revolution broke out in the evening of 2 August at Ilinden[15] in the Bitola (Monastir) vilayet, which remained its focal point. The insurgents attacked estates and properties owned by Muslim *beys*, destroyed telephone and telegraph lines, blew up bridges and important official and strategic buildings, and, in some places, attacked local garrisons. One of their earliest successes was the capture on 3 August of Kruševo, a picturesque mountaintop town 1,250 meters above sea level, with a largely Macedonian and Vlach population of about 10,000. There, under socialist Nikola Karev, the rebels established a provisional government, issued a fiery manifesto reiterating the revolution's aims, and declared the Kruševo Republic.

Large-scale revolutionary actions took place elsewhere in the Bitola vilayet, in the counties of Kastoria (Kostur) and Florina (Lerin); in various localities in the counties of Ohrid, Kičevo, and Prilep, revolutionary authorities emerged. The vast majority of the non-Muslim inhabitants of the vilayet supported the revolution. As Henri Noel Brailsford, a British journalist who was in Macedonia in 1903 and 1904, wrote: "there is hardly a village [in the Monastir vilayet] which has not joined the organization."[16]

Elsewhere in Macedonia, undertakings were far less intense and widespread. In the Salonika, Seres, and Skopje regions, the smaller numbers of rebels attacked railway lines, especially the Salonika-Skopje and Skopje-Bitola lines and railway bridges over the Vardar. Exact and impartial statistics on the number of active participants in the uprising are not available. An official publication of the VMRO in 1904 claimed that

26,408 fighters took part in the period from 29 July to 19 November 1903. More than two-thirds of them, or 19,850, fought in the Bitola vilayet, 3,544 in the Salonika, and 1,042 in the Skopje.[17]

The extent and intensity of the revolt surprised the European powers, the neighboring Balkan states, and the Ottoman authorities. However, it was also obvious from the outset that without external assistance—a decisive diplomatic intervention by Europe or military help from the Balkan neighbors, particularly Bulgaria—the premature, badly organized, poorly armed uprising would fail. Europe wished to preserve the status quo; each of the Balkan states claimed Macedonia and the Macedonians. Hence the rebels had to face alone the Ottoman empire—a declining giant, but one with substantial military power.

The Turks, with 350,931 soldiers by mid-August, concentrated in Macedonia 167,000 infantrymen, 3,700 cavalrymen, and 444 guns.[18] The offensive aimed at isolating and eliminating the focal points of the uprising. The first attack was against the town of Smilevo; after its capture, they concentrated on Kruševo, the seat of the republic, the uprising's greatest achievement. The operation there began on 9–10 August, and by 12 August, according to some estimates, the 1,200 rebel defenders faced 20,000 Ottoman soldiers with heavy artillery. Battle continued throughout 12 August; by evening, the remaining rebels and the leaders of the republic fled, fighting through the siege.

After defeating the insurgents at Kruševo, the Ottoman army moved systematically against the other centers and gains of the revolution in the Bitola vilayet and elsewhere in Macedonia. They faced vigorous and stubborn resistance, and the conflict continued throughout September and well into October, until the final suppression of all traces of the uprising.

For nearly three months, Macedonia writhed in the throes and flames of Ilinden. The immediate consequences were disastrous for Macedonia and its people, especially the Macedonians and the Vlachs. Data concerning death and destruction vary greatly, but it appears that as many as 8,816 men, women, and children died; there were 200 villages burned, 12,440 houses destroyed or damaged, and close to 70,836 people left homeless. The Ottoman army and police and armed bands of Muslims continued a terror campaign against Christians even after the uprising ended.[19]

The psychological and political impact of the ill-timed and failed uprising is beyond calculation. The optimism, high hopes, and expectations for a free and better life that the VMRO and the revolt generated gave way to "panic, demoralization, disillusionment and hopelessness."[20] The VMRO fragmented into antagonistic factions keen to destroy one another and never regained its pre-Ilinden strength, prestige, and unity of purpose.

Nonetheless the Ilinden Uprising represented a landmark in the history of the Macedonians. It was the first such organized effort bearing the Macedonian name, taking place throughout the territory, and calling for a free state encompassing the whole of geographic Macedonia. It helped to redefine the so-called Macedonian question at home and in the rest of the Balkans and Europe. Thereafter people would view the problem no longer as Bulgarian or Greek or Serbian, as each of the neighbors claimed, but first and foremost as Macedonian.

The uprising and its disastrous end changed the national movement and long helped shape national identity. For the Makedonisti, Ilinden confirmed all their worst fears and forebodings. In their view, the revolt was a huge mistake—certain to fail because it involved only the Exarchist Macedonians. Further, expecting Bulgarians to offer armed support was totally unrealistic, because they saw the two lands' interests as divergent and would not risk their own to aid the Macedonians.

The Makedonisti now believed more than ever that the real enemy was the neighboring Balkan nationalisms, including the Bulgarian, which claimed Macedonia and divided its people against each other. They saw salvation only in the termination, with Ottoman help, of all their activities and their expulsion. This might facilitate the normal and natural unification of all Macedonians. A standardized language and a common culture, church, and political and economic interests would ground that unity and safeguard their land's territorial integrity. In short, what the Makedonisti wanted, and what Krste Misirkov and the other leaders stressed repeatedly, was unification of all Macedonians on a strictly domestic basis of patriotism and within the context and with the help of the Ottoman state. Otherwise, they warned, their ambitions and greedy neighbors would conquer and partition Macedonia.[21] They proved true prophets in both respects. Force of arms partitioned Macedonia in the Balkan Wars of 1912–13, but a Macedonian nation would also complete its formation on a Macedonian ethnic basis.

The events of 1903 and their aftermath even more profoundly affected the Macedono-Bulgarians—the political separatists—particularly the right-wingers who tended to be extremely pro-Bulgaria and expected its aid. The defeat of the uprising was in fact their own defeat, and it plunged their Macedonian national orientation into a crisis from which it never fully recovered. However, in 1904, only a year after Ilinden, Bulgaria appeared to consider in principle a Serbian proposal to divide Macedonia into spheres of influence. This came as a shock to the pro-Bulgarians, who looked up to that country and expected it to protect Macedonian interests.

The Macedono-Bulgarians' crisis, which spurred fratricidal infighting and assassinations within the VMRO, was deep, and there was no easy way out. Those on the Macedonian left had to acknowledge that the Makedonisti were right: the interests of Bulgarianism and Macedonianism were divergent, Macedonian patriots could not rely on Bulgaria, and victory would be virtually impossible without Macedonians' uniting on strictly domestic terms. It was becoming obvious that Macedono-Bulgarians would have to choose between the two nationalisms, which had become irreconcilably contradictory; they could not be Macedonians and Bulgarians. This predicament helped split the VMRO between its Macedonian left and its pro-Bulgarian right—a divide that had existed since 1893.[22] The post-Ilinden crisis launched the prolonged and agonizing end of Macedono-Bulgarianism.

The VMRO's organizational network throughout Macedonia and the Ilinden Uprising affected the masses as well, enhancing their awareness of their land and of themselves as Macedonians. The concepts "Macedonia" and "Macedonian" had already acquired national connotation and coloring for the intelligentsia and the better educated, but not necessarily for the peasants, especially in rural areas.

The latter still tended to identify most often with a particular region—Bitolčani, Kosturčani, Prilepčani, and so on—and naš for them embraced inhabitants of neighboring regions. The recent turbulent events, which placed Macedonia on the map of Europe, also made them more conscious of the idea of Macedonia, which was larger and more abstract than their own region. And their understanding of naš broadened and widened to include many people speaking Macedonian dialects akin to their own. This was true of Exarchist villagers but also of Patriarchists and adherents of the Serbian church. This was a critical development in the transformation of the peasant, the naš, into a Macedonian, which took place between the turn of the century and the Second World War and its revolutionary aftermath in Macedonia.[23]

Finally, the VMRO of Ilinden became an integral part of national folk culture and mythology. Folk songs and tales and fictional and political writings glorified the original leaders and the uprising, which became national symbols that resonated with people from every walk of life, along with the VMRO and its program for a free land (slobodna Makedonija). The failed revolution metamorphosed into a glorious national epic, a myth that inspired all future generations of Macedonian patriots, revolutionaries, and nationalists.

PART THREE

STRANGERS IN THEIR HOMELAND (1913–1940)

For half a century before the Ilinden Uprising, Macedonian nationalism was illegal, recognized neither by the theocratic Ottoman state nor by the two established Orthodox churches in the empire: the Patriarchist (Greek) and, after its establishment in 1870, the Exarchist (Bulgarian). Moreover, as I repeatedly emphasize, the neighboring Balkan nationalists—Bulgarian, Greek, Serbian—who had already achieved independence with the aid of one or more of the great powers, denied the existence of a separate Macedonian identity; indeed, each claimed Macedonia and the Macedonians as their own. They fought for Macedonia, first using propaganda and then, after the suppression of the revolution, increasing force against each other and the nascent Macedonian nationalists and peasant population in general. That prolonged struggle culminated in 1913 with the forceful partition of Macedonia after the Second Balkan or Inter-Allied War between Bulgaria, on the one side, and allied Greece and Serbia, on the other.

The partition created a new and an even more oppressive environment for the Macedonians. The new rulers scorned them; they were unwanted strangers in their Macedonian homeland. After the partitioning powers consolidated their control over their respective parts of Macedonia and throughout the interwar years, they inaugurated and implemented policies that were intended to destroy any manifestation of genuine Macedonianism.

Consequently, until the Second World War, unlike the other nationalisms in the Balkans and eastern Europe more generally, Macedonian nationalism continued to develop without the aid of legal political, church, educational, or cultural institutions. Notwithstanding the largely opportunistic flirtations of fascist powers with Macedonian rightists and of the Comintern with Macedonian leftists, Macedonian movements lacked the international sympathy, aid, and, most important, benefits of open and direct diplomatic and military support accorded other Balkans nationalisms. Indeed, for an entire century Macedonian nationalism, illegal at home and illegitimate internationally, waged a precarious struggle for survival against overwhelming odds: against the three expansionist and, after 1913, partitioning Balkan states and their respective patrons among the great powers.

8 Decline and Partition (1903–1919)

Patriotic Macedonians have traditionally considered the period 1903–19 and, more particularly, the decade 1903–13 as the most tragic in their history. For Macedonian patriots and nationalists, the partition of their land—which the VMRO fought and the Ilinden Uprising sought to prevent but the European powers approved in 1913 and the Allies confirmed in the peace settlement in 1919—represented a tragedy. In Macedonian mythology, it represents the greatest injustice that Macedonia and its people have ever suffered.[1]

Three sections make up this painful chapter. First, the VMRO declined rapidly and by 1908 became virtually irrelevant. Second, the resulting political vacuum in Macedonia allowed the neighbors free rein, and in the Balkan Wars of 1912–13 the armies of Bulgaria, Greece, and Serbia partitioned the territory. Third, another conflict over Macedonia erupted in 1915 during the Great War and led to repartition, and the post-1918 peace settlement confirmed, with minor modifications, the original division of 1913.

The VMRO's Decline and Split (1903–1908)

In the decade after Ilinden, instability, turbulence, and violence became permanent features in Macedonia. For patriots, who sought the preservation of territorial integrity, it proved calamitous. Major developments, internal and external, harmed their cause and paved the way for partition.

As we saw in chapter 6, the defeat and the bloody suppression of the uprising unnerved the VMRO. Many of its leading activists perished, and many survivors fled to Bulgaria. The aftermath saw destruction or disruption of its institutions and organizational networks. Defeated, disorganized, and demoralized, the remaining leaders had to examine themselves, search their own souls, and reconsider the VMRO.

Calls for reexamination of the organization surfaced by late 1903. From the outset, the debates were heated, divisive, and full of violent accusations and recriminations. The leaders' first major gathering, in Sofia in January–February 1904, attracted the most notable figures from all parts of Macedonia. They debated the VMRO's past, present, and future and failed to agree on anything. Two major groupings emerged, which historians usually consider "left" and "right." However, these terms related more to views about Macedonia's future than to ideological beliefs. In general, the left represented a pro-Macedonian orientation, and the right, a pro-Bulgarian.

The stronghold of the left was the Seres revolutionary district, which Jane Sandanski led. It was much more unified and homogeneous in its views than the right. It called for radical changes in the VMRO's structure: for decentralization and democratization, including elections. It also sought to diversify the social base to bring in the growing urban elements and to curb the predominance of teachers, most of whom worked for the Bulgarian exarchate. Its national and political program reflected the VMRO's traditional ideals: continued faith in a general uprising, but only under favorable internal and external conditions; protection of the movement's independence; and rejection of all foreign interference. The ultimate aim remained "Macedonia for the Macedonians" (i.e., preservation of territorial integrity and achievement of one of the following: autonomy within the Ottoman empire, outright independence, or equal partnership in some future Balkan federation).

The right was more heterogeneous and less unified on most issues. It included activists whose aims were identical with those on the left, but who felt that outside help was essential and looked toward Bulgaria. However, Macedonians who were openly pro-Bulgarian or even considered themselves Bulgarian led and dominated it. They seemed to focus their activities on Exarchist Macedonians. Their leaders Hristo Matov

Map 5 Partitioned Macedonia

and Dr. Hristo Tatarčev resided in Sofia, and their stronghold after Ilinden was the Skopje revolutionary district. They embraced centralization and opposed major changes in organization.

Most of the right's leaders had no confidence in a planned and well-prepared internal uprising. They favored continuation of armed strikes against Ottoman targets in order to provoke outside intervention by Bulgaria or the great powers or both. In their writings, declarations, and proclamations, they also put forth autonomy as their ultimate aim, undoubtedly the main reason why they attracted support in Macedonia and especially among the many Macedonian refugees and immigrants in Bulgaria.

However, Macedonian autonomy embodied different meanings for the right's various elements. For some, as with the left, it meant a truly self-governing state with equality for all its ethnic elements. For others, it implied some sort of association with Bulgaria. And for still others, it represented but the first step toward annexation by Bulgaria and creation of a Great, or San Stefano Bulgaria.

The leaders' strong pro-Bulgarian orientation received no open publicity; it remained a "hidden agenda" but gradually became even stronger and better known. As a result, many observers came to identify the VMRO's right with the ideas and aims of the former, Sofia-based, Supreme Macedonian Revolutionary Committee, which had emerged in Sofia in 1895 and served Bulgarian state interests in Macedonia. Opponents on the left would designate people on the right as "Vrhovists" (Supremists) and their pro-Bulgarian program and aims as "Vrhovizam" (Supremism).

A general congress was to determine the VMRO's future. Preliminary congresses took place in the five revolutionary regions—Bitola, Salonika, Seres, Skopje, and Strumica—between May 1904 and July–August 1905. The heated debates there only confirmed the deep divisions between the Macedonian left and the pro-Bulgarian right. The left prevailed at Salonika, Seres, and Strumica. The Bitola region leaned left, and the Skopje region, right. However, all five agreed on a general congress to deal with the post-Ilinden malaise. Although the statutes required general congresses in Macedonia, long debates decided that, because of the difficult situation there, this conclave would take place at the Rila Monastery in Bulgaria, very near the Ottoman border in Macedonia.

The historic Rila Congress met at the beginning of October 1905, attracted 21 delegates from all over Macedonia, and lasted a month. The left prevailed: the new central committee included Dame Gruev, Pere Tošev, Todor Popantov, and Dimo Hadžidimov, the rising ideologist of the left and editor of the VMRO's *Revolucioneren list* (Revolutionary Newspaper). The gathering endorsed liberation as the ultimate aim and, to that end, a well-prepared popular uprising. It condemned neighbors' interference and stressed the VMRO's determination to resist it by all possible means. It specifically warned against the dispatch of Vrhovist armed bands into Macedonia and against the exarchate's encouraging "Bulgarian state nationalism" in Macedonia.

However, the apparent unity soon proved ephemeral. The old divisions resurfaced, and the movement fractured permanently. The right declined to implement the decisions, and the polarization erupted in heated discussions over the meeting place for the next annual general congress. Contrary to the Rila agreement, the right insisted on Sofia. Although a compromise proposal for Rila passed, the congress never met. Shortly before it was to convene, the right issued a declaration insisting that the VMRO coordinate its activities with, and accept financial aid from, Bulgaria. These demands ran against the strongest ideals of the left. The gap between left and right was unbridgeable.

The right, which usurped the name "VMRO," held a congress under Bulgarian auspices in Kiustendil, Bulgaria, in 1908 and revised the decisions from Rila. A congress of the left met in Macedonia in May 1908, shortly after the Young Turk Revolution; attending were representatives of the Salonika, Seres, and Strumica revolutionary regions, and they reconfirmed their ideals. The split marked the beginning of a vicious struggle. The assassination, or "liquidation," in November 1907 of Boris Sarafov and Ivan Garvanov, two leaders of the right, turned into a war of extermination that lasted until the late 1940s.

The revolution in Istanbul in 1908 marked the end of the VMRO as the original Macedonian national and revolutionary movement. The left, under Sandanski, supported the Young Turks, and in the following year it became the legal Popular Federalist Party. The Young Turk regime promised to reform and modernize the empire along liberal-democratic lines and hoped and expected that a united Macedonia would become one of its administrative and autonomous units.

The right aligned itself even more with Bulgaria and, with its support and the exarchate's guidance, set up the Union of Bulgarian Clubs as its own legal front. Unlike the left, however, it did not support the Young Turks and did not give up its arms and armed actions or the VMRO name. With the regime's total failure to fulfill its promises and the outbreak of the First Balkan War in 1912, the Union came under direct control by Sofia. During the Balkan Wars and the Great War, Bulgaria used it to recruit Macedonians for the Bulgarian war effort and supposedly to liberate Macedonia.[2]

Intervention, Wars, and Partition (1903–1913)

After Ilinden in 1903, the mid-decade decline of the VMRO—the only organized defender of Macedonian interests—created a political vacuum. It opened the door to more intense intervention by the great powers and the neighboring kingdoms. Two Balkan wars followed in 1912–13, leading to partition of Macedonia; a third during the First World War repartitioned Macedonia; and the postwar settlement ratified partition.

Before final supression of Ilinden in autumn 1903, the European powers intervened to stabilize the situation, in line with the Russian-Austro-Hungarian understanding of 1897 "to keep the Balkans on ice." Already in October 1903, St. Petersburg and Vienna, the two capitals most concerned with the Balkans, prepared the so-called Mürzsteg reform program. It recommended that Russian and Austro-Hungarian representatives accompany the Ottoman inspector general on his tour of Macedonia and report on conditions there; reorganization of the *gendarmerie* under a foreign general and officers; reform of the judiciary; and financial aid for return of refugees and rebuilding of villages. The other powers approved the program, and the sultan accepted it, but virtually nothing happened.

In March 1908, Sir Edward Grey, the British foreign minister, proposed an autonomous Macedonia. Tsar Nicholas II and his and his wife's uncle King Edward VII discussed it when they met at Reval (Tallinn, Estonia) in June. The Young Turk Revolution in July ended any further discussion of reform in Macedonia.[3]

Armed Supremist bands expanded operations in Macedonia. They coordinated their efforts with the right wing of the VMRO until the two virtually merged before the revolution in Istanbul. Their targets were no longer solely Ottoman symbols and authorities, but almost as frequently leftist leaders and followers in the VMRO.

Serbs also intensified their activities. By 1905, there were eleven Serbian armed bands operating in Macedonia. In the same year, a supreme committee in Belgrade, with branches in Skopje and Bitola, took control of them; the Serbian General Staff took over the entire movement. Serbia aimed to entrench its influence in central Macedonia, along the Vardar valley, as a base for its future drive for unhindered access to the Aegean.

Greek armed bands grew in number, had better organization, and were much more aggressive. They were under the direction of various local organizations throughout southern Macedonia, in the Salonika and Bitola vilayets, which took orders from the Macedonian Committee in Athens. Wealthy Greeks in Macedonia and Greece funded them generously, but the state budget provided most of the money. Locally recruited bands seemed not very reliable, and most of the armed men and officers came from Greece and many from Crete. The Greeks fought both wings of the VMRO and sought to terrorize and force the Exarchists and their communities to return to the patriarchate. Greek efforts in Macedonia were under more direct government control and were better organized than those of Serbia and even of Bulgaria.[4]

The Young Turk Revolution in July 1908, restoration of the 1876 constitution, and decisive defeat of the conservative Muslim counterrevolution in April 1909 appeared to signal a new and promising era in the Ottoman empire. The resulting general euphoria temporarily ended foreign-inspired armed actions in Macedonia.

Bulgaria, Greece, and Serbia had to change tactics and adapt. They replaced armed bands with political associations that continued the struggle by legal means. As we saw above, the Bulgarians sponsored the Union of Bulgarian Clubs, which brought Bulgarians and Bulgarophile Macedonians together with the right wing of the VMRO. Serbia launched the Associations of Ottoman Serbs, which operated not only among the Serbs in Old Serbia proper, but primarily in Macedonia. Likewise, the Greeks founded numerous political clubs and many supposedly nonpolitical societies, brotherhoods, and unions, all under the well-established Greek elite in Constantinople (Istanbul).

Withdrawal of armed bands and suspension of armed struggle soon ended. Once in power, the Young Turks proved unwilling to abandon Muslim hegemony and to grant real political representation and religious equality throughout the empire, let alone decentralization and local autonomy. They implemented a program that called for Turkish hegemony, greater centralization of power, and Turkiezation. On 16 August 1909, the Law of Association banned ethnically or nationally based political organizations; on 27 September, the Law for the Prevention of Brigandage and Sedition forbade armed bands in the European provinces.

The new regime's nonintroduction of promised reforms, which outcome the neighboring Balkans states expected and indeed hoped for, gave them a pretext to renew armed intervention in Macedonia. In the two years preceding the First Balkan War in 1912, acts of violence by these armed bands or by the special "pursuit battalions" that the Young Turks created, spilling of blood, and destruction of property increased dramatically. It seemed as if the Balkan states were intent on solving the Macedonian issue by provoking war with the Ottoman empire. They sought to impress public opinion in the great powers that the only solution for Macedonia was its liberation from Ottoman rule—that is, the end of Turkey in Europe. Austria-Hungary's annexation of Bosnia-Herzegovina in 1908, and the resulting "Annexation Crisis," which broke out only months after the revolution in Istanbul and pushed the divided great powers to the brink of war, seemed only to propel the Balkan states further in that direction.[5]

The powers of the Triple Alliance (Austria-Hungary, Germany, and Italy) and the Triple Entente (Britain, France, and Russia) avoided war over the Annexation Crisis. However, the triumph of Austria-Hungary and the capitulation and humiliation of Russia destroyed the two empires' entente, which Goluchowski and Muraviev had arranged in 1897 "to keep the Balkans on ice." The Dual Monarchy's gains endangered Russia's traditional aims in the Near East, threatened Serbia and Montenegro's independence, and challenged the expansionist aims of all Balkan states.

Hence the crisis initiated a chain of developments that pushed Serbia and Bulgaria together, forced Russia to seek the cooperation of a united bloc of Balkan allies to check Austro-Hungarian influence and its spread to the south, and emboldened the Balkan states to contemplate taking the Eastern Question, and thus the Macedonian issue, into their own hands. Finally, the threat from Austria-Hungary and the prospects of dazzling gains from a war against the Ottoman empire made Balkan unity very attractive.[6]

Protracted discussions between Bulgaria, Russia, and Serbia and between Serbia and Bulgaria culminated in the Serbian-Bulgarian Treaty of Alliance on 13 March 1912. This relationship constituted the core of the Balkan System of Alliances of 1912, which became complete when Greece allied with Bulgaria on 29 May and Montenegro reached a verbal understanding with Bulgaria on 28 August and a treaty of alliance with Serbia on 6 October.[7]

The new system aimed to destroy the status quo and expand the allies' territory at the expense of the Ottoman empire. The Secret Annex of the Serbian-Bulgarian treaty set out the territorial settlement and the division of Macedonia into uncontested Serbian and Bulgarian zones and a contested zone for the Russian tsar to arbitrate.

Bulgaria and Serbia allied not because they both feared the Dual Monarchy—Bulgaria had no quarrels with Austria-Hungary—but to expand territorially. The new partners saw the offensive clauses of their agreement as its primary consideration. The ultimate success or failure of their rapprochement would depend on the realization of these ambitions. Serbia sought to expand to the south and southwest into Macedonia, Old Serbia, and Albania and thus win an exit to the Adriatic to secure its precarious existence. Bulgaria looked south and southwest, to Macedonia and the Aegean, and as far east as possible, toward Constantinople (Istanbul) and the straits of the Bosphorus and the Dardanelles.

The main weaknesses of their alliance, and hence of the Balkan system, were apparent from the outset. The allies still could not resolve the perennial puzzle—dividing territorial spoils—particularly Macedonia. Although Bulgaria and Serbia had finally agreed, with Russia's aid, on partition, there were political circles in Belgrade, including Prime Minister Nikola Pašić, who felt that Serbia had paid too high a price in Macedonia to win Bulgaria's friendship and sought revisions. More important, Bulgaria and Greece could not reach an accord before the war and side-tracked the issue.

Above all, Russia, protector of the delicate entente, had ideas that differed from those of the Balkan states. It failed to grasp the parties' real intentions and saw the arrangement as a defensive tool against the Dual Monarchy. For the allies, it allowed an immediate war against the Ottoman empire. Moreover, they expected Russia, which was not ready for and opposed such a war, to protect them against the certain hostility of Austria-Hungary.

Encouraged by the outbreak of the Italo-Turkish, or Tripolitan, War in September 1911 and citing growing violence and instability (which they helped create) in Ottoman Europe, the Balkan states decided on war too. They called on the great powers to force the High Porte to implement reforms in Europe in accordance with article 23 of the Treaty of Berlin. On 13 October 1912, they handed a collective note, or rather an ultimatum, demanding the same to the Ottoman representatives in Athens, Belgrade, and Sofia. As they hoped and expected, the empire rejected both the powers' démarche and their own collective note, and on 17 October Bulgaria, Greece, and Serbia broke off all diplomatic ties with the empire. The declaration of war and the opening of hostilities followed the next day, starting the First Balkan War.

The allies' swift and decisive victories, which soon terminated Ottoman rule in Europe, transformed the war into a European crisis. The winners, especially Serbia and Montenegro, now needed and expected

Russia to safeguard their gains against Austria-Hungary. The fate of the alliances, which were so important to Russia, depended on this.

In the course of the great powers' deliberation on the peace settlement in southeastern Europe, St. Petersburg endeavored alone or with whatever support it could muster from its Triple Entente partners, Britain and France, to uphold the Balkan states' aims. However, facing determined opposition by the Triple Alliance led by Austria-Hungary, Russia surrendered on the central issues: first, the Albanian question and the Serbian exit on the Adriatic and, second, Scutari (Shkodär). By so doing, Russia avoided a possible European war for which it was not ready and thus attained one of its major objectives. But it jeopardized its primary aim: preservation of the Serbian-Bulgarian alliance and thus the entire Balkan system.

Even while the allies were fighting the Ottoman empire in the First Balkan War of 1912–13, and long before the climactic Treaty of London of 30 May 1913, differences over Macedonia were undermining the Balkan alliances. The Greeks and the Serbs engaged the Ottoman forces primarily in Macedonia, occupied most of its territory, and claimed most, if not all, the areas under their military control. The Bulgarians, who carried the brunt of the fighting in the east in Thrace, near the center of Ottoman power, occupied only a small part of Macedonia but claimed most if not all of it on the basis of the alliance with Serbia.

A deadlock ensued, lines became rigid, and a negotiated resolution was not possible. For with the collapse of Serbia's pretensions in Albania and on the Adriatic, Belgrade sought recompense in Macedonia, where it met Sofia's unyielding opposition. The consequent territorial conflict intensified the dispute in Macedonia between Bulgaria and Greece, which in turn exacerbated rivalry between Bulgaria and Serbia. Greece and Serbia drew closer together and on 1 June 1913 signed a defensive treaty of alliance against Bulgaria. They also began to curry favor with Romania, the only nonalliance Balkan state.

The secret Greek-Serbian Treaty of Alliance on 1 June 1913 in effect ended the Serbian-Bulgarian alliance and the Balkan System of Alliances. Its primary aim was to subvert the territorial settlement in Macedonia to which Bulgaria and Serbia agreed in 1912 and to impose on Bulgaria, if necessary by force, the new arrangement. It left no room for debate or for a negotiated settlement and virtually ensured another conflict: the Inter-Allied, or Second Balkan War in the summer of 1913, which finally destroyed the Serbian-Bulgarian rapprochement and with it the Balkan system.

The summer war violated the territorial integrity of modern Macedonia, which comprised a natural economic and, in the main, ethnocultural unity. Bulgaria and the allied Greece and Serbia forcibly partitioned their neighbor. Greece acquired Aegean Macedonia, the largest territory, and Serbia, Vardar Macedonia, with the largest Macedonian population. The defeated Bulgarians, whose influence in Macedonia had grown steadily since 1870 and who wanted desperately to annex it all and thus create a Great Bulgaria, ended up with the smallest part, Pirin Macedonia. The Peace Treaty of Bucharest of 10 August 1913 sanctioned this arrangement and ended the Second Balkan War.[8]

Sequel: The Great War and the Peace Settlement

The Bucharest treaty in August 1913, however, only set the stage for yet another war over Macedonia, which erupted during the First World War. The 1913 settlement was not acceptable to the Macedonians, and Bulgaria was keen to overturn it. Sofia moved into the sphere of influence of the Central Powers (Austria-Hungary and Germany) and probably saw the Great War as mainly a continuation of the Second Balkan. In September 1915, Bulgaria intervened on the side of the Central Powers by attacking Serbia primarily because of its frustrated ambitions in Macedonia.

The Serbian army was active on the Austro-Hungarian front, and the Bulgarians quickly overran the newly Serbian part of Macedonia. They reached the Greek-Serbian border, which, with brief exceptions, was until 1918 to separate the two belligerent sides in the Balkans, on the so-called Salonika, or Macedonian front. To the north of this line, the Central Powers had deployed 600,000 troops, and over time the Allies—Britain, France, and Russia—concentrated a similar force to its south. For three years, Macedonia and its people suffered under these huge forces of occupation and war.

The Central Powers handed over to Bulgaria the area of Macedonia under their control. The Bulgarians treated it as their own: they imposed martial law and declared general mobilization. They sent Macedonians to the front or forced them to perform military duties on the home front. Aegean, or Greek Macedonia, which the Allies controlled, was nominally under Greek administration but in fact under the various national forces of occupation. This situation led to frequent conflicts between the Greeks and the Serbs, who had their own designs even on this part of Macedonia.

This divided and competing administration made life worse for the Macedonians than that under the Bulgarians. In any case, both parts of occupied Macedonia suffered terribly: exploitation of material and human resources, requisitioning, martial law, and forced mobilization. Cities and towns such as Kastoria (Kostur), Florina (Lerin), Bitola, Dojran, and Edessa (Voden) near to and on both sides of the front lines experienced daily air and ground bombardment. Many villages in the heart of Macedonia, in the fertile area between Florina and Bitola, underwent total destruction.

During the Great War, the Macedonian question did not preoccupy the great powers of the two belligerent camps. True, both sides at first used Macedonia as a bargaining chip to entice strategically located Bulgaria into their respective ranks. However, once Bulgaria accepted the generous offers of the Central Powers and entered the war on their side in September 1915, the question lost its importance.

It came to the forefront again after Russia's two revolutions in 1917 and its withdrawal from the war. The collapse of Russia—in effect, of the eastern front—forced Britain and France to turn their attention again to Bulgaria. They considered offering it a separate peace to draw it away from the enemy camp. However, unlike in 1915, when they offered Bulgaria virtually the whole of Vardar (Serbian) Macedonia, they now considered two alternative solutions. At first they thought of ceding to it Macedonia east of the Vardar; in the first half of 1918, they seemed to favor Macedonia as an autonomous Balkan state under the protection of the great powers.[9]

Although Macedonians could not voice freely their views, an autonomous state—the principal demand of all patriotic organizations since 1878—had received support since August 1914 from organized Macedonian émigré groups, especially in Russia and Switzerland. The Macedonian colony in St. Petersburg (Petrograd) called on the Entente Powers to take up Macedonia's liberation as the only solution that would contribute to peace and stability in the Balkans and Europe.[10] The Macedonian Society for an Independent Macedonia, formed in Switzerland in

1918, rejected the Bulgarian, Greek, and Serbian claims and called for an independent state—a Macedonia for the Macedonians.[11]

Nothing came of the strong British and French proposals of 1917 and 1918. Both the Greek and Serbian governments, their wartime allies, disapproved very strongly and made it clear that they would not relinquish any of their Macedonian gains. As the war neared its end, both were hoping and planning additional gains in Macedonia at each other's expense or at the expense of the once-again-defeated Bulgaria.

In the period between war's end and conclusion of the treaties comprising the peace settlement in the Balkans, the future of Macedonia surfaced repeatedly in Macedonian organizations in Bulgaria as well as in Switzerland and the United States. Except for some extreme Bulgarophile elements and the right of the former VMRO, which had identified completely with the Bulgarian cause during the Balkan Wars and the Great War and would have liked annexation to Bulgaria, most Macedonian patriotic organizations called on the Paris Peace Conference of 1919 to establish a united, autonomous state under the powers' protection. As a last resort, some even approved of a united, autonomous Macedonia in the emerging southern Slav state—the kingdom of the Serbs, Croats, and Slovenes, later Yugoslavia.

At Paris, the Macedonian question fell to the Committee on the Formation of New States. In its thirty-second sitting, on 10 July 1919, the Italian delegation proposed a "special administration in Macedonia," and in the following sitting it suggested autonomy for Vardar (Serbian) Macedonia. Despite energetic support from France, Serbia rejected the Italian initiatives as well as a British compromise proposal at the thirty-ninth sitting.

The peace treaties forced Serbia and Greece to act only vis-à-vis minority rights. Article 51 of the Saint-Germain Treaty with Austria (10 September 1919) obliged Serbia, and article 9 of the Convention for the Protection of Minorities required Serbia and Greece, to protect the rights of all minorities in lands that they conquered and annexed after 1 January 1913—that is, in the Balkan Wars and the Great War. The Yugoslav kingdom did not fulfill this obligation; Greece has not, to the present day.[12]

Otherwise, the peace conferences and treaties confirmed the partition of Macedonia and the Macedonians that the Treaty of Bucharest laid out in 1913, with some minor modifications at Bulgaria's expense. There was no resolution of the Macedonian question. It remained the central issue, the apple of discord, dividing the Balkan states and peoples throughout the interwar period—and even down to current times.

9 Macedonia in Three Parts (1920s and 1930s)

Partition and Assimilation

For all Macedonians, the Balkan Wars and partition shaped the period between the two world wars. The peace conferences and treaties of 1919, which allowed self-determination for many other "small," "young" peoples of central and eastern Europe, denied this right to the Macedonians. Except for a few minor adjustments that harmed Bulgaria, they confirmed the partition that the Treaty of Bucharest set out in August 1913.

The victorious Allies, especially Britain and France, thought that the Macedonian problem was over. They could satisfy two of their clients, pillars of the new order in southeastern Europe: Greece and Serbia, now the dominant component of the new kingdom of Serbs, Croats, and Slovenes, or Yugoslavia. Even though those two states did not obtain as much of Macedonia as they had hoped, they too pretended that Macedonia, its people, and their problem had ceased to exist. Serbia proclaimed Vardar Macedonia to be South Serbia and its inhabitants South Serbs; for Greece, Aegean Macedonia became simply northern Greece, and its residents Greeks, or at best "Slavophone" Greeks.

Although Bulgaria had enjoyed the greatest influence among the Macedonians, its defeat in the Inter-Allied and the First World Wars left it with only Pirin Macedonia, or the Petrich district, as it called the area.

Its ruling elite did not consider the settlement permanent; but lacking sympathy from the victorious great powers and with revolution threatening at home, it had to acquiesce for the moment.

The peace conferences upheld the decision of the London Conference of Ambassadors, in December 1912, to give the new state of Albania small parts of Macedonia: Mala Prespa (Little Prespa), west of Lakes Ohrid and Prespa, and Golo Brdo, further to the north, where most inhabitants were Macedonian.

The three partitioning states denied the existence of a distinct Macedonian identity—ethnic, political, or territorial. Greece and Serbia claimed the Macedonians within their boundaries as Greeks and Serbs, respectively; Bulgaria continued to claim all Macedonians as Bulgarians. Hence the Macedonians in all three areas constituted unrecognized and repressed minorities. They found themselves in much more oppressive circumstances after their "liberation" from Ottoman rule. Under the latter they had communicated and prayed freely in Macedonian, could declare who they were, and could choose their political-church affiliation. Under the Balkan 'liberators,' they had to accept the national identity of the ruling nation or face excommunication and its political, economic, social, and cultural consequences.

Forced assimilation had two significant results. It enhanced assimilation among those Macedonians who for reasons of necessity or advantage embraced the new national identity temporarily or permanently. It also hastened the growth of Macedonianism, the development of national consciousness and identity, among those who rejected forced assimilation and were subject to repression and discrimination.

Macedonians sympathized with, and many of them actually joined, the activists, nationalist and communist, who rejected partition and called for a free Macedonia *(slobodna Makedonija)*—an autonomous or independent, but united, state. This was the central tenet of rightist nationalism, which the revived VMRO (Internal Macedonian Revolutionary Organization, or Vnatrešna Makedonska Revolucionerna Organizacija) represented under Todor Aleksandrov and then, after his assassination in 1924, Ivan (Vančo) Mihailov.

It also became the fundamental principle of leftist nationalism, as we can see in the new VMRO (*obedineta*, United), or VMRO (ob.), of 1924 and its sponsors and supporters, the Communist International (Comintern), the Balkan Communist Federation, and the Communist parties of Bulgaria, Greece, and Yugoslavia. The Balkan Communists made up the only political parties in the three partitioning states to recognize a distinct Macedonian national identity and to defend the Macedonians and their national cause.

Consequently, throughout the interwar years Bulgaria, Greece, and Yugoslavia faced a Macedonian problem. In differing ways, the matter helped destabilize all three. Moreover, since Greece and Yugoslavia approved of this settlement, and Bulgaria sought to destroy it, it was the primary cause of regional instability. It remained the stumbling block and doomed to failure any attempt at interstate cooperation. We now look in turn at the situation in Yugoslav (Vardar) Macedonia, in Greek (Aegean) Macedonia, and in Bulgarian (Pirin) Macedonia.

Yugoslav (Vardar) Macedonia

Vardar, or Yugoslav, Macedonia covered 25,713 square kilometers, or about one-tenth of Yugoslavia, at its founding in 1918–19. According to the first Yugoslav census, it had 728,286 inhabitants. Although the vast majority of them were Macedonians, we have no exact figures for them or for the various ethnic minorities. As Ivo Banac observes: "though it [the census] reveals a great deal about the official ideology [unitarism and centralism], it is not particularly helpful as a statistical guide to the size of each national community. . . . For one thing, nationality was not a census rubric. The religion and the maternal language of the population are therefore our only guides to nationality. But here also, official attitudes got in the way of clarity. As far as Slavic population was concerned there were only three possibilities: (1) 'Serbian or Croatian,' (2) 'Slovenian,' (3) 'other Slavic.' "[1]

Since the Macedonians were officially Serbs, officials counted them as "Serbian or Croatian." They grouped Macedonians with all the Orthodox believers in Yugoslavia, and the Macedonian Slav Muslims (Torbeši), with all the country's Muslims. It is equally difficult to determine the number of Albanians, Jews, Turks, Vlachs, and so on. Officials counted them together with their fellow coreligionists or conationals in the kingdom.

The first Yugoslav basic law—the Vidovdan Constitution—came into force on Saint Vitus Day, 28 June 1921. It passed "without the participation and against the will of most of the non-Serb parties."[2] Nikola Pašić, premier since 1903 of Serbia and now of Yugoslavia, and the leading advocate of Great Serbianism, pushed it through the constituent assembly (which the people elected on 22 November 1920) by 223 of 419 votes. Almost all the votes in favor were Serbian (183); Pašić virtually bought the rest from the Muslims (32) and the Slovene Peasant Party (8). The Croatian Peasant Party, under Stjepan Radić, the dominant (and nationalist) Croatian representative, boycotted the conclave; the Communist Party of Yugoslavia (KPJ), which won the most votes and seats in Macedonia, could not take part. Yugoslavia outlawed it at the end of December 1920, and it would remain illegal throughout the 1920s and 1930s.

The Vidovdan Constitution based itself on unitarist Yugoslavism. The Serbs saw the new state as an extension of 'Greater Serbia'; it "was to be strongly centralized, Serbian dominated, and ruled by the Karadjordjević dynasty."[3] Until 1928, under a barely functioning parliamentary system, Serbian centralist-dominated governments ran the kingdom. They arranged the necessary majorities in the Skupština (assembly) by "buying" the support usually of Muslim deputies, but also of the Slovene People's Party, and in 1925–26 of Stjepan Radić himself. This unworkable system, which constantly pitted decentralizers against their opposite numbers and which the Croatian Peasant Party almost always boycotted, ended in 1929.

In 1926, Nikola Pašić died. In 1928, a Montenegrin deputy from the Radical (Pašić's) Party shot the Croatian powerhouse Stjepan Radić in the Skupština, and he soon died.

Centralists, including King Alexander, used the resulting crisis to abolish the Vidovdan Constitution, "aiming to preserve centralism [instead] by extra parliamentary means."[4] Alexander abolished the constitution, dissolved the assembly, and made himself dictator. On 3 September 1931, he issued a new constitution, which nominally ended his personal rule. But, as Stavrianos notes: "This document, which remained in force to the 1941 German invasion, was merely a legal fig leaf for the royal dictatorship which continued as before."[5] The electoral laws announced a few weeks later guaranteed huge majorities in the assembly for the government party. They abolished proportional representation and provided that the party that received a plurality in a national election—the government party—would receive two-thirds of the seats. They accomplished exactly that goal in the elections of 1935 and 1938.

On 9 October 1934, Vlado Černozemski, a Macedonian terrorist with Italian, Hungarian, and Croatian Ustaša (far-right, fascist) connections, assassinated Alexander in Marseilles, together with Louis Barthou, the French minister of foreign affairs. However, the king's "system" remained intact during the regency (1934–41) of his young cousin Prince Paul and the premiership (1935–39) of Milan Stojadinović. The twelfth-hour negotiations in late 1938 and 1939 of Prime Minister Dragiša Cvetković with Vladko Maček, new leader of the Croatian Peasant Party, could not resolve the country's profound problems. True, on 26 August 1939, only days before the outbreak of war, the two men signed the Sporazum, which granted most Croatian demands. It came too late, did not satisfy extremists on either side, and further complicated national and political divisions and antagonisms that had built up over two decades.

The interwar struggle over (de)centralization of the Yugoslav state and between Great Serbian demands and those of Croatia and Slovenia involved leaders of the Serbs, Croats, Slovenes, and, to a lesser extent, Muslims. This conflict affected Macedonians as well, but they were not direct participants. They had no formal representation and could not voice their demands legally. However, they waged their own battle with Belgrade, which related to their very existence and their national, political, and economic survival.

As we saw above, the ruling elite in Belgrade officially declared and considered Vardar Macedonia a Serbian land, an integral part of Serbia, and the Macedonians, Serbs or South Serbs. However, since Macedonians rejected this designation, Belgrade treated their land as a Serbian colony and its inhabitants as objects of Serbianization. Thus the new Serbian rulers initiated policies that would have been inconceivable even under the old Ottoman regime and aimed to destroy all signs of regionalism, particularism, patriotism, or nationalism.

They acted on several fronts, totally controlling political life and repressing any dissent, deporting "undesirables" or forcing them to emigrate, transferring Macedonians internally in Yugoslavia, assimilating and denationalizing others by complete control of education and cultural and intellectual life, colonizing the land, and practicing social and economic discrimination.[6] They divided Yugoslavia arbitrarily into thirty-three districts *(županija)*, including three in Macedonia—Bitola, Bregalnica, with its center in Štip, and Skopje. Under Alexander as dictator, the kingdom had five large regions *(banovini)*, with Vardar Macedonia and parts of South Serbia proper and Kosovo forming the Vardar banovina, with its center in Skopje.

The local administration meant no more to Macedonians than the government in Belgrade. They had no real representation in either. Unlike the Serbs, Croats, Slovenes, Muslim Slavs of Bosnia-Herzegovina, Muslims of Kosovo and Macedonia (Albanians and Turks), and even ethnic minorities in the north, they could not establish political parties or any other ethnic organizations. Only Serbian or Serb-dominated Yugoslav parties could form and function legally in Vardar Macedonia.

From the outset, Macedonians rejected Serbian rule and domination. They showed their discontent in the election for the constituent assembly on 22 November 1920, which "was eminently fair; a quality that was not to be characteristic of later elections."[7] As Banac pointed out, the Communist Party (KPJ) won almost two-fifths, or about 37 percent, of all Macedonian votes. In local elections on 22 August, the Communists had won in some of the principal towns: Skopje, Veles, Kumanovo, and Kavadarci. Both polls revealed a strong protest vote from economically backward Macedonia.[8]

The KPJ would enjoy a strong following in Macedonia even after Belgrade outlawed it in late 1920. As an illegal and underground organization, it and its front attracted new, younger Macedonian intellectuals on the left who studied and matured under Serbian rule.[9] Otherwise, Macedonians who voted tended to support the opposition Democratic Party during the 1920s. Under the 1931 constitution and new electoral laws, elections became meaningless, and their results tell us little about the political situation and trends in Yugoslavia and even less about those in Vardar Macedonia. Moreover, we can detect the sizeable discontent and opposition to Serbian rule in the 1920s and early 1930s in widespread support, passive and active, for the anti-Yugoslav (-Serbian) underground and terrorist activities of the reestablished and reorganized VMRO.[10]

Belgrade appointed the chief administrators and officials in Macedonia—usually Serbs with proven nationalist credentials. They imposed on the Macedonians Serbian administrative and legal codes without regard to local conditions or requirements. Their behavior was even more offensive. D. J. Footman, the British vice-consul at Skopje, described it as invariably harsh, brutal, arbitrary, and corrupt. "Officials depend for their promotions and appointment on the service they can render their political party," he wrote. "It is therefore natural for them to make what they can while they are in office. I regard this as the factor which will most militate against improvement in administration."[11]

The British Foreign Office echoed these sentiments. Its lengthy review of 1930 stated: "At present Jugoslavia lacks the material out of which to create an efficient and honest civil service. This want is especially felt in the new and 'foreign' provinces such as Serb-Macedonia. To make matters worse, the Jugoslav Government . . . are compelled to pursue a policy of forcible assimilation and, in order to 'Serbise' the Slavs of Serb-Macedonia, must necessarily tend to disregard those grievances of the local inhabitants which spring from the violation of their local rights and customs."[12]

Forcible Serbianization began during the first Serbian occupation (1913–15). The new rulers acted fast to eliminate all vestiges of Patriarchist (Greek) influence in the south of Vardar Macedonia and particularly the widespread Exarchist (Bulgarian) presence. The policy ended in September 1915, when Bulgaria entered the war, occupied Vardar Macedonia, and introduced forcible Bulgarianization. At the end of the war, again under Serbian occupation, the Vardar Macedonians experienced their third "baptism by fire" in five years.

Many members of the Exarchist-educated elite and numerous Macedonian activists felt they had to leave with the retreating Bulgarian army and sought refuge in Bulgaria. Remaining Exarchist clergymen and teachers lost their posts; some suffered expulsion and ended up in Bulgaria as well. Their places went to nationally proven individuals, mostly Serbs, but in some cases to Serbophile Macedonians.

All Bulgarian signs gave way to Serbian; all Bulgarian books, to Serbian. Various Serbian social and cultural clubs, societies, and organizations replaced Bulgarian counterparts. The government Serbianized personal names and surnames for all official uses and, whenever possible, inserted Serbian equivalents in place of local Macedonian place names. In September 1920, the Orthodox churches of the new state united, and the Macedonian Orthodox community in Vardar Macedonia transferred to the Serbian Orthodox church.

Most important, Yugoslavia did not recognize the Macedonian language and forbade its writing and publishing. It declared Serbian the official language of Vardar Macedonia and the maternal tongue of Macedonians there. Serbian became the language of instruction at all levels of the educational system, from kindergarten to the Faculty of Philosophy in Skopje—a branch of the University of Belgrade and Vardar Macedonia's only interwar institution of higher learning. Serbian was also compulsory for all official purposes and in all official dealings.

In fact, Serbian was to serve as the major carrier of the Serbian national ideology and thus as the instrument for Serbianization. The chief guarantors of this effort were to be a strong armed presence and new colonists and settlers. Yugoslav (Vardar) Macedonia became a veritable armed camp. Anywhere between 35,000 and 50,000 armed men from the Yugoslav (Serbian) army, *gendarmerie*, and armed bands of the state-sponsored Association against Bulgarian Bandits, with headquarters in Štip, were active in Macedonia. Over 70 percent of the Yugoslav military police force—12,000 men out of 17,000—was there as well.

Moreover, Belgrade had far-reaching plans for colonization: it hoped to settle 50,000 Serbian families and create Serbian oases and bridgeheads throughout the region. It encouraged Serbian speculators to purchase huge tracts of the best land from departing Turkish landowners and make it available to colonists.

For various reasons, however, by 1940 only 4,200 households, many of them families of veterans of the Salonika front in the First World War, had settled. One of their main duties was to help maintain "law and order," or "pacify," the restive land. They were to fight the frequent attacks and incursions by armed bands from the reestablished VMRO operating from bases in Pirin (Bulgarian) Macedonia. More important, they were under orders to punish severely local VMRO leaders and sympathizers. Indeed, they were to eradicate any sign or evidence of passive or active Macedonianism or Macedonian activity, which Serbia equated with "Bulgarianism" and Communism and hence with treason and made subject to death, imprisonment, internment, exile, and so on.

During the depths of the royal dictatorship, between 1929 and 1931, and as part of efforts to promote Yugoslav nationalism, the regime also founded in Macedonia "national organizations"—Yugoslav sports, social, and cultural societies and associations. However, these groups remained primarily Serbian and did not win over Macedonians, nor did the National Guard, a network of paramilitary bands, or the association that Serbia promoted as the Yugoslav Youth of the Vardar Banovina.[13]

Finally, the regime also discriminated economically against Macedonians. In all Balkan countries, "The high birth rate, the low agricultural productivity, the inability of industry to absorb the population surplus, and the lack of domestic market adequate to support industrial expansion—all these condemned the peasants and the urban workers to a low living standard and no hope for the future."[14]

But extreme poverty worsened these problems in Macedonia. The long struggle for Macedonia under Ottoman rule, the two Balkan wars, and the military campaigns of the First World War in Macedonia caused enormous human and material losses. They damaged or destroyed many towns and villages. War stopped cultivation of large tracts of land; ruined animal husbandry, an economic mainstay; damaged railway links and bridges; and rendered useless means of communication.

The partition had devastated the economy of all parts of Macedonia. Historically and traditionally, the whole area comprised an economic unit, which the Vardar valley, along with the Bistrica and Struma rivers and the Aegean littoral, linked together. The new, artificial borders severed traditional markets from trade routes and sources of supply and destroyed economic unity that had existed since ancient times.

Interwar Vardar Macedonia was probably Yugoslavia's least developed region. In 1921, when Yugoslavia's illiteracy rate was 51.5 percent, and Slovenia's only 8.8 percent, Macedonia's was 83.8 percent. In the same year, the urban population counted only 27 percent of the total; and, in 1931, 75 percent of Yugoslavs still worked in agriculture, with probably 43 percent of that figure active and the rest surplus. There were many landless households, and many others owned less than a hectare. The methods of cultivation were primitive, and the yield of grain crops on 81 percent of the cultivated land was among the lowest in Europe. After the Great War, more land switched to industrial crops, such as cotton, tobacco, and opium poppies. Yet cotton growing declined after the war, because partition and new boundaries deprived it of its traditional market, the textile industry in Aegean Macedonia. Production of tobacco and opium poppies fell dramatically when demand for and prices of both collapsed during the Depression.

The industrial sector, or the urban economy, was equally backward. After the war, there were only 16 industrial enterprises left in Yugoslav Macedonia. By 1925, their number grew to 27; the state owned 11, and Serbs and Czechs 16. The following five years saw 25 new firms, mostly small power stations and food-processing plants, with the participation of local investors. The banking system expanded modestly as well. In addition to existing branches of Serbian banks in Skopje and Bitola, new banks opened in Skopje, Štip, and other towns. The craft industry—an urban staple—was in decline; it lacked resources to modernize, and many craftspeople had also to work on the land.

The Depression hit the small, underdeveloped industrial sector even harder than the agrarian economy. By 1932, about thirty plants shut down. During a recovery of sorts in the late 1930s, some new enterprises started up. Overall, however, on the eve of the Second World War, industrial plants in Macedonia were small and technologically backward. In industrial development, Macedonia ranked last in Yugoslavia.[15]

Serbia was not to blame for Macedonia's historic economic backwardness. No progress, however, occurred between the two world wars; Belgrade did hardly anything to alleviate Macedonia's economic situation, and its discriminatory practices tended to exacerbate its peoples' plight. As O. C. Harvey of the British Foreign Office reported after a visit to Yugoslav and Greek Macedonia in April 1926: "Such discontent as exists springs from genuine economic distress . . . And wherever else the Serb is spending his money, he does not seem to be spending it in Macedonia. Yet this country is perhaps really the biggest problem for the Serbs."[16]

It needed radical land reform: redistribution to landless and poor peasant households of properties of large landowners, mostly departed or departing Turks. However, Belgrade repeatedly postponed promised reforms, and when it acted in 1931 it aimed first at colonization. The laws on land reform favored colonists—veterans from the Salonika front, members of Serbian bands, military policemen, frontier guards, financial officials. Belgrade gave them the best lands and encouraged them to settle in Macedonia.

By 1940, of 381,245 hectares up for distribution, the government had given 142,585 hectares to 17,679 colonists and Serbian volunteers and only 85,511 hectares to 30,582 agricultural tenants and peasants. At the same time, it continued to exploit the agrarian economy even during the depths of the Depression through state monopolies of industrial crops such as opium, tobacco, and silk cones. For example, the export price of opium fell by only 42 percent in 1927–35, but the purchase price of crude opium dropped by 77 percent.[17]

Furthermore, Macedonia lacked infrastructure for industrial development. Yet the government did virtually nothing to initiate even small-scale industrial growth. In the 1930s, it constructed the Veles-Prilep-Bitola roadway with French financial aid. Such limited and isolated undertakings could not stimulate industrial development, which would have absorbed the surplus rural poor.

On the eve of Yugoslavia's collapse in 1941, R. I. Campbell, British minister at Belgrade, summed up the sad history: "Since the occupation by Serbia in 1913 of the Macedonian districts, the Government has carried out in this area, with greater or lesser severity, a policy of suppression and assimilation. In the years following the Great War land was taken away from the inhabitants and given to Serbian colonists. Macedonians were compelled to change their names . . . and the Government did little or nothing to assist the economic development of the country."[18]

Greek (Aegean) Macedonia

Greece acquired the largest territory in the partition of 1913: Aegean Macedonia covered 34,356 square kilometers. The Greek state preserved the region's territorial unity but not its Macedonian name. Aegean Macedonia formed the core of the new Greek province of Northern Greece, which also included western Thrace and southern Epirus, and its chief administrative officer, or governor, was the kingdom's minister for Northern Greece.

Greece further subdivided Aegean Macedonia into three directorates, or provinces: the central, with its seat in Salonika, included the districts of Salonika, Chalcidice (Chalkidiki), Kilkis (Kukuš), Edessa (Voden), and Vereia (Ber); the eastern, with its capital in Kavala, included Seres, Drama, and Kavala; and the western, with headquarters in Kozani (Kožani), included Kozani, Florina (Lerin), and Kastoria (Kostur).

As we saw in previous chapters, statistics on the ethnic composition of Ottoman Macedonia are notoriously unreliable and confusing. Nonetheless, all sources except Greek ones agree that the Slavic speakers, the Macedonians, constituted the majority before partition.[19]

The competing statistics on Aegean Macedonia are equally problematic, yet all but Greek sources find the Macedonians its largest single group before 1913. The figures range from 329,371, or 45.3 percent, to 382,084, or 68.9 percent, of the non-Turkish inhabitants, and from 339,369, or 31.3 percent, to 370,371, or 35.2 percent, of the area's approximately 1,052,227 people.[20]

Todor Simovski prepared one of the most detailed breakdowns for the region just before the Balkan Wars. Using Bulgarian and Greek sources, he estimated 1,073,549 inhabitants: 326,426 Macedonians, 40,921 Muslim Macedonians *(pomaks)*, 289,973 Turks, 4,240 Christian Turks, 2,112 Cherkez (Circassians), 240,019 Christian Greeks, 13,753 Muslim Greeks, 5,584 Muslim Albanians, 3,291 Christian Albanians, 45,457 Christian Vlachs, 3,500 Muslim Vlachs, 59,560 Jews, 29,803 Roma, and 8,100 others.[21]

The number of Macedonians in Aegean Macedonia began to decline absolutely and relatively during the Balkan Wars and particularly after 1918. The Treaty of Neuilly, 27 November 1919, provided for the "voluntary exchange" of minorities between Bulgaria and Greece. According to the best estimates, between 1913 and 1928 Greece forced 86,382 Macedonians to emigrate from Aegean Macedonia, mostly from its eastern and central provinces, to Bulgaria.

More important still, under the Treaty of Lausanne, 24 July 1923, which ended the Greek-Turkish war of 1920–22, the compulsory exchange of minorities forced 400,000 Muslims, including 40,000 Macedonians, to leave Greece, and 1.3 million Greeks and other Christians to depart from Asia Minor. In the years up to 1928, the Greek government settled 565,143 of the latter refugees, as well as 53,000 Greek colonists, in Aegean Macedonia.

Thus, by removing 127,384 Macedonians and settling 618,199 refugees and colonists, Greece transformed the ethnographic structure of Aegean Macedonia in fifteen years.[22]

However, available evidence on Macedonians after 1928 is even shakier. The official Greek census of 1928 sought to present an ethnically homogeneous state and minimized all minorities, especially Macedonians, or "Slavophone" Greeks, and the census cited only 81,984 of them. That figure is far too low when we compare it to all non-Greek pre-1913 statistics.

Stojan Kiselinovski, a Macedonian historian who has evaluated pre-1914 statistics, migrations of the 1920s, and the Greek census of 1928, offered a more credible and realistic figure. He estimated that at least 240,000 Macedonians remained in Aegean Macedonia before the Second World War.[23] Furthermore, the overwhelming majority inhabited the western part—the districts of Kastoria (Kostur), Florina (Lerin), Kozani (Kožani), and Edessa (Voden)—which the population shifts little affected; unlike the eastern and central parts, its people preserved their

Macedonian character. The population movements of the 1920s rendered Macedonians a minority in their own land—and an unwanted, unrecognized, and oppressed minority at that. This group bore the brunt of the Greek state's policies of forced denationalization and assimilation.

The Treaty of Sèvres of 10 August 1920 required Greece to protect "the interests of the inhabitants who differ from the majority of the population in nationality, language or faith." It had to provide non-Greeks with equal political and civil rights and allow them to use their native tongues in the press, courts, churches, and primary schools.

In September 1924, Bulgaria and Greece concluded the Kalfov-Politis Agreement, in which Greece recognized the presence on its soil of "Bulgarians." This arrangement provoked a crisis in traditionally amicable relations between Greece and Serbia/Yugoslavia, which feared that Greece's recognition of its Macedonians as Bulgarians would only justify Bulgaria's claims that even Vardar Macedonians—indeed, all Macedonians—were Bulgarians. Consequently, Yugoslavia threatened to abrogate its 1913 alliance with Greece unless the latter recognized the Macedonians of Aegean Macedonia as Serbs. In any event, the strong protest from Belgrade provided the Greek parliament with a welcome and suitable pretext not to ratify the agreement, and in January 1925 the Greek government pronounced it null and void.[24]

Greece now changed its approach to its Macedonian problem. After frequent criticism at the League of Nations in Geneva that Greece was not protecting minority rights as Sèvres required, Greece promised maternal-language instruction in the primary schools of areas with compact groupings of Macedonians.

Athens appointed a three-member commission in the Ministry of Education to prepare a primer for the schools. *Abecedar* (ABC) appeared in Athens in 1925[25] in the Florina (Lerin)-Bitola dialect but in the Latin rather than the Cyrillic alphabet. Ostensibly, it was for Aegean Macedonia, and Greece submitted it to the League to show its compliance with its treaty obligations. "The Bulgarian representative described it as 'incomprehensible' but the Greek representative to the League, Vasilis Dendramis, defended it on the grounds that the Macedonian Slav language was 'neither Bulgarian nor Serbian, but an independent language' and produced linguistic maps to back this up." However, the Greek government never introduced the *Abecedar* in schools, and it confiscated and destroyed all copies of the text.[26]

Greece proclaimed Aegean Macedonians as Greeks or Slavophone

Greeks. Denial of their identity and forced assimilation took on institutional form and remains official Greek policy.

There is little scholarship in the West on interwar Macedonians of the Aegean region. They suffered isolation from the world, even from relatives in Albania, Bulgaria, and Yugoslavia. Few Westerners, including diplomats, ever ventured into their area, west of Edessa (Voden), until the early 1940s. Most academic and nonacademic observers were Grecophiles and readily accepted Greek claims for ethnic homogeneity; for them Aegean Macedonians did not exist.

The Macedonians were never part of Greek life. The ruling elite and its bourgeois parties accepted ethnic homogeneity, Macedonians' nonexistence, and forced assimilation, discrimination, and oppression—and this situation still continues. Furthermore, most Greek scholars have agreed. Hardly anyone has undertaken serious research or published scholarly studies on the political, social, economic, or cultural life of Macedonians or other minorities in the country. And dissenting scholars, domestic or foreign, do not gain access to archives and primary sources on Macedonian themes in research institutions in Greece. The Macedonian question was and remains the "Achilles' heel" of Greek politics and scholarship.

Only the Communist Party of Greece (KKE), in accord with the general line of the Comintern, took up the cause. As with the other Balkan Communist parties, in the 1920s it recognized the Macedonians in all three partitioned regions as a distinct Slav nation with its own language, history, culture, territory, and interests. *Rizospastis*, the main newspaper of the KKE's central committee—the only official organ of a Balkan Communist Party to appear legally through most of the 1920s and 1930s—was until 1936 Greece's only major publication to write about the Macedonians and hence constitutes an invaluable source.[27]

Between the world wars, the Macedonians in Aegean Macedonia, a minority in their own land, were overwhelmingly rural and scattered in mountainous villages and small towns. They no longer formed a majority in any large urban center. And, since Greece had expelled virtually the entire Exarchist (Bulgarian)-educated intelligentsia and most Macedonian activists to Bulgaria or distant places in Greece, especially the islands, they lacked an elite. Well-educated Macedonians remained few in number; their Greek education in now totally Greek Salonika and especially in Athens estranged many of them from their Slavic roots and cultural traditions.

As I indicated above, political life in Greece excluded Macedonians. The perennial struggle between royalists and republicans, which dominated interwar politics at least until General Ioannis Metaxas became dictator in 1936, little affected their lives. After 1936, official neglect and oppression gave way to open persecution. The regime deported many Macedonians from their native villages near the Yugoslav border to Aegean islands; interned many on uninhabited islands, where they perished; and tortured tens of thousands in prisons or police stations. Their "crime" was to identify themselves as Macedonians, to speak or be overheard speaking Macedonian, or to belong to or sympathize with the KKE, the only party to take any interest in their plight.

Macedonians had direct contact with officialdom only through the local administrator, priest, teacher, policeman, and tax collector, all state appointees. Most such officials were Greeks from other regions, and some were assimilated Macedonians, whom other Macedonians derisively called *Grkomani* (Grecocized Macedonians). They and refugee families from Asia Minor who received the best land controlled the native Macedonians.

Like the Serbian administration in Vardar Macedonia, the Greek in Macedonian areas of Aegean Macedonia seems to have been harsh, brutal, arbitrary, and totally corrupt. Colonel A. C. Corfe, a New Zealander and chair of the League of Nations Mixed Commission on Greek-Bulgarian Emigration, reported in 1923: "One of the Macedonians' chief grievances is against the Greek Gendarmerie and during our tour we saw many examples of the arrogant and unsatisfactory methods of the Gendarmerie, who commandeer from the peasants whatever food they want. . . . One visits few villages where some of the inhabitants are not in Greek prisons, without trial."[28]

Captain P. H. Evans—an agent of Britain's Special Operations Executive (SOE), who spent eight months of 1943–44 in western Aegean Macedonia as a British liaison officer (BLO) and station commander—described the attitude "even of educated *Greeks* toward the *Slav* minority" as "usually stupid, uninformed and brutal to a degree that makes one despair of any understanding ever being created between the two people."[29]

Greece was a poor agrarian society. Its new northern territories, in Macedonia and Thrace, were more backward and became even more desperately so with the settlement of hundreds of thousands of destitute refugees from Asia Minor. However, discriminatory Greek policies worsened the situation of the Macedonians, who benefited not at all from wide-ranging agrarian reforms in the 1920s. The government gave Greek peasants state and church lands, and lands that it purchased from larger estates that departing Turks or expelled Macedonians vacated.

Nor did ambitious and costly government-sponsored projects that drained five swamps and lakes and recovered thousands of hectares of land help Macedonians. On the contrary, Athens confiscated arable land from Macedonian peasants and villages and gave it to newcomers for economic and political reasons. Peasants—most of the Aegean Macedonians—became marginal, in subsistence farming. Their plots were too small and infertile, their methods primitive, their yields too low. They barely eked out an existence.

The few nonpeasant Macedonians—shopkeepers, craftspeople, and tradespeople in villages and small provincial towns (Kastoria, Florina, Kozani, and even the larger Edessa) were not much better off. However, there was virtually no industrial sector to employ surplus labor and improve economic conditions. There was no local capital, and the government did not invest in this region. There were a few large-scale government projects such as construction of the Metaxas line of defense, but they excluded Macedonians unless they joined extreme nationalist, right-wing, or fascist organizations.

The industrial recovery in central and eastern Aegean Macedonia—involving textiles, food processing, and tobacco in Salonika, Seres, Drama, and Kavala—which began before the Depression and continued in the later 1930s, provided work for some refugees from Asia Minor but not for Macedonians in western areas. The latter remained neglected and poor in this beautiful, picturesque, virtually unknown corner of Europe.

The only way out appeared to be emigration, and many of the Macedonians left in search of a better life in Canada and the United States in the late 1920s and the 1930s. Such large-scale emigration undoubtedly delighted Athens, for it facilitated Hellenization of the area that had the most Macedonians.[30]

The situation of Greece's Macedonians was hardest of all in culture. As in Vardar Macedonia, people here could no longer decide their own identity—the "liberators" demanded total assimilation. Aegean Macedonians had to embrace the national identity, become Greek in every respect, or suffer the consequences. The state employed all its resources—including military, churches, schools, press, cultural institutions and societies, and sports organizations—to further the cause.

Before the Balkan Wars, there had been many Slav schools throughout Aegean Macedonia. The Exarchist church controlled 19 primary schools in towns and 186 in villages, with 320 teachers and 12,895 pupils. There were also four Serbian schools and about two hundred other community-run Slav primary schools in villages. After partition, Greece closed all the Slav schools and destroyed their libraries and other teaching aids. It replaced them with an inadequate number of Greek schools. The education was poor, especially outside district centers. Illiteracy remained prevalent, and even students at village schools were at best only semi-literate.

Athens, like Belgrade with Serbianization, "Grecocized" names or replaced them with Greek. In November 1926, a new law ordered replacement of all Slavic names of cities, villages, rivers, mountains, and so on. Athens sought to eradicate any reminders of the centuries-old Slavic presence in Aegean Macedonia. In July 1927, another decree ordered removal of all Slavic inscriptions in churches and cemeteries and their replacement with Greek ones. This campaign reached its most vicious in the later 1930s under Metaxas. The government prohibited use of Macedonian even at home to a people who knew Greek scarcely or not at all and could not communicate properly in any tongue but their own.[31]

As in Serbia/Yugoslavia, so in Greece assimilation failed. Western Aegean Macedonia remained Slav Macedonian, and the Macedonians there stayed Macedonian. As Captain Evans emphasized: "It is predominantly a *Slav* region, not a *Greek* one. The language of the home, and usually also the fields, the village street, and the market is *Macedonian*, a *Slav* language. . . . The place names as given on the map are *Greek*, . . . but the names which are mostly used . . . are . . . all *Slav* names. The *Greek* ones are merely a bit of varnish put on by *Metaxas*. . . . *Greek* is regarded as almost a foreign language and the *Greeks* are distrusted as something alien, even if not, in the full sense of the word, as foreigners. The obvious fact, almost too obvious to be stated, that the region is *Slav* by nature and not *Greek* cannot be overemphasized."[32]

Bulgarian (Pirin) Macedonia

Bulgaria, the third partitioning power, enjoyed the greatest influence among Macedonians, but its defeat in two wars left it with the smallest part, Pirin Macedonia, or the Petrich district. The region covered 6,788 square kilometers and had 235,000 inhabitants. According to one source, after the First World War and the various exchanges or expulsions of populations, 96 percent of its residents were Macedonians.[33] Moreover, there were many refugees and émigrés from Macedonia, perhaps hundreds of thousands, who had settled all over Bulgaria, especially in urban centers such as Sofia, Varna, Russe, and Plovdiv, following post-1870 crises in Macedonia. They tended to keep their Macedonian memories and connections alive; or, as Stavrianos puts it: "Some had been assimilated, but many remained uprooted and embittered."[34]

Until the Balkan Wars, Pirin Macedonia was part of the Seres *sanjak,* which had six administrative districts: Nevrokop, Razlog, Gorna Dzhumaia, Melnik, Petrich, and Demir Hisar. Partition brought division of the Seres sanjak: the city of Seres and the district of Sidirokastron (Demir Hisar) became part of Aegean (Greek) Macedonia, and the rest comprised Pirin Macedonia. Until the coup d'état in Sofia in 1934 and the military dictatorship, Pirin Macedonia remained united—a Bulgarian administrative region with five districts and with its capital in Petrich. The new regime split the area into two parts: one in the Sofia administrative region, and the other in the Plovdiv.

The Macedonians' situation in Bulgaria,[35] where the major nationalist trends thrived in Pirin Macedonia and among the many Macedonians in its capital, was radically different from that of compatriots in Greece and Serbia/Yugoslavia. Sofia assumed a more ambiguous position: continuing paternalism vis-à-vis Macedonians in all parts of Macedonia, toward whom it acted as patron but whom it claimed as Bulgarians. This approach left Pirin Macedonians to do what they wanted. Unlike Athens and Belgrade, Sofia tolerated free use of the name "Macedonia" and an active Macedonian political and cultural life.

Organized activity, which virtually ceased in the other two parts of Macedonia, reemerged in Bulgaria immediately after 1918. The ranks of Exarchist-educated Macedonians and Macedonian activists in the Pirin region, in Sofia, and elsewhere in Bulgaria gained émigrés and refugees from the other parts of Macedonia. After an agonizing, bitter, divisive struggle, by the early 1920s they again regrouped into left and right, in the VMRO tradition.

The left consisted of organizations such as the Provisional Representation of the Former Internal Macedonian Revolutionary Organization, the Ilinden Organization, the Macedonian Federative Organization, and the Émigré Communist Union, which had links with the Bulgarian Communist Party (BKP). It identified with the left of the original VMRO and the Sandanists (Jane Sandanski's followers) of the post-Ilinden period.

Intellectuals of the original VMRO led it—for example, Dimo Hadžidimov, Ǵorče Petrov, and Petar Poparsov, who survived the uprising and partition. As with the original VMRO and the Sandanists, they sought a united, independent homeland; but now they hoped for aid from the Balkan and European left, or "progressive forces." In the early 1920s, they enjoyed considerable support in Pirin Macedonia as well as among Macedonians in Sofia and elsewhere in the country. They allied with the Agrarian government of Aleksandŭr Stamboliski. Unlike most Bulgarian politicians, he was not a proponent of a Great Bulgaria and, while pursuing rapprochement with Yugoslavia, was sympathetic to the Macedonian national cause.[36]

After the coup d'état of 9 June 1923 installed a reactionary, revisionist, authoritarian regime, and especially after suppression of the Communist revolt in September, the new government outlawed the Macedonian and the Bulgarian left. Those groups went underground, and their organizational center moved to Vienna. Leaders of the old political parties, the military, and the Macedonian right had planned the Bulgarian coup to reestablish the traditional ruling elite and pursue a revisionist foreign policy. The Macedonian right played a critical role in both the June coup and suppression of the Communist revolt. Macedonian terrorists carried out the bloody and gruesome murder of Stamboliski and launched a murderous campaign against the leaders of the Macedonian left that forced survivors underground or out of the country.

The Macedonian right grouped itself around the VMRO, which had resurfaced in 1919 under its reactivated central committee—Todor Aleksandrov, Petar Čaulev, and Bulgarian general Aleksandŭr Protogerov. Until his murder in 1924, the charismatic Aleksandrov led and dominated the right and hence the VMRO. He was a schoolteacher by training and "the last of his kind, a combination of a hajduk, warlord and politician."[37]

Like the left, the right claimed the name, tradition, and heritage of the original VMRO, adopting its statutes and rulebooks and calling for a united, autonomous homeland. Between the world wars, people commonly called it the "autonomist" VMRO and its followers, Macedonian "autonomists." Unlike the left, however, the right waged armed struggle. From secure bases in Pirin Macedonia, the VMRO regularly dispatched armed bands into Aegean and Vardar Macedonia. They hoped to undermine the status quo by striking at Greek and Serbian symbols and authorities. However, they also depended on Bulgaria, or rather its revisionist, nationalist right.

As a result, the VMRO projected a confusing double image—a Macedonian patriotic revolutionary organization fighting for the national cause, but also an instrument of Bulgarian revisionism pursuing a Great Bulgaria. In the early 1920s, dual identity and aims helped win it widespread support among Macedonians and Bulgarians. By the late 1920s, however, the duality was undermining its strength and following among both groups.[38]

Except for the brief, abortive attempt to unite the Macedonian left and right in the spring of 1924,[39] the VMRO until 1934 served loyally and was a junior partner of Bulgaria's authoritarian and irredentist regimes. After Alkesandrov's murder in August 1924, which Sofia instigated to avenge his rapprochement with the left, the VMRO became even more dependent on the regime. His young, ambitious, and scheming private secretary and successor, Ivan (Vančo) Mihailov (1896–1990), who lacked his charisma and élan, transformed the VMRO into a terrorist organization serving Bulgarian irredentism and the interests of its leader and his cronies, who ruled Pirin Macedonia.

In return for its loyalty and services, Sofia rewarded Mihailov's VMRO with a free hand over the Macedonians in Bulgaria. The VMRO established its rule in the Pirin region and control over the many Macedonian societies, associations, and other organizations in Bulgaria, which served as its legal front and facade and suppressed its opponents. From 1924 to 1934, Pirin Macedonia was the VMRO's private domain—"a state within a state," or "a Macedonian kingdom," within Bulgaria. The presence of Bulgarian institutions and officers was only nominal, for they depended totally on Mihailov's lieutenants, who exercised power on behalf of the VMRO, which controlled every aspect of the inhabitants' lives.

Through its local chieftains, the VMRO oversaw the poor agrarian economy and exploited it, supposedly for "the national cause." The chieftains collected taxes from everyone, insisted on "donations" (protection payments) from owners of larger estates and representatives of major tobacco firms, and in turn allowed "donors" to exploit the peasants. They tightly supervised the small urban and industrial labor force; strikes were not legal in the Petrich district.

The overall standard of living was noticeably lower there than in the rest of Bulgaria: the average income was lower, and the cost of goods of daily consumption higher. Moreover, residents had a heavier tax burden. In addition to taxes to Sofia, they had to pay an "autonomy tax"—a sort of sales tax on all goods—as a contribution to the "national cause," the liberation of Macedonia. As Stavrianos puts it: "The unfortunate inhabitants were required to pay two sets of taxes, one for the Sofia treasury and the other for the IMRO."[40]

The VMRO's control of political life was no less rigid. The inhabitants enjoyed only political rights and activities that its leadership allowed them. Nominally there were political parties and a multi-party system, but all candidates in local and parliamentary elections had to receive VMRO approval. The region's members of the Bulgarian parliament (Sobranie) formed a separate group, or caucus, and obeyed the VMRO's dictates. Moreover, these "Macedonian" parliamentarians led the various Macedonian organizations in Bulgaria—the Ilinden Organization, the Macedonian Youth Union, the Vardar Student Society, and, most important, the Macedonian National Committee (MNK) of the Macedonian Brotherhoods in Bulgaria. Through the MNK, the VMRO controlled the numerous and well-organized brotherhoods, or benevolent associations, that embraced the many refugees and émigrés from Aegean and Vardar Macedonia throughout Bulgaria.

The MNK was in effect the VMRO's legal front in Bulgaria and beyond. By the mid-1920s, Mihailov's VMRO had established its presence abroad. The newspaper *La Macédoine,* from Geneva, was its official organ in western Europe. The Macedonian Political Organization (MPO) of the United States and Canada, with headquarters in Indianapolis, Indiana, modeled itself on the MNK in Sofia. This umbrella organization brought together the numerous village, town, or district brotherhoods of Macedonian immigrants, primarily from Aegean but also from Vardar Macedonia, who settled in those two countries. The MPO and its *Macedonian Tribune–Makedonska Tribuna* dictated the VMRO's line to the brotherhoods, lobbied on its behalf in Washington, in Ottawa, and at the League of Nations, and collected from poor Macedonian immigrants substantial sums for the liberation of the homeland—or rather for Mihailov's VMRO.

The VMRO's precarious unity under Mihailov lasted only until 1927, when the coalition, the so-called democratic accord, which had governed Bulgaria after 1923, split over foreign policy. Andrei Liapchev, prime minister since 1926, favored a pro-British and -Italian course. Aleksandūr Tsankov, a former prime minister, wanted a pro-French and hence a pro-Yugoslav Balkan policy. Mihailov sided with Liapchev, a Macedonian by birth from Resen in Vardar Macedonia; General A. Protogerov, his rival in the leadership of the VMRO, sided with Tsankov, whom the majority of Bulgaria's officer corps seemed to support. Mihailov used this disagreement to purge the Protogerovists, whom he now blamed for the murder of Aleksandrov in 1924. Protogerov became the first victim, murdered on 7 July 1928. His group responded by killing Mihailovists, and this "Macedonian fratricide" continued for six years in Pirin Macedonia, Sofia, and other towns in Bulgaria.

The Mihailovists reclaimed the VMRO and, at least nominally, the Macedonian movement in Bulgaria. However, by liquidating or driving into exile outstanding leaders of the left and then of the Protogerovists, Mihailov and his henchmen weakened the national movement in Bulgaria and in the other parts of Macedonia. Many Protogerovists and their sympathizers in the legal Macedonian organizations moved toward the illegal, underground Macedonian left in Bulgaria.

The bloodletting and useless armed incursions into Greek and Serbian Macedonia undermined the VMRO's mass support. Moreover, the VMRO and Macedonian activists were becoming isolated in Bulgaria. Bulgaria's educated public resented their constant interference in politics and even more the frequent, well-publicized murders and assassinations, often in Sofia, which tarnished Bulgaria's image abroad. By the early 1930s, Mihailov's VMRO and its most loyal adherents in the legal organizations—the most Bulgarophile elements within the Macedonian movement—had become totally dependent on Sofia's reactionary governing elite.

After the coup d'état in May 1934, the new regime of Kimon Georgiev must have decided that Mihailov's VMRO was more trouble than it was worth. It outlawed the organization, liquidated its networks, and arrested or expelled leaders who did not escape.[41]

The new government took direct control of Pirin Macedonia. It abolished the Petrich administrative district and split it into two parts: it annexed one to the Sofia province and the other to the Plovdiv. More important, it liquidated the VMRO's de facto "state within the state" and integrated the region into Bulgaria. The new order was not much better for the residents. However, the old VMRO regime found very few defenders.

Macedonianism Survives

The interwar attempts by the partitioning states to eradicate all signs of Macedonianism failed. Forcible assimilation in Greece and Serbia did produce some of the desired results. Some Macedonians accepted or felt they had to embrace the host's national ideology and constructed Greek or Serbian identities. However, many more reacted negatively and helped to form the ethnic Macedonian national identity. Bulgaria's more tolerant and paternalistic policies fostered continuation of Bulgarophilism among Macedonians. However, neither official Bulgaria nor the VMRO could reconcile the conflicting interests of Bulgarian irredentist nationalism and of Macedonian patriotism and nationalism. When they had to choose, Macedonians opted for their native Macedonianism.

Early in 1941, the British vice-consul at Skopje claimed that most Macedonians belonged to the national movement: "90 percent of all Slav Macedonians were autonomists in one sense or another." Because the movement was secret, however, gauging the relative strength of its various currents was difficult, although clearly the VMRO had lost ground since its banning in Bulgaria and the exile of its leaders. While the diplomat acknowledged the close relationship between Communism and "autonomism," or nationalism, he downplayed the contention that Communists used the Macedonian movement for their own ends. As he saw it, since every Macedonian was an autonomist, almost certainly "the Communists and autonomists are the same people," and Macedonian Communists were not doctrinaire and were "regarded by other Balkan communists as weaker brethren." "My opinion," he wrote, "is that they are autonomists in the first place and Communists only in the second."[42]

10 Macedonian Nationalism: From Right to Left (1920s and 1930s)

The interwar period represented, according to Ivan Katardžiev, "a time of maturing" of Macedonian national consciousness and national identity.[1] These two decades saw the three major nineteenth-century trends—the intelligentsia's Macedonianism and Macedono-Bulgarianism and the masses' Macedonianism (našizam)—coalesce in a clearly articulated and unambiguous Macedonianism and Macedonian nationalism on the left. In the history of the Macedonian people (i.e., the Slav speakers), this outcome marked the culmination of a long, complicated, but continuous process of national development and affirmation.

This chapter considers in turn three stages in interwar Macedonian nationalism. First, there reemerged in Bulgaria in the early 1920s rightist and leftist Macedonian organizations, which tried unsuccessfully to merge in 1924. Second, the VMRO's terrorist activities and aims represented Macedonian nationalism on the right and appeared dominant in the 1920s. Third, the organizational work and the platform of the VMRO (obedineta, United) represented Macedonian nationalism on the left and was in the ascendancy in the 1930s.

Unification Aborted (1924)

As we saw in the previous chapter, the partition of Macedonia and the settlements of 1913 and 1919 came as a shock to the Macedonian people. Instead of experiencing liberation, they found themselves under new and harsher regimes. Educated Macedonians and activists, especially in Bulgaria, where the largest number of them now lived, felt confusion, low morale, and deep divisions. An agonizing process of soul searching eventually led to their regrouping into a political and national right and left.

In order to win popular support throughout Macedonia, each wing presented itself as the true successor of the original VMRO. The pro-Bulgarian right used the name "VMRO" after the 1907 congress, when the organization split. It continued to claim and use the name after reestablishing the organization in late 1918. Nominally, it had three equal, joint leaders—Todor Aleksandrov, Aleksandūr Protogerov, and Petar Čaulev. It was obvious from the outset, however, that the youthful, handsome, resourceful, energetic, and charismatic Aleksandrov was in charge; many people used the label "Aleksandrov's VMRO."

The reestablished VMRO became a formidable organization, with Pirin Macedonia as its stronghold. From its secure and protected bases there, it launched frequent armed incursions and propaganda campaigns into Aegean and particularly Vardar Macedonia. Although it appeared to be and was far better organized and more united than the left, it had its own left wing, former Sandanists, and experienced its own share of divisions and splits. In December 1922, left-leaning deserters formed the Macedonian Emigré Federalist Organization (MEFO); another group of former Aleksandrov supporters formed the Macedonian Federalist Revolutionary Organization (MFRO). Those 'federalists' who survived Aleksandrov's wrath moved toward or eventually joined the Macedonian left.[2]

The left too wrapped itself in tradition. The VMRO of Goce Delčev and the Ilinden Uprising, or its mythology, provided the sole legitimation for any leader and movement seeking the hearts and minds of Macedonians. In late 1918, a group of former leaders of the Seres revolutionary district called for a united, independent homeland. Dimo Hadžidimov epitomized their views in a brochure, *Back to Autonomy* (1919).[3] It proposed reestablishment of the original VMRO and its national program. Since the name "VMRO" had become the property of the right, the left had to settle on a modified version of that name. Its organization bore the rather awkward name "Provisional Representation of the Former United Internal Macedonian Revolutionary Organization" (PPBOVMRO). It brought together many close friends and associates of Goce Delčev's, such as Ǵorče Petrov, Dimo Hadžidimov, and Petar Poparsov, and former comrades of Sandanski's in the Seres district. Like the right, the left sent emissaries and appeals to the Paris Peace Conference, but it had no more success. The two groups' open antagonism and confusing demands probably did more harm than good for Macedonian unification and autonomy.

In the years just after the war, the left fared much better in Bulgarian domestic politics. In the parliamentary and local elections of 1919, the PPBOVMRO (or PP) supported the candidates of the Bulgarian Communist Party (BKP), who fared surprisingly well both in Pirin Macedonia and in areas with many émigrés. Although its leaders were on the left, and some of them were even members of the BKP, Bulgarian Communist leaders did not approve of their Macedonian preoccupation and disregard of social and economic issues. The BKP thought the PP too nationalist and sought to take it over—in fact to transform it into its own department or section.

In 1920, the BKP did just that: it dissolved the PP and replaced it with the Emigrant Communist Union (EKS). It planned to dominate Macedonian, Thracian, and Dobrudjean émigrés. However, because it dwelt on ideological issues rather than on national problems, many Macedonians deserted it. Some members and followers of the PP refused to join the new organization and carried on as independent Communists, independent even of the BKP; others joined Aleksandrov's VMRO or organizations that it controlled. The latter strengthened the left wing of the Macedonian right.

Other non-Communist groups on the left emerged after 1918. The Macedonian Federalist Revolutionary Organization included leading intellectuals and some seasoned revolutionary activists such as Pavel Šatev and Todor Panica. The Ilinden Organization attracted and hence reactivated some of the old revolutionary stalwarts. It had ties with the left wing of Aleksandrov's VMRO and considerable influence even with Aleksandrov himself. At least until the mid-1920s, the Macedonian left was not a united movement: unlike the right, it did not have a single, powerful leader operating through a centralized and tightly controlled organization.[4]

After the defeat of the Communist uprising of September 1923 in Sofia, the new authoritarian regime outlawed the BKP and the Agrarian Union and repressed leftist Macedonian organizations. A number of leftist activists departed Bulgaria and established headquarters in Vienna, which was becoming a center for Balkan political émigrés. Dimitar Vlahov (1878–1953), a VMRO veteran and former Bulgarian diplomat, helped coordinate the activities of Macedonians there. Assisting him were Todor Panica, Rizo Rizov, and Dr. Filip Atanasov, and they won over Petar Čaulev, the third member of the VMRO's central committee.

Dimitar Vlahov established contacts with the Communist International—the Comintern—in Moscow, which provided moral and material support. The central committee of the VMRO was also seeking ties and alliances with other Balkan parties and movements that favored a more radical and acceptable solution of the peninsula's national problems. Aleksandrov made contact with Stjepan Radić, leader of the Croatian Peasant Party, who was already in touch with the Comintern.

The Comintern realized the great potential of a united Macedonian revolutionary movement under its influence and worked to bring the two sides together. Serious negotiations began in Vienna, in the autumn of 1923, between the VMRO's central committee and representatives of the Macedonian left and the Comintern. They ended successfully in April–May 1924, with accords calling for unification on the basis of a program similar to that of the original VMRO. The most significant document—the so-called May Manifesto—had an initial text drafted by two people: Vlahov, a representative of the Comintern, and Nikola Kharlakov, a BKP leader. The three members of the VMRO's central committee then corrected and revised the text and signed it. It appeared in Vienna as Manifesto of the United VMRO on 6 May 1924.

The document declared that history showed that the Macedonian people could rely on only Europe's progressive revolutionary movements, which also fought against their governments' imperialist policies, against the unjust peace treaties, and for the self-determination of their own and other peoples. In the Balkan context, the VMRO would cooperate with those who struggled against the expansionist policies of European imperialism, which Balkan governments also helped implement. The VMRO would welcome and accept "the moral, material and political support of the USSR, the only power fighting for the liberation of all oppressed peoples, for their self-determination and federalization, and whose Balkan policy does not seek any imperialist aims."

The manifesto stressed the need to work for democratization of Macedonia's neighbors and their unification in a Balkan federation, which would pave the way for just resolution of the Macedonian question. It defined the VMRO's goal as liberation and unification of Macedonia into an independent state in its natural, geographic, and ethnographic boundaries. Until that happened, Macedonians in their temporary countries should fight for their minority rights on the basis of equality with other national groups.

The May Manifesto concluded by declaring that the central committee of the VMRO would terminate all persecutions and revoke all executive measures against individual activists, groups, and organizations. It called on all patriotic Macedonians to join the common struggle for a free, independent homeland as a pillar of the future Balkan federation.[5]

There was little in the document that was radically new. Its aims resembled those of the original VMRO but reflected the changed circumstances of partition. However, it proposed a revolutionary transformation—unification of left and right and creation of a strong front for national liberation. Moreover, the united movement should ally itself with and depend on Europe's "progressive forces," which rejected the political and in some cases the territorial status quo; more specifically, it should form a working alliance with the Comitern and the Soviet Union.

The events in Bulgaria in 1924 that followed release of the May Manifesto have not received adequate investigation and explanation. However, there is no doubt that the three VMRO leaders who signed the document came under intense pressure and threats from Aleksandūr Tsankov's government, which compelled Aleksandrov and Protogerov to revoke their signatures. On 1 August 1924, the two men issued a declaration, which the official Bulgarian press publicized widely; it stated that they "did not sign any manifesto and that the published manifesto is a mystification of exalted communists."

This humiliating recantation, however, could not save Aleksandrov; on 31 August, a VMRO assassin ambushed and murdered him on Mount Pirin. The plot—which the minister of the army, General Ivan Vūlkov hatched, with the knowledge of Protogerov, Aleksandrov's leadership rival—had Tsankov's approval. The government blamed the Macedonian left for the murder and used it as a pretext for a bloody campaign of liquidation in Bulgaria and Pirin Macedonia.[6] It took place systematically and efficiently under the direction of Vančo Mihailov, Aleksandrov's ambitious private secretary in Sofia and successor as leader of the VMRO.

The VMRO and Macedonian Nationalism on the Right

The renunciation of their signatures, and thus of the accords, by two of the VMRO's three leaders finalized the movement's split, which had existed from its inception in 1893. Under Mihailov's leadership, from 1924 until the organization's demise about 1945, the right retained the VMRO name and embraced the somewhat opaque program of Aleksandrov's organization. As Katardžiev observes,[7] until the May Manifesto the VMRO had no clearly defined political program, and, like Aleksandrov's character and personality, its pronouncements and tactics were full of real or apparent contradictions.

The program had its basis in the well-known and popular slogans and aims of the original VMRO. Its core plank was an autonomous Macedonian state. Its long-term aim was the liberation and unification of all parts of Macedonia into one independent country. Its short-term goals were, first, recognition of the minority rights of Slav Macedonians (whom both Aleksandrov and Mihailov considered a Bulgarian ethnic, or Macedono-Bulgarian, minority), and, second, recognition of Macedonia as an equal and autonomous member in a South Slav or Yugoslav or wider Balkan federation.[8]

On 12 February 1933, the so-called Great Macedonian Assembly in Blagoevgrad (Gorna Dzhumaia) revised and reformulated the program. Supposedly 20,000 people attended, representing Macedonian associations in Macedonia, the Balkans, the rest of Europe, and North America. They decided to abandon the minimal aim and to reformulate the maximal one into a "Free and Independent United Macedonia—the Switzerland of the Balkans." One formula captured its essence: "To be under no-one. To be ourselves. To govern ourselves." *(Da ne bideme pod nikogo. Sami da si bideme. Sami da se upravuvame.)*[9]

The VMRO hoped to achieve its own revolutionary struggle against the occupiers of Aegean and Vardar Macedonia and was willing to accept the aid of any outside party willing to aid the cause. This explains, for example, Aleksandrov's constant shifts as he searched for allies among opponents of the status quo on both the ideological left and the ideological right. In early 1921, he ceased activities against the Macedonian left; in June 1920, he urged the VMRO in Vardar Macedonia to vote in municipal and parliamentary elections for the Communists and all those who promoted federal reorganization of Yugoslavia. In July 1923, he even expressed readiness to accept incorporation of Aegean Macedonia into Yugoslavia on condition that Macedonia receive autonomy. During 1922, he declared that the VMRO would not interfere in the internal affairs of Bulgaria and would not even oppose organized Communist work in Pirin Macedonia, since national liberation did not preclude social change. From 1920 until his assassination in 1924, Aleksandrov kept contacts and negotiated with representatives of the BKP and the Comintern, and in 1924 he even signed the May Manifesto.

Yet he also engaged in seemingly contradictory activities. He maintained close ties with the reactionary political, military, and court opposition to Stamboliski's regime in Bulgaria and its allies on the Macedonian left, whom he suspected of seeking rapprochement with Pašić's Yugoslavia at the expense of the cause. In October 1922, he launched an attack on Nevrokop, stronghold of the Sandanists, the federalists, and Todor Panica. A year later, he ordered the murder of Ǵorče Petrov, a theoretician of the Macedonian movement and Stamboliski's confidant, and that of several other associates of the Bulgarian prime ministers.

And, as we saw above, in the prolonged struggle between the Agrarian government and Tsankov's reactionary opposition, Aleksandrov's VMRO directly assisted in the latter's victory and assumption of power. The VMRO helped suppress the Communist uprising in September 1923 probably because Aleksandrov believed that the Communists acted too late, were poorly prepared, and had no chance of success. It was wiser to be on the side of the victor, Tsankov's new regime.

Aleksandrov's renunciation of the May Manifesto and other documents that he signed in Vienna in 1924 strongly suggests that he was running out of options. Tsankov and the Bulgarian conservatives were in full control: for them, Aleksandrov's free and independent VMRO had outlived its usefulness—it no longer served their interests.[10] Their murder of him proves that he was their captive.

Perhaps Aleksandrov did not act out of ideological considerations but considered himself a Macedonian patriot fighting for Macedonian autonomy. "That meant not only against Serbs and Greeks but also against Bulgarians, like Stamboliski, who tried to extinguish the patriot game. Anyone who offered aid to the 'cause' was welcome; when necessary, Aleksandrov worked with the Communists, and took money from Mussolini."[11]

Aleksandrov's successor, the authoritarian, bureaucratic, secretive, ruthless Ivan Mihailov, played the "patriot game" in a more straightforward manner. From the moment he took power, he allied the VMRO very closely with the Bulgarian nationalist and revisionist right. He also cooperated actively with the other revisionist powers—Benito Mussolini's Fascist Italy, Admiral Horthy's right-wing Hungary, and Adolf Hitler's Nazi Germany—and with right-wing movements, such as the Croatian Ustaša.

Under Mihailov, the VMRO identified itself so closely with Bulgaria and its irredentist aims that one could legitimately question his Macedonian patriotism, the independence of his organization, and its devotion to autonomy for the homeland. Moreover, the VMRO's organizational, propaganda, and military activities in the other two parts of Macedonia declined. Incursions by armed bands into the Vardar region gave way to terrorist acts against individual Yugoslav officials. Otherwise, the VMRO employed whatever armed strength it possessed in terrorist acts against, and murders and assassinations of, its opponents on the Macedonian left and, after 1928, among the Protogerovists, as well as to maintain its grip over Pirin Macedonians.

Despite its patriotic Macedonian slogans, the VMRO had become radically different and appeared so to observers in Bulgaria and abroad and among Macedonians. It had turned into a Bulgarian-based, émigré terrorist organization serving primarily the interests of the Bulgarian state, its own fascist patrons, and its own leaders. By the late 1920s, its influence in Aegean and Vardar Macedonia was declining, and it was losing support in Bulgaria, in the Pirin region, and among the large Macedonian emigration. It no longer looked to be, as in Aleksandrov's time, a popular Macedonian movement for national liberation.

Probably Mihailov's realization of the VMRO's increasing irrelevance forced him and his colleagues in the early 1930s, especially at the Great Macedonian Assembly in Gorna Dzhumaia, to redefine the organization. They attempted to restore its former image as a Macedonian movement independent of the Bulgarian state and fighting for a united, independent homeland—the "Switzerland of the Balkans." Yet this attempt clearly convinced Sofia's ruling elite, as well as many Bulgarians, that the VMRO had become an embarrassment—that their country should pursue its interests in Macedonia on its own. And, as we saw above, after May 1934 the new regime banned and liquidated Mihailov's VMRO.

The great ease with which authorities did so revealed the weakness of rightist Macedonian nationalism. Through its control of the Pirin region and widespread terrorist activities, the VMRO looked like a powerful force for national liberation. During the early 1920s, many confused and disoriented Macedonians had been searching for leadership and direction; and Aleksandrov, who seemed to offer those, had used Bulgaria and other supporters and sympathizers to further the national cause. Under Mihailov, however, the weaker VMRO became totally dependent on Bulgaria and Italy, which used it as a terrorist group to further their own revisionist aims.

The source of the VMRO's weakness under both men, and hence of right-wing Macedonian nationalism, was the lack of a meaningful program. Neither leader offered a coherent, comprehensive political, social, economic, and particularly national platform to attract and hold Macedonians throughout their divided homeland. Of course, the VMRO called constantly for a free, united, independent homeland, but it never presented a realistic strategy to reach that virtually impossible goal. Nor did it ever elaborate coherently and convincingly on the future state's political system, its social and economic organization, or its cultural set-up.

In view of Mihailov's close association with the authoritarian regimes in Sofia, which claimed Macedonia for Bulgaria, and with the fascist powers and movements in Europe, what could the VMRO offer the oppressed, overwhelmingly poor Macedonian peasants? Or rather, what could they expect from it?

However, the most vulnerable part, the "Achilles' heel," of the VMRO's general political program was Aleksandrov and Mihailov's national agenda. Both leaders considered and declared themselves Macedonian patriots. They claimed to possess a political and civic Macedonian consciousness. But they also thought of themselves as Macedono-Bulgarians—Bulgarian speakers. Since, in the age of nationalism in the Balkans and in eastern Europe as a whole, language was the chief determinant of ethnicity, hence nationality, the two men defined themselves also as Bulgarians. They did not recognize a separate Macedonian language and hence ethnic identity.

Their official platform recognized the existence of Macedonians—of a Macedonian people (narod)—and that it consisted of various ethnic elements: Bulgarians, Turks, Greeks, Jews, Vlachs (Romanians), and so on. They were all Macedonians; they constituted the Macedonian people, the Macedonian political, civic nation. That nation had its own interests, aspirations, territory, and destiny, and their realization required an independent state. Moreover, Balkan political reality necessitated such a solution of the Macedonian question. It was the only way to end intra-Balkan rivalries and guarantee peace.

Hence the spokesmen of Mihailov's VMRO gave the term "Macedonian people" *(Makedonski narod)* great symbolic and practical significance. They stressed repeatedly the need to propagate it constantly and widely in order to cultivate common political ideals and a common political identity and nation. As Katardžiev observes, they understood and defined "Macedonian" in the same way as they did "Swiss." It was not ethnic, but it was not solely geographic either. It denoted Macedonians' political belonging; it manifested not their ethnic, but rather their civic national consciousness.[12]

It is difficult to determine whether Aleksandrov and particularly Mihailov were naive or cynical; most probably the former was more naive, and the latter, more cynical. Needless to say, neither the Balkans nor Macedonia constituted a Switzerland. That declared conception of the Macedonian nation would have seemed out of place before Ilinden, as K. Misirkov pointed out in 1903. It appeared—and was—even more unrealistic in the 1920s and 1930s. Contrary to the expressed hopes of Aleksandrov and Mihailov, the non-Macedonian ethnicities did not, and did not wish to, identify themselves as Macedonians. The Albanians, Greeks, and Turks in particular identified ethnically, that is linguistically and culturally, as well as politically, with their "maternal" nations and had already formed or were forming their respective non-Macedonian ethnic national identities.

Moreover, Macedono-Bulgarianism and the Macedono-Bulgarian identification of the Macedonians, which Aleksandrov and Mihailov's VMRO propagated, was becoming a relic of the past. As we saw in an earlier chapter, it had never resonated with Patriarchist Macedonians and adherents of the Serbian Orthodox church under Ottoman rule. The elimination of all Bulgarian presence and influence in Aegean and Vardar Macedonia after partition in 1913 and particularly after 1919 and the expulsion from there of many Exarchist-educated Macedonians undermined Bulgarophilism and Macedono-Bulgarianism in those two regions.

For the growing majority of Macedonians there, especially those born after 1900, Macedono-Bulgarianism was a strange concept. Many were illiterate or semi-literate, attended Greek or Serbian schools only briefly, and spoke Macedonian at home, on the street, and in the marketplace. Literary Bulgarian was as foreign to them as Serbian and Greek. Even more than under Ottoman rule, such people's Macedonian identity, Macedonianism (našizam), was a product of attachment to their homeland, identification with its language and folklore, and reaction against their rulers' discriminatory and repressive policies. By the early 1930s, Macedono-Bulgarianism was evaporating in Aegean and Vardar Macedonia. The identity survived there only in part of the older generation.

For obvious reasons, the situation was much more complex among Macedonians in Bulgaria. However, even there, the hybrid Macedono-Bulgarianism was on the way out. Some well-established émigrés, whose families had been in the country for generations and had embraced Bulgarianism and formed a Bulgarian national identity, considered Macedonia a Bulgarian land and like most Bulgarians suspected VMRO's Macedonianism, which seemed too Macedonian for their liking. Educated Macedonians—many intellectuals in the Pirin region and in Bulgaria—belonged to the political left. They rejected Mihailov's VMRO both on ideological grounds—it associated with and depended on Bulgaria's authoritarian regimes and on Europe's fascist powers—and on national grounds, because of its national agenda. By the late 1920s, they were joining the Makedonisti and, as did the Comintern and the Balkan Communist parties, embraced Macedonianism and recognized a separate ethnic nation.

The peasants of the Pirin region, who suffered under Mihailov's VMRO, supported its patriotic appeals, which reflected their Macedonianism (našizam). But even they were suspicious of its close ties with official Bulgaria and hence of its Macedono-Bulgarianism. Moreover, they were feeling increasing alienation because of the VMRO's violence, terror, oppressive political rule, and economic exploitation.[13]

VMRO (ob.): Macedonian Nationalism on the Left

By the late 1920s, Mihailov's VMRO was facing challenges in all parts of Macedonia, particularly in Bulgaria, from the reorganized Macedonian left in the form of the Internal Macedonian Revolutionary Organization—United (Vnatrešna Makedonska Revolucionerna Organizacija—obedineta), or VMRO (ob.).[14] Leftists founded the organization in 1925, after the failed attempt in 1924 to unite all Macedonian factions in the spirit of the original VMRO. For the Macedonian left, it was the successor of the various groupings that sustained the left until then. It had its headquarters in Vienna; its best-known leaders—including émigrés Dimitar Vlahov (1878–1953), Metodija Šatorov-Šarlo (1897–1944), and Vladimir Poptomov (1890–1952)—had been active in Pirin Macedonia or elsewhere in Bulgaria.

The Comintern and the Balkan Communist parties—Bulgarian (BKP), Greek (KKE), and Yugoslav (KPJ)—recognized VMRO (ob.) at once, and the Balkan Communist Federation (BKF) accepted it as a partner. It was illegal in all partitioning states, because it was both Macedonian nationalist and pro-Communist. It sought to win over progressive intellectuals in the Balkans and in western Europe. Its publications—the newspapers *Balkan Federation–Federation Balkanique* and *Makedonsko delo*, and its frequent pamphlets, which it had printed in Vienna—were distributed in western Europe and among Macedonians in the United States and Canada. Its newspapers and pamphlets also reached all three parts of Macedonia clandestinely through its own organized network of groups and through the underground channels of the three countries' Communist parties.

In Bulgaria, VMRO (ob.) had numerous and dedicated followers in Pirin Macedonia and elsewhere among emigrants, especially after liquidation of the Mihailovist VMRO. It was also making inroads into Aegean and Vardar Macedonia. Indeed, it sought to act as a Communist Party of Macedonia and attempted to serve as a Communist-led national or popular front, until the Comintern, which had adopted the "Popular Front" policy, dissolved it in 1937.

The Comintern, the Balkan Communist parties, and the VMRO (ob.), like the original VMRO, had emphasized a Macedonian political and civic consciousness and nation and embraced the cause of liberation and reunification. This was to occur through a socialist revolution, paving the way for a Balkan Communist federation, with reunited Macedonia as an equal partner.

Their heightened interest brought Balkan Communists into closer contact with the Macedonian masses, whose support they sought. They learned about the Macedonians' local loyalties, language, customs, and social and economic interests—that is, their Macedonianism. Moreover, the Communists recruited young Macedonians, who, unlike their parents and grandparents, had while growing up experienced not the patronizing ways of competing outside propaganda, but the harsh realities of foreign misrule. And these young recruits introduced the Macedonianism of the masses into party organizations.

Both the masses and the Macedonian recruits pushed the VMRO (ob.) and the Communist parties toward Macedonianism. By the late 1920s, the Balkan Communist parties, after long, heated debates, embraced Macedonianism and recognized the Macedonians as a distinct Slav ethnic nation with its own language, history, culture, territory, and interests.[15] The Comintern's recognition came in 1934.[16]

The role of the VMRO (ob.) in Balkan Communist politics and in grounding and organizing the development of Communism and nationalism in Macedonia has received little attention from Balkan Communist historians, including Macedonians. The reason lies in the ambivalence of the three states' Communist parties toward the Macedonian question, as well as in their relationship with the VMRO (ob.). The Communist parties, under pressure from Moscow, paid lip service to the cause but relegated its resolution to a hypothetical Balkan Communist federation. The limited available evidence suggests that they did not think seriously about parting with their Macedonian lands. Their primary interest, like the Comintern's, was in using Macedonia for ideological purposes—to further the class struggle and the socialist revolution.

In contrast, the VMRO (ob.) and Macedonian Communists in general, while taking ideology, class struggle, and revolution seriously, focused on the national cause. Also, the Balkan Communist parties, to whom many, if not most, of its active followers belonged, did not approve of the parallel and divided loyalties of their Macedonian comrades. Consequently, the VMRO (ob.), although the Comintern supported it, never gained full acceptance by the fraternal Communist parties in the peninsula. The Comintern's change in tactics triggered its dissolution in 1937, but the Balkan parties welcomed its demise—they always had sharp differences on Macedonia and between their respective national interests and Macedonia's. These differences later seriously harmed the cause of Macedonian liberation and unification.

In the meantime, the official Comintern and Balkan Communist line on Macedonia spurred its nationalism. Acceptance of a Macedonian ethnic nation represented its first official recognition by an international movement led by a great power, the Soviet Union. During the late 1920s and particularly the 1930s, the Communist parties, the VMRO (ob.), and their numerous legal, semi-legal, and illegal organs and front organizations in divided Macedonia encouraged and supported the growth of class and of national consciousness.

The party cells and the numerous Macedonian political, cultural, literary, and sports groups, clubs, societies, and associations that the VMRO (ob.) and the Communist parties sponsored and supported, especially in Skopje, Sofia, Belgrade, and Zagreb, became the training ground, the schools, of nationally conscious leftist Macedonian intellectuals. They provided Macedonian nationalism with its first systematic legal or semi-legal institutional infrastructure, with a home, and with organized bases, which, in the absence of a national church, earlier generations could not establish in the theocratic Ottoman empire. Such a network and its members helped the movement's three major trends—the masses' Macedonianism *(našizam)* and the intellectuals' Macedonianism and Macedono-Bulgarianism—to coalesce gradually into a leftist Macedonianism and nationalism.[17]

All in all, their endeavors strongly affirmed Macedonian national life, consciousness, and thought. They prepared the ground for a literary language and facilitated growth of a national culture and political thought. This process did not develop at the same pace and with the same intensity in all three parts of divided Macedonia.

Conditions for national development were least favorable in Aegean Macedonia, which had contributed so much to the Macedonian awakening. Macedonians now had no large urban center that they could call their own; most of them lived in small, isolated, mainly mountainous towns and villages. For the few who had had a good education, their schooling in Greek tended to estrange them from their Slavic roots and cultural traditions. Moreover, the VMRO (ob.) had started there rather late, and its activities lagged behind those in the other two parts of Macedonia. It was also virtually impossible to establish even elementary printing facilities in the Cyrillic script, and use of Macedonian was illegal even at home while Metaxas was dictator.

Rizospastis, the newspaper of the central committee of the Communist Party of Greece—the only official organ of a Balkan Communist party to appear legally through most of the interwar years—was before 1936 the sole major publication in Greece to recognize and defend the Macedonians. In addition to condemning the bourgeois regimes in Athens, it also consistently attacked their repressive treatment of the Macedonians,[18] who saw it as their sole defender.

Macedonians frequently addressed their many letters and other communications to it affectionately: "Dear Rizo," or "our only defender"; they sometimes wrote in Macedonian—"the only language we know"—though in the Greek script; and most of them signed "a Macedonian" or "a group of Macedonians from . . ." They used *Rizospastis* as their mouthpiece—their only platform for declaring their national identity and the existence of their nation—and to demand their national rights.

A letter from the village Ksino Neron (Ekši-Su), from "many Macedonian-fighters," stated: "We must declare loudly to the Greek rulers that we are neither Greeks, nor Bulgarians, nor Serbs, but pure Macedonians. We have behind us a history, a past, rich with struggles for the liberation of Macedonia, and we will continue that struggle until we free ourselves."

And, rejecting remarks by A. Pejos, a parliamentary deputy, the leader of a VMRO (ob.) group in Giannitsa (Ǵumendže) wrote: "We declare to you that we are neither Greeks, nor Bulgarians, nor Serbs! We are Macedonians with our language, with our culture, with our customs and history. . . . Do you think, Mr. Pejos, that they [Gruev, Tošev, Delčev, and so on] were Bulgarians? No, they were Macedonians and fought for a united and independent Macedonia."

The aims of the Macedonians in Greece find elegant expression in a lengthy communication from "G. Slavos," writing on behalf of a VMRO (ob.) group in Voden (Edessa):

> We, Macedonians here, held a conference where one of our comrades spoke to us about the program of the VMRO (ob.) and about how the minorities live in the Soviet Union.
>
> He told us that the Macedonians in Bulgaria and Serbia are fighting under the leadership of the Communist parties for a united and independent Macedonia.
>
> We declare that we will fight for our freedom under the leadership of the Communist Party of Greece and [we] demand that our schools have instruction in the Macedonian language.
>
> We also insist on not being called Bulgarians, for we are neither Bulgarians, nor Serbs, nor Greeks, but Macedonians.
>
> We invite all Macedonians to join the ranks of the VMRO (ob.), and all of us together will fight for a free Macedonia.[19]

Although Yugoslavia was as keen as Greece to stamp out all signs of Macedonianism, conditions in Vardar Macedonia proved more conducive for its development. Cities such as Skopje, its administrative capital, and district centers such as Bitola, Ohrid, Prilep, and Veles retained their Macedonian character. The number of educated Macedonians was growing each year, in high schools, the Philosophical Faculty in Skopje, and universities elsewhere in Yugoslavia, especially in Belgrade and Zagreb. True, they studied in Serbian or Croatian, but Macedonian remained the language of home and of everyday life. An antidote to the Great Serbian content of their education lay in Macedonianism, for towns, high schools, and especially institutions of higher learning were hotbeds of leftist radicalism.

As we saw above, use of the national name was illegal, as was publishing Macedonian material in the national language or even in Serbian/Croatian. Nonetheless in the 1930s Macedonian intellectuals were no longer only proclaiming the existence of their nation and language. Despite oppression, they worked to create a literary language and a national culture. They even found a way to evade the official ban, wrote on national themes in Serbian/Croatian and in Macedonian, and published at least some of this material in leftist publications in Skopje, in Belgrade or Zagreb, or in illegal publications of the KPJ.[20]

V. Il'oski, R. Krle, and A. Panov wrote plays in Macedonian, and performances became national manifestations in Vardar Macedonia.[21] The Communist activist and talented essayist and poet Kočo Solev Racin (1908–1943) published on the Macedonians' political and cultural history in such leftist Yugoslav periodicals as *Kritika*, *Literatura*, *Naša stvarnost*, and *Naša reč*. But his greatest work, possibly the most influential prewar literary achievement in Macedonian, was *Beli Mugri*, a collection of his poetry that appeared illegally in Sambor, near Zagreb, in 1939.[22] Young and gifted poets V. Markovski (1915–1988) and K. Nedelkovski (1912–1941) grew up in Vardar Macedonia but ended up in Sofia and before 1939 published collections in Macedonian.[23]

In the late 1930s, journals such as *Luč* (Skopje, 1937–38) and *Naša reč* (Skopje, 1939–41), which focused on national affairs, published scholarly and literary pieces, many in Macedonian, by a growing number of younger intellectuals. Finally, on the eve of war, the KPJ's Regional Committee for Macedonia put out its short-lived, illegal, occasional publications, *Bilten* (1940) in Serbian/Croatian and Macedonian and *Iskra* (1941) in Macedonian.

But Macedonian life was most vibrant in Bulgaria, particularly in Sofia, which housed many activists and intellectuals from all over the partitioned homeland. Although official Bulgaria still hoped to harness

Macedonian patriotism to Bulgarianism, its traditional patronizing attitude allowed for a more tolerant milieu. There, unlike in Vardar Macedonia, people could use the national name freely, many institutions and organizations identified with Macedonia, and numerous publications carried the national name. This atmosphere also accounts for the wide-ranging influence of the VMRO (ob.) among Macedonians there.[24]

Young, nationally conscious intellectuals dominated the so-called Macedonian Progressive Movement (MPD) in Bulgaria and its many, often short-lived, newspapers and journals.[25] In 1935, a young intellectual, Angel Dinev, ran perhaps the decade's most significant Macedonian publication: *Makedonski vesti* (1935–36), a journal covering history, learning, and literature.

The circle that formed around *Makedonski vesti* embraced an entire generation of leftward-leaning Macedonians. They published sources and studies on Macedonian history and on national, cultural, and economic issues, as well as literary prose and poetry. Even though they used mostly Bulgarian, their language at school, they affirmed the reality of a Macedonian nation and sought to create a national culture. Like their counterparts in Vardar Macedonia, they emphasized the need for a literary language, and they always treated national themes with piety, but with a greater, much more certain national revolutionary zeal.[26]

The group around *Makedonski vesti* prepared the ground for the illegal Macedonian Literary Circle (MLK) in Sofia (1938–41)—focus of the most remarkable interwar national cultural activity.[27] Its founding members included some of the most promising Macedonian literary talents living in Bulgaria, with roots in all three parts of their native land. The chair and guiding force was the proletarian poet Nikola Jonkov Vapcarov (1909–1942), whose cycle "Songs for the Fatherland" in *Motorni Pesni* (Sofia, 1940) testified to his national consciousness.[28]

The members of the MLK maintained contact with their counterparts in Vardar Macedonia, whose writings they knew of; for instance, they read, discussed, and admired Kočo Racin's poetry in Macedonian. Like Racin, they were familiar with the work and ideas of K. P. Misirkov, the ideologist of Macedonianism of the Ilinden period. They took on tasks that Misirkov had set: to crate a literary language and culture and to enhance national consciousness. As Vapcarov declared to the MLK, the last task was to let the world understand that "we are a separate nation, a separate people, with our own particular attributes which distinguish us from the other South Slavs."[29]

In such organizations in all three parts of Macedonia, with support from the VMRO (ob.) and the Balkan Communist parties, the youthful intellectuals nurtured national ideas and devotion to the national cause. They also elaborated a cohesive, leftist national ideology, which, while explaining their people's past and present, also advanced a national program for the future. Their conceptions were not all new, but largely a synthesis of the earlier views of the Makedonisti and the left wing of the original revolutionary movement, but they amalgamated that heritage with many contemporary Communist doctrines. They rejected Bulgarian, Greek, and Serbian claims on Macedonia and denials of its identity. A declaration by the VMRO (ob.) in February 1935 stated:

> Just as the Macedonians under Greek rule are neither "Slavophones" nor "pure" Greeks, [just] as the Macedonians under Serbian rule are not "pure" Serbs, so too the Macedonians under Bulgarian rule are not Bulgarians and nor do they wish to become [Bulgarians]. The Macedonian people have their own past, their present and future, not as a patch attached to imperialist Bulgaria, Greece and Serbia, but rather as an independent Slav element which possesses all the attributes of an independent nation, [and] which, for decades now, has been struggling to win its right to self determination, including secession into a political state unit independent from the imperialist states that now oppress it.[30]

These intellectuals argued that Macedonians possessed all the attributes of an ethnic and independent nation: their own territory and economic unity, language, national character, and history. "All these elements, taken together," wrote V. Ivanovski, a well-known Macedonian publicist in Bulgaria, "make up the Macedonian nation. They are irrefutable proof that we, Macedonians, do not belong to the Serbian, nor to the Bulgarian or Greek nation. We are a separate nation."[31]

The long historical process that led to that nation began with the Slavs' arrival and settlement in Macedonia and their amalgamation with the remnants of the ancient Macedonians, and it continued well into the nineteenth century—indeed, to their own time. It reached its height with the national awakening in the nineteenth century, which, according to the publicist and historian K. Veselinov, was "independent"—"it followed its own path"—despite various outside interventions.[32] Furthermore, K. Racin, the Communist activist and poet, claimed that this separate and independent Macedonian awakening was in fact much like what happened with Bulgarians and Serbs. Responding to charges by

Professor N. Vulić, a prominent archaeologist and proponent of Great Serbianism, that even the Macedonian name was an invention, Racin maintained that it was no more so than "Bulgarian" and "Serbian." These historic names, he went on,

> were taken from the treasure chest of history. The Serbs took from their history that which they once had. The Bulgarians did the very same thing. What did our Macedonians do? They did the very same thing! . . .
>
> There was an awareness among the Macedonians that this land had at one time been called Macedonia. They took from their historical treasure chest their name just as the Serbian and Bulgarian ideologists did. In this manner they inscribed their Macedonian name on the banner of their national revival. I think that our Macedonian revolutionary movement under the Turks did the same thing as your Serbs as well as the Bulgarians had done in the course of [their] struggle.[33]

The history of the Macedonian people and particularly the memory of the original VMRO and its Ilinden Uprising of 1903 became essential components of this leftist nationalism. The study and knowledge of the Macedonians' past were to inspire their own and future national struggles. In concluding his history of the Macedonian people, A. Dinev declared:

> The people who gave the alphabet to the entire Slav world, who emitted from its womb the great revolutionary reformer Bogomil and the Puritan warrior Samuil, who lived in a revolutionary republic formed secretly on the territory of the Sultan's state for 19 years from 1893 to 1913; who selflessly created for itself the Ilinden epic; who carried on a bloody armed struggle against the armed propagandas; who clashed with the Sultan's troops in the streets of Constantinople; That people will never, never forget its own historical past and, despite the absence of any freedom, will not lose its ethnic character, nor its spirit, nor its mother's speech.[34]

To repeat, this largely youthful Macedonian national intelligentsia suffered rejection, denial of recognition, and persecution by state and society in Bulgaria, Greece, and Yugoslavia. It had nowhere else to turn, except to the Communist ideology of protest that recognized their existence. Consequently, although not all of its adherents were Communists—formal members of one of the three Balkan Communist parties—

they were all leftists,[35] whose view of the world the teachings of Marxism-Leninism largely shaped.

They saw and understood the world as being divided into two antagonistic fronts engaged in a life-and-death struggle. As the MPD program in Bulgaria stated: "On one side is the front of the *imperialists*; who hold under national slavery many European and colonial peoples and who oppress their own working masses; and on the other side is the common front of the *socially and nationally oppressed*."[36] Macedonians endured both national and social oppression under Bulgarian, Greek, or Serbian imperialists, who had assistance from their agents of Macedonian origin. And the only way out for them, as for apostles of the original Macedonian movement, was a mass revolutionary struggle.

This endeavor was to involve above all a collective effort to achieve national liberation and unification, since only such conditions would permit social emancipation. "The Macedonian Progressive Movement is national, for it has as its aim the national liberation of Macedonia," declared *Makedonsko zname*. "It is not a party, or a social or a class [movement]; it is popular, democratic, because its very aim [national liberation] is a popular, democratic task."[37] The same sentiments appeared in its program: "The Macedonian Progressive Movement is an independent national movement. . . . It is not struggling for socialism, but for the national liberation of Macedonia. In what kind of economic form will be organized Macedonia—that will be decided by the Macedonian population after its national liberation."[38]

The Macedonian intellectuals expected a difficult struggle, because they were working against three oppressor-states, as well as against Vrhovism, the rightist VMRO, which they believed had betrayed the legacy of Ilinden. Nonetheless they remained confident, for they considered their effort an integral part of "the common front of the oppressed against imperialism." They felt as one with all the enslaved nations and with the working-class movement of the ruling states; this alliance was "especially close with the enslaved nationalities and the socially oppressed in the three Balkan countries among whom Macedonia is partitioned."[39]

As we saw above, they tended generally to identify their national liberation with the Comintern slogan: "Independent Macedonia in a Federation of Balkan People's Republics." They placed far greater emphasis on their national question than the Communists did, however, and were thus unwilling to leave it to the uncertain future and a Balkan

Communist federation. In 1933, *Makedonska pravda,* an organ of the emigration in Sofia, published a series of articles calling for "the federalization of the South Slavs on the basis of full equality and equal respect for the rights of all peoples and for the creation out of the existing Yugoslav chaos a free state of free autonomous regions." Realization of such an entity would require destruction of the Serbian dictatorship and establishment of a people's government. "Only such a truly people's government would be in a position to resolve not only the Macedonian problem, but also the great problem of the unification of South Slavdom in one great, people's, Yugoslav republic without dictators and hegemons." Such a government would present the final resolution of "our Macedonian question and *Macedonia will be free.*"

When a reader asked whether it fought for a Balkan or for a South Slav federation, *Makedonska pravda* replied: "Our ideal and [the ideal] of all good Balkanites *is and must be the Balkan federation.*" Only such an arrangement could reconcile the cultural, economic, and political interests of the Balkan peoples and overcome their antagonisms. "We talk about a South Slav federation as *one stage toward the future Balkan federation*, which would be easier to attain after the realization of the first."[40]

Yugoslavia restricted the activities of the VMRO (ob.) to a far greater extent, and the organization's influence was not as widespread in Vardar Macedonia as in Bulgaria. Macedonian students and intellectuals there felt much more the influence of the Communist Party (of Yugoslavia) and tended to focus on their part of Vardar Macedonia. They sought national liberation and equality for their region in a restructured, federated Yugoslavia on the way to national unification and presumably to a Balkan Communist federation.[41]

A more searching and critical analysis of the Comintern's position on Macedonia appeared from the Macedonian Progressive Movement (MPD) in Bulgaria and its newspaper, *Makedonsko zname*. They argued that the Comintern defined the Macedonian national struggle "too vaguely and inconcretely," assuming that the revolution would "come only as a common Ilinden of all Balkan peoples"—as a result of the simultaneous struggle of the nationally and socially oppressed in all the Balkan countries. The Comintern also suggested that liberation of Macedonia would depend on formation of the Balkan federation.

This stance was obviously not acceptable to the MPD and its newspaper, which were unwilling to postpone liberation indefinitely. Moreover, they complained that the Comintern ignored the fact that "the uneven decline of imperialism" would result in the "uneven development of the liberation struggle" in the Balkans. That endeavor "could succeed first in one of the oppressor states and thus the liberation be achieved first in one of the three partitions of Macedonia which would establish the beginning and become the base for the liberation of the entire Macedonia."

D. Dinkov, one of the MPD's representatives, pointed to the contradiction implicit in the two halves of the Comintern slogan: "Balkan Federation" and "Independent Macedonia." He argued that the former restricted self-determination to autonomy, thus denying the possibility of a separate, independent state. The latter, in contrast, was very separatist and rejected in advance the autonomous or federal unification of Macedonians with other newly free peoples. Dinkov dismissed both conceptions as "incorrect" and did not want the national endeavor to be in a straitjacket. "How the Macedonian people will use its right to self-determination up to separation will depend on the concrete conditions after the masses win their struggle for liberation." Consequently, the MPD replaced the old Comintern position with a call for "the right of the Macedonian people to self-determination up to its separation into an independent state–political unit."[42]

Accordingly, the MPD called on Macedonians in each partition to insist on self-determination and to work with all the nationally and socially oppressed in their state. After the expected victory in one of the partitioning states, the Macedonian national region within it would constitute itself as an autonomous small state *(dūrzhavitsa)*. That autonomous Macedonian small state would serve as "a base in the struggle for a *united Macedonian state*. It will serve as an example, will encourage, and will provide support to the other Macedonian regions to do the same in order to attain the national liberation of the whole." "*Which [part] would start first will depend on whether the required conditions will mature first in Yugoslavia, in Greece or in Bulgaria*. We will follow this path until the liberation of the three Macedonian regions in one united Macedonian People's Republic."[43] Thus, despite differences and debates among Macedonian leftists over short-term tactics, generally speaking they shared a final aim: national liberation and unification, a free Macedonia.[44]

Such aims inspired the many conscious Macedonians, both Communists and bourgeois nationalists, who joined the Communist-led resistance movements in Bulgaria, Greece, and Yugoslavia during the Second World War. Long before the conflict ended, however, the Macedonian question had again become "the apple of discord," this time dividing the Balkan Communists, who locked themselves in silent competition over Macedonia. They continued in that mode during the war's turbulent aftermath—through abortive Yugoslav-Bulgarian negotiations for a federation, the Civil War in Greece, and the Soviet-Yugoslav conflict.

PART FOUR

STATEHOOD AND INDEPENDENCE (DURING AND AFTER THE SECOND WORLD WAR)

In the Balkans, the Second World War began with Italy's failed invasion of Greece in October 1940, but it engulfed the region only with the German blitz against and speedy occupation of Yugoslavia and Greece in April 1941. Its outbreak caught the Macedonians angry and restless, but divided and wholly unready for common action. While they had no reason for loyalty to the oppressive Greek and Serbian/Yugoslav regimes or to regret their collapse, they soon discovered that their new rulers, Italian or Albanian, German, and Bulgarian, were no better and in many respects worse. Like all other occupied peoples in Europe, they faced some stark choices. They had to decide their attitude toward the occupiers: accommodation, collaboration, or resistance. And they had to think about their postwar future.

However, answering these dilemmas was much more difficult and confusing for them than for all other occupied peoples. For almost three decades, three Balkan states had separately oppressed them. Now they were under four foreign occupiers: Italian, Albanian, German, and Bulgarian. They had no government-in-exile to represent their interests among the Allies. They did not have even a quisling administration to represent or pretend to speak for them among the Axis occupiers. Even more devastating, they had no single, all-Macedonian organization, legal or illegal, active in all parts of Macedonia, that could legitimately claim to lead or represent them in all parts of their homeland. Bulgaria's dissolution of Mihailov's VMRO in 1934 and the Comintern's dismantling of the VMRO (ob.) in 1937 left Macedonians leaderless and lacking national representation.

The right, especially Mihailov's VMRO, had been losing ground to the left throughout the 1930s. Mihailov himself was in exile and would spend the war years in Zagreb, waiting and hoping that the Axis powers, or rather Hitler, would treat Macedonia like Croatia and establish a satellite state under his stewardship.Extreme Bulgarophiles had taken over direction of Macedonian organizations in the Pirin region and throughout Bulgaria, and they favored annexation of Macedonia by Bulgaria and creation of a Great Bulgaria. The Mihailovist organizational network in Greek (Aegean) Macedonia had been rather weak all along and was virtually nonexistent on the eve of the war. The VMRO appeared stronger in Yugoslav (Vardar) Macedonia; many of its principal activists were still there, and they had a following but no active and functioning organization ready and willing to lead.

Although the VMRO (ob.) no longer existed, the left seemed stronger, at least potentially. Many Macedonian leftists, its former members, also belonged to the Communist parties of Bulgaria (BKP), Greece (KKE), and Yugoslavia (KPJ). All three parties recognized the existence of a Macedonian nation and had to accept the Comintern's policy calling for a Macedonian state in a future Balkan Communist federation and Macedonians' right to their own state.

Whatever the three parties thought of the Comintern's long-range and hypothetical policies, the outbreak of war in 1939 forced them and their national liberation movements to tackle the Macedonian question. It immediately became obvious that that issue would divide them more than any other cause. At the same time, their vicious struggle for that territory and its people forced Macedonian party members to choose between their party and their national cause—for most, the primary consideration. All these factors influenced developments in Macedonia during the war and its revolutionary aftermath in the Balkans. They affected collaboration, resistance, and the fight for national liberation in the three parts of divided Macedonia.

11 War and Revolution (1940–1949)

This chapter's first four sections look at Macedonians' situation between 1941 and 1944, and the fifth, at the new postwar "Macedonian questions." The first considers Macedonians' plight under the new partition, and the second, their "hostile neutrality" toward the occupiers. The third, about Vardar Macedonia, examines their leftward, Macedonianist drift, declaration in November 1943 of a federal Yugoslavia with a Macedonian republic, and the republic's formal establishment in August 1944. The fourth section details Macedonians' wartime situation in the Greek and Bulgarian partitions. The fifth outlines the position of Macedonians in a substantially Communist Balkans, as Greece's Civil War reached its right-wing dénouement.

A New Partition (1941–1944)

Following the collapse of Yugoslavia and Greece in April 1941, occupying powers again partitioned Macedonia. Bulgaria occupied most of Vardar (Yugoslav) Macedonia and eastern and a small part of western Aegean (Greek) Macedonia. The central, most strategic regions of Aegean Macedonia, including Salonika and the coast, remained under direct German control. The most westerly region of Vardar Macedonia, which included the towns of Tetovo, Gostivar, Kičevo, Debar, and Struga, became part of Italian-occupied Albania. Italy occupied the rest of western Aegean Macedonia—the districts of Kastoria (Kostur), Florina (Lerin), Kozani, and Grevena—until its collapse in September 1943.

Once again, most Macedonians—in Bulgarian and Italian-Albanian areas—were under foreign masters that imposed their own national ideologies and identities. Bulgaria presented its occupation as the realization of its "historic right," as the liberation of "its own national territories." It did not treat the lands as a protectorate and did not set up a special administration; it strove to absorb them. Accordingly, Sofia introduced the Bulgarian political, administrative, judicial, and police systems there. It gave all responsible positions to trusted people from Bulgaria with proven ideological and nationalist credentials. In order to maintain law and order under German supervision, Bulgaria deployed a large military and police presence in the "newly liberated lands" throughout the war. According to one source, the Bulgarians and Italians concentrated 120,000 men in Vardar Macedonia.[1]

Moreover, Bulgaria declared all Macedonians in the occupied lands to be Bulgarians and embarked on a policy of "Bulgarianization." The Directorate for National Propaganda spearheaded the drive and sought to eliminate all reminders of Serbian rule. Standard Bulgarian became the official language, and the vastly expanded educational system, the chief instrument of Bulgarianization. In the 1941/42 academic year, occupation authorities opened 800 primary schools, 180 middle schools *(osmoletki)*, and 17 secondary schools *(gymnasia)*.[2] They also planned a university in Skopje, which opened in 1943/44 as Tsar Boris University. They staffed the educational system too with "proven" people from Bulgaria. All levels of education focused instruction on Bulgarian studies—language, history, and culture—which of course included Macedonia and its people.

The Directorate of National Propaganda also supervised a number of institutions—philological, historical, ethnological, and so on—which published only works proving that Macedonia and its people were Bulgarian. Sofia mobilized all institutions and media under its control and influence, such as radio, press, theaters, museums, and churches, to serve the national cause, to spread and entrench Bulgarianism among Macedonians. It also expected all public servants to serve as eyes and ears and to report on any dissent in word, thought, or deed.

Its policies toward other, non-Macedonian ethnicities, which it did not expect or even try to win over, were much harsher, more ruthless, and more devastating. The Bulgarians tolerated the Muslims, Albanians, and Turks in Vardar Macedonia, but ignored their rights and needs. While they saved the Jews of Bulgaria proper, they transferred to the Nazis those of Macedonia, who ended up in death camps.

In eastern Greek (Aegean) Macedonia, east of the River Strimeon (Struma), the Bulgarians were ruthless toward Greeks, by then the majority there. As we saw earlier, Greek authorities forcefully relocated the area's Macedonians, its Slavic-speaking inhabitants, after the Balkan Wars and the Great War. They expelled most of them to Bulgaria and resettled the area with Greek refugees, whom the Turks had expelled from Asia Minor. "Since there were few Slavs in those regions, the Bulgarians here sought not to convert the local population but to eliminate it in one way or another and to replace it with Bulgarian colonists."[3] Or, as Hugh Poulton stated: "In their own portions the Bulgarians imported settlers from Bulgaria and acted in such a way that even a German report of the time described their occupation as a 'regime of terror.'"[4]

At the start of the occupation, in May—June 1941, the Italians administered western Vardar Macedonia directly. In July 1941, they attached the territory to Italian Albania and transferred its administration to the Ministry for the Newly Liberated Albanian Lands, in Tirana. In February 1943, when they abolished this ministry, they passed its functions to the appropriate ministries of the quisling Albanian government. They consolidated their rule with the support of proponents of Great Albanianism, with whom they staffed the administrative, judicial, and police systems. Albanian Fascists received the highest positions, and local collaborators, the lower offices.

Just as Bulgaria sought to Bulgarianize the areas under its occupation, Albania aimed to do something analogous for western Vardar Macedonia. And its measures and policies resembled those of the Bulgarians. The school system and education in general were to assist forced Albanization. All Serbian schools gave way to Albanian, and all Serbian or Macedonian teachers who taught in Serbian, to teachers from Albania. All non-Albanian pupils—Macedonian, Serbian, and so on—had to attend these schools, and their instruction inculcated Great Albanianism and fascism. All jobs in public service required Albanians speaking the language. All signs, even on private buildings, had to be in Italian and Albanian. The names and surnames of non-Albanians had to take on an

Albanian form. Even telephone conversations in a language other than Italian or Albanian were illegal.[5]

Paradoxically, Macedonians and other inhabitants of central Aegean Macedonia, which was under direct German control, and the western, under Italian, fared better. The two occupying powers allowed the Greek quisling government to administer the area under their supervision. While the economic situation there, as elsewhere in Macedonia and occupied Europe, worsened, the political situation improved. The Germans and particularly the Italians passively neglected them; Greek officials could no longer enforce the oppressive measures of the Metaxas regime. Early in the war, the Macedonian-populated western Aegean region became a stronghold of the Communist-led Greek resistance, which displayed far greater understanding and tolerance vis-à-vis the Macedonians.[6]

Hostile Neutrality and Beyond (1941–1944)

The vast majority of Macedonians, overwhelmingly peasants, knew very little, if anything at all, about Italian Fascism or German Nazism or the intentions of each, but they did expect relief from the Bulgarians. The occupation authorities, especially the Bulgarians, posed as liberators and exploited opposition to the repressive prewar Greek and Serbian/Yugoslav regimes to at least neutralize many Macedonians. Traditional Bulgarophilism also helped their cause at the start.

Generally speaking, however, most Macedonians felt a sort of hostile neutrality toward their new overlords. As far as they knew or could remember, their land was always under occupation, but their patriotism would not countenance *foreign* occupiers. As Captain P. H. Evans in western Aegean Macedonia wrote in December 1944: "The Macedonians are actuated by strong but mixed feelings of patriotism. . . . There is . . . thriving and at times fervent local patriotism; and a feeling, hard to assess because rarely uttered before strangers, and because it fluctuates with the turn of events and of propaganda, for *Macedonia* as such, regardless of present frontier-lines, which are looked upon as usurpation."[7]

Yet, lacking organization, leadership, and arms, they could not even think of standing up to the occupiers, let alone defeating them. In order to survive, they pretended to adjust. As an old man told Captain Evans:

"You see, we have had so many different masters that now, whoever comes along, we say (placing his hands together, but smiling and making a little bow) 'kalos oriste' [welcome]." "It was most eloquent," continued Evans. "It is this perfect duplicity of the *Macedonians* which makes them difficult to know. It is hard to find out what they are thinking."[8]

Macedonians were traditionally suspicious of all foreigners—that is, of everyone who did not belong to them, who were not *naši*, who did not belong to their land, did not speak their language, did not sing their songs, did not practice their customs, did not eat their food, did not celebrate their festivals, did not suffer their sufferings. They maintained this hostile neutrality toward the occupier until its rule became unbearable, or until they felt sure that active opposition had a realistic chance of success, and then they fought as bravely and ruthlessly as any peasant people. Survival was of the essence.

Active collaboration with the occupation authorities was not widespread—it involved only certain groups and regions. In Italian-occupied western Vardar (Yugoslav) Macedonia, by then part of Great Albania, many ethnic Albanians collaborated actively. They joined the Albanian Fascist Party, the reactionary Albanian National Front (the Bali Kombetar), or other Italian-sponsored organizations, which were keen to wipe out Macedonians and all non-Muslims in the area. The Macedonians there struggled to survive.

In Aegean (Greek) Macedonia, the German and Italian occupiers offered little to satisfy the Macedonians' patriotic impulses. Their vague promises of a free Macedonia won over some disorganized Bulgarophile groups belonging to Mihailov's VMRO—at least while they appeared to be winning the war. With the aid of the Bulgarian Club in Salonika and of Bulgarian officers attached to the German garrisons there and in Edessa (Voden), Florina (Lerin), and Kastoria (Kostur) in central and western Aegean Macedonia, they set up the Komitet or the Komitadži movement. This political and military organization of Macedonians attracted approximately ten thousand followers in about sixty villages in the district of Kastoria. Members formed their own bands, or paramilitary units, which the occupiers armed, and were to defend their own villages against attacks from neighboring Greek refugee villages, as well as from bands belonging to both the Greek Communist-led resistance and the nationalist resistance.

The Komitadži movement was more anti-Greek and anti-Communist than pro-German, -Italian, or -Bulgarian. By late 1943 and early 1944, the Greek Communist-led resistance, the National Liberation Front—the Greek Popular Liberation Army (EAM-ELAS), with the aid of its Slav-Macedonian National Liberation Front (SNOF), the Macedonian liberation organization in Greece—had defeated and neutralized the Komitadži movement. After the tide in the war began to change in 1943, many of the armed komitadži, as well as other active Macedonian collaborators, switched over to the Macedonian or primarily Macedonian units of EAM-ELAS and thus to the struggle for national emancipation of the Macedonians of Aegean Macedonia.

The situation in Bulgaria's new parts of Macedonia was much more complex. As I noted above, Macedonians who had formed a Bulgarian identity welcomed the occupiers as liberators. The Macedonian right, followers of Mihailov's VMRO, hoped to follow Croatia's example and attain a united and autonomous or independent country with Bulgaria's aid. Members of both groups collaborated actively with the new authorities. The Macedonian left opposed the occupation on both national and ideological grounds. For the majority of Macedonians, Bulgarian occupation initially represented welcome relief from brutal Greek and Serbian rule and appeared more tolerable and less repressive. Passive acceptance or benevolent neutrality, and a wait-and-see attitude, greeted the Bulgarian occupiers.

Early in the war, however, the Bulgarians began to exhaust their welcome even among the most pro-Bulgarian elements. They could not long sustain the material benefits, such as regular supply of basic necessities and orderly rationing, especially in a lengthy war. And their freeing of Macedonians, including Communists, from the former regimes' jails could not mask their nationalist, anti-Macedonian, dictatorial rule.

Moreover, the occupiers treated Macedonia as a colonial extension of Bulgaria proper. They ignored its regionalism, which even the most Bulgarophilic Macedonians had respected, as well as its traditional (and overwhelming) demands for autonomy or statehood. They showed remarkable disdain and distrust for all Macedonians, including the most Bulgarophilic leaders of the Mihailovist VMRO. They excluded the latter from senior positions, which they awarded to Bulgarians or occasionally to Macedonians who were natives or longtime residents of Bulgaria and were solid Bulgarian nationalists.

Forcible Bulgarianization offended the vast majority of Macedonians. In July 1942, even a group of very prominent Bulgarophiles and representatives of Mihailov's VMRO, who worried deeply about mass disillusionment with and alienation from Bulgaria, sent a representation to the Bulgarian tsar. The group complained about continued partition, lack of Macedonian representation, total neglect of agrarian reform, disorderly supply and provisioning, ruthless police and bureaucrats, and contempt for the native intelligentsia.

The occupiers' attempts to draw many Macedonians into active collaboration failed. The Bulgarian nationalist and rightist organizations that they established in 1941 for virtually every age group attracted few members. Their effort in 1942 to create and underwrite a military organization, the *kontračeti*, produced even worse results. The kontračeti were military units of Macedonians, whom Bulgaria recruited from among followers of Mihailov's VMRO and of other rightist, pro-Bulgarian groups who accepted the Bulgarian stand on Macedonia. The occupiers organized and paid them to fight the Communist-led National Liberation Army and Partisan Detachments of Macedonia (NOV i POM) and to frighten the populace from joining or aiding it. They set up only eight such units, with twenty to thirty members each. In the following year, 1943, most of them underwent defeat and dispersal, and many members joined partisan units.[9]

Conscious of Germany's coming, unavoidable defeat, in the summer of 1944 Sofia approached the Allies for separate peace talks. It also toyed with setting up, with German aid, an autonomous Macedonia under Bulgarian influence. At the end of August, the Germans dispatched Vančo Mihailov, who had spent the war years in Zagreb, to Macedonia to survey the situation and declare an "Independent Macedonia." The rugged mountains around Skopje were already in partisans' hands, and, after a brief sojourn with trusted lieutenants, Mihailov wisely decided to accept defeat and departed Macedonia for good.[10] Moreover, this capitulation marked the final defeat of Macedono-Bulgarianism in the long struggle for Macedonians' loyalty. Macedonianism would prevail.

Toward a Yugoslav Republic (1941–1944)

Although Macedonians passively accepted occupation, the new rulers had no political, socioeconomic, or, most important, national program and vision for Macedonia, so they could not win active collaboration.

Consequently, even before the tide of war turned, they could not compete with the Communists of the three original Balkan partitioners and the resistance movements that they organized and led. The Communist parties in Bulgaria (BKP),[11] Greece (KKE), and Yugoslavia (KPJ) pushed clearly and strenuously their vision: adaptations of the Comintern program for Macedonia. They offered their traditional, ideologically inspired social and economic transformation, with the promise of equality and justice. More significant, they advanced a Macedonian-driven national program of self-determination that promised national liberation and equality, even statehood.

The three parties did not necessarily agree on the ultimate outcome and would not unconditionally promise their respective countries' Macedonian possessions. In reality, the KPJ and the BKP each hoped for Macedonian unification under its own auspices, or within its own country, or within a south Slav or Balkan federation that it hoped to dominate. The KKE, which would obviously not join a south Slav federation and could hardly expect to dominate a Balkan federation, may therefore have wanted Aegean Macedonia out of plans for a united Macedonian state. In any case, its leadership emphasized equality for and protection of national rights of Macedonians in Greece, rather than Macedonian statehood.[12]

Unlike the Balkan Communist parties, which manipulated the Macedonian question to further their ideological and political aims, Macedonian Communists, all members of one or another of those parties, saw national liberation as the primary aim. This stance frequently forced them to choose between their party's position and their own dream—liberation, unification, and statehood. While some adhered to their party's discipline and position, many others at critical times broke ranks and shifted to the political party that seemed closest to Macedonian aims.[13] Metodija Šatorov-Šarlo (1897–1944)[14] exemplifies this predicament. He was born in the Ottoman empire, in Prilep, in what became Vardar Macedonia. Before 1918, he emigrated to Bulgaria. In 1920 he joined the BKP and in 1925 the VMRO (ob.), and he became a leader in both. In the 1930s, he worked in Moscow for the Comintern and became an authority on Balkan national revolutionary movements. In 1939, he returned to Macedonia, and in the following year he became leader of the Regional Committee for Macedonia of the KPJ (PK na KPJM). He immediately changed the body's name from "for" to "in" Macedonia, replaced Serbo-Croatian with Macedonian as its working language, and sought to win autonomy for it. In 1940, at the KPJ's fifth conference in Zagreb, he joined its central committee, the only member from Macedonia.

After the collapse of Yugoslavia and the Bulgarian occupation of Vardar Macedonia in 1941, the KPJ and BKP argued over control of the regional party organization in their struggle for Macedonia. The KPJ called for armed struggle against all occupiers and restoration of Yugoslavia's territorial integrity. It envisaged a new, Communist Yugoslavia in which Vardar Macedonia would join a federation of equal republics. The BKP continued to advocate the Comintern position—a united Macedonia in a Communist Balkan federation.

What were Šatorov-Šarlo and other nationally minded Macedonian Communists, former members of the dissolved VMRO (ob.), to do? They could side with the KPJ, which they felt the Serbians dominated and which had embraced the Comintern position unwillingly; it now offered only liberation of one part of Macedonia under KPJ auspices. Or they could choose the BKP, sponsor and most vocal supporter of the Comintern policy, national liberation and unification. That position embodied traditional maximal Macedonian aims, and after the German invasion of the Soviet Union in June 1941, Šatorov-Šarlo and his allies felt that those goals were realizable. They believed, like most Communists, that the Soviet Union would win the war and spark Communist revolutions in the Balkans. Unification of most of Macedonia under Bulgarian occupation paved the way for the eventual united Soviet Macedonia.

Such reasoning and the traditional Comintern principle "one state—one party" led Šatorov-Šarlo to agree with his Bulgarian comrades, to remove the party organization in Vardar Macedonia from the KPJ's control, and to place it under the BKP. After he ignored orders from the KPJ's central committee in July 1941, its politburo accused him of anti-party and counterrevolutionary activities and dismissed him from the KPJ. In early September, Josip Broz Tito, the party's leader, appealed to the Comintern in Moscow. To its executive committee, he denounced the "old Bulgar" Šatorov-Šarlo as an opponent of the armed struggle, attacked the BKP for taking over the PK KPJM, and demanded its return to the KPJ.

The Comintern ruled in favour of the KPJ, which promptly appointed new leaders for the PK KPJM. The KPJ named as head Lazar Koliševski (1914–2000), a strong, pro-Serbian loyalist.[15] The Bulgarian police soon arrested him; he would spend most of the war in prison in Bulgaria but would become the dominant figure in the postwar republic of Macedonia in the Communist Yugoslav federation. After rejection by the KPJ, and now suspect to the BKP, Šatorov-Šarlo perished as a ranking commander in the resistance in Bulgaria in 1944. The circumstances of his death lack adequate explanation.

The Comintern's historic ruling marked a turning point in the long history of the Macedonian question. It transferred the initiative from the Bulgarian Communists, the dominant such group in the Balkans but whose country had joined the Axis, to the Yugoslavs, whose homeland the Axis had partitioned and occupied. In search of wider support among Macedonians, the KPJ, during the following year or year and a half, seemed to embrace at least in theory Macedonian national liberation and unification in Yugoslavia or in a Yugoslav-dominated south Slav or Balkan Communist federation. Yugoslav (Vardar) Macedonia would soon claim to be the Piedmont of Macedonian unification. Yugoslavia would dominate the Macedonian question until its bloody disintegration in 1990–91.

Many Macedonians joined the Communist-led resistance in Bulgaria, Greece, and Yugoslavia because they believed that their victory would bring national liberation and social and economic justice. However, since the Macedonian resistance in each partition was only a component of a larger movement, its growth and development in each responded to local conditions and circumstances.

In Vardar Macedonia, the KPJ's regional committee began preparations for organized resistance in the summer of 1941. It formed partisan units in Skopje, Prilep, and Kumanovo. The attack on 11 October 1941 by the Prilep partisans on the local police station and other symbols of the occupation launched Macedonia's revolution and struggle for national liberation, and Macedonians still celebrate it. In the following year, the leadership of the KPJ and the Anti-Fascist Council for the National Liberation of Yugoslavia (AVNOJ), in Bosnia-Herzegovina, restructured Macedonia's KPJ regional committee several times to speed up and intensify armed resistance.

In the second half of 1942, the regional military headquarters for Macedonia became "supreme" headquarters of the National Liberation Army and Partisan Detachments of Macedonia (NOV i POM), which organized new and larger armed units. It named these units after Dame

Gruev, Jane Sandanski, Ǵorče Petrov, and other VMRO leaders of the Ilinden period, with whom the KPJ and its regional leaders identified themselves. Armed clashes with the occupiers became larger and more frequent. Regional party leaders also established front organizations, such as the National Liberation Front (NOF), the Anti-Fascist Front of Women (AFŽ), and the Anti-Fascist Youth (AM) to mobilize the masses in support.

However, in 1941 and throughout 1942, the armed struggle in Macedonia lagged behind that in other parts of Yugoslavia. The continuing KPJ-BKP conflict over control of the party, which divided and confused local leaders and the rank and file, was only one inhibitor. As well, Bulgarian rule was markedly more paternalistic than harsh and was certainly less repressive than the previous Serbian/Yugoslav. More important, however, communication was virtually nonexistent between leaders of the armed fight in Macedonia and AVNOJ supreme headquarters in Bosnia-Herzegovina.

Here geographic distance and hostile terrain played a role, but above all there were no Macedonians in the top leadership of AVNOJ. The aims of AVNOJ, even as its first session in Bihać formulated them in late November 1942, were not familiar to Macedonians. Its chief goal—national liberation of Yugoslavia—could not inspire and attract Macedonians, who saw it as reestablishment of Yugoslavia and Serbian rule—a prospect even less enticing than the Bulgarian regime. Supreme headquarters of AVNOJ knew even less about the actual situation and mood in Macedonia and about the traditional aims of its liberation struggle.

The situation began to change by the end of 1942 and particularly after February 1943, when Svetozar Vukmanović-Tempo arrived in Macedonia representing the KPJ's central committee and AVNOJ. Supreme headquarters of AVNOJ soon realized that securing mass participation of Macedonians would require that it pay attention to conditions, sensibilities, aims, and aspirations in their region, as it had done vis-à-vis other parts of Yugoslavia, such as Croatia and Slovenia. It would have to "Macedonianize" the struggle's form and content—give it a Macedonian facade as well as aims and aspirations.[16]

In the crucial first step, it dissolved the regional committee (PK) of the KPJ in Macedonia and replaced it in March 1943 with the central committee of the Communist Party of Macedonia (KPM). A separate Macedonian Communist party would lead the effort for national liberation—not restoration of old Yugoslavia—but above all liberation of Macedonia and a new federal union of Yugoslav peoples. Both the KPM and supreme headquarters stressed the Macedonian character of the National Liberation Army and the Partisan Detachments. Macedonian officers ran the organization, and Macedonian was their language of command; they propagated national liberation of all Macedonians and, more subtly, national unification. During 1943 and 1944, this appeal attracted more and more young Macedonians to the armed resistance.

In its session on 2 August 1943, the KPM's central committee ordered the formation of larger partisan units capable of bigger operations. On 18 August, the supreme headquarters of the NOV i POM formed the Mirče Acev battallion, the first regular unit of the Macedonian army; and on 11 November, the first brigade, the Macedonian-Kosovo brigade, with 800 troops. It set up the first division in August 1944, and by November, when Skopje, the capital, was free again, there were seven divisions in the field, with 66,000 people under arms.[17]

The growth in strength of armed resistance facilitated larger military operations and liberation or partial liberation of areas of western Vardar Macedonia in 1943. Activities expanded further after Fascist Italy capitulated on 9 September 1943. The first liberated territories allowed bases for additional military efforts and represented the start of the future Macedonian state. The National Liberation Front established its authority in these areas. It introduced initial organs of local self-administration—the national Liberation Councils—and the first Macedonian elementary schools and religious services in Macedonian.

The "Macedonianization" of the push for liberation in the Vardar region culminated in the first half of October 1943 with the stirring Manifesto of the Supreme Headquarters of NOV i POM. The document appeared in the village Crvena Voda, in liberated territory in the Debar region. It appealed to the Macedonian people to join the struggle for independence; to build statehood through self-determination, in unity and equality with the other peoples in the new Yugoslavia; and thus to establish the basis for national unification.[18]

The manifesto did not gain immediate approval from all leading activists in Vardar Macedonia. Activists and intellectuals around the National Liberation Action Committee (ANOK) in Skopje prepared a sweeping critique *(prigovor)* of the document. They criticized it most of all because it ignored the plight of Macedonians in the Greek and Bulgarian partitions and hence national unification. They argued that such unification was not solely a Yugoslav problem, but rather a Balkan question, involving Albania, Bulgaria, Greece, and Yugoslavia and their Communist parties, and therefore required a Balkan solution. They questioned whether national unification was realizable on a Yugoslav basis and thus wondered about the authors' sincerity.

Through direct and indirect contacts, supreme headquarters convinced the skeptics of its sincerity and dedication. However, it stressed that—in view of the conflicting Balkan interests of the Soviet Union and of Britain and the United States and because the Balkan neighbors (and their Communist parties) had incompatible aspirations in Macedonia—a Balkan solution might not prove possible during the war. It emphasized repeatedly that the Macedonians could achieve unity only with the help of the other Yugoslav peoples and that, even though AVNOJ embraced the aim, its leaders could not broach it publicly and officially because of its "sensitivity."[19]

This very delicate issue would divide Macedonia's nationalists and the leaders of AVNOJ and later of Yugoslavia, including Tito, for years: through the war, its revolutionary aftermath, the Civil War in Greece, and the Soviet-Yugoslav dispute. For while Tito and the KPJ hoped for unification of Macedonia within Yugoslavia, they thought it a maximal aim. For them, liberation of Yugoslavia, preservation of its territorial integrity, and the regime's stability were the primary concerns, which they would not risk for the sake of Macedonian unification. Independently minded Macedonian nationalists, Communist and non-Communist, considered unification their principal aim—within Yugoslavia, if that country would help, or outside it, with aid from other supporters.

In any event, NOV i POM's manifesto of October 1943 was historically significant for the Macedonians. It was the first comprehensive declaration of aims in the effort for national liberation. It bore the names of the entire top leadership of the Macedonian movement. It helped legitimize the Communist-led struggle among the overwhelmingly patriotic but non-Communist population; it convinced doubters that the movement sought first and foremost Macedonians' liberation and creation of a new Yugoslavia. Finally, it affected Macedonians' thinking and developments in Aegean and Pirin Macedonia. The second session of AVNOJ, meeting in Jajce, Bosnia, on 29–30 November 1943, confirmed the manifesto's most significant promise: it proclaimed the new federal Yugoslavia, with Macedonia equal to five other federal units.

What form would the new republic take? Four months earlier, on 2 August 1943, the Prespa meeting of the KPM's central committee had agreed to prepare for the Macedonian equivalent of AVNOJ—the Anti-Fascist Assembly for the National Liberation of Macedonia (ASNOM). Sometime between the appearance of the NOV i POM's manifesto (in the first half of October) and the second session of AVNOJ (late November)—most probably in early November—the KPM's central committee created its organizational council (Iniciativen odbor). That body included senior leaders of the national struggle and until August 1944 acted as the government of Macedonia. In the spring and early summer of 1944, it organized the first elections of village, town, and district National Liberation Councils (NOOs) and selection of delegates to the first session of ASNOM on 2 August.

In the first half of 1944, especially in wintry January through March, the Macedonian army and partisan units undertook some of the most difficult operations of the war. They fought large-scale clashes with the Germans, the Bulgarian army and police, and *četnik* units of Draža Mihailović, leader of the Serbian nationalist resistance. They expanded the liberated territories in western Macedonia, reached the Greek border in the south and contacted the EAM-ELAS in Aegean Macedonia, and began freeing areas in central and eastern Vardar Macedonia, all the way to the Serbian border. These successes made possible the historic first session of ASNOM.

The gathering took place on 2 August 1944—anniversary of the Ilinden Uprising of 1903—in the St. Prohor Pčinski monastery near Kumanovo, in the liberated territory in the northeast. Some 115 delegates and guests attended, including S. Vukmanović-Tempo, delegates from the Serbian liberation movement, and heads of the American and British military missions to Macedonian supreme headquarters.

This conclave—the so-called Second Ilinden—represented the culmination of the long and difficult road to statehood. It proclaimed the People's Democratic Republic of Macedonia in federal Yugoslavia, declared itself its constituent assembly, assumed full legislative and executive powers, and began to build the new state. It approved previous decisions and actions of supreme headquarters and the organizational council, guaranteed basic human rights for all citizens and national rights for minorities, proclaimed Macedonian the official language and 2 August the national holiday, set up a legislative commission and a commission to investigate enemy acts, and elected representatives to

AVNOJ. Finally, it chose a presidium of 22 members to perform all legislative and executive tasks until the next, the second session of ASNOM.[20] The presidium's first president was Metodija Andonov-Čento (1902–1957).

Čento was an exceptional political figure. He was not a Communist Party member; he was a businessman from Prilep. He was a high-profile and popular Macedonian activist in his native city and before the war had been a representative and candidate on the electoral list of the United Opposition. Yugoslav authorities arrested and imprisoned him in 1939 and in 1940; the occupiers interned him in Bulgaria in 1941 and in 1942. On 1 October 1943, he crossed into liberated territory and joined the armed struggle. Although he was not a member, party leaders gave him a position at supreme headquarters of NOV i POM because of his popularity among the masses. Later he headed the organizational council for the first session of ASNOM and was a Macedonian delegate to the second session of AVNOJ in November 1943. He was the most charismatic Macedonian leader and the most open and vocal proponent of national unification. In short, he was the most independent-minded and popular national wartime leader, and for that he would pay a heavy price at the end of the war.[21]

Greek and Bulgarian Macedonia (1941–1944)

The Macedonian question was from the outbreak of war much more than a Serbian/Yugoslav issue, concerning as it did Greek and Bulgarian Macedonia and neighboring states. The first session of ASNOM in August 1944 and its formal establishment of the Macedonian republic within Yugoslavia had far-reaching repercussions throughout the Balkans, but its impact was direct and immediate among Macedonians in Greece and Bulgaria, as we now see.

Like the KPJ in Yugoslavia, in Greece the KKE was the only political party to recognize Macedonian national identity and have a public policy on the national question. And, like its Yugoslav counterpart, it organized and led its country's most powerful resistance movement, the National Liberation Front (EAM), and its military arm, the Greek Popular Liberation Army (ELAS). While maintaining its commitment to social revolution, like the KPJ, the KKE also defended the traditional national interest of Greece. It attracted many non-Communist patriots and planned to seize power after liberation.

At the beginning of the war, the KKE paid no particular attention to the Macedonians. The sixth and the seventh plenums of its central committee, in June and September 1941, respectively, called on all citizens to fight the occupiers, but they did not mention the minorities. The eighth plenum, in January 1942, and the All-Greek Conference of the KKE, in December 1942, went further. They urged Macedonians to join Greeks in a common effort with Bulgarians and Serbians against the fascists and for Soviet victory, as well as for their own national and social liberation. Many Macedonians joined the EAM-ELAS; according to official KKE information, 6,000 served in its regular units and 20,000 in its reserves.[22]

However, the KKE and EAM-ELAS faced stiff competition for Macedonians' allegiance. After years of neglect, oppression, and repression, this predominantly peasant people felt alienated from the Greek state. It was difficult for them to show loyalty to it or to believe vague promises of equality in a future "people's Greece." Many responded instead to the Italian, German, and Bulgarian occupation authorities and to Mihailov's VMRO, which promised them liberation from Greek rule in a "free," "autonomous," "independent," or "united" Macedonian state. Such propaganda and coercion appealed to their traditional and profound distrust of Greeks; as we saw above, these bodies armed many villages and recruited and equipped paramilitary bands, the so-called *komiti*, or *kontračeti*, to fight on their side.

By 1943, however, the KKE and EAM-ELAS faced much stronger competition. Overshadowing these rightist and largely non-Macedonian influences were powerful events in the Vardar region, which influenced the Aegean partition. Many people, including loyal members of the KKE and followers of EAM-ELAS, were in awe of the region's apparent autonomy within Tito's movement in Yugoslavia. Moreover, they savored its clearly Macedonian character. It had its own supreme headquarters and a Macedonian partisan army with Macedonian officers; it used Macedonian as the language of command and a Macedonian flag; it propagated openly national liberation of all Macedonians and, more quietly, national unification.

This situation stood in sharp contrast to practice in Greece, where, as Captain P. H. Evans, SOE, wrote: "ELAS . . . have always officered their *Macedonian* units with *Greeks* and this made a bad impression on the Slavophone Andartes in ELAS. It has made them feel, as the civilians also feel, that the millennium announced by EAM/ELAS, with the Slav

Macedonians enjoying equal privileges and full freedom, is just a sell-out after all; *Greece* will go on excluding them from state posts, from promotion in the army and so on."[23]

With the Yugoslav example inspiring them, Macedonian leftists began to demand a liberation movement in Aegean Macedonia. This stance, as well as recognition of their right to self-determination, as Yugoslav practice showed, was invaluable for drawing Macedonians into the Communist-led Balkan resistance.

However, the KKE rejected all such proposals. Its leaders feared that raising the Macedonian question in Greece would alienate Greeks from the KKE and EAM-ELAS. Nonetheless, from then on and throughout the Civil War (1947–49), the KKE sought to maintain and enhance its support among Greeks while attempting to conciliate Macedonians. Since divisions were so deep and reconciliation was so difficult, Greek Communist leaders manipulated the issue to assist their own party. Whenever the KKE needed Macedonians' support, it paid lip service to their demands and made halfhearted concessions without giving up control over them. When it no longer required their support, it cancelled the concessions and downplayed their demands and the Macedonian problem in Greece.

In 1943, relations between EAM-ELAS and smaller groups in the nationalist resistance deteriorated dramatically. After ELAS fought with units of the National Republican Greek League (EDES) in early autumn—the so-called first round of the Civil War—the Communists courted the Macedonians in order to draw them away from Bulgarian influence and into their own ranks. In September 1943, ELAS created a Macedonian unit, Lazo Trpoviski. In October, the KKE reluctantly sanctioned a Slav-Macedonian National Liberation Front (SNOF) and its military arm, the Slav-Macedonian National Liberation Army (SNOV), under the direct authority of EAM-ELAS.

For the more radical Macedonian leaders, this was clearly but a first step: they hoped that SNOF-SNOV would become a movement for national liberation—autonomous, perhaps even independent of EAM-ELAS, with its own organization, leadership, and command structure throughout Aegean Macedonia. Such a movement, with a program of self-determination, would appeal to most Macedonians.

In fact, even the SNOF-SNOV won immediate acceptance and widespread support among Aegean Macedonians. The KKE wanted only an obedient and subservient, token instrument to draw Macedonians into the EAM-ELAS and thus away from the various "free" and "autonomous" Macedonian bands that the Bulgarians and Germans supported. It was not willing to tolerate, let alone accept as partner, an authentic, leftist Macedonian liberation movement with popular mass following and an independent power base. While the movement was still organizing, party leaders severely curtailed its independence, restricting and hindering its activities, and they suppressed it in April–May 1944. They ordered the arrest of some of its top figures, but eighty partisans under Naum Pejov fled to join the Macedonian army in Vardar Macedonia.[24]

In the summer, the KKE had once again to conciliate the Macedonians. A temporary solution emerged with the help of Macedonian leaders in Yugoslavia when the KKE promised to permit separate Macedonian units within the ELAS. However, it allowed only two battalions—the Edessa (Voden) in June and the Kastoria (Kostur)-Florina (Lerin) in August. It tightly controlled their activities and restricted their numbers. As the secretary of the party's Macedonian bureau confessed cynically: there would be two bands "so that the Slav Macedonians are not deceived by an eventual plot by the Bulgarians."[25]

Tense relations reached a crisis by October, when, facing liquidation, the two Macedonian battalions revolted and crossed into Vardar Macedonia. The flight of the two units, which included the most prominent Macedonian leftists, represented an open break between the Communist-led resistance and the Macedonians in Greece. The rebels enjoyed mass support, which troubled KKE leaders. They denounced the rebels as traitors, komitadjis, kontračetniks, and instruments of the Gestapo and the "intelligence service."

The Macedonians in turn accused the KKE and EAM-ELAS of Greek chauvinism and opportunism and refused further cooperation unless the KKE corrected its policy on the Macedonian question and met their demands. The rebels wanted separate units; a Macedonian national front with representation in the central committee of EAM; Macedonian institutions; local self-government; and freedom to conduct their own propaganda and education, even on subjects such as Macedonian self-determination and unification. Until then, "the Macedonian national fighters will not subordinate themselves to dictatorship and discipline of EAM-ELAS; [they] will carry on an independent policy and struggle for national justice."[26]

This split, which also chilled KKE-KPJ relations, occurred at an awkward moment for EAM-ELAS: on the eve of the so-called second round (December 1944–January 1945) in Greece's Civil War. The Greek left's defeat in the Battle of Athens by the British, who had the support of the previously discredited Greek right, and its acceptance of the humiliating Varkiza Agreement on 12 February 1945 only widened the rift. Macedonian leaders in Greece and victorious Communists in Yugoslavia considered Varkiza a shameful capitulation.

The wartime situation of Macedonians in Pirin (Bulgarian) Macedonia differed entirely from that of their conationals in Yugoslavia and Greece. As a signatory of the Tripartite Pact of 1936 allying Germany, Italy, and Japan, Bulgaria was an Axis ally and therefore not an occupied land. Consequently, Bulgarians did not suffer the deprivations—existential, political, economic, cultural, and so on—that the peoples of the conquered and occupied countries underwent. Bulgaria made large territorial acquisitions in Macedonia—virtual fulfillment of the dream of San Stefano—and it gained economically at least for as long as its allies, especially Germany, were winning on the battlefields and providing a stable market for Bulgaria's expanding output.

Under such circumstances, the resistance in Bulgaria was very modest in comparison with that in occupied Greece and Yugoslavia. The first armed bands emerged after the German attack on the Soviet Union in June 1941. Communists organized and led most of them; the entire resistance depended almost totally on the Communist underground. The Communists retained effective control of the bands even after mid-1942, when they set up the Fatherland Front (OF), a leftist coalition, together with the Social Democrats, the left-wing Agrarians, and the intellectuals and military officers of the elitist Zveno group.[27]

The aims and tactics of the Bulgarian resistance were equally modest. Party leaders, most of whom had spent the 1920s and 1930s in Moscow and would remain there throughout the war, decided that "classical" conditions for an armed partisan uprising did not exist in their homeland and therefore called on members to engage solely in sabotage and diversionary activities.

The resistance was more extensive in the Pirin region than elsewhere in the country. In the interwar years, the traditional parties, including the Communists' OF partners, had hardly any following in the Pirin region. Mihailov's VMRO controlled the political right and center. After its dissolution in 1934, its disorganized followers continued to support the authoritarian government and, during the war, the pro-Fascist regime. Only the Communist Party (BKP), most of whose Macedonian followers also belonged to the VMRO (ob.) and its auxiliaries, represented the organized opposition in Pirin Macedonia. Between the world wars, it enjoyed a greater following in the region than in other parts of Bulgaria and had a solid underground network there. Moreover, unlike elsewhere in Bulgaria, the Communist resistance had a Macedonian dimension. Both the BKP and the VMRO (ob.) advocated the Comintern platform—a united Macedonia in a Balkan Communist federation. A successful outcome—a Communist revolution and takeover of power—would result in a united Macedonia as an equal partner in a reconfigured Balkans.

The region's first partisan units appeared shortly after Germany invaded the Soviet Union in June 1941, under leading activists of the former VMRO (ob.). By the end of 1942, they operated throughout Pirin Macedonia. The success of the Allies, particularly the Red Army, in 1943, and new contacts with Communist-led movements in Yugoslavia and Greece inspired them. In the final year of the war, they consolidated into larger fighting detachments and intensified their diversionary attacks on police, military targets, and public buildings; obstructed the regime's requisitioning of foods and livestock; and punished people who closely identified with the regime.[28]

Macedonians in a New Balkans (1944–1949)

There is no doubt that the national liberation movements—AVNOJ in Yugoslavia and EAM-ELAS in Greece—aided in the liberation of their countries. Yet Allied successes in France and Italy, and the Soviet advances in Poland and southeast Europe, were the decisive factors. Communists ruled in most of the Balkans at war's end. Macedonians had their new Yugoslav republic, but potential unification with Pirin Macedonia went nowhere after the Soviet-Yugoslav break in 1948. In Greece, British intervention in 1944–45 and American in the Civil War (1947–49), which conflict cost Macedonians there dearly, swayed that contest toward the extreme right, which triumphed in 1949.

The Red Army crossed the Pruth River in early spring 1944, and Romania capitulated on 23 August 1944. The Red Army's push into the Balkans provoked the collapse of the Axis-dominated regime in Sofia. The Soviet Union declared war on Bulgaria on 5 September, and three days later the Red Army entered the country. That same night, the Communist-dominated Fatherland Front (OF) seized power in Sofia. Moreover, the Red Army's inexorable march westward through the peninsula threatened the Germans' only escape route, through the vital Morava-Vardar valley and the Salonika–Skopje–Belgrade railway.

The Germans began evacuating Greece in September 1944. By early October, when the first British units landed in Greece, the Germans were in full retreat. On 14 October, the British reached Athens, which ELAS already controlled. In the following two weeks, as the Germans retreated north, ELAS units attacked them constantly and took one town after another.

By early autumn 1944, most of rural Vardar (Yugoslav) Macedonia was free. The National Liberation Army and Partisan Detachments—three army corps with nine divisions—took the principal towns about mid-October. In the eastern and southeastern areas, they had help from units of the Bulgarian army. The resistance liberated Strumica on 5 November, Štip on the eighth, and Kumanovo on the eleventh. Pelagonia and the lake district fell at the same time: Prilep on 2 November, Bitola on the fourth, Resen on the fifth, and Ohrid on the eighth. The Germans fought back with far greater determination in the battle for Veles, a transportation junction on the Vardar. After two days of heavy fighting, the liberators took the city on 11 November. That advance opened the way for them to Skopje, soon to be capital of the Macedonian republic, where German units made up more than a division. Skopje became free on 3 November. From there, fighting moved toward Tetovo, which capitulated on 19 November. After the liberation of Macedonia, units of the National Liberation Army continued north toward Kočanik and Kosovo and helped free the rest of Yugoslavia.

The ending of the Axis occupation of Macedonia and the end of the war—the fourth in modern times by neighbors for control of the country—did not resolve the perennial Macedonian question. The general outline of the postwar political settlement came from the Allied powers, particularly Britain and the Soviet Union.

The "percentages agreement" to divide east central Europe into spheres of influence, which Winston Churchill offered and Josef Stalin graciously accepted in Moscow in October 1944, formalized the military situation and again left Macedonia in parts and the Macedonians separated. Britain maintained control of Greece, "the most important Balkan country from the point of view of British interests," and was determined to keep it and neighboring Turkey "within the British postwar sphere and to defend them against the possible or probable expansionist tendencies of a vast Soviet sphere of influence on their northern borders."[29]

In order to guarantee its own part of the bargain, Britain intervened militarily in Greece, which the Communist-led left had already practically liberated and now virtually controlled. The Greek left's defeat by the British in the Battle of Athens in December 1944–January 1945, its acceptance of the Varkiza Agreement on 12 February 1945, and the rise to power of the extreme nationalist right devastated the national aspirations of the Macedonians in Greece.

The Churchill-Stalin bargain left Bulgaria, which the Red Army had already liberated and occupied, in the Soviet sphere of influence. Yugoslavia, which they were to share equally, was free now thanks mostly to the Communist-led national liberation movement and was under its control and administration and so at least nominally in Moscow's sphere.

Although at war's end Macedonia continued to belong to its three neighbors, Macedonians' situation in the three partitions differed radically. In Greece, the British-installed reactionary government reverted to the prewar policy. It launched a violent campaign against the left, and Macedonians became primary targets of this so-called white terror. It victimized Macedonians partly because so many of them had supported the left—the EAM-ELAS—during the war, but mainly because they had raised national demands ranging from minority rights to outright separation from Greece.

In Bulgaria, the BKP, which led and dominated the Soviet-backed Fatherland Front (OF) government, recognized the separate national identity of the Macedonians, but had not yet determined the future of the Macedonians in Bulgaria and in Pirin Macedonia.

The Federal People's Republic of Yugoslavia, as we saw above, had in November 1943 recognized Vardar Macedonia as an equal republic and the Macedonians as a constituent nation. The first session of ASNOM (August 1944) had set up a Macedonian Communist government and administration—the People's Republic of Macedonia.

The dramatic events of the war transformed the Macedonian question. Vardar (Yugoslav) Macedonia won not only national recognition, but also legal equality in the new federation. With the new Macedonian state, Tito's victorious regime consolidated its dominant role in Macedonian affairs. It had won the support of activists, Communist and non-Communist, not only in Vardar but also in Aegean and Pirin Macedonia.

However, the activists' loyalty was not unconditional. Victory in Yugoslavia, the Red Army's successful march through eastern Europe, and the ascendancy of the Communist-dominated left made many activists see the new republic as the Piedmont of Macedonian unification, as the beginning of the national unification of Macedonia and the national unification of Macedonians. They rarely ever distinguished between the two options—unification of Macedonia and unification of the Macedonians. Greater Macedonia was their priority, and they expected the new Yugoslavia to spearhead the drive for its attainment.

Even before war's end, the confident leaders of victorious Yugoslavia began to impose their Macedonian solution on the weak and uncertain Communist-dominated Fatherland Front (OF) government of defeated Bulgaria. Throughout negotiations for a Yugoslav-Bulgarian federation, which began in November–December 1944 and climaxed with Tito and Georgi Dimitrov's meetings in Bled, Slovenia, in August 1947 and at Evksinograd, near Varna, in November 1947, Macedonia was the focus. The Yugoslavs sought to impose on the divided and hesitant Bulgarians the unification of Pirin Macedonia with the new Yugoslav republic or in a Yugoslav-dominated south Slav federation. Unlike some of his fellow leaders of the Bulgarian party and particularly leaders of the government's other parties, Communist leader and prime minister Dimitrov, both of whose parents were born in Macedonia, "was receptive to the proposed plan of unifying the constituent parts of Macedonia, and signed the Bled agreement of August 1947 between Yugoslavia and Bulgaria which was tantamount to union of Pirin and Vardar Macedonia. The agreement abolished entry visas and envisaged a customs union. However, Dimitrov opposed immediate formal union until after the proposed Yugoslav-Bulgarian federation had been realised. This proved something of a stumbling block as Tito wanted Bulgaria to join on a basis of equality with the other constituent republics of Yugoslavia (i.e., Serbia) while the Bulgarians wanted equal status with Yugoslavia."[30]

Meanwhile, and in accordance with the Bled agreement, which had reconfirmed the resolution of the tenth plenum of the BKP's central committee in August 1946, Dimitrov's government was giving Pirin Macedonia virtual cultural autonomy. The resolution had stated the party's general line on Macedonia—the right of other parts of Macedonia to unite with the Yugoslav republic—and declared that creating conditions for such unification, especially vis-à-vis the Pirin region, was the task not only of Macedonians but of Bulgaria's Fatherland Front and People's Federal Yugoslavia. In the interim, the BKP would move the Macedonians of Pirin culturally closer to the Yugoslav republic. To facilitate unification, it would popularize the standard Macedonian language and literature and the history of the Macedonian people; facilitate contacts and open the region's borders with the republic; and enhance the region's cultural autonomy and thus Macedonian consciousness there. The resolution called on all party members, especially in the Pirin region and among Macedonians elsewhere in Bulgaria, to support strengthening of the republic and preparations for merger in the context of Bulgarian-Yugoslav union.[31]

The Macedonians in Pirin Macedonia and in Bulgaria in general had in effect won the right to cultural autonomy. The Bulgarian census of December 1946 for the first time permitted Macedonians to declare their nationality. Macedonians organized their own educational and cultural societies and published their own newspapers and journals. *Makedonsko zname*, the newspaper of Macedonian émigrés in Bulgaria, and *Pirinsko delo*, that of the OF in Pirin Macedonia, were published in Macedonian and became mouthpieces of cultural autonomy.

The Bled agreement speeded up implementation of cultural autonomy. In August 1947, the Narodno sūbranie (parliament) in Sofia introduced the Macedonian language and national history in schools in Pirin Macedonia, and the government asked Skopje to send teachers and other qualified cultural workers to the region. Early in the autumn, a large group of teachers, professors, writers, and actors arrived there. At the same time, the Macedonian government organized special language centers for teachers from the Pirin region and accepted and funded students from there in its secondary schools and at the University of Skopje. These efforts were preparing the ground for introduction of Macedonian as the language of instruction in Pirin Macedonia.

Furthermore, cultural contacts and exchanges between the region and the republic increased markedly throughout the autumn and winter of 1947–48. The Macedonian national theater in Gorna Dzhumaia presented Macedonian plays. Macedonian bookstores, Makedonska kniga, opened in major towns, and exhibitions of Macedonian books and publications, with accompanying lectures, took place in towns and larger villages. Prospects for cultural autonomy and even for unification with the republic appeared promising indeed.[32]

Leaders of the KPJ and the Macedonian republic closely observed developments in Greece. They hoped that Communist victory there would pave the way for a Yugoslav resolution of the Macedonian question: Aegean Macedonia or its Macedonian-populated areas would unite with the Yugoslav republic or in a Yugoslav-dominated Balkan Communist federation that would include Greece.

As we saw above, during the wartime occupation, Yugoslavia, or rather the movement for national liberation in Vardar Macedonia, had helped rally Macedonians in Greece and their organizations behind the EAM-ELAS. The KKE and Macedonian activists in Greece had major differences. The KKE saw in Macedonian nationalism disloyalty to the Greek state; Macedonians saw in their Greek comrades' strong patriotism and nationalism a betrayal of their national rights. The split in autumn 1944 between the Macedonian leadership in Greece and the EAM-ELAS, British intervention and victory in the Battle of Athens (December 1944–January 1945), and the capitulation of the Greek left at Varkiza in February 1945 set back the Macedonian cause and Tito's designs.

However, the Yugoslav leaders remained confident that the KKE would depend on them in any attempt to seize power. But they also realized that the liberation of the Aegean Macedonians depended on the victory of the KKE—the only party in Greece that recognized their identity and existence. They were aware too that the KKE, to win, would need direct or indirect aid from Communist neighbors to the north, especially in Yugoslavia. Direct aid from Yugoslavia, where the Macedonians already had a republic, would not come unless the Greek Communists could win active support from Macedonians in Greece. These incompatible allies would have to fight together; the success of each depended on the other.

The Greek extreme right aimed its terror campaign after Varkiza especially hard against Macedonians. In addition to supporting EAM-ELAS, the Macedonians did not consider themselves Greek, so the fanatical right condemned them as "Bulgars," "komitadjis," "collaborators," "autonomists," "Sudetens of the Balkans," and so forth and threatened to exterminate them.[33] And Macedonians suffered armed attacks on their villages, murders, arrests, trials, jail, and exile; confiscation of property and movable equipment; burning of homes and villages; economic blockades of villages; forcible expulsions; discriminatory use of taxes and aid from the United Nations Relief and Rehabilitation Administration (UNRRA); and restrictions on movement.

Macedonian activists, particularly the leaders who broke with the KKE and crossed into the republic in autumn 1944, realized the need to organize the Macedonians in Greece. With the undaunted encouragement and support of Skopje and Belgrade, in April 1945 they founded the Communist-led National Liberation Front (NOF) as a direct successor of the wartime SNOF and as a single, united organization of all Macedonians in Greece. The new body not only appealed to Macedonians who had sided with EAM-ELAS but also wished to draw in Macedonians, the so-called autonomists, whom occupation authorities had armed. The NOF sought and soon established a vast organizational network that reached all Macedonian-populated areas.

The primary aim of NOF, as of SNOF, was self-determination and thus national liberation; for its Communist leaders, this could mean only ultimate unification with free Macedonia in Yugoslavia. However, in the conditions of post-Varkiza Greece and the Balkans in general, the NOF had to play down, or set aside until the victory of the Greek left, this maximal aim, which was anathema to all Greeks. Instead, it focused on safeguarding Macedonians in Greece, which goal the Communist-led left apparently supported. This minimal program remained its declared policy until its second congress in March 1949—that is, virtually until the end of the Civil War in Greece.

NOF leaders were fully conscious of their isolation in Greece and called repeatedly for collaboration with the Greek left. But a basis for cooperation did not exist; Varkiza had exacerbated the existing split. Macedonian leaders denounced the agreement because they were sure that the KKE could seize power only through armed struggle. The KKE, however, endorsed the accord and as a legal party embraced political struggle to win power in Greece. The two positions were not compatible and precluded meaningful cooperation. Hence, in the year and a half following Varkiza, the KKE and EAM, while protesting anti-Macedonian terror, also rejected the NOF, denouncing it as an "autonomist" and "fascist" tool of the "Intelligence Service" and equating it with the Bulgarian-sponsored wartime autonomist movement.[34]

The KKE's attitude toward the NOF, and the struggle for power in Greece, did not change as long as KKE leaders thought political victory possible. The first indications of possible reorientation surfaced in late 1945 and early 1946, when KKE leaders recognized the NOF as "an anti-fascist organization of the Slav Macedonians" and called for Greek-Macedonian unity, which Varkiza had disrupted. Conciliation of the NOF intensified after 12 February 1946, when the second plenum of the central committee decided to begin preparations for a possible armed struggle.

These overtures set the stage for a formal rapprochement. The long, difficult discussions commenced in May 1946. Agreement finally emerged with the aid of Belgrade and Skopje on 21 November 1946. The accord did not fully satisfy either side. Under pressure probably from the KPJ, the NOF abandoned its demand for separate Macedonian units in the rebel army, the Democratic Army of Greece (DSE), and left appointments and promotions to the KKE. However, the KKE made some concessions as well. It wanted to decapitate the NOF, to do away with its central leadership, and to take control of district and local organizations, as token instruments for mobilizing Macedonians. In the end, it had to accept the NOF's right to retain its own central leadership, which meant de facto recognition of that group as the highest organ of the Macedonians in Greece.[35]

The two sides concluded the agreement not because they trusted each other but because they needed and depended on each other to realize their respective ends—namely, seizure of power for the KKE and national liberation for the NOF. Although the NOF was no longer voicing it openly, the KKE suspected that its real aim remained self-determination and unification of Aegean Macedonia, or at least of those areas with Macedonians, with the Yugoslav republic. The KKE distrusted the NOF's leaders, and past experience inspired the NOF's leaders to question the KKE's Macedonian program and, above all, the sincerity of its leaders. It is unclear how each side hoped to tackle the challenge that the other posed after the common struggle. However, NOF leaders probably counted on Yugoslav support, while the KKE hoped to neutralize the NOF as a factor in future relations with Yugoslavia.

In any event, the Macedonians of Greek Macedonia made a critical contribution to the Communist side during the Civil War in Greece. They bore the brunt of the war. They inhabited central and western Aegean Macedonia, which bordered on Yugoslavia and Albania and was site of the heaviest fighting, including the decisive battles. Throughout the Civil War, this area served as a base for the political and military operations of the so-called democratic movement. The KKE and its military arm, the Democratic Army of Greece (DSE), both maintained headquarters there. The area also embraced the so-called liberated territories—lands under DSE control that formed its home front and supplied or were expected to supply most if not all of the provisions. As one participant and close observer stated: "[They] were turned into military workshops for the DSE, where everyone, young and old, male and female, served the needs of the DSE."[36]

Even more notable was the Macedonians' contribution to the fighting strength of the left. Throughout the struggle their participation in the ranks of the rebel army was high, far out of proportion to their relatively low numbers in the Greek population. Their estimated representation in the DSE ranged from more than a quarter in April 1947 to more than two-thirds in mid-1949. According to Colonel C. M. Woodhouse, chief of the British Military Mission to occupied Greece, "they numbered 11,000 out of 25,000 in 1948, but 14,000 out of less than 20,000 by mid-1949."[37] In the most critical theaters, they constituted an even higher percentage. As early as October 1947, they made up three-quarters of the manpower of the command of central and western Macedonia. Vasilis Bartzotas, a member of the Politburo and political commissar of DSE general headquarters, paid a tribute to "this heroic people [which] gave everything . . . ; it sacrificed its children, its property, its homes. Every household has a wounded or a dead [member]."[38]

Tito became the principal patron of the Greek Communists in their struggle for power. The Yugoslavs not only offered moral support but helped rally the Macedonians to the Communist side. They also became the crucial source of practical aid. They provided food, transport facilities, and use of camps, arms, artillery, and ammunitions. They hoped for a Communist victory in Greece for ideological reasons but perhaps primarily because they expected such a victory, and federation with Bulgaria, to pave the way for Yugoslav resolution of the Macedonian question—unification of Macedonia under Yugoslav auspices.

Stalin stopped both the south Slav federation and Macedonian unification. As we saw above, in 1941 the Soviet Communist Party sided with the KPJ on Macedonia. Later Stalin endorsed the initial moves toward a Yugoslav-Bulgarian federation. As the war wound down, however, he began to suspect Tito, who, unlike other eastern European Communist leaders, enjoyed an independent base of power at home and did not depend on Moscow.

Stalin's distrust must have grown after the war with Tito's persistent independence in foreign relations. As Phyllis Auty has noted, this stance "endangered the fundamental basis of Soviet foreign policy and challenged the communist theory that had been used to cloak Russia's national aims."[39] Stalin feared that a Yugoslav-Bulgarian or a Balkan federation centered in Belgrade could easily challenge Soviet hegemony in the Balkans, throughout eastern Europe, and in the international Communist movement. Consequently, Stalin vetoed the plans for federation at the end of 1947 and, with the outbreak of the historic Soviet-Yugoslav dispute in the spring of 1948 and the Cominform's expulsion of Yugoslavia on 28 June 1948, destroyed any chances the Communist left had in the Civil War in Greece. Macedonian unification died in the ashes of the Stalin-Tito conflict—the first cold war dividing the Communist bloc.

The Cominform reintroduced the interwar Comintern program on Macedonia—a united Macedonian state in an illusory future Balkan Communist federation. This approach mirrored the ideals and dreams not only of the SNOF and the NOF, but also of earlier Macedonian patriotic and nationalist leftists. Yet Stalin acted only out of expediency. The Cominform reembraced the old slogan exclusively as short-term propaganda, for tactical gains, and as an integral part of its campaign against Tito's Yugoslavia. Stalin turned Macedonia into an instrument of his anti-Yugoslav endeavors.

Although the KKE did not declare its support for the Cominform resolution right away, it was obvious that it would follow the Bulgarian example and side with Stalin and his party. Both parties were subservient to Stalin, and the Cominform resolution emboldened Bulgarian and Greek Communist leaders who resented Tito's overbearing tactics as well as his work for a Yugoslav solution on Macedonia.

Thus, after its expulsion from the Cominform in June 1948, Yugoslavia worried about its own survival. Macedonian unification was not a priority; Yugoslavia left the NOF and the Macedonians in Greece to their own devices. The KKE's alienation of Yugoslavia, its sole major patron, and Yugoslavia's gradual withdrawal of support decided the fate of the KKE and its struggle in Greece. The victory of the U.S.-supported Greek nationalist right and the capitulation of the left a year later, in 1949, also eviscerated the national aspirations of the Macedonians in Aegean Macedonia.[40]

The dramatic events of the Second World War and its revolutionary aftermath in the Balkans transformed the Macedonian question. To be sure, the Macedonians failed to achieve national unification, and those in Aegean (Greek) and Pirin (Bulgarian) Macedonia did not even win lasting official recognition.

After the Communist defeat in the Civil War, the pro-Western royalist government in Athens equated expressions of Macedonianism with Communism, which became illegal in Greece. It denied even more vociferously than before 1939 a Macedonian identity and national minority and continued to call Macedonians in the republic "Serbs" or "Skopjans."

Communist Bulgaria found itself in an even more awkward situation. Despite having recognized a separate Macedonian identity, accepted Macedonian cultural autonomy in the Pirin region, and endorsed in principle Macedonian unification, after Yugoslavia's expulsion from the Cominform Bulgaria reverted to the traditional royalist position. It negated the existence of a Macedonian national identity and claimed all Macedonians as Bulgarians.

However, the Macedonians of Yugoslav (Vardar) Macedonia, the largest Macedonian group, won not only national recognition but also legal equality within the new, Communist-led, federal Yugoslavia. They became a constituent republic and Macedonian one of four official languages. Federal Yugoslavia claimed the role of champion of all Macedonians, enjoyed a dominant say in Macedonian affairs until its collapse in 1991, and placed Bulgaria and Greece on the defensive.

12 Yugoslav Macedonia: Politics and Government (1944–1991)

Creation in 1944 of the People's Republic of Macedonia[1] in the Communist Yugoslav federation was of great symbolic and practical significance for the Macedonians. It was the first state since the Roman conquest of Macedonia in 168 BC to bear the territorial name and to carry the ethnic-national name of its Slavic majority. Its establishment represented the culmination of an almost-century-long drive for a state.

Yet founding of the republic represented only partial fulfilment of the traditional national program. At the end of the war, it was unclear how much autonomy or self-rule the new government would enjoy in the Communist-led Yugoslav federation. Moreover, Macedonians had not achieved the dream of territorial or national unification, no matter how unrealistic the political and ideological divisions plaguing the Balkans and the rest of Europe made it. In fact, the Macedonians in Greece and Bulgaria did not even gain lasting national recognition and still remain unrecognized and repressed.

The People's Republic of Macedonia (after 1974, the Socialist Federal Republic of Macedonia) was one of the smallest constituents of the People's Federal Republic of Yugoslavia. It covered 25,713 square kilometers, or about 10 percent of the country's territory, and 38 percent of geographic Macedonia. It had no outlet to the sea: it shared a border with Serbia, another Yugoslav republic, in the north and with Bulgaria in the east, Greece in the south, and Albania in the west.

The republic was a multi-ethnic state in a multi-national federation. Its people represented just over 8 percent of Yugoslavia's population. Ethnic Macedonians made up just over two-thirds of the republic's inhabitants. The 1971 census counted 1,647,308 inhabitants: 1,142,375 ethnic Macedonians (or 69.35 percent of the total), 279,871 Albanians (16.99 percent), 108,552 Turks (6.59 percent), 46,465 Serbs (2.82 percent), and 70,045 others (4.25 percent).[2]

As we saw above, Macedonia formed one of six equal Yugoslav republics. Ethnic Macedonians were also a constituent nation, and Macedonian was one of four official languages. Throughout its existence as a federal republic, its political history responded to the political development of the Communist-ruled federation itself.

In this chapter, we consider in turn the new Communist system in Yugoslavia from 1943 to 1948, the resulting suspension of Macedonia's national dream, the evolution of one-party government in Yugoslavia from 1948 to the late 1980s, and Macedonia's place as a junior partner in the federation. The next chapter examines the republic's economy, culture, and national minorities.

Yugoslavia's New Dispensation (1944–1948)

At the end of November 1943, at its historic second session, the AVNOJ transformed Yugoslavia into a federal state. In the following months and with Allied victory approaching, the Communist-dominated partisan army defeated its domestic ideological opponents in a bloody civil war. By the time liberation arrived, the Communists controlled all of Yugoslavia. However, determined pressure from Britain, the United States, and the Soviet Union prevented them from immediately setting up government. Instead, the Communists launched a series of well-thought-out compromises that appeased the Allies and legitimized their formal takeover of the government.

The second session of the AVNOJ had constituted itself as a provisional government and vested executive power in the People's Liberation Committee that it elected. These new organs of government challenged the authority of King Peter and the government-in-exile in London. As a sign of his willingness to "cooperate" with the latter, Josip Broz Tito, the Communist leader, allowed two of his nominees to join the reorganized government-in-exile, which Ivan Šubašić formed in London in July

Map 6 The Republic of Macedonia in Federal Yugoslavia (1944–1991)

1944. In November, in another move of "cooperation," Tito concluded an agreement with Šubašić that prevented the king's return until after a referendum on the monarchy's future; in the meantime, a three-man regency would act as head of state. The king's renunciation of this agreement early in 1945 had no effect on any of the concerned parties.

But in another move to conciliate the Allied powers, the KPJ enlarged the AVNOJ assembly by adding non-Communist members and included five nonpartisans in the cabinet of March 1945. The new government's main task was to prepare elections in November for the constituent assembly. Until that conclave approved a new constitution, the

Communist-controlled provisional government would govern in terms of legislation from AVNOJ and the Communist-dominated provisional assembly.

For the Communists, the election campaign against their real or potential opponents merely continued the wartime civil war by different, yet ruthless, means. The National Liberation Army, soon to become the Yugoslav National Army (JNA), remained under the KPJ, protecting the country's security and the party's political interest. The pervasive and efficient wartime police system became a Yugoslavia-wide secret political police in the Department for the Protection of the People (OZNa). The OZNa was part of the Commission, later Ministry, of National Defense. After the 1946 proclamation of the People's Federal Republic of Yugoslavia, the reorganized police relocated to the Ministry of Internal Affairs as the Administration of State Security (UDBa). It was the KPJ's most powerful instrument of control, and until 1966 it was responsible only to Aleksandar Ranković, a Serb and one of Tito's closest and most trusted lieutenants.

The regime unleashed the feared secret police against all "collaborators"—enemies of the people and class enemies. These elastic terms could include any and all political opponents. The victims of the OZNa faced "people's justice" in "people's courts." Like the OZNa, these courts appeared originally in liberated territories and after the occupation throughout the country. Using the army, the political police, and the courts, the Communists liquidated or silenced their most vocal and determined opponents.

The Communists also launched a social transformation. Ideology shaped their measures, which represented the initial moves in state direction of postwar reconstruction and planning of the economy. But these actions also aimed to undercut the economic viability of the government's enemies. A decree of 21 November 1944 called for expropriation of all property in the hands of Germans, war criminals, and collaborators. It placed under state control about 55 percent of the country's industry. In the first half of 1945, a series of financial measures, a special tax on war profits, a drastic increase in general taxes on small businesses, and new price controls crippled or bankrupted all segments of the middle class, whose businesses the state took over.

To appeal to the peasants—close to 80 percent of the population—in August 1945 the provisional government introduced radical land reform. The guiding principle was that land belongs to those who till it, which had been one of AVNOJ's resolutions. The maximum size of a private holding for a farmer cultivating it with his or her family depended on its quality—no less than 20 hectares or more than 35 hectares. All properties that the state confiscated, including those of owners who fled the country, absentee landlords, and foreigners, banks, other private companies, churches, monasteries, charitable foundations, and so forth, entered a state-controlled land fund. Only half of these lands went to needy peasants who had joined or supported the partisans; the rest would go later to the planned socialized sector of agriculture, comprising state, collective, and cooperative farming.

On 11 August 1945, the provisional assembly passed a new electoral law. It gave voting rights to men and women over the age of eighteen and to all partisans regardless of age. It denied the right to vote to a quarter million people, alleged collaborators of one sort or another. It set 11 November as the election date. In November, the KPJ reorganized the People's Liberation Front as the Popular Front (NF). The KPJ controlled the NF, which included many non-Communist organizations and individuals who had joined or supported the Communist-led liberation movement in all parts of Yugoslavia. It approved a single list of candidates.

The campaign was a contest between two unequal sides. The KPJ, or rather its NF, represented the victors in the war and enjoyed international recognition and the prestige that went with it. The KPJ was the only national, Yugoslavia-wide party with a disciplined, multi-level organizational network in the form of party organizations and NF committees. As we saw above, the KPJ controlled the provisional government, the army, the police, the trade unions, and the media and was only too ready to use them to silence or intimidate "class enemies."

Its main rivals were regional parties: Milan Grol's Democratic Party, with support in Serbia, and the faction of the Croatian Peasant Party under Stjepan Radić's widow in Croatia. They lacked unity, organization, and morale. Official and unofficial limitations on their freedom to organize supporters and to campaign frustrated them, and so the three non-Communist members of the provisional government—M. Grol, I. Šubašić, and J. Šutej—resigned and boycotted the election.

The results on 11 November were predictable. The NF list received 90 percent of the votes, and the announced turnout was also about 90 percent. When the new constituent assembly convened on 29 November, it deposed the king and adopted the country's new name, People's Federal Republic of Yugoslavia. On 31 January 1946, it approved the new constitution and transformed itself into the federation's first parliament.[3]

The 1946 constitution[4] imitated Stalin's Soviet constitution of 1936. It declared the federation of six equal republics—Bosnia and Herzegovina, Croatia, Macedonia, Montenegro, Serbia, and Slovenia. Serbia had two autonomous regions or provinces: Vojvodina and Kosovo-Metohija. "The Constitution defined the individual republics as the sovereign homelands of sovereign nations. These were five nations: Serb, Croat, Slovene, Macedonian and Montenegrin; the Muslims were not recognized as a nation until 1981."[5] Changes to the boundaries between republics required approval of those republics. The constitution also recognized national minorities in various parts of Yugoslavia as nationalities *(narodnosti),* which, unlike nations *(narodi),* did not have their own republics. Like Stalin's 1936 model, it recognized the right of the sovereign republics and nations to self-determination, even though exercise of that formal right was politically inconceivable.

The federal assembly *(skupština)* consisted of a federal council *(savezno veće)* elected by universal suffrage and a council of nationalities *(veće naroda)* "composed of equal number of representatives chosen by the assemblies of the six republics and the two autonomous units."[6] The assembly elected its presidium, which decided day-to-day activities and also acted as a corporate head of state. The federal executive council *(savezno izvršno veće)* was a cabinet under a chair *(predsedatel),* a premier, and consisted of heads of ministries. Tito became the first premier.

The federal government in Belgrade "was responsible for defence, foreign policy, economic planning, the currency and banking system, communications, law, and maintenance of the social system."[7] The "sovereign" republics had few noncultural powers and responsibilities—in effect, the right to use the national language. Republican sovereignty was formal rather than substantive, theoretical rather than practical. The system was centralized and hierarchical. Local and republican governments were not really responsible to their electors, the people, but instruments of the central government in Belgrade. In fact, they constituted the link, or *smychka* (a Leninist term), between the constituent nations and the federal government, which in turn was responsible to the KPJ, the only legal and real political force, which controlled it.

Although the constitution did not mention the KPJ or socialism, the party enjoyed an exclusive monopoly of power. In line with Leninist "democratic centralism," the Politburo, the party's highest organ, made decisions, and its "orders flowed downwards . . . to the lower strata of the party, whose members exercised day-to-day supervision over the organs of government. There was a close interlocking of party and state functions, symbolized at the summit by Tito's positions as head of the government, of the army and of the party. . . . [This formed the basis] of a bureaucratic, centralized and fundamentally undemocratic system . . . of the dictatorship of the proletariat, exercised by the party in the name of the workers. The controlling hand of the party was evident at all levels of political, economic and cultural life."[8]

Finally, the constitution provided for the equality of all Yugoslav citizens irrespective of race, nation, language, creed, education, or social position. It guaranteed individual freedom and freedom of religion and conscience, speech, the press, assembly, and association, as well as the right to private property and private enterprise. However, as with the Stalinist model, a one-party state would not implement these provisions and guarantees. It planned to build revolutionary socialism by subordinating individual rights and freedoms to the good of society and of the working people, as the Communist Party defined that good.

The election on 11 November 1945 and the proclamation of the constitution on 31 January 1946 legitimized internally and internationally the KPJ's hold on power. The Communists now inaugurated construction of the "dictatorship of the proletariat," or rather of the KPJ acting in the name of the proletariat. This first phase lasted until just after the Soviet-Yugoslav dispute and split in 1948.

The Communists pursued their opponents with vengeance. They rounded up the remnants of their defeated wartime enemies, the Croatian Ustaša and the Serbian Četniks; they shot some of them and jailed others with or without trials by regular courts. They silenced, intimidated, or suppressed their political critics outside the Popular Front (NF), imposed the KPJ's program on all elements in the NF, and placed the NF under tight control.

Resorting to similar repressive tactics, the one-party state forced its authority and control on the major established churches. The conflict with the Catholic church was intense, but the state crippled it by depriving it of its wealth and its traditional role in education and social life. The Orthodox church did not mount as determined a resistance. Internal divisions and ethnic wrangling had already weakened it: the lower clergy fought the hierarchy, and Macedonians opposed Serbians. The Muslim establishment resisted least; it was traditionally dependent on the state financially.

With its political power secure, the new regime quickened postwar reconstruction and revolutionary transformation. It followed very closely the Stalinist model. By the end of 1946, reconstruction was progressing. Wartime damage had disappeared, the economy was functioning, production was rising, and national incomes reached 1938 levels. On 6 December 1946, the government nationalized most industry. Private enterprise came to a virtual end in April 1948, with nationalization or closing down of remaining small enterprises and workshops.

In 1947, the government's First Five-Year Plan called for rapid industrialization of the predominantly agrarian country. It set some very ambitious targets, especially vis-à-vis heavy industry. By 1952, it expected, heavy industry would be producing at 552 percent of 1938 levels, and consumer production, at 174 percent. The plan also set the stage for transformation of the agrarian economy. Agricultural output was to increase by 52 percent above 1939 levels through Soviet-style collectivization via large, mechanized farming enterprises. However, fear of peasant opposition forced the KPJ to move cautiously. Collectivization did not begin until 1949. In the meantime, the government made private farming difficult by introducing compulsory delivery orders, forcibly requisitioning grain, and prohibiting sale of land, private purchase of machinery, employment of village labor, and so on.[9]

By early 1948, "sovietization" had moved more rapidly in Yugoslavia than in other countries in the Soviet sphere of influence in eastern and central Europe. Yugoslavia's break with the Soviet Union and its dismissal from the Cominform (28 June 1948) halted its construction of a Stalinist dictatorship of the proletariat. Yugoslav Communists underwent agonizing self-examination, purging of Stalinists and Cominformists, and the search for a new, Yugoslav model for socialism.

Macedonia: Putting Dreams on Ice (1945–1948)

Postwar developments in Macedonia, and in the other federal republics, reflected exactly those in Belgrade; top KPJ leaders dictated them. The wartime ASNOM continued with its legislative and executive functions in Macedonia. In mid-April 1945, ASNOM turned into a regular republican parliament, the national assembly *(narodno sobranie)*. The executive functions went to the republic's new government, under Lazar Koliševski (1914–2000), leader of the Communist Party of Macedonia (KPM), who was in prison in Bulgaria for most of the war, until 9 September 1944. State-building reached completion on 31 December 1946 with passage of the republic's first constitution by the constitutional assembly.[10]

There was hardly any organized national opposition to establishment of this first modern Macedonian state. People equated statehood, or autonomism (the popular term in the 1930s and 1940s), with a free Macedonia, the dream of patriots since the 1860s. It was the official program of the entire left. It was also the aim of the rank and file of the right who had joined or supported Mihailov's VMRO. They too were passionate about Macedonian nationalism, patriotism, *našism*, separatism, particularism, and so forth, and by 1943, when they no longer questioned the national orientation of Macedonian Communists, many of them actually joined or aided the effort for national liberation.

The exceptions were those people, mostly higher in Mihailov's VMRO, who had acquired Bulgarian national consciousness, identified Macedonians with Bulgarians, and sought annexation to Bulgaria or status as a second Bulgarian state. By war's end, many of them had left Macedonia; those who did not escape faced rounding up and execution or imprisonment with or without trial. The same fate befell those unfortunate individuals, sincere Macedonian patriots, who had suffered under Serbian or Greek authorities between the wars, lost confidence in the Macedonian cause, and let their anti-Serbianism or -Hellenism drive them into active collaboration with the Bulgarian occupiers.[11]

Moreover, unlike in Croatia, Serbia, and Slovenia, Communists in Macedonia did not face an organized political or so-called democratic opposition. Serbian leaders had not permitted Macedonian political parties in interwar Vardar Macedonia; Serbian parties monopolized politics there. The latter had enjoyed passive acceptance before the war, but hardly any support afterward. There was no Macedonian Orthodox church, but there was a popular movement for separating the Macedonian eparchies from the Serbian Orthodox church (SPC) and for a separate national church. The separatist movement tended to undermine whatever little influence the SPC still enjoyed in Macedonia. As we saw above, the disorganized remnants of Mihailov's VMRO were totally ineffective as a political force. Their leadership's subservience to Bulgarian authoritarianism, Italian Fascism, and German Nazism compromised, discredited, and defeated them.

Although the Communists were—and presented themselves successfully as—the chief proponents of the Macedonian national cause and interests and had a widespread following, other individuals and groups sought a non-Communist, democratic, and preferably united and independent Macedonian state. However, in postwar Yugoslavia they could not establish a functioning organizational network. Such groups formed secretly in the principal towns, especially among students, in the short period between liberation and the immediate aftermath of the split with the Soviet Union.

These anti-Communist nationalist groups have not received sufficient attention, but they appear to have identified themselves with their understanding of the original VMRO of the Ilinden years. They used names such as "Democratic Front of Macedonia—Ilinden 1903," "VMRO—Independent Democratic Republic of Macedonia under the Protection of America," and "VMRO—Truth," and they did not survive for long. Their members could not escape surveillance by the UDBa or Communist justice.[12]

The Yugoslav Communists' greatest challenge in consolidating their rule in Macedonia, however, came from within the Macedonian Communist-led movement for national liberation. Top KPJ leaders had long differed with Communist and non-Communist Macedonian leaders, and with the rank and file in the Communist-led national liberation movement, over Macedonia's future. The disagreements simmered during the struggle and surfaced as peace and a Balkan settlement approached. They concerned two issues: Macedonia's unification and its place in the Yugoslav federation.

First, patriots felt that unification of Macedonia and/or the Macedonians—they hardly ever made the distinction—was the only acceptable resolution; the KPJ considered it very desirable, but only if achievable without great risks. During the war, the KPJ and AVNOJ had made implicit and explicit promises of uniting Macedonia or the Macedonians. In return for such pledges, Macedonian leftists in Vardar Macedonia and some in Greece and Bulgaria embraced the Yugoslav solution—equal partnership in the new federation. Thus they accepted the Yugoslav solution only conditionally. They expected Yugoslavia to deliver on its commitments. Many leftists would not give up on unification solely for the sake of the federation.

Undoubtedly, promises from the KPJ and AVNOJ powerfully stimulated growth of the wartime partisan movement in Macedonia. However, as I have stressed above, for Yugoslav Communist leaders, including Tito, Macedonian unification within Yugoslavia was desirable but never a primary aim. They sought above all to safeguard the territorial integrity of Yugoslavia, including Vardar Macedonia, and the regime that they planned. There is no indication that they were ever willing to risk those aims to unify Macedonia within Yugoslavia, let alone give up the Vardar region to a united Macedonia outside Yugoslavia.

Second, Macedonia's position in the federation depended on the measure of self-rule and autonomy that it would gain; here again patriots differed from the KPJ on how much was appropriate. There were no Macedonians among the KPJ's top leaders, and none participated in designing the federal system. Many of the Macedonian leaders seemed to hold an idealized view of Communist federalism and the Soviet federal system. They, Communists and non-Communists alike, expected far greater autonomy, more freedom in internal affairs, and a larger say in foreign relations than the highly centralized, one-party federation could allow or deliver.

During the war, KPJ leaders encouraged such expressions of "greater" Macedonian nationalism in order to monopolize support among Macedonians not only in Vardar, but also in Aegean and Pirin Macedonia. After liberation, Tito and his closest advisers, who did not include a single Macedonian, became arbiters of the republic's future. They demanded total loyalty and obedience from the leadership there, which could no longer include nonparty members or people who questioned the party line on the Macedonian question. Such personalities had to go, giving way to party loyalists.

Lazar Koliševski (1914–2000), Tito and the KPJ's "man in Skopje" and Macedonian strongman through most of the Communist period, directed the purge. Born in Macedonia, he spent his formative years in Kragujevac, Serbia, where he joined the KPJ and served as local organizational secretary until the collapse of Yugoslavia in 1941. He was most noteworthy for his loyalty and obedience to the party and its leadership, which, until Tito's arrival in 1937, was synonymous with the Serbian party and leaders.

In 1941, the KPJ's central committee sent Koliševski for party work to Macedonia, where he clashed with and helped engineer the ouster of

Šatorov-Šarlo and, in September 1941, replaced him as organizational secretary of the KPJ's regional committee (PK) in Macedonia. Two months later, in November, the Bulgarian police arrested him; the authorities tried him and sentenced him to death. However, they commuted his sentence to life imprisonment, and he served his sentence in Pleven, Bulgaria. He remained there until pro-Fascist Bulgaria collapsed and the Fatherland Front (OF) seized power on 9 September 1944.

While Koliševski was in prison, in March 1943 the KPJ appointed him secretary of the central committee of the new Communist Party of Macedonia (KPM) and a member of the presidium of the second session of AVNOJ. After the liberation, he quickly took power. In addition to leading the KPM, at the second session of ASNOM (28–31 December 1944) he became Metodija Andonov-Čento's first deputy in the ASNOM presidency, and, in mid-April 1945, he took over the new government, as premier of the Macedonian republic.[13]

Koliševski's foremost task was to purge the ruling elite in the republic of real or potential nationalist critics of the KPJ's policies on Macedonia's future. This opposition did not represent organized resistance to the KPJ or Yugoslavia. Its members had been active in the push for national liberation, and many played leading roles; most of the leaders belonged to the party. What united them and distinguished them from other party members was their open and unconditional devotion to Macedonian liberation and unification. For them, this was the prime wartime aim; the overly cautions and tentative Yugoslav moves disappointed them, and the very circumscribed autonomy for the republics in the federation troubled them.

The guiding spirit of nationalists in the wartime liberation movement was Metodija Andonov-Čento (1902–1957), introduced above. As we saw, in the 1930s he was a well-to-do merchant and a popular Macedonian activist in his native Prilep. He did not belong to either the illegal organized right, the Mihailovist VMRO, or the left, the VMRO (ob.) and the KPJ. He was perhaps a bourgeois nationalist. Since organized political activity in interwar Vardar Macedonia was illegal, he acted independently as the unelected representative of the Macedonians in the Prilep region. In the late 1930s, Serbian authorities arrested and incarcerated him twice; in 1941 and again in 1942, the Bulgarian occupiers did the same.

Sure that the Communist-led movement—AVNOJ and NOB—was

fighting for a free Macedonia in a federal Yugoslavia, on 1 October 1943 Andonov-Čento crossed into the liberated territory in western Macedonia. The movement's top leaders immediately made him a member of the supreme headquarters of NOV i POM. He was the most charismatic figure in the drive for national liberation—the best known, most trusted, and popular even among the still relatively few party members. The historic first session of ASNOM, on 2 August 1944, elected him president of its presidium—in effect, first head of government for the new Macedonian state. The second session, on 29–30 December 1944 in Skopje, re-elected him.

In 1945, Andonov-Čento joined the federal parliament in Belgrade and the republican in Skopje, where he continued to call for Macedonian unification and greater autonomy for the republics. In mid-April 1945, Koliševski, leader of the KPM, became head of the Macedonian government, and Andonov-Čento, powerless president of the ineffective national assembly *(narodno sobranie)*. In 1946, he had to resign all his positions. On 13 July 1946, he returned to his native Prilep, where he made it known that he planned to plead for a united Macedonia at the United Nations and at the Paris Peace Conference.

In November 1946, authorities arrested him on charges of having been a member of Mihailov's VMRO and of "working for a 'completely independent Macedonia.'"[14] A staged trial sentenced him to 11 years of hard labor. Andonov-Čento left prison in September 1955, ill and broken, a shadow of the vigorous and charismatic leader. He died in July 1957. The democratically elected government of the independent republic of Macedonia "rehabilitated" him in 1991.[15]

Andonov-Čento was not alone—other leaders in the drive for liberation felt the same way. They included the elderly Dimitar Vlahov, founder of the VMRO (ob.) and Macedonia's representative in the presidium of the AVNOJ, and his son Gustav; General Mihailo Apostolski, a former major of the Royal Yugoslav Army and chief of supreme headquarters of NOV i POM; Cvetko Uzunovski, political commissar of supreme headquarters; Venko Markovski, the poet and wartime party propagandist; and the young Kiro Gligorov, later independent Macedonia's first democratically elected president (1991–99). Others of that view included Blagoja Fotev, Panko Brašnarov, Kiril Petrušev, Petre Piruze, Emanuel Čučkov, and Lazar Sokolov.

After Andonov-Čento's incarceration in November 1946, the regime in Skopje demoted and marginalized some of these figures; it sent others out of Macedonia, to serve the KPJ and the Yugoslav regime in Belgrade or elsewhere. Koliševski launched a thorough purge of real or alleged Čentovites (*Čentovci*) from the party and government apparatus.

Another purge of proponents of unification took place after expulsion of Yugoslavia from the Cominform in June 1948. The victims belonged to the party; many were former members or sympathizers of the prewar VMRO (ob.), who still believed or allegedly believed in the old Comintern policy of a united Macedonia in a Balkan Communist federation. In 1948, Stalin and the Communist Party of the Soviet Union revived this policy, which appealed to Macedonian leftists, as an instrument in the Cominform campaign against Yugoslavia. The KPJ accused such proponents not of Macedonian nationalism or "Great" Macedonianism, of which sentiments many people would have approved, but rather of Bulgarianism, Cominformism, and Stalinism (i.e., anti-Yugoslavism). They lost their positions and many went to prison; Panko Brašnarov, Petre Piruze, Venko Markovski, and others ended up in Yugoslavia's Gulag—the camps on Goli Otok, a barren island in the Adriatic.[16]

Andonov-Čento's imprisonment and the purge of so-called Macedonian nationalists warned Macedonians, most of whom wanted national unity, that any settlement could emerge only within federal Yugoslavia and on the KPJ's terms. By December 1948, when the first congress of the Macedonian Communists convened, Koliševski's party, the new KPM, which had silenced or liquidated all independent voices and expanded more than fourfold with new recruits—loyalists of the KPJ and Yugoslavia—had already adopted the KPJ's terms. Koliševski's KPM accepted and remained loyal to the Leninist principle of "democratic centralism," always aware that the real center was Belgrade. This did not necessarily mean that the KPM abandoned Macedonians elsewhere.

However, Skopje turned over the initiative on the Macedonian question to the KPJ's leaders. The KPJ would continue to safeguard primarily its own interests and those of its regime in Belgrade, not the rights of the Macedonian minorities in the neighboring Balkan states. Koliševski's new KPM accepted this reversal of priorities and subordinated itself to the KPJ and Belgrade.

Yugoslav Communism (1948–1991)

The historic Soviet-Yugoslav dispute and split shook up the Communist bloc and international relations in a cold war world. Yugoslavia, seeking to become more Stalinist than the Soviet Union, suddenly found itself in dangerous political and economic isolation. Survival of the country and the regime dictated complete reorientation of foreign and domestic policies.

Facing ostracism by the Soviet-dominated Communist bloc, Yugoslavia turned toward the West. In February 1953 in Ankara, Yugoslavia signed a treaty of friendship and cooperation with Greece and Turkey, two members of the North Atlantic Treaty Organization (NATO). A few months later, a military agreement concluded in Bled, Slovenia, supplemented the treaty. By the early 1960s, Yugoslavia defined itself as a nonaligned country, and Tito claimed leadership of the bloc of like-minded countries. Nonalignment supposedly meant neutrality in the cold war, but Communist Yugoslavia more often than not enjoyed better ties with the West, its major trading partner and the source of its economic aid and financial credits, than with the Soviet bloc.

By the early 1950s Tito's regime had discarded the Stalinist model for building socialism. The KPJ began to seek and to define a separate, independent road to socialism, which became "Tito's Way," or the Yugoslav model. Throughout this forty-year experiment, Yugoslav Communists tried to preserve one-party dictatorial rule and their own hegemony. Otherwise, they showed remarkable flexibility, changing the system and experimenting with new ideas and approaches, but always within a one-party state. Generally speaking, they intended the frequent changes to reconcile the political and economic interests of the six republics and two autonomous provinces and hence the federation's nations and nationalities. The survival of country, regime, Yugoslavism, and Titoism, or Yugoslav Communism, depended on that strategy.

Titoist Yugoslavia, as it emerged and evolved after 1948, remained a single-party Communist dictatorship. However, for its citizens, especially from the 1960s through the 1980s, it was a much more liberal, tolerant, and open society than the Communist dictatorships in the "Bloc countries." However, it did not, and perhaps could not, reconcile all of its groups' conflicting interests.

The collapse of so many Communist regimes in 1989–91 doomed the Titoist variant as well. And the latter's fall in turn doomed the federation, which had always linked Yugoslavism inexorably with Yugoslav Communism. The resulting ideological and political vacuum created openings for traditional nation-states to search for territorial aggrandizement under the guise of national unity. The federation of *bratstvo i edinstvo* (brotherhood and unity) disintegrated in a quagmire of bloody, fratricidal conflicts.

The first major systemic reforms came after the tumultuous events of 1948. The constitution of 13 January 1953 differed radically from the 1946 constitution and its Soviet original. These reforms inaugurated decentralization or de-étatization and controlled liberalization within a one-party state, which continued until 1990. The most original and significant reform established workers' self-management as the basis of Yugoslav Communism. The means of production, which the state owned, became "social property." Workers would manage their social properties through elected workers councils. Such economic decentralization went hand in hand with political decentralization: enhancing the autonomy of municipal and district administrations and, indirectly, of the six republics and two autonomous provinces.

The constitution of 1953 also altered state institutions. The federal assembly *(savezna skupština)* now had a federal chamber and a producers chamber. The federal house absorbed the former chamber of nationalities and consisted of appointed deputies from republics and provinces and elected representatives from single-member territorial ridings. Workers councils selected members of the other chamber. The federal assembly chose the federal executive council *(savezno izvršno veće),* which was to include representatives of all republics and provinces. The head of state was to be the president; Tito became the first and only incumbent: the federation abolished the post after his death in 1980.

The introduction of workers' self-management accompanied political changes. At its sixth congress, in Zagreb in November 1952, the party became the League of Communists of Yugoslavia (Savez Kommunista Jugoslavije, or SKJ). A year later, the People's Front became the Socialist Alliance of Working People of Yugoslavia (SSRNJ). The republican and provincial counterparts followed suit. SSRNJ was larger than the SKJ. In addition to the SKJ, which controlled it, the former included affiliated organizations such as trade unions; youth, student, and women's organizations; and the veterans' association. The SKJ retained its monopoly of political power and remained the leading political force. However, unlike the KPJ, it sought to rule through its control of SSRNJ and its affiliated organizations and workers councils rather than directly by force or administrative fiat.

Reforms, limited economic and political decentralization, and controlled liberalization of everyday life distinguished Titoist Yugoslavia from the Stalinist system elsewhere in central and eastern Europe. It also brought more relaxed political stability and impressive economic growth. From 1952 to 1957, the Yugoslav economy grew at an average annual rate of 8.5 percent, the industrial sector at 12.6 percent, and the agricultural at 5.9 percent. As Singleton has pointed out: "The sustained growth and industrial output during the 1950s was faster than that achieved during the same period by any other country in the world."[17]

However, the economy, especially industry, grew not by increases in productivity and greater efficiency. Rather, artificial measures protected domestic industries against foreign competition at the expense of agriculture and consumers. This policy could not last forever, and the crisis came in 1961. The rate of growth dropped by half, imports rose dramatically, and exports stagnated. Like the shock of 1948, this economic crisis sparked another heated debate involving federal, republican, and provincial elites. At the start, it focused on economic questions, but a one-party, centralized state cannot change the economy in isolation from the political and social system and life of the country. The debate lasted until the purge of liberal reformers in 1972, after the crackdown and suppression of the Croatian Spring of 1970.

Already in the very early 1960s, it was becoming obvious to liberal and reform-minded elements in the ruling elite that, for economic reasons, controlled decentralization and liberalization would have to continue. They worried only about the extent and character of both processes. Theoretically, there were two major routes: through democratic reform or through decentralization.

Democratization would have required the SKJ to give up its monopoly of power and introduce a multi-party system and a free market economy. This option received no serious attention. It was not acceptable to the ruling elite, including liberal decentralizers, who, like the leaders of the Prague Spring in 1968, sought to reform the system, not to destroy it.

Decentralization, in contrast, would have devolved power to the republics and provinces, which pretty much coincided with rival national divisions. Party and state would have switched some responsibilities to the republican and provincial party organizations and administrations. This process would have safeguarded the Communist monopoly of power, but in a more liberal atmosphere, and attracted younger, reform-minded, liberal decentralizers.

Conservative centralizers, however, believed in old-style party rule, control, and discipline from Belgrade. They felt that political relaxation and economic decentralization had already gone too far; further change would threaten the unity of country and party. They blamed economic problems on the "reforms" and sought return to a centralized, centrally planned economy.[18]

The liberal decentralizers scored significant successes in the 1960s. The new constitution of 1963 allowed for further economic and political decentralization and liberalization. It changed the country's name to the Socialist Federal Republic of Yugoslavia. It reorganized the legislative branch and chambers, and the republics and provinces followed suit. More important, it made self-management the cornerstone of the socialist society. Self-management was to extend to everyone in social, cultural, and other activities. "Workers' self-management was to become social self-management."[19]

The 1963 constitution called for further separation of party and state and greater respect for law. It pretended to be a step on the road to the state's eventual withering away; it actually weakened federal structures, but not republican. This devolution continued with the constitutional amendments of 1967, 1968, and 1971. In 1974, all these changes informed a new constitution.

Like the constitution of 1963, the party's eighth congress in December 1964 distanced itself from "unitarism"—Serbian hegemony and centralism—and supported greater authority for the republics and provinces. In line with this statement, the congress decided that republican and provincial party congresses should precede the federal; delegates to the latter would attend as representatives of the former, with full republican programs. This change shifted power from the SKJ to the republican and provincial parties.

The liberal decentralizers experienced their greatest victory in July 1966 with the fall of Alexsandar Ranković, one of Tito's closest and most trusted aides and wartime head of the Department for the Protection of the People, or OZNa. After 1945, he headed the Ministry of the Interior and the new State Security Administration, or UDBa. In 1963, he became as well the country's first vice president. In the debates of the 1960s, he led the old guard and the conservative centralizers. He viewed liberalization and decentralization as threats to the SKJ, the system, and the country. Accusations of gross abuse of power hit Ranković and the SDB (Service for State Security—the UDBa's name from 1964 on), and on 1 July 1966 he lost all his posts and his places in the federal assembly and the SKJ.[20]

His fall led to a purge of his supporters and reorganization of the SDB and the party. The SKJ's ninth congress in 1969 revised its statutes and, by adopting the "ethnic key" principle, transformed its chief committees into confederate bodies. "The members of the Executive Bureau and the collective presidency which replaced the old Central Committee saw themselves as representatives of the interests of their home areas, where their real power bases lay . . . the real focus of activity was in the economic and governmental organization within the republics."[21]

In 1971, Yugoslavia set up a similar collective presidency, with three representatives elected by each republican assembly and two by each provincial assembly. Each year, in rotation, the presidency chose one of its members as president of the federal presidency. Tito was to remain president of the republic for life, but this new organ gradually took over some of his responsibilities. Finally, during the Croatian Spring in April 1970, the SKJ recognized the sovereignty of the republics and provinces in all affairs "not specifically reserved for the federal constitution."[22]

The radical political and economic changes went hand in hand with controlled liberalization of life in general. By the late 1960s, Yugoslav citizens saw their country as substantially freer than the other Communist states in eastern and central Europe—the "Bloc countries." Nonetheless Yugoslavia remained a one-party, authoritarian state, and the SKJ held on to power as fiercely as the Communist parties in the Soviet satellites did. The liberalization in Yugoslavia ended with Tito's suppression of the Croatian Spring in 1971.

His crackdown in Zagreb dissolved the liberal coalition of younger, reforming Croatian, Slovenian, and Macedonian Communists, which was splintering before 1970. Next came dismissal of liberal Communist republican leaders in Croatia, Serbia, Slovenia, and Macedonia and in Vojvodina province. Older, more conservative party stalwarts replaced most of them.

The purge of the reformers terminated liberalization but not decentralization. The latter had acquired a distinctly ethnic-national character, had aligned itself with republican and provincial interests, and had become irreversible and unstoppable. Devolution of power continued with the blessing of the SKJ's top leaders as long as disciplined, conservative party cadres controlled the republican and provincial governments. Before Tito's death in 1980, the republics were becoming "the real loci of power and thus the indispensable power base for the newer generation of politicians."[23] Decentralization and devolution, in line with constitutional reforms in the late 1960s and early 1970s, crystallized in the 1974 constitution.

The 1974 document was complex and lengthy, with 406 articles. It gave the two provinces the same rights as the republics. All eight received sovereignty in internal affairs. The nine-person collective federal presidency, with representatives from all republics and provinces, was to replace Tito, with each member in turn acting as president. Provincial representatives to the collective presidency received the same right of veto as their republican counterparts.

The constitution of 1974 established indirect elections by occupational and interest groups, which chose delegations to the three chambers of the assemblies of every commune, province, and republic. The republican and provincial assemblies in turn named deputies to the new, bicameral federal parliament.

The smaller, more powerful Chamber of Republics and Autonomous Provinces had 88 members—12 from each republic and 8 from each province. It considered all legislative measures affecting republican and provincial interests. No measure could go into effect without agreement of all eight sets of delegates. Each set had to vote in accordance with the instructions of its electors—the republican or provincial assembly. The larger, but less important federal chamber consisted of regional delegations. Each republic sent 30 deputies, and each province 20, for a total of 220. Although its deliberations were less significant and its decisions required majority votes, its members responded to the interests and directions of the home republic or province.

Hence no significant federal legislative proposal could become law without the approval of all republics and provinces, and so each republic and province could veto important legislation. While remaining a single state and economy, Yugoslavia in effect no longer had a central or federal government. Rather, it was a confederation of eight republican and provincial one-party regimes, most of which would increasingly define and embrace their own interests.[24]

Yugoslavia's political tranquillity in the 1970s derived largely from its prosperity. As long as this situation continued, parties and governments could reconcile their differences. Whenever it was necessary and as a last resort, Edvard Kardelj, architect of Yugoslavia's constitutions and Tito's oldest and most trusted confidant, or Tito himself would intervene and resolve the quarrel.

The death of Kardelj in 1979 and especially that of Tito in May 1980 symbolized the passing of this "golden age"[25] of Titoist Yugoslavia. The years of prosperity ended in the early 1980s as a result of internal economic factors and the worldwide oil crisis of the 1970s. The period of easy borrowing abroad and reckless spending at home was over. Difficult economic challenges emerged: a shrinking economy, rising unemployment, uncontrolled inflation, and a deteriorating standard of living. An extreme manifestation of growing discontent was the prolonged and violent uprising by the Albanian majority in the province of Kosovo.

Because of traditional political, socioeconomic, and cultural differences among republics and provinces, their problems, especially in the economic sphere, were not the same, and neither were the solutions. They could not easily reconcile their differences, and the central leadership was too weak to establish a consensus or to impose common solutions. From the debates of the early 1980s, two alternative solutions evolved within the ruling elites. One, which Serbia championed, called for recentralization of party and state. After 1986, Slobodan Milošević, Serbia's new, young, ruthless, ambitious, and unpredictable leader, seemed its chief spokesman. The other stance advocated the status quo or further decentralization. Slovenia was its foremost proponent, and after 1986 Milan Kučan, its new, young, liberal party leader, was the major defender.

In late 1988, Milošević began his drive to dismantle the constitution of 1974 and rebuild Yugoslavia according to his vision and under Serbian direction. He mobilized Serbian nationalism, reduced the autonomy of Vojvodina and Kosovo, and brought them under Serbian control. Using similar tactics, he forced out the leadership in Titograd, replaced it with his loyalists, and seized the whip hand in Montenegro. These coups gained Milošević control of four of the eight votes in the federal presidency.

Milošević's unilateral and unitarist approach crippled the SKJ and Titoist Yugoslavia and destroyed any possibility of compromise and a negotiated solution to the crisis. His tactics, his mobilization of militant Serbian nationalism, and his vision of a recentralized, Serbian-dominated Yugoslavia frightened the ruling elites and people in the remaining four republics. Even though Bosnia-Herzegovina, Croatia, Macedonia, and Slovenia had not agreed on a common alternative, they all strongly opposed recentralization, which they equated with Serbian hegemony. The Yugoslav drama had reached deadlock; as Sabrina Ramet observed, "The system had dead-ended."[26]

This hopeless polarization dominated the SKJ's fourteenth extraordinary congress in Belgrade in January 1990. The Slovenes proposed the framework for an even looser confederation, while Milošević, as everyone expected, called for something tighter and more centralized. Since neither proposal could win a majority, the Slovenes left. Milošević now controlled four votes, but the three remaining republics refused to continue without Slovenia. The Croatians walked out next, and their counterparts from Bosnia-Herzegovina and Macedonia followed them.

Two weeks later, the Slovenian party formally left the SKJ and reinvented and renamed itself as the Party of Democratic Renewal. So ended, unceremoniously, Yugoslav Communism as an organized political party. The SKJ, the party of Tito, did not dissolve itself formally, and others did not terminate it: it just ceased to exist.[27]

The SKJ's effective collapse also marked the end of federal Yugoslavia. The party founded this state and gave it legitimacy and its legitimizing doctrine. Yugoslav Communism, or Titoism, was not just any ideology; it was the state ideology. Yugoslav Communism, or Titoism, and Yugoslavism were inseparable. They were one and the same; there was no other Yugoslav state idea or ideology. The federation survived for another year and a half, but only in name and as a ticking bomb.

In the second half of the 1980s, other, non-Communist approaches to the Yugoslav crisis were emerging. As in all other Communist states in central and eastern Europe, even in the more liberal Yugoslavia there was growing disillusionment with Communism and one-party rule. Yugoslav intellectuals in Belgrade and the republican and provincial capitals began to challenge the SKJ's monopoly of power. They started by debating reform and evolved into a political opposition working for transformation or even destruction of the system. They paved the way for, and some led in, formation of alternative parties in the late 1980s.[28]

Moreover, the international situation was rapidly changing. The ascendancy of Mikhail Gorbachev in the Soviet Union and his policies of *glasnost* and *perestroika* signaled the beginning of the end for the cold war and for Communism in central and eastern Europe. In this new world, security considerations that helped maintain unity among Yugoslavia's constituent nations rapidly dissipated. The Macedonians feared their neighbors to the east and south, but the Croats, Serbs, and Slovenes faced no external threats.

Even more important, the Croats and the Slovenes no longer deemed Yugoslavia necessary, let alone indispensable for their security and survival. The growing anti-Communist opposition in these two republics was not necessarily calling for destruction of Yugoslavia. Yet it was obvious that these republics would not remain in Yugoslavia on unfavorable terms. By the late 1980s, critics were seriously contemplating secession, independent statehood, and eventual membership in the European Community, which seemed a successful federation of free peoples and states.

In 1990, the first multi-party elections took place in the six republics. In Bosnia-Herzegovina, Croatia, Macedonia, and Slovenia, the opposition to the Communists scored victories. These results showed clearly that Milošević, the Serbian strongman, who earlier failed when he sought to restructure Yugoslavia on his own terms, could never convince or force the new governments.

However, Milošević saw only two choices: a centralized, unitary, Serbian-dominated Yugoslavia or a Greater Serbia, uniting all the Serbs or all the Yugoslav lands that the Serbs claimed as Serbian. His dogmatic insistence on the first doomed Yugoslavia; his equally fanatical determination to create a Greater Serbia in its place devastated all the peoples of Yugoslavia, including the Serbs. He could establish a Greater Serbia only at the expense and against the will of Bosnia-Herzegovina, Croatia, Montenegro, possibly Macedonia, and the Albanians in Kosovo—and only by war. Milošević's pursuit of a Greater Serbia destroyed any possibility for a negotiated and peaceful dissolution of Yugoslavia. It made unavoidable its bloody disintegration and the Balkan wars of the 1990s.[29]

Macedonia: A Junior Partner (1943–1991)

Macedonia was legally an equal partner in the Yugoslav federation but in fact a junior partner. At no point did it have an equal say with Croatia, Serbia, and Slovenia, the "big three" of Yugoslav politics and economics, in determining internal or external policies. The respective leaders of all three lacked knowledge about and even interest in Macedonia's complex national development, and they, particularly the Serbs, who had claimed the Macedonians as their own, were distinctly patronizing toward them, as we see in this section.

Only during the heated debates on restructuring in the late 1960s and early 1970s did Macedonia, as a partner of Croatia and Slovenia in the short-lived liberal coalition, play a significant role in the highest organs of the party and state. But even then it felt awkward as a partner of Croatia and Slovenia. On the one hand, it fully shared their fears of Serbian hegemony and supported political decentralization. On the other hand, its economic backwardness and need for financial aid pushed it to preserve a centralized, regulated Yugoslav economy. On economic policies, the Macedonian leadership seemed closer to the centralizers of the economically less advanced republics, Bosnia-Herzegovina, Montenegro, and Serbia.

After suppression of the Croatian Spring in 1971 and the purge of liberal reformers throughout Yugoslavia, in 1974 Krste Crvenskovski (1921–2001), the relatively young Macedonian party leader, and his liberal, reform-minded advisers, Slavko Milosavlevski, Milan Nedkov, Tomislav Čokrevski, Dimitar Mirčev, and Čamuran Tachir, were thrown out of power. From then until multi-party elections in 1990, the League of Communists of Macedonia (SKM) was under the colorless, conservative disciples and followers of Lazar Koliševski: Angel Čemerski (1974–82), Krste Markovski (1982–86), and Jakov Lazarovski (1986–89). They reverted to Macedonia's more traditional and passive role in the federation. Similarly, Macedonia did not play a significant part in the federation's bloody breakup.[30]

Macedonia was small and economically backward and proved very vulnerable within the federation and the Balkans, but, as we see in this section, lack of leadership weakened its position even further. I end this section with a discussion of two major failures of leadership.

The republic was small in size and population and economically backward and underdeveloped. Although it had made great economic advances during the Communist period, the gap with Slovenia, the most advanced republic, widened, and it remained one of the more underdeveloped regions until the federation collapsed.

Macedonia was also, at least after the Soviet-Yugoslav split in 1948, the most vulnerable and insecure region of Yugoslavia and perhaps of the entire southern Balkans. Political and ideological opponents of Yugoslavia—Greece, Bulgaria, and Albania—surrounded it. Bulgaria and

Greece were also national opponents of the Macedonians, refusing to recognize their national identity. They, as well as Albania, had claimed part or all of the republic, and many observers thought that they still harbored such ambitions. The external threats and dangers made the Macedonians less secure nationally and, hence, more dependent on the Yugoslav federation for national survival.

More important, however, the Macedonians usually lacked strong, experienced, well-connected national leaders who could have raised a powerful voice in party and state. They did not have a single such leader on the Communist left even at the end of the war, no Kardelj, Djilas, Pijade, Ranković, Kidrić, Bakarić, or Vukmanović-Tempo, all close and trusted lieutenants of Tito's. There was no Macedonian in Tito's inner circle.

The Communist Party soon sidelined two men—Andonov-Čento and Dimitar Vlahov—who might have galvanized the republic; in contrast, longtime leader Lazar Koliševski was completely unprepossessing, as we see below. Metodija Andonov-Čento (1902–1957), as we saw above, was the most popular, able, energetic, experienced, and charismatic Macedonian leader in 1945. He rose to senior positions during the drive for national liberation, but he was not a party member, was too independent, possessed his own strong views on the Macedonian issue, and never achieved full acceptance by and the trust of the rulers of Communist Yugoslavia. His fall from grace, even more rapid than his rise, and his tragic end created a vacuum at the top in Macedonia that remained throughout the Communist era.[31]

Also prominent during and after the war was Dimitar Vlahov (1878–1953). Born in Kilkis (Kukuš) in what would become Aegean, or Greek Macedonia, he studied in Bulgaria and attended university in Switzerland. He became a professor in a Bulgarian lyceum, an activist in the original VMRO, a member of the Ottoman parliament, a Bulgarian diplomat, and a founder and leader of the VMRO (ob.). Between the world wars, he had close links with the BKP, worked for the Comintern, and lived in Moscow. He wanted above all to see the liberation and unification of Macedonia.

Early in the Second World War, Vlahov moved or was sent from Moscow to Yugoslavia, where he served as vice president of the first session of AVNOJ. Throughout the war, he remained at AVNOJ headquarters as a nominal and powerless Macedonian representative. His experience had not prepared him for a high role in Communist Yugoslavia and kept him out of Tito's inner circle. Moreover, he was much older than its members; communicated with greater ease in Bulgarian, French, and Russian than in any of the Yugoslav languages, including Macedonian; and was unknown and had no political base in Yugoslavia, not even in Macedonia. He became dependent on the KPJ, was useful to it, and represented no threat to its interests. As a result, he survived as a token Macedonian representative in Belgrade, holding high-sounding but powerless posts virtually until his death in 1953.[32]

The KPJ in 1943 chose one of its own, Lazar Koliševski (1914–2000), a loyal and devoted member, to execute its orders and consolidate its position in Macedonia. Unlike other Macedonian leaders who joined or supported the KPJ or one of the other Balkan Communist parties primarily because of national considerations, Koliševski, who spent his formative years in Kragujevac, Serbia, was not active in Macedonian national or revolutionary organizations. He showed virtually no interest in Macedonia before the summer of 1941, when the KPJ sent him to Skopje to rid the regional party of Šatorov-Šarlo and his followers.

Thus began his rise to power, with the aid of Serbian KPJ leaders who knew him well. In September 1941, he succeeded Šatorov-Šarlo as head of the regional KPJ organization in Macedonia. Shortly after the Bulgarian occupation, authorities arrested him, and he spent time in a Bulgarian prison but nonetheless in 1943 became first leader of the new Communist Party of Macedonia (KPM). After the liberation of Bulgaria in September 1944, he returned to Skopje and, with KPJ backing, consolidated his control over party and state.

Although Koliševski long dominated Macedonian politics, there is little scholarly writing about him even in Macedonia. His lengthy so-called memoirs convey the impression that perhaps there is not very much that one could or would need to say about him. He was born into a poor family in Macedonia and became a metalworker in industrial and proletarian Kragujevac in Serbia, where he came under Communist influence and at twenty-one joined the local party in 1935. He had had only an elementary education, and his ideas, including his views on Macedonia, reflected the teachings of the KPJ.

He did not lack for Macedonian patriotism but saw it as inseparable from Yugoslav Communism. The KPJ was, he thought, infallible, and in that spirit he accepted its changing line on Macedonia. He was first and foremost a loyal and obedient instrument of the KPJ/SKJ. He received rich rewards for his loyalty: the immense material benefits that came with his political positions, the exercise of personal political power in Macedonia, and the right to mingle and rub shoulders with the real wielders of power in Yugoslavia.[33] All in all, Koliševski appears to have been a reliable executor of the policies of the KPJ/SKJ and Belgrade in Macedonia and on its future.

Krste Crvenkovski, a young, dynamic, reforming liberal, succeeded him as party leader in 1964. Three of Koliševski's conservative, colorless protégés followed him: Angel Čemerski (1974–82), Krste Markovski (1982–86), and Jakov Lazarovski (1986–89).

Skopje's lack of authority in the federation is clearest in connection with two crucial issues—Macedonians' rights in Bulgaria and Greece and creation of a Macedonian Orthodox church.

First, denial of all national rights to the Macedonian minorities in Bulgaria and Greece could trouble Yugoslavia's relations with the two neighbors. As we saw above, during the Second World War and its revolutionary aftermath, the Communist leadership in Yugoslavia became the most vocal champion of Macedonian unification within Yugoslavia and of the national rights of Macedonians elsewhere.

After Yugoslavia's break with the Soviet Union and reorientation of its foreign policy toward the West, which included a treaty of friendship and cooperation with Greece, Yugoslavia abandoned the Macedonian minorities. Belgrade withdrew from any public airing of the issue in or outside Yugoslavia. This official silence was acceptable to Koliševski and his colleagues in Skopje, and they enforced it in Macedonia. To Macedonians, especially nationally minded intellectuals and the many Aegean Macedonian refugees in the republic, it looked like total Yugoslav indifference and as if the Serbs in particular sought to expand economic ties with Greece and Bulgaria rather than defend Macedonians' rights there. Even more troubling, their own leaders did not do anything to influence Belgrade. The official silence halted during Krste Crvenkovki's tenure in Skopje but resumed afterward.[34]

However, by the 1980s official silence proved unenforceable. In 1981, Greece entered the European Community, and Macedonians in Greece, with the aid of international and European human rights organizations, began to insist on their national rights. Their counterparts in Bulgaria followed suit after Communist rule ended in that country.[35]

The other issue concerned establishment of the Macedonian Orthodox church (Makedonska Pravoslavna Crkva, or MPC). International recognition of the MPC was and still is a complex matter involving the patriarchate of Constantinople and the other national Orthodox churches in Europe. However, in the Yugoslav federation its status was an internal matter that affected the Serbian Orthodox church (SPC). Although the Communist leaders in Macedonia were declared atheists, they realized that religion and the church were central to national formation and key elements of each nation in the Balkans. Hence they fought hard for an independent Macedonian Orthodox church.

Attempts to reestablish the historic Ohrid archbishopric as a Macedonian Orthodox church had occurred in the nineteenth century. They failed because of opposition by national orthodox churches in Bulgaria, Greece, and Serbia, which controlled the Macedonian dioceses and whose states were fighting for Macedonia. After partition in 1912–13, each of the three national churches seized control of the dioceses in the respective part of the land. In Vardar Macedonia, the Serbian Orthodox church (SPC) took over churches and monasteries and all their wealth, most of which belonged earlier to the Bulgarian exarchate, and began to direct the religious lives of the Macedonian Orthodox.

During the Second World War, creation of an independent, or autocephalous Macedonian Orthodox church became part of the struggle for national liberation. In October 1943, Macedonian clerics met in liberated western Macedonia and demanded its establishment. The political leadership responded by placing a Macedonian, the Reverend Veljo Mančevski, in charge of religious affairs in the liberated areas. After the liberation, in March 1945, the first national convention of the Macedonian clergy petitioned the Serbian patriarch to grant independence to the church in Macedonia, but the SPC's Holy Synod rejected the petition. The church in Macedonia enjoyed and exercised some autonomy, but it remained an integral part of the SPC.

Calls for independence surfaced again in 1951 from the Association of Macedonian Clergy and in 1955 at the congress of the Orthodox Priests Federation of Yugoslavia. The SPC's hierarchy in 1957 accepted a compromise, which included use of Macedonian in administration and preaching and of Old Church Slavonic for the liturgy; appointment of native Macedonians as officials and bishops in Macedonia; and creation of church seals with "People's Republic of Macedonia" and the name of the diocese in Macedonian around the church coat of arms. The compromise never went fully into effect: in 1958, SPC leaders insisted on appointing Serbian bishops for the Macedonian dioceses.

In the same year, and no doubt with Skopje's approval, a Macedonian National Convention of Clergy and Laymen met 4–6 October in Ohrid and reestablished the historic archbishopric of Ohrid as the autonomous Macedonian Orthodox church (MPC). It elected as its head Bishop Dositej, a Macedonian and the vicar general of Patriarch Vikentije, who had died on 5 July. Dositej became archbishop of Ohrid and Skopje and metropolitan of Macedonia. The convention also decided that the Macedonian church would "remain in canonic unity" with the SPC; the Serbian patriarch would be patriarch of both churches.

The new Serbian patriarch and the Serbian hierarchy did not approve this fait accompli but had to accept it. However, they obstructed the Macedonian church whenever and however they could. They refused to introduce it to other autocephalous Orthodox churches; the patriarch did not call himself "patriarch of Serbia and Macedonia" but continued to refer to "South Serbia" and "Serbian brothers and sisters."

In the 1960s, growing discontent over continuing SPC control became part of the SKJ's bitter conflict between liberal decentralizers and conservative centralizers. The rise to power in Macedonia of young, national-minded, liberal decentralizers under Krste Crvenkoski (party leader, 1964–74) and the fall from power in June 1966 of A. Ranković—chief of the secret police, leader of the conservative centralizers, and patron of Serbian nationalism—emboldened the MPC's hierarchy to prepare for complete autocephaly. In May 1966, the SPC prohibited the Macedonian National Church Convention from changing the MPC's constitution without the approval of the SPC's Holy Synod.

Obviously, the MPC would have preferred a negotiated, amicable separation and twice in late 1966 formally asked the SPC to recognize the MPC's autocephaly. However, the Holy Synod rejected both requests, and the Macedonian National Church Convention met in Ohrid on 17–19 July 1967 and unilaterally declared the church autocephalous. It elected Dositej archbishop of Ohrid and Macedonia and its first head *(poglavar)*. The MPC's declaration of independence terminated another obvious remnant of Serbian hegemony in Macedonia. Even the republic's Communist rulers understood and celebrated it as such.

In view of the running dispute with Bulgaria and Greece over Macedonians' ethnicity, SPC recognition of the MPC was crucial to Macedonians nationally and to Yugoslavia politically. However, Macedonian leaders, from the pro-Serbian Koliševski, through the nationally minded Crvenkovski, to his pro-Belgrade successors, failed to secure that official acknowledgment. They could not convince the SPC directly or through the highest authorities to accept the latest fait accompli.

The Serbian patriarchate rejected reason and to the present day considers Macedonia "South Serbia" and its inhabitants "Serbian brothers and sisters." By the same token, Serbian leaders, Communist and post-Communist, have chosen to heed the SPC's irrational views over the MPC's legitimate demands. In any event, achieving recognition for the MPC was one of many burdens that the small, independent Macedonian state took on after the collapse of federal Yugoslavia.[36]

This section's emphasis on Macedonia's position as a junior partner does not imply that the republic remained stagnant, did not progress, or derived no benefits from its membership in the federation. In fact, as we see in the next chapter, Macedonians entered the modern world in the Yugoslav republic. They went through a virtual social and economic transformation; most important, their impressive cultural development consolidated their long, difficult national formation and integration.

13 Economics, Culture, Minorities (1944–1991)

Creation of the republic of Macedonia in the Communist Yugoslav federation in 1944 was a defining event in Macedonians' modern political history. It also launched a shift in their social and economic development, from an underdeveloped agrarian to a more modern, semi-industrial society. It was undoubtedly also the most historic occurrence in the evolution of their culture since the Slavic renaissance in medieval Macedonia. The existence of a state facilitated the rise and development of a national culture using the standardized Macedonian literary language—the official language of the republic and one of four of Yugoslavia. The relatively free milieu allowed for completion of the nation-building process that began in the second quarter of the nineteenth century.

This chapter examines these three facets of national life in Yugoslav Macedonia: the economy, especially industry and agriculture; culture, particularly language, education, and the arts; and treatment of national minorities.

The Economy: Agriculture and Industry

During the interwar years, in the first, or royal Yugoslavia, Vardar Macedonia, or South Serbia, or the Vardar banovina (region) was probably one of the most backward and underdeveloped, and certainly the most economically neglected, region. It was predominantly a rural society. Except for Skopje, its administrative center, it had few towns with a developed urban life. The communication system was primitive or nonexistent. There were hardly any modern roads and few railway links. Most areas lacked electricity, running water, telephones, and so forth.

Agriculture dominated the economy. In 1946, after restoration of prewar economic activities, industry and mining made up 15 percent of the economy, and agriculture and animal husbandry, 58 percent. Most people depended on agriculture for their livelihood. The agrarian economy consisted principally of small, subsistence family farms. There were very few properties with either several tens of hectares of arable land or herds of several hundred sheep. The agrarian sector had a surplus of labor, primitive methods of cultivation, low productivity, and inadequate incomes.[1]

Industrialization began in Macedonia at the end of the nineteenth century, but it grew very slowly. In 1945, 140 factories could employ 8,873 workers but actually had jobs for only 3,391.[2] About half of these factories were "monopolies"—storage buildings for drying and fermenting purchased tobacco.

The new Communist regime, acting primarily in terms of ideological considerations, sought to create a modern, socialist, industry-based economy and society. According to Nikola Uzunov, the economic and social transformation between the mid-1940s and 1990 passed through six phases, which corresponded roughly to the federation's political evolution.[3]

In the first, brief phase, 1946–47, the government aimed to restore all economic activities to prewar levels. Since Macedonia had not suffered enormous physical destruction during the war, it reached the targets in most areas: for example, commerce, transportation, trades, construction, industry, and farming. But in livestock breeding, numbers had fallen badly, and restoration took longer.

During the second phase, 1947–52, the regime introduced measures to establish the new, socialized economy. It "nationalized"—that is, expropriated—the privately owned means of production, including small trades, and formed larger, state-owned commercial and industrial enterprises. In the countryside, in addition to its postwar land redistribution, it now attempted, frequently by force, to collectivize family farms into village cooperatives. However, peasants' widespread opposition and resistance seriously hindered its efforts on that front. In the early 1950s, it decided to terminate the program and even allowed forced collectives to disband.

In this phase, the government also inaugurated rapid industrialization to ameliorate extreme underdevelopment. It directed all available investment capital to the building of factories, at the expense of other economic activities, particularly agrarian. Furthermore, it did away with the free market, took control of domestic and foreign trade, and introduced detailed planning for the entire economy and state administration and direction of all enterprises.

The one-party, centralized state used all its power to implement its policies, which aimed to establish socialism in Macedonia, as in all the other republics. The results were uneven, if not disappointing. Although industry, building, and construction expanded, farming production and crafts and trades declined sharply. And the overall standard of living dropped substantially.

The third phase, 1953–64, coincided with the first major reforms of the socialist economy: introduction of worker self-management in enterprises; formation of a market for goods and services; partial decentralization of planning; and introduction of legal protection for private property in agriculture, trades, and housing, despite strict limits on the scale of such operations.

Targets in this phase were higher, and the accomplishments greater, than those in the previous two. The economic plan called for growth throughout the economy. Industry expanded through the addition of many sizeable enterprises in textiles, leather, and metalworking; greater generation of electrical power; and higher production in forestry, metallurgy, and chemical industries. A few large construction companies emerged, each with several thousand workers; and the state built a network of major highways and roads. In farming, production expanded in traditional crops—tobacco, rice, poppies, wheat, corn—in a new crop, sugar beets, and in sheep breeding.

However, productivity remained low, and the economy could hardly compete with outside suppliers. Nonetheless, overall expansion in production and economic activity, and growth in the workforce and its buying power, helped increase the standard of living.

Debates on decentralization and democratization turned the fourth phase, 1965–71, into a liberal interlude. The primary aim of the economic planners changed. They sought not further expansion of economic capacity but rather reconstruction and modernization of existing capacity, higher productivity from labor, more-efficient production in all sectors, and greater specialization. Accompanying this new orientation were measures to liberalize foreign trade and give the banks greater autonomy.

The aim of all these undertakings was to make enterprises competitive with foreign firms. Some improvement undoubtedly occurred—probably as much as could have taken place under existing socialist self-management. Macedonia found it difficult to compete even with the more developed Croatia, Slovenia, and Vojvodina, let alone with Western economies. The best results came in agriculture, particularly in private family farms specializing in greens, vegetables, and fruits for the market.

During the fifth phase, in the 1970s, the government, without changing fundamentals, sought to secure economic growth through intensified investment in all sectors. It built large mining-industrial complexes, many food-processing plants, and a number of livestock farms, banks, tourist hotels and resorts, shopping centers, and so forth. The domestic economy, still developing and suffering from low productivity, could not generate enough capital for such expansion. The government had to depend on financial resources from the other, more economically developed regions, on the Federal Fund for the Accelerated Development of the Less Developed Regions, and on foreign investment. As a result, Macedonia accumulated a huge debt at a time of rising interest rates and of fuel costs skyrocketing because of the worldwide energy crisis.

This rise in investment went hand in hand with reforms aiming toward a "consensual economy." The goal was to deregulate the economy and to permit self-managed enterprises to negotiate business deals among themselves. In actual practice, however, party and state hindered any local initiative, and so economic efficiency did not increase. Hence, any economic growth was the result primarily of borrowing.

A general, nationwide economic crisis dominated the sixth and final phase in the 1980s. Macedonia had a huge debt, lacked new investment, and experienced stagnant production, high and rising inflation, growing unemployment, and a declining standard of living. Macedonia, like many other small, developing economies, had borrowed very heavily to modernize and now could not meet payments on the accumulated debt. The world energy crisis of the 1970s compounded its problems. The sharp increase in the price of oil virtually crippled economies such as

Macedonia's that imported all their oil. However, the long-term weaknesses and shortcomings of the existing system did even more to bring about the crisis. The system offered ineffective direction; was not very productive; wasted much of the national income on unsustainable, politically motivated endeavors; replaced tried and proven economic regulators such as supply and demand with administrative measures; and interfered constantly in economic life.[4]

We cannot know how the republic of Macedonia would have fared under a different dispensation. However, despite the system's shortcomings and uneven development, and particularly from 1947 to 1980, it made remarkable economic advances. The improvements amounted to a minor industrial revolution and turned Macedonia into a semi-developed country. The gross national product was nine times higher in 1980 than in 1947, with average annual growth an impressive 6.5 percent.

Like Yugoslavia as a whole, the republic aimed at rapid and forced industrialization. As a result, by 1990 it had transformed the very structure of its economy. While in the late 1940s farming dominated the economy, by 1990 industry was predominant. Industry and mining grew from 15 percent of the economy in 1947 to 54 percent in 1990, and agriculture declined from 58 percent to 17 percent. Industrialization, however, occurred at the expense of agriculture, especially its private sector, which suffered neglect and remained premodern. As a result, while overall economic output grew by 5.7 times between 1953 and 1990, and industry and mining by 21.1 times, agriculture increased by only 2.5 times.[5]

At war's end, the rural economy had consisted largely of small, private family farms. Agriculturalists worked the land in traditional ways, and yields were very low. Basically villagers engaged in subsistence farming; there were too many people working on the land and too many mouths to feed. Between 1946 and 1948, agrarian reform brought confiscation of land above 25 hectares per household and nationalization of large herds of sheep. The state distributed some of the land and livestock among the poorest peasants to help ameliorate their economic situation. The reform, however, did not necessarily increase productivity or output.

In 1948, the KPJ dramatically altered its agrarian policy. It introduced forced collectivization and establishment of rural cooperatives or collectives as large agricultural enterprises. The KPM carried out collectivization in Macedonia with particular vengeance. However, it immediately became obvious that collectivization in the republic would be a failure. The large collectives possessed no modern machinery and had to work the land in the traditional, primitive ways with hand implements and harnessed animals. More important, however, peasants rejected the new organization of labor and the new administration and distribution of output and income.

Thus, instead of improving the situation, forced collectivization created a crisis: it dislocated the farming economy and slashed productivity and overall output. In 1953, Belgrade acknowledged that the policy had been a mistake, abandoned it, allowed the co-ops to dissolve, and returned the land to its former owners. In Macedonia, only a few voluntary co-ops with small properties continued.[6]

However, Macedonia's postwar socially owned agricultural sector, which slightly antedated forced collectivization, proved much more successful and survived past 1990. Such enterprises had begun in 1946 on lands that the state confiscated. After that, they expanded through purchases from private owners, acquisition of uncultivated lands, or rehabilitation of marshlands. They became large enterprises cultivating hundreds of hectares or even several thousand and with hundreds or thousands of livestock. "In 1990 there were 147 such enterprises in Macedonia with a total of 144,000 hectares of cultivated land, 21,200 employees, 3,438 tractors, 27,500 heads of cattle, 160,000 sheep, etc."[7]

From the very beginning, the state favored these establishments. It equipped them with modern machinery and implements, professional administrators and agricultural specialists, and employees who worked on the same basis and under the same conditions as people in other sectors; these enterprises produced more than individual household farms. In time, they expanded, set up industrial plants to process their products, and became agricultural-industrial complexes. Throughout the Communist period, they helped modernize farming production in Macedonia.

Nevertheless, individual peasant households dominated Macedonian farming. They lacked up-to-date machinery and know-how, and their productivity was low, but they were responsible for the largest part of the republic's agricultural output. About 1990, they owned 70 percent of the cultivated land and 85 percent of the livestock and produced 61 percent of the agricultural output.[8]

Industrialization and the consequent decline of farming continued throughout the Yugoslav period. The great demographic changes reflected that shift. The proportion of agriculturalists was 63 percent in 1953, 57 percent in 1961, 40 percent in 1971, 22 percent in 1981, and 15 percent in 1991. Migration to the cities was one cause, but so were nonagricultural jobs. Over time, more rural inhabitants found these without having to leave the countryside. By 1980, more than half of the rural population had such positions. Further, many village households became mixed, with some members in agriculture and others working in other sectors.[9]

All in all, the Macedonian republic underwent a major economic and social transformation. It followed a zigzag pattern, and various sectors performed unevenly. However, a solid basis emerged for the further, less wasteful, and more economically rational modernization that became possible after 1990 under pluralist democracy and a free market.

Culture: Language, Education, and the Arts

The cultural situation in Vardar Macedonia up to 1941 was even drearier than the economic one. Since the Macedonians had no national recognition and it was illegal to use their language in educational and cultural institutions and in public life, their culture virtually stagnated. In interwar Yugoslav Macedonia, the official culture was that of the Serbian minority—colonists, officials, teachers, security personnel, and so on—and of some educated and assimilated Macedonians. The handful of Serbian-educated, nationally conscious Macedonian intellectuals partook of the Serbian culture but did not consider it their own and did not identify with it. Macedonian-language culture existed only in the form of the rich folk/popular culture and in illegal or semi-legal publications. Consequently, in this cultural sphere, the new Macedonian republic had virtually to start from scratch.

The growth and development of a national culture depend on many factors. A people's determination to ground it in its 'mother tongue' is indispensable. But external factors are also essential: a free and tolerant environment and supportive institutional infrastructure. In Macedonia's case, such external supports were totally absent from the start of the nineteenth-century national awakening. Ottoman authority and competing Balkan nationalisms prevented any domestic cultural initiatives up to 1912; from then until 1940, Bulgaria, Greece, and Serbia/Yugoslavia blocked such efforts.

The 1941 collapse of the old order in Greece and Yugoslavia and the rise of powerful Communist-led resistance transformed conditions in Aegean and Vardar Macedonia. In the liberated territories of Aegean Macedonia under EAM-ELAS, that group allowed use of the language, and its Macedonian organizations encouraged and directed Macedonian cultural activities.

This freedom ended after EAM-ELAS capitulated at Varkiza in February 1945 and remained nonexistent during the white terror and reaction that followed. It emerged again, more widespread and organized, in the heavily Macedonian areas that the Communist-led left controlled during the Greek Civil War (1947–1949).[10] The Communist defeat in 1949 ended Macedonians' cultural aspirations in Greece. Ever since, Athens has refused to recognize Macedonian identity, people, language, and so forth anywhere and has treated any Macedonianism in Greece as treason.

In Yugoslavia and hence in Vardar Macedonia, the victory of the Communist-led National Liberation Movement laid the groundwork for development of Macedonian national culture. As we saw above, the second session of AVNOJ (November 1943) recognized Macedonia as an equal partner in a Yugoslav federation and Macedonian as one of the state's four official languages. In Vardar Macedonia, the national liberation movement used Macedonian and made it the official language for education and cultural expression in the areas under its rule. The first session of ASNOM (2 August 1944) proclaimed Macedonian the literary and official language of the new republic.

Generations of patriots and nationalists had dreamed of a Macedonian-language national culture. However, such an aspiration was also critical for Communist leaders in both Macedonia and federal Yugoslavia. It would represent and symbolize the existence of the Macedonian ethnic national identity. And this in turn would counter and discredit the persistent Greek and, after 1948, Bulgarian negation of that identity and those countries' claims and aspirations in Macedonia.

Consequently, while the new republic, like the other partners in the federation, had limited sovereignty, its inhabitants enjoyed far more cultural freedom. As long as they did not question Titoist doctrine and Macedonia's status, they were free and could help develop a national culture. And quite quickly exactly that emerged and flourished. Its remarkable successes surprised even its most ardent champions—to say nothing of its traditional Balkan detractors.

The Macedonian government sought first to standardize and codify the language. Between late November 1944 and early May 1945, three official Commissions on the Macedonian Language and Orthography, with some overlapping membership, dealt with the issue. The basis was to be the so-called central Macedonian dialects, which were along the lines of Veles-Prilep-Bitola. These dialects were equally distinct from Bulgarian and Serbian and most free of their usages. Krste P. Misirkov had chosen them in 1903 as the ground for his proposed Macedonian literary language. Furthermore, Kočo Racin and Venko Markovski used them in their poetry and prose of the 1930s and wartime.

However, the alphabet proved divisive. Some people sought a Cyrillic alphabet with its own characteristics or peculiarities distinct from and equidistant between the Bulgarian and the Serbian (Vuk Karadžić's). Others, for practical and political reasons, advocated Karadžić's Serbian alphabet.

The first commission, which consisted of intellectuals, decided on a Macedonian alphabet on 4 December 1944. Where the presidium of ASNOM considered the proposal, it expressed satisfaction with the body's work but did not announce its decision. Instead, on 15 February 1945 it formed another commission, which added representatives of other interested parties. This second group split badly but recommended the Serbian alphabet. This situation and delays in resolving the question threatened the country's political stability, and even the central committee of the KPJ called for speedy agreement.

A third commission, again with politicians and intellectuals, adopted the Serbian Cyrillic. It submitted the proposal on 3 May 1945, and the government approved the idea the same day. Standardization was complete within a month. On 2 June, the commission recommended a Macedonian orthography, and on 7 June the government approved it. The first grammar of the newly codified Macedonian literary language and the first schoolbooks in that language soon appeared.[11]

The standardization and codification were a historic achievement, representing national affirmation and laying a solid foundation for education and growth of a national culture.

The speedy creation of a Macedonian-language educational system was essential to the new regime. Education spread national consciousness, Communist ideology, and know-how for economic modernization. Consequently, support for it remained strong in federal Macedonia.

However, the republic suffered from high rates of illiteracy, a lack of books in Macedonian, and shortages of teachers and of schools. According to one source, 75 percent of its inhabitants were illiterate in 1939.[12] Another claimed that in 1946 illiteracy among people ten years of age or older stood at 67.5 percent.[13] Since use of Macedonian had been illegal in all three partitions before the war, there were no schoolbooks, textbooks, or any other educational aids in the language, and very few literary works used it. Furthermore, there were no instructors who could teach in Macedonian. In December 1944, just after liberation, the republic had only 337 trained treachers for primary schools and 140 for high schools, and many of them were active in the liberation movement or public service. Estimates for the 1944/45 school year suggested the need for 3,000 primary and 450 high school teachers.[14] And facilities were totally inadequate. In the late 1930s, there had not been enough schools, and during the war 18 percent of primary-school buildings had become barracks for military, police, or other security forces.[15]

The first Macedonian primary schools opened for 1944/45 in the liberated territories. The network expanded rapidly, along with courses in libraries and special reading rooms for the many illiterate adults. By December 1944, nine academic high schools (gymnasia) were operating in larger towns, as well as more specialized music, fine-arts, and teacher-training schools in Skopje, the capital.

To ease the shortage of teachers, the authorities engaged young people who had at least some high school education and started intensive training in large cities, paying special attention to the teaching of Macedonian language, geography, and history. During the first half of the 1944/45 school year, some two thousand individuals completed those courses and immediately received teaching positions.[16]

After the difficult launch, the educational system continued to expand on all levels. According to one authority, Macedonia underwent a veritable educational "boom," or "explosion."[17] Illiteracy, rampant under the old Serbian regime, virtually disappeared, declining from 75 percent of the population in 1939 to 35.7 percent in 1953, 26.5 percent in 1961, 18.1 percent in 1971, and 10.9 percent in 1981. The 1994 census found only 5 percent of people illiterate, most of them seventy years of age or older and belonging to particular ethnic groups. This decline was largely the result of effective adult education, which also provided training and qualifications for work.

The school system grew dramatically in facilities and enrollment. In 1939, there were only 39 kindergartens; by 1987 there were 627, with 41,217 pupils. In 1939, 817 primary schools enrolled 100,000 pupils; in 1951, 1,591 schools had 167,000. By 1993, 261,127 children were attending primary schools. Between 1951 and 1966, the number of high schools increased from 112 to 163, and enrollment from 19,836 students to 52,697. By sometime in the 1970s, 80 percent of those who had completed primary education went on to secondary school.

Postsecondary education saw even greater growth. Before the war, Yugoslav Macedonia had no university. The Philosophical Faculty in Skopje, a branch of the University of Belgrade, reopened at the end of 1946 with Macedonian-language instruction and 199 students. The first Macedonian university, SS Cyril and Methodius in Skopje, began in 1949 with 1,092 students; by 1974, it had enrolled 37,449. In 1979, a second university opened in Bitola.

In addition to training and graduating thousands of students every year, these institutions also established postgraduate programs and awarded many master's and doctoral degrees in all academic disciplines.[18] Creation of academic infrastructure culminated on 23 February 1967 with the founding of the Macedonian Academy of Sciences and Arts (MANU) as the nation's highest institution of learning and culture.

The emergence of a Macedonian state, and its codification of the language and granting of official status to it, accelerated cultural development. For the first time in their modern history, Macedonians could freely develop their own culture, as the other "new" nations of central and eastern Europe had done. With Skopje's support and encouragement, and Belgrade's, Macedonians sought to catch up culturally with the other Yugoslav peoples and, even more important, with neighbors such as the Bulgarians and the Greeks, whose governments continued to deny their national existence.

The rich traditional folk culture—music, songs, dances, crafts, and so on—continued to flourish; but governments focused on contemporary arts: music, fine arts, literature. Before the war, some struggling artists trained elsewhere and partook in Yugoslavia's cultural life, but at home there was little organized activity, let alone of the Macedonian variety. After 1945, the state founded schools, professional societies, and associations to enhance Macedonian music, performing arts, visual arts, theater, cinema, and especially literature.

There soon appeared the first Macedonian symphonic compositions, operas, and ballets. Macedonian painters and sculptors were exhibiting at home and in leading galleries and museums in Yugoslavia and abroad. By the 1970s, talented directors were making feature films that attracted attention beyond Yugoslavia and the Balkans; Milčo Mančevski's *Before the Rain* (1993) won international acclaim. All in all, the achievements of Yugoslav Macedonians in all these areas of cultural endeavor were striking—comparable to those of the other Balkan peoples, whose state-sponsored cultural development began a century or more earlier.

Even more notable, however, were Macedonian accomplishments in poetry, prose, and drama. In the Balkans and, indeed, in central and eastern Europe as a whole, ethnic or linguistic nationalism prevailed. There, with few exceptions, the so-called mother tongue defined people. The nation and its language were inseparable: one could not exist without the other; literature in that language was the most recognizable and undeniable proof that both existed.[19] Consequently, for Macedonians, the rapid flowering of their literature—poetry, prose, drama—was probably the defining cultural accomplishment, and the most notable writers have traditionally enjoyed national recognition and prestige.

The poets led the way. They found inspiration in the rich oral tradition of carefully collected and compiled Macedonian folk songs and verse. Modern Macedonian poetry started before standardization of the language at war's end. During the 1930s and the fight for national liberation, poets such as Kočo Racin, Kole Nedelkovski, and Venko Markovski were already writing in Macedonian. Joining Markovski after the war were younger colleagues such as Blaže Koneski, Aco Šopov, and Slavko Janevski, who used standardized Macedonian.

From this modest beginning, Macedonian poetry grew in quantity and quality. By the late 1960s and the 1970s, its practitioners were attaining world standards through the "middle generation" of poets such as Matej Matevksi, Gane Todorovski, Vlado Uruševič, and Cane Andreevski. Their younger contemporaries, such as Bogomil Ǵuzel, Mihail Rendžov, Dušica Todorovska, and Radovan Cvetkovski, showed even greater artistic and thematic originality. Translations of their work were appearing elsewhere in Yugoslavia and central and eastern Europe but also in the major world languages.[20]

There was no tradition of fiction in Macedonian before standardization. No short stories or novels appeared in the language before 1945. In the first issue of the journal *Nov Den*, in 1945, Blaže Koneski, the new republic's leading linguist, writer, and intellectual, lamented this gap. "Macedonian literature is represented today almost exclusively by poetry," he wrote. "Only in that field we have good results and proven names such as Kočo Racin, Venko Markovski, Kole Nedelkovski. On the other side, our short story, our prose, finds itself still in its very beginning. It would appear that we have taken to writing poems and searching for rhymes and have forgotten prose writing or even set it aside, in the face of the triumph of the poetic words."[21]

However, the first generation of Macedonian prose writers—Vlado Maleski, Slavko Janevski, Jovan Boškovski, Kole Čašule, and Giorgi Abadžiev—soon began to publish fiction. The first collection of short stories, *Rastrel*, by Jovan Boškovski, appeared in 1947; the first novella, Slavko Janevski's *Ulica,* in 1950; and the first full-length novel, Janevski's *Selo za Sedumte Jeseni*, in 1952. By the 1970s, fiction claimed equality with other forms of literary creativity and was the most popular literary genre; prose writers were achieving recognition in the other lands of Yugoslavia and on the wider world stage. Anthologies of Macedonian prose, short stories, and novels appeared in other countries; translations of the best works of Slavko Janevski, Stale Popov, Dimitar Solev, Živko Čingo, Kole Čašule, Simon Drakul, Božin Pavlovski, Taško Georgievski, and others were published in Yugoslavia, other parts of Europe, and beyond.[22]

As with poetry, drama had a proud tradition in Macedonia that went back to Vojdan Černodrinski (1875–1951) and especially to the three interwar playwrights, Vasil Il'oski, Anton Panov, and Risto Krle. However, stage or radio performances of drama could strongly influence the masses, and so the Communist regime applied its rigorous ideological controls more stringently on plays and theater than on other literary endeavors. These crackdowns tended to stifle creativity and hinder the development of dramatic literature. The recovery did not begin until the mid-1950s, under the prolific Kole Čašule and Tome Arsovski. A flowering and achievement of European standards emerged in the numerous plays of the younger generation, especially those by Goran Stefanovski, Jordan Plevneš, Mitko Mandžukov, and Dejan Duklovski. Stefanovski and Plevneš have dominated for the past twenty years, with their plays in production continuously in the major cities of Europe, and they have achieved world renown.[23]

All in all, during the Yugoslav republic's four and a half decades, Macedonians enjoyed relative freedom and engineered a veritable cultural renaissance—the "Macedonian cultural miracle"[24]—to cap more than a century of national awakening. This development must have shocked those neighbors who denied Macedonians' existence and called their language "Tito's artificial creation." This rapid flowering debunks all their claims and misconceptions and renders delusional their refusal to accept Macedonian identity, people, and nation.

National Minorities

As I have stressed many times above, Macedonia has always been a multi-ethnic region. However, before the nineteenth century and the age of nationalism, religion and class tended to determine relations between the state and ethnic groups or among ethnic groups. During the era of nationalism, ethnicity became increasingly influential in those relations. Nevertheless, as long as foreign rule continued in Macedonia—Ottoman before 1912 and Bulgarian, Greek, or Serbian thereafter—the overlords largely shaped those relations.

A Macedonian state in Communist Yugoslavia created a completely new situation in what had been Vardar Macedonia. The Communist Party of Macedonia (KPM) came to power; throughout its history (1943–90), it was under the control of Macedonians, who made up most of the membership. Under the direction of the Communist Party of Yugoslavia (KPJ), it regulated the new republic's relations with ethnic-national minorities and between them and the Macedonian majority.

According to the 1948 census, Macedonians comprised 68.5 percent of the republic's people (789,484 persons), Albanians 17.1 percent (197,389), and Turks 8.3 percent (95,940).[25] The more-detailed 1981 census gave the total population as 1,912,257: 1,281,195 Macedonians, 377,726 Albanians, 86,691 Turks, 47,223 Roma, 44,613 Serbs, 39,555 Muslims, and 7,190 Vlachs. The remainder belonged to other ethnic groups and included 1,984 Bulgarians.[26]

Unlike Bulgaria and Greece, which sought forcefully to assimilate their Macedonian minorities, and Albania, which was ambiguous and inconsistent, Communist Yugoslavia, including its Macedonian republic, recognized all national minorities. The successive Yugoslav and Macedonian constitutions designated three categories of national minorities:

nations, nationalities, and ethnic groups. The Torbeši—Macedonian-speaking Muslims—together with the Serbo-Croatian-speaking Muslims of Yugoslavia, became a nationality of Yugoslavia in 1961 and a separate Muslim nation of Yugoslavia in 1971. The Albanian and Turkish minorities were nationalities because their national "homes" were outside Yugoslavia. The Roma and the Vlach minorities were ethnic groups. After 1981, in theory at least, the Roma in Yugoslavia as a whole gained the status of nationality.

Within the limitations of a one-party system, the successive constitutions of Macedonia guaranteed to everyone—the Macedonian majority and the minorities—equality before the law and religious equality. The national minorities also had cultural rights: use of their national language, formation of cultural associations, organizations, clubs, publishing, and broadcasting in their languages, and so on. The "nationalities" possessed rights to primary and, where numbers warranted, secondary education in their languages.

In the 1944/45 school year, there were 60 primary schools with Albanian as the language of instruction, 37 with Turkish, and 2 with Serbo-Croatian. Attendance at the Albanian schools increased from 25,645 in 1952/53 to 54,801 in 1971/72 and to 72,121 in 1991/92. Turkish numbers stabilized at about 55,000 in 1959/60. Enrollment also grew in Albanian and Turkish secondary schools. To prepare teachers for these schools, the republic created in Skopje departments or institutes of Albanian and Turkish language and literature in the Philosophical Faculty at the SS Cyril and Methodius University and in the Pedagogical Academy. In 1980, there were 2,365 students of Albanian nationality in institutions of higher learning.[27]

The constitutional guarantees of equality and cultural and educational rights did not fully satisfy all members of these minorities or harmonize all relations between them and the majority. The roots of the problem were political and psychological. Like national majorities in multi-ethnic central and eastern European states, the Macedonians viewed their republic as a national state. They had long worked against overwhelming odds for national recognition and a "free Macedonia." Statehood in at least part of Macedonia represented for them its culmination.

Without denying the support of traditional allies and sympathizers—Vlachs and members of the Jewish, Turkish, and Roma minorities—Macedonians considered the victory their own. They controlled the KPM/SKM, which led the struggle's final and decisive phase, and hence dominated every aspect of life in the one-party state. Until 1965, Macedonians held almost all offices of the government and party.

The republic's executive council—the government—included only one Albanian or Turk or at times one of each. The party's executive committee consisted only of Macedonians; its central committee, with as many as ninety-nine members, never included more than one Albanian and two Turks. As one observer concluded: "Although Serbian advisors and centralized party control limited an independent exercise of power, there was a feeling that Macedonians were governing their own republic."[28] And there is a great deal of truth in Poulton's statement: "The minorities of Macedonia were not keen to join the ruling L.C. [League of Communists] and it appears that the Socialist Republic of Macedonia was a state effectively run by Macedonians to a greater extent than their demographic position merited."[29]

After its fourth congress in 1965, the SKM sought to boost minority representation in the highest bodies of state and party; indeed, it moved toward proportional representation. Such an effort helped appease the smaller minorities or at least their leaders. The same happened vis-à-vis the Turks, whose numbers had declined by the 1960s. Many of them had left Macedonia after Yugoslavia and Turkey signed an emigration agreement in the early 1950s.

The Albanians—the largest minority nationality—constituted a special case and challenge. The Muslim Albanians were distinctive in language, religion, and culture. Moreover, unlike all other ethnic minorities, they had a nearby "national home": Albania. During the Second World War, Fascist Italy sponsored a "Great Albania" incorporating lands of prewar Yugoslavia, including northwestern Macedonia. Nationalist Albanians in Macedonia fought alongside the Italians against Yugoslav and Macedonian liberation; they would have preferred to be part of a Great Albania.

Although the Albanians of Macedonia were better off than their conationals in Kosovo or in Albania, many remained dissatisfied. After the fall of Ranković in 1966, growing Albanian nationalism in Yugoslavia came into the open. There were large-scale demonstrations in Kosovo in November 1968, and even longer, more widespread unrest and violence erupted in 1981. The Albanians of Kosovo called for republican status for their autonomous region. The unrest in Kosovo inspired similar, but smaller, Albanian nationalist outbreaks in the neighboring Tetovo region in Macedonia. Their leaders insisted that Albanian-inhabited areas of western Macedonia should join Kosovo as a seventh Yugoslav republic. Many people in the federation viewed such a change as the first step on the road toward separation and unification with Albania and thus creation of Great Albania.

Moreover, Albanian nationalists' demands posed a mortal danger to the Macedonian state. As Hugh Poulton pointed out: "The proposed seventh republic comprising the Albanian dominated areas of Western Macedonia would have severely truncated SR [Socialist Republic] Macedonia and almost certainly have revived Bulgarian (and even Serbian and Greek) claims to the rump. Thus the growth of Albanian nationalism in SR Macedonia was seen as possibly fatal, not only to the territorial integrity of the republic but even to the very existence of the Macedonian nation."[30]

Seeming Albanian disloyalty and Macedonia's severe suppression of Albanian unrest exacerbated mutual distrust, and the standoff persisted after 1991 in newly independent Macedonia.

The Titoist system shaped Macedonia's policies toward its national minorities, which were more tolerant and liberal than those of the Soviet-bloc countries. Macedonia, just like its partners in the federation, did not deny the existence of minorities as Greece did; nor did it claim to have resolved all the minorities' problems as members of the Soviet bloc did. When Yugoslavia collapsed in 1991, Macedonia avoided the bloody conflicts that engulfed the rest of the country. But how would the democratically elected leaders—Macedonian and non-Macedonian—of the independent republic deal with those intractable issues?

14 Independent Republic (1991–2004)

Macedonia and its people played little role in the disintegration of Yugoslavia in 1990–91. Most Macedonians valued the benefits of the federation. Membership gave them a sense of security both against unfriendly, even antagonistic neighbors Bulgaria, Greece, and, to a certain extent, Albania and against condescending and patronizing Serbia.

Until the very end of Yugoslavia, Macedonian leaders in Belgrade and Skopje sought to bring together the Serbs and the Croats and Slovenes and preserve a reformed, looser, democratic federation or confederation. The attacks in the north of the country by the Yugoslav National Army (JNA) in June 1991 and the spilling of blood in Slovenia and Croatia, however, made it clear that the federation, which allowed Macedonia a balance of sorts between external security and limited but clear autonomy, had ceased to exist. The Macedonians needed alternative routes to national survival.

This chapter explores the first years of independence, examining in turn the creation of the republic, the difficult search for foreign recognition, the rightward drift of political life in the late 1990s, pressing economic problems, and relations between Macedonians and the large Albanian minority, which reached a crisis in 2001.

Setting Up an Independent Republic

The discourse on the future of Macedonia and its people began in the Yugoslav republic—part of the growing democratic challenge to the Communist monopoly of power and of the intense, federation-wide debate on Yugoslavia's future. By April 1989, the Macedonian Sobranie (assembly) had, over a year, adopted thirty-two constitutional amendments, which in effect sanctioned multi-candidate elections and privatization in the economy. A few months later, the League of Communists of Macedonia (SKM) promised a multi-party system and opened the door for pluralism.

On 4 February 1990, respected Macedonian intellectuals formed the Movement for All-Macedonian Action (MAAK) and chose as its leader the poet Ante Popovski, head of the Writers Union. MAAK's aim was to defend Macedonian interests in Yugoslavia as well as in neighboring states, but it disclaimed any territorial ambitions. In August 1990, it announced its support for secession from the federation. Two months earlier, on 17 June, a more radical, better-organized nationalist party had held its founding congress in Skopje. It chose to call itself by the highly evocative name Internal Macedonian Revolutionary Organization–Democratic Party of Macedonian National Unity (Vnatrešna Makedonska Revolucionerna Organizacija–Demokratska Partija za Makedonsko Nacionalno Edinstvo, or VMRO-DPMNE). Ljubčo Georgievski, a young, politically inexperienced, aspiring poet became its leader. It promised to work for the principal aims of the Ilinden Uprising of 1903. Like MAAK, it also called for independence.

The national minorities also used political relaxation to set up parties. The main Albanian group became the Party for Democratic Prosperity (PDP). Nevzat Halili, a teacher of English from Tetovo, formed it in nearby Poroj in April 1990 and became its leader in August. Although he denied that the PDP was an ethnic party, it claimed to represent the Albanians of Macedonia. As well, the Democratic Alliance of Turks emerged in 1990 before the first multi-party election. It later took another name, the Democratic Party of Turks (DPT).

Macedonia was to hold its first democratic election in November 1990. Before the voting, the SKM transformed itself into the League of Communists of Macedonia–Party for Democratic Renewal (SKM-PDP). At its congress in April 1991, it adopted its present name, the Social Democratic Union of Macedonia (SDSM). To meet the challenge of

Map 7 The Republic of Macedonia in East Central Europe, 2007

Communists or reformed Communists, whom many observers thought would do well, the MAAK and the VMRO-DPMNE formed the nationalist Front of Macedonian National Unity.

More than twenty parties took part in the election, and a remarkable 80 percent of eligible voters cast ballots. No single party or bloc won a majority in the 120-seat national assembly. The VMRO-DPMNE took 38 seats with 31.7 percent of the vote. The reformed Communists (SKM-PDP, or SDSM after 1991) obtained 31 (with 25.8 percent of the ballots). The PDP, allied with another, smaller Albanian party, the People's Democratic Party (NDP), won 22 (with 18.3 percent), and the

Alliance of Reform Forces of Macedonia, the party of Ante Marković, the last effective prime minister of Yugoslavia, took 11 (with 9.2 percent). Smaller parties and three independent candidates won the remaining 18 seats (with 7.2 percent).[1]

Following in the footsteps of Croatia and Slovenia, the democratically elected national assembly on 25 January 1991 declared sovereignty, but it reserved the right to determine future relations with the other Yugoslav states.[2] Two days later, it elected Kiro Gligorov as first president.

Kiro Gligorov was born on 3 May 1917, in Štip, where he received his schooling. He completed his legal training in the Law Faculty of Belgrade University. Before the Second World War, he was active in the Macedonian Communist student movement, and he joined the push for national liberation in 1942. During the war, he belonged to the majority leftist section of the Macedonian intelligentsia, which acted in terms more of national considerations than of the KPJ's Marxist-Leninist teachings. He drafted and cosigned the critique (prigovor) that the National Liberation Action Committee (ANOK) in Skopje prepared vis-à-vis the Manifesto of the General Headquarters of NOV i POM (October 1943).[3] He served as secretary of the organizational committee for the landmark first session of ASNOM (2 August 1944) and participated as a delegate.

After the liberation, or rather after Koliševski's consolidation of power in Macedonia, Gligorov was not exactly persona grata in Skopje. Koliševski and his colleagues distrusted and feared him, and Gligorov spent virtually the entire Communist era in Belgrade. He held various federal offices, including secretary of finance, deputy chair of the federal executive council, and president of the federal assembly, and built a reputation as a liberal economic reformer. He followed events in Macedonia very closely, but, except during the reform period under Crvenkovski in the late 1960s and early 1970s, he had no direct influence there.

The election of the almost-74-year-old Gligorov was fortunate for Macedonia. It is difficult to think of a contemporary who possessed his expertise in and understanding of Macedonian, Yugoslav, and Balkan politics and major international trends. His personal attributes suited him ideally to guide the small, insecure, and isolated republic on its dangerous road to independence. He was reasonable, patient, cautious, and flexible, yet wise, shrewd, cunning, determined, decisive, and, when necessary, extremely stubborn. He knew how to win friends and, more important, how not to offend unnecessarily Macedonia's many opponents. He sought and listened to all opinions, then withdrew to ponder and analyze all the available information and everything he had heard before making his final decision. Above all, he had no personal ambitions that could interfere with his difficult task.

His opponents liked to accuse him of being authoritarian, and there was an element of personal rule during his presidency. However, this was not due to any lust for power or disrespect of democratic principles. Rather, he perceived such an extremely delicate situation that he shrouded some negotiations and decisions in the utmost secrecy. Just a few weeks before the referendum on independence in September 1991, while standing on a terrace of the presidential retreat (Tito's former villa) on beautiful Lake Ohrid, he told a visitor: "I am already an old man. There is nothing in politics for me any longer. I have accepted the presidency solely to serve my people in these very dangerous circumstances."[4]

Nikola Kljusev, a professor of economics, formed the first democratic cabinet. This "government of experts" survived for more than a year and under Gligorov's leadership supervised the tense transition to independence and the difficult start of political democracy and a market economy. Even after the declaration of sovereignty (25 January 1991), Macedonian leaders hoped to preserve some form of association for the Yugoslav republics. Gligorov worked on a compromise to reconcile the growing differences between Croatian and Slovene confederalism and Serbian centralism. The draft proposal that he prepared and proposed with Bosnia-Herzegovina's Alija Izetbegović went nowhere. It could not even serve as a basis for further discussions.

On 25 June 1991, the Yugoslav army attacked Slovenia, and a month later it opened hostilities against Croatia. The spilling of blood sealed the fate of Yugoslavia, and on 26 June the Macedonian national assembly discussed independence; its members divided, as did the population in general.

But the disagreement was not, as many people have assumed, between nationalists and "Yugoslavists." Rather, it was between moderate, or cautious, nationalists under Gligorov, who in view of grave internal and external threats urged restraint, and the radical, or "impatient," nationalists, whom the VMRO-DPMNE led and who tended to minimize the threats and wanted independence immediately. However, once the northern fighting widened to include Croatia and threatened

Bosnia-Herzegovina, even the cautious had to agree that the Yugoslav idea was dead. Macedonian sovereignty and independence even within a loose association no longer formed a viable option.

At this point, Macedonians had only two possibilities. First, they could, as Belgrade and Athens wanted them to do, join a third, or "reduced," Yugoslavia. In a new federation without the Croatians and the Slovenes to counterbalance the Serbs, however, they could have become extremely weak and vulnerable. Consequently, they rejected this option from the outset. Second, they could declare complete sovereignty and independence—the only route acceptable to most of the population, including the Albanians.[5]

The political leaders resolved to give the people the final say. In the referendum on 8 September 1991, 72.16 percent of 1,495,080 registered voters cast ballots; 95.08 percent of voters, or 1,021,981 people, supported independence, and only 3.63 percent, or 38,896, opposed it. Unfortunately—a sign of internal troubles to come—Albanians boycotted the referendum to protest their constitutional status. On 17 September 1991, the national assembly passed the declaration of independence, and on 17 November it adopted a new constitution. The official proclamation of independence took place on 20 November.

The preamble of the constitution of 1991 describes Macedonia as a "national state of the Macedonian people in which full equality as citizens and permanent co-existence with the Macedonian people is provided for Albanians, Turks, Vlachs, Romanies and other nationalities."[6] This was a compromise formulation aiming to appease proponents of both a "national" and a "citizens" state. The body of the document refers not to a "national state," but rather to "an independent, sovereign, democratic, and social state" of equal citizens (article 1) and to "rights and duties in accordance with the concept of a 'citizens' state.'"[7]

The constitution specified parliamentary government. The head of state—the president of the republic *(pretsedatel na državata)*—must be at least forty and have been a resident and citizen for at least ten of the preceding fifteen years. A direct and secret ballot chooses this official for five years and permits only two terms. The head of state may not initiate legislation but has considerable power, serving as commander in chief of the armed forces and head of the national security council; he or she also proposes members for the constitutional court, appoints and dismisses ambassadors, and nominates the head of government, or prime minister.

Legislative power lies with the 120-member Narodno Sobranie, the national assembly, or parliament, which voters choose for four years in "general, direct, and free elections and by secret ballot." The deputies elect from their own ranks the president of the assembly and one or more vice presidents. This body's most important functions include making laws, adopting the state's budget, ratifying international agreements, deciding on war and peace, electing judges whom the state president recommends to the constitutional court, and appointing and dismissing public officials other than ambassadors.

The government wields executive power, and its head is the prime minister *(pretsedatel na vladata)*. The president of the republic nominates that official, who in turn selects ministers and must secure the assembly's approval. Deputies may not serve as ministers. The government initiates and directs domestic and foreign policy. The assembly may remove the government by a vote of nonconfidence.

In the months following the declaration of independence, the government moved to secure and safeguard the new state. It ruled out association with the reduced federation and withdrew representatives from all Yugoslav institutions. It introduced a separate Macedonian currency, the *denar,* and began the search for a new flag, coat of arms, and national anthem.

Gligorov initiated secret and intense negotiations with Slobodan Milošević, the Serbian strongman, and Serbia agreed to withdraw all Yugoslav army units from Macedonia by 15 April 1992. Although Yugoslav forces stripped military installations of all equipment, in violation of the agreement, they completed a peaceful withdrawal by 26 March. By mid-March, the Macedonian Territorial Defence Forces took control of the republic's borders, and the government began building a new army.

Macedonia was the only one of the four republics to withdraw from Yugoslavia and attain independence peacefully—a remarkable achievement and a triumph of Gligorov's diplomacy.[8] Skopje had also begun seeking international recognition, which proved more difficult and which complicated the transition far more than even the most pessimistic observers expected.

Seeking Foreign Recognition (1991–1995)

As I emphasized above, all of Macedonia's neighbors had at one time or another denied the existence of a Macedonian people and its right to a state, claiming its people and territory as their own. All of them viewed the small, independent republic as a threat to their past gains or future aspirations there and rejected it as an artificial creation. Consequently, speedy recognition by other powers, particularly by the European Community (EC) and the United States, was critical; the state and nation's survival depended on it.

Shortly after adoption of the new constitution, on 29 November 1991, Macedonia joined Slovenia, Croatia, and Bosnia-Herzegovina seeking recognition from the European Community. That body's arbitrator—the Badenter Commission—soon ruled that only Slovenia and Macedonia met the minimum requirements. However, to the Macedonians' surprise and disappointment, by April 1992 the European Community had recognized the other three applicants but not Macedonia. Both it and the United States, as Sabrina Ramet put it, "singled out [Macedonia] for discriminatory treatment";[9] Greece's determined opposition convinced them. Macedonia, EC members, and the United States became hostages of Greece's unwillingness to accept its own smaller role in post-Communist, post–cold war Europe.

At the outset, Athens claimed that the new republic represented a security threat. How the small, poor, militarily powerless state could threaten Greece—one of the region's larger states, a member of the European Community and of the North Atlantic Treaty Organization (NATO), and a modern military power—was difficult to grasp. Greece demanded guarantees that Macedonia had or would have no designs on southern, or Aegean, Macedonia.

Greece also objected to articles 3 and 49 of the Macedonian constitution. Article 3 provided that the borders "may be changed only in accordance with the Constitution," and Greece suspected irredentist ambitions. Article 49 expressed interest in "the status and rights" of Macedonians in unnamed neighboring countries, which Greece saw as interference in its internal affairs. This was paradoxical because Greece had always denied the existence of Macedonians in its country.

The European Community accepted Greece's demands and insisted on resolution of them as its condition for recognition. The national assembly met early in January 1992 and adopted the requisite changes and declarations. Although the Badenter Commission on 15 January "issued a judgment declaring that among the Yugoslav successor states, Slovenia and Macedonia fulfilled all conditions for diplomatic recognition," the

European Community again deferred to the Greeks and "did not honor its implied promise to the Republic of Macedonia."[10]

At the core of the Greek-Macedonian dispute lay the Greek claim to exclusive ownership of all things and matters Macedonian: geography, history, traditions, symbols, and, most important, the Macedonian name itself. This became a highly volatile and emotional issue in Greece because its romantic-nationalist mythology identified and linked it not only with the glories of the ancient city-states, but also with the heritage of the dynastic ancient Macedonian kingdom and empire and the medieval multi-ethnic Byzantine Orthodox Commonwealth. This mythology grounded the Megali Idea (Great Idea), the ideology of modern Greek imperialism.

For Macedonians, the Greeks' claim was not only irrational but unacceptable. The Greeks were asking them to give up their land's name, which, as part of geographic and historic Macedonia, it had possessed for 3,500 years. They were also insisting that the Macedonians sacrifice their national name, under which, as we have seen throughout this work, their national identity and their nation formed in the nineteenth century. They were asking Macedonians to surrender their history, tradition, and culture, which were all inseparable from their national name. In other words, they were telling the Macedonians to scrap their national identity and cease being a nation. As President Gligorov told EC foreign ministers: "to comply with the Greek demand that Macedonia change its name would mean that the people of that republic would also lose their name, from which it would further stem that this people have no right to a state at all."[11]

Behind Greece's stance lay more immediate and pragmatic considerations: one internal, the other external. First and foremost, recognition of the republic would also implicitly extend to national identity and nation. Greece could then hardly continue to deny the existence of the Macedonian minority in Aegean Macedonia. Recognition of the latter would in turn create pressure on it to do justice to its other minorities—Turks in Thrace, Albanians and Vlachs in Epirus—which would destroy its long-standing assumption of its ethnic homogeneity.

Second, Greece wanted to preserve a common border with its traditional ally Serbia. Except during the mid- and late 1940s, its alliance of 1913 with Serbia and an informal rapprochement dating back to the 1890s had grounded Greece's Balkan policy. The potentially unreliable new republic would control land routes to Serbia and the rest of Europe.

For Greece, as for Milošević's Serbia, that territory should be under Serbia's control.

The decision of EC members and the United States to withhold recognition until settlement of the Greek-Macedonian dispute (i.e., siding with Greece) influenced other states. On 15 January 1992, Bulgaria became the first country to recognize the new state, even though it continued to deny the existence of a Macedonian nation. But by summer, only six others joined it: Croatia, Slovenia, Turkey, Bosnia-Herzegovina, Lithuania, and the Philippines. Russia also extended recognition but decided not to exchange ambassadors until the European Community formalized relations.

Moreover, the stand of the EC and United States rendered Athens even more inflexible and aggressive. The simplest solution for the Greeks would have been for Macedonia to join Serbia's reduced Yugoslavia. The most drastic scenario, which the most extreme nationalists advocated, sought to destabilize the republic and to carve it up with Serbia and, if necessary, with Bulgaria, as had happened in 1913. If these options proved unattainable, Athens would force Macedonia to change its name and its people to invent a new national identity. As one Greek diplomat commented, "We will choke Skopje into submission."[12]

To achieve its aims, Athens resorted to a campaign of intimidation. Hundreds of thousands of Greeks demonstrated in Salonika and in Athens against the "counterfeit nation," "Skopjans," and "pseudo-Macedonians."[13] In early December 1992, dignitaries of church and state led an estimated 1.3 million people at a rally in Athens. The Greek military executed maneuvers on Macedonia's border and repeatedly violated its airspace. Greece interfered with shipments to the republic, including foreign aid passing through the port of Salonika, and in August 1992 imposed a partial economic embargo, which it lifted early in 1993. In late 1993, however, Andreas Papandreou, the socialist prime minister again, reimposed a more sweeping embargo, which lasted eighteen months. The Greeks closed southward trade, and United Nations (UN) sanctions against Serbia and the wars in Croatia and Bosnia-Herzegovina disrupted trade to the north. Macedonia lost about 60 percent of its trade and approached economic collapse.[14]

Greece and Serbia also launched a joint political campaign against the republic. Milošević's Serbia supported Greece in its dispute, and Greece, despite UN sanctions, aided Serbia in its wars. The two states maintained frequent high-level contacts and had regular bilateral discussions. In 1992 and 1993, under the New Democracy, Prime Minister Konstantinos Mitsotakis and Foreign Minister Antonios Samaras, the cabinet's leading anti-Macedonian, discussed the issue with Milošević several times. The two nations' close collaboration continued after Papandreou returned to power in October 1993.

Reliable reports and unconfirmed rumors suggested that talks concerned a "joint Serbian-Greek border," partition (perhaps with Albania and Bulgaria as well) of Macedonia, formation of a Serbian-Greek confederation, and other ideas. Details of the talks may not surface for some time, but perhaps the most significant item on the agenda was Macedonia's fate. Takis Michas, the most serious investigator into the Greek-Serbian axis of the early 1990s, has argued convincingly that the two governments were actually conspiring to destabilize and partition the republic by force. "There is now," he wrote, "much hard evidence indicating that political leaders in Athens and Belgrade seriously entertained this adventurous scenario."[15]

It was this scheme that finally compelled EC members and the United States (and thus NATO) to blow the whistle on Greece's demands and assume a more realistic stance. A war over Macedonia would have been much wider than the wars in Slovenia, Croatia, and Bosnia-Herzegovina. It would have involved those new states, all of Macedonia's neighbors, and possibly Turkey. And since Greece and Turkey would be on opposite sides, it would have become the first armed conflict between two NATO members. Obviously, a war over Macedonia was inconceivable; the new state needed security guarantees through international recognition.

The process began with its admission to the United Nations on 8 April 1993 as—temporarily and demeaningly—the Former Yugoslav Republic of Macedonia (FYROM). This advance paved the way for the UN to station, in July 1993, a protection force along the Macedonian-Serbian border, which grew to some 1,300 members by October. In December, weeks before Greece was to assume the revolving EC presidency on 1 January, most European countries, including Britain, France, and Germany, as well as Japan, recognized the Former Yugoslav Republic of Macedonia.

On 9 February 1994, the U.S. State Department announced its intention to recognize Macedonia. However, a month later, after Papandreou's government unilaterally imposed a total trade embargo and the powerful U.S. Greek lobby caught the ear of U.S. president Bill Clinton, he backed down. His country did not recognize the republic until early 1996 but made up for this flip-flop under President George W. Bush. Immediately after his reelection on 8 November 2004, the United States became the first major Western power to recognize Macedonia under its constitutional name, the Republic of Macedonia.

Under growing pressure from its EC partners and the United States, Greece finally came to terms with the new reality and recognized the new state to its north. The two countries established contacts and after protracted negotiations partially resolved their differences. On 13 September 1995, their foreign ministers signed the Interim Accord in New York. Greece agreed to lift the trade embargo, which it did on 15 October, and not to veto Macedonia's admission into international organizations. The Macedonians were to change their flag; they promptly replaced the Vergina star at the center with an eight-ray sun or star. In addition, as they had promised, they forswore claims on any Greek territory (i.e., Aegean Macedonia).

The two states set aside the most divisive issue—the new republic's name; UN mediators would work with them later. Skopje insisted that the constitutional name was not negotiable and that the state would remain the "Republic of Macedonia." Athens continued to protest, mostly for domestic consumption, and insisted on a mutually acceptable name.

In the meantime, Greece kept using "Former Yugoslav Republic of Macedonia"; most countries, however, including Russia, China, and more recently the United States, recognized Macedonia by its constitutional name. Many other nations, including EC members, referred to the "Republic of Macedonia" in bilateral relations and to "Macedonia" in other contexts.

Greek-Macedonian relations improved under the Interim Accord of September 1995. Trade soon increased, as did Greek investment in its neighbor's economy. By mid-November, Macedonia had joined the Organization for Security and Co-operation in Europe (OSCE) (15 October), the Council of Europe (9 November), and NATO's Partnership for Peace Program (15 November). The search for recognition ended with the opening of diplomatic relations with the new federal Yugoslavia (Serbia and Montenegro) early in 1996, after the signing of the Dayton Accords.[16]

Politics in the 1990s: From Left to Right

The withholding of Western recognition sapped Macedonian morale. The government and the people were conscious of their delicate situation; they feared their neighbors' intentions. President Gligorov's policy of maintaining "equal distance" from all of them aimed to avoid giving them any pretexts to interfere and to win the powers' support. Macedonians certainly did not expect the West's discriminatory treatment of their republic, alone among the Yugoslav successor states. They sought and expected the West's support and could not understand why it would side with Greece and against them on the only name that they had.

The withholding of recognition, the resulting years of isolation, and *the name questioning, which still continues*, were demeaning to the Macedonians, in addition to creating great uncertainties and insecurities. They compounded the new republic's problems and dissipated the popular enthusiasm and energy that followed the declaration of independence and that were essential in building the new state. The resulting atmosphere also diverted the government and the ruling elite from the pressing problems that threatened internal stability.

Nikola Kljusev's "government of experts" led Macedonia successfully through the initial transition in 1991–92. However, it failed to secure international recognition, and the leaders of the major parties in the national assembly, who wanted a "political" government, forced it to resign. Gligorov asked Ljubčo Georgievski, leader of the VMRO-DPMNE, the largest party in the assembly, to form the new government. After he failed, Gligorov turned to Branko Crvenkovski, the thirty-year-old leader of the SDSM, the second party. In 1992, he formed a coalition with the Reformed Forces–Liberal Party (RS-LP), the Socialists, and two Albanian parties, the PDP and its ally, the NDP. His new cabinet included four Albanian Macedonians.

The coalition brought a greater semblance of security and stability to the country. Under Gligorov's watchful eye, Crvenkovski and the leaders of the Albanian parties worked together to resolve some of the issues that divided Macedonians and Albanians. In 1993, the government introduced and began to implement economic privatization. It also scored some qualified successes in foreign policy. Most countries recognized Macedonia, albeit in many cases under its temporary name, and negotiations leading to the Interim Accord with Greece were well under way.

Before the 1994 presidential and parliamentary elections, the three governing Macedonian parties—the SDSM, the Liberals, and the Socialists—formed a new coalition, the Alliance for Macedonia, under Gligorov himself. The first round of elections took place on 6 October 1994. Gligorov won the presidency with 52.4 percent of the votes against Ljubiša Georgievski, a well-known theater director and candidate of the VMRO-DPMNE.

However, the parliamentary contest became very controversial. In the first round, an impressive 78 percent of eligible voters cast their ballots; of the 176 candidates representing 37 political parties and independents, only 10 won office. However, the Alliance for Macedonia did extremely well and appeared to be heading for victory in the second round. But the VMRO-DPMNE and the Democratic Party fared much worse than they had expected. Their leaders, Ljubčo Georgievski and Petar Gošev, respectively, declared the vote fraudulent, appealed to their supporters to boycott the last round, and called for a totally new election.

On 30 October, 57.5 percent of eligible voters went to the polls. The Alliance for Macedonia took 95 seats, the SDSM 58, the Liberal Party 29, and the Socialist Party 8. The two Albanian parties won 14 seats—the PDP 10 and the NDP 4; small parties took 4 seats, and independents 7. Foreign observers and monitors, including OSCE representatives, pointed to some minor irregularities but all in all considered the elections and results valid.

Branko Crvenkovski headed the new coalition cabinet, which included the three Alliance for Macedonia parties and a number of Albanians. It faced virtually no effective opposition; two parties had boycotted the second round, and their leaders, Georgievski and Gošev, dismissed the assembly as unrepresentative and challenged the government's legitimacy.

Seeking popular support, the government proposed wide-ranging political, social, and economic reforms to put Macedonia on the path to integration with Europe. The prime minister worked to conciliate the Albanians by increasing their numbers in high positions in the judiciary, the army, and the diplomatic service. Sadly, the cabinet implemented many changes, especially relating to privatization, unfairly and dishonestly, and the opposition pounced on corrupt practices. Concessions to Albanian demands, which many Macedonians thought unreasonable or unrealistic, also eroded popular support. The government's internal divisions over its economic program and policies toward the Albanians weakened it, as did personal differences between its two leading figures.

Crvenkovski and Stojan Andov, the Liberal president of the assembly, did not like each other. They were both ambitious, jealous of the other's political power, and determined to expand his own. They also had significant differences on major issues. Their struggle for power reached a crisis after 3 October 1995, the day of an assassination attempt on President Gligorov. Gligorov survived but was incapacitated; Andov automatically became acting president of the republic and served until Gligorov returned in January 1996.

The following month, Crvenkovski radically shuffled his cabinet. He excluded Andov's Liberals and added two more Albanian ministers. After it secured the confidence of the national assembly on 21 February, Andov resigned from that body's presidency, and his party became the effective opposition. The Liberals joined the VMRO-DPMNE and the Democratic Party in calling for new elections.

The government was on the defensive over corruption, privatization, economic performance, and mounting Albanian demands, and the 1996 local elections indicated declining public support. All political leaders began to plan for the next parliamentary election. In the meantime, both the Albanian and Macedonian camps realigned their forces.

In 1994, the main Albanian group, the Party for Democratic Prosperity (PDP), split over internal differences. Abdul Rahman Aliti replaced the founding leader, Nevzat Halili, as head of the official faction, which retained the party name. The more radical, splinter segment became the PDP-A and in 1996 the Democratic Party of Albanians (DPA). Its leader was Arben Xhaferi, and his deputy, Menduh Thaci, was even more strongly nationalist.

On the Macedonian side a new party, the Democratic Alternative (DA), emerged. Its founder was Vasil Tupurkovski, a former president of the League of Communist Youth of Yugoslavia and Macedonia's last representative on the rotating presidency of Communist Yugoslavia. He was a university professor of law in Skopje, and his political ambitions were far greater than his foresight. In preparation for the expected election, Tupurkovski, the former rising star of Communist Yugoslavia, joined with Georgievski of the VMRO-DPMNE, a leading nationalist and anti-Communist. Their two parties formed the right-wing coalition For Change to contest Crvenkovski's left-of-center Alliance for Macedonia.

The elections took place on 18 October and 1 November 1998. For Change won 59 of the assembly's 120 seats, the VMRO-DPMNE 47, and the DA 12. The governing SDSM elected only 29 deputies, and Xhaferi's DPA 11. Ljubčo Georgievski, as leader of the largest group, formed a coalition government with the DA and the DPA, the most nationalist Albanian party.

Political life in Macedonia was changing. After six years in power, Branko Crvenkovski became leader of the opposition. In the presidential election in 1999 (Gligorov could not seek a third term), Tito Petkovski, for the SDSM, led after the first round, but the second round elected Boris Trajkovski of the VMRO-DPMNE with the support of many Albanian voters. Thus power shifted peacefully from the Social Democrats, who had dominated politics since 1991, to a party on the right: nationalist, anti-Communist, and anti-Socialist and claiming the legacy of the right wing of the historic Macedonian revolutionary organization.[17]

Economic Problems

The independent republic's economic development was complicated and difficult. The transition from a primarily state-owned to a free market economy, which all former Communist states faced, was only part of the problem. Regional instability worsened the situation. The bloody breakup of Yugoslavia took away protected markets for more than 80 percent of Macedonia's exports, as well as substantial transfer payments from Belgrade. The war in Bosnia-Herzegovina and international sanctions on Serbia (1992–96) also hit Macedonia's trade-dependent economy; Greece's trade embargoes (1992–95) were equally damaging. The sanctions against Serbia may have cost Macedonia about $2.9 billion, and the Greek embargoes $1.5 billion.[18] The U.S. Department of State concluded that "as a result of these border closures [Macedonia's] 1995 GDP declined to 41 percent of its 1989 level."[19]

The 1999 crisis in Kosovo was particularly devastating for neighboring Macedonia. "At the height of the crisis, Macedonia sheltered more than 350,000 Kosovo refugees, straining fiscal accounts and increasing social pressure."[20] Foreign investment dried up, unemployment reached 33 percent, and living standards plunged.

Before the war in Kosovo, about 70 percent of Macedonia's economy depended on imports from and exports to, or transport through, the new federal Yugoslavia (Serbia and Montenegro). At the height of the crisis, total exports had dropped to about 70 percent of the 1998 level. Exports to Yugoslavia had declined by 80 percent.[21] Macedonians found alternative routes for some exports through Bulgaria, Romania, and Greece, but increased transportation costs and delivery times made Macedonian goods less competitive. One estimate for three months of the Kosovo conflict placed the cost to Macedonia at $630 million in lost exports.[22]

Although the regional crises strained the country's economy and distracted government from internal reform, the economic transition proceeded apace. Macedonia embarked on a comprehensive program of stabilization and reform. Until the Kosovo conflict, it attained some positive results, which met with the approval of the International Monetary Fund and the World Bank. Financial austerity stabilized the denar, reduced the fiscal deficit, and tamed runaway inflation. However, austerity and privatization led to the closing of some large but outdated industrial enterprises, increased corruption, and slow economic growth in the first half of the 1990s.

The late 1990s saw modest economic recovery, in 1998 3.4 percent growth. The Kosovo conflict did not hit the Macedonian economy as hard as many experts predicted, but it reduced growth to about 2.7 percent in 1999. The situation improved throughout the following year and until the Albanian insurgency in Macedonia began in the spring of 2001.

The crisis of 2001, which faced Macedonia with possible interethnic war, threw the economy into crisis. All economic indicators pointed downward: in 2001 real gross domestic product (GDP) declined by 5 percent instead of the projected 2.2 percent; inflation averaged 5.5 percent; the budget deficit reached 5.8 percent; foreign direct investments, credits, and donations dropped; and the country lost about $200 million of its foreign currency reserves.[23]

Recovery after 2001 was slow. Real GDP grew by 0.3 percent in 2002. In 2003, financial help began to arrive from the international community; GDP grew by 3.1 percent, inflation remained low, and the budget deficit fell to 1.1 percent, but unemployment remained high, at 36.7 percent.[24]

Moreover, the government began implementing the internationally mediated Ohrid Framework Agreement, which ended the domestic conflict (more on this later). It introduced economic and political reform to stimulate the economy and attract more foreign investment. Fulfilling the agreement's terms stabilized the political and security situation—an indispensable precondition for further economic growth and development.

Macedonian-Albanian Relations

The most pressing domestic task facing the newly independent and democratic Macedonian state and its government was winning the loyalty of the various non-Macedonian ethnicities and maintaining interethnic peace. The Macedonians comprised about two-thirds of the population in 1991. Although they controlled both the executive and the legislative branches of government, the ruling elite realized that, unlike in authoritarian Communist Yugoslavia, the new democratic state would have to win the minorities' support and allegiance. The survival of the state—the only homeland, or Heimat, of the Macedonians—and of the nation depended on it.

From the start, the independent republic recognized all the national minorities and guaranteed them legal equality politically, economically, socially. Its protection of their cultural and educational rights went beyond the requirements of either the UN or the European Union charter. In fact, its policies, which were more liberal and tolerant than those of other multi-ethnic states in eastern Europe, contrasted sharply with nonrecognition of Macedonians in the neighboring Balkan states.

These guarantees of equality and rights won over the Turkish, Vlach, and Roma communities and, after the Dayton Accords in 1995, even the Serbians; but they did not appease the large Albanian minority, confounding the state's internal stability.

Although Macedonians and Albanians differ in ethnicity and religion, their mutual suspicion and distrust are primarily political. The Macedonians identify with and are very possessive of the republic: it is, as I stressed above, the only homeland they have or could have. Their survival as a people and nation, and that of their language and culture, depends on the continuing existence of their state. For the Albanians of Macedonia, this small state does not embody such significance. They feel deep attachment to the areas that they inhabit, but many of them identify with Albania proper or with Kosovo, now apparently a second Albanian homeland in the making, or they like the idea of unifying Albania, Kosovo, and the areas of Macedonia, Serbia, Montenegro, and Greece where Albanians live into a "Great Albania."

All these trends—pro-Albania, pro-Kosovo, and pro–Great Albania—have a following in Macedonia. Although it is impossible to determine the extent of support for each, their existence colors Macedonians' perception of and attitude toward their Albanian fellow citizens. They tend to question their loyalty and to see separatism and threats to national survival in all Albanian demands, whether major, as in federalization, cantonization, or bilingualism, or less sweeping, as in greater numbers in the civil service, more and better educational and cultural institutions, and greater use of Albanian in local administrations.

The mutual distrust is not new. It was present in the Communist period, but authorities sought to hide it. However, with independence, democratic pluralism, and nationalist parties on both sides, all the divisive issues came into the open. Lively debates occurred in private discussions, in the media, and in the national assembly.

In general elections, Albanians have tended to vote as a bloc for ethnic parties and have normally elected about one-fifth of the deputies—roughly corresponding to their proportion of the population. All governments since 1991 have been coalitions and included at least one of the leading Albanian parties.

No government could act on the most extreme demand and recognize the Albanians as a second constituent nation, which could lead to a federal system or to cantons and bilingualism. The Macedonian majority as well as the other minorities would oppose this, and internal chaos and collapse and external interventions would almost certainly follow.

However, governments in Skopje have been fully conscious of the problem's seriousness and during the 1990s sought to address some of the Albanians' more feasible demands. Some advances occurred, such as hiring more of them in the civil service, especially in the police forces; using their language more in areas where they form a majority; providing more and better education facilities for them; and reforming and empowering local self-administration. Perhaps Skopje should have done more about their moderate demands as it dealt with a raft of other issues: international recognition, economic transition and corruption, Kosovo, and Macedonian-Albanian divisions.[25]

Extreme Albanian nationalists, mostly in Kosovo and responding to NATO's military intervention and defeat of Milošević's Serbia there, used Albanian grievances as a pretext to launch armed incursions against Macedonia. Their real aim was to destabilize the new state, detach its northwestern Albanian areas, and annex them to Kosovo and eventually to a "Great Albania." In February 2001, they carried out armed provocations near the Kosovo border, which soon escalated into an insurgency. Claiming to fight for greater rights for Albanians in Macedonia, the rebels seized nearby territory and attacked police and military forces. The insurgency spread through parts of northern and western Macedonia during the first half of 2001. As fighting intensified and tension grew throughout the country, by the early summer there were fears of full-scale civil war.[26]

The tragedy of civil war and possible foreign intervention eased after tardy but firm political intervention by the United States and the European Union, whose mediation led to a cease-fire in July 2001. The same month, Georgievski's governing coalition had to add representatives of all the major Macedonian and Albanian parties. With aid and under great pressure from American and EU diplomats, the Macedonian and Albanian leaders in this "grand" coalition worked out the Ohrid Framework Agreement of 8 August 2001, which ended the fighting.[27]

The Ohrid accord called for constitutional and legislative changes to expand civil rights for minority groups. Such rights included greater representation in the civil service, the police, and the army; official use of Albanian in districts with an ethnic Albanian majority; and stronger local self-government. It also provided for deployment of 3,500 NATO troops to disarm the rebels (the National Liberation Army) who instigated the conflict.[28]

The agreement was a compromise. Albanian negotiators enhanced minority civil rights or, more precisely, forced their expansion. Macedonian negotiators protected the Macedonians' status as a constituent nation of the republic. As Phillips points out: "In general both sides found the agreement unsatisfactory but workable, provided they could be persuaded that the other side would act in good faith."[29]

The national assembly ratified the requisite constitutional changes on 16 November 2001. The grand coalition had already disbanded, and a narrower coalition emerged under Georgievski's VMRO-DPMNE that included Xhaferi's DPA, both of which parties had been in power during the crisis and received substantial blame for it from both sides. However, in the general election in September 2002, the coalition partners suffered decisive defeats.

A coalition led by SDSM won half the 120 seats. Branko Crvenkovski, leader of the Social Democrats, became prime minister again and governed with the new Albanian Democratic Union for Integration (DUI), under Ali Ahmeti, former leader of the rebels and now a democratic politician. President Boris Trajkovski died on 26 February 2004 in an airplane crash in Bosnia-Herzegovina, and the second round of new presidential elections on 28 April chose Branko Crvenkovski as his successor. Both as prime minister and as president, Crvenkovski guided the governing coalition in implementing the Ohrid Framework Agreement and in preparing for Macedonia's eventual membership in the EU and NATO.[30]

A permanent and perfect relationship between a national majority and a substantial minority is virtually unobtainable. Such minorities tend to be overprotective of their rights, and majorities oversensitive about the stability of the state with which they identify their own survival. Striking a mutually acceptable balance is difficult, and keeping the relationship stable and peaceful requires a great deal of mutual understanding.

The crisis of 2001—the armed attempt to destabilize the new state—worsened Macedonian-Albanian relations. It nullified for a time the small but real gains of the 1990s and again heightened mutual distrust and suspicion. In the long run, stable and mutually beneficial relations would require the Albanians to show greater acceptance of and loyalty to the state, and the Macedonians, more respect for and trust in their compatriots. This result would take time and a great deal of work and understanding by leaders and elites on both sides. Safeguarding the state is in the interest of both; its destabilization would represent a tragedy for both, as well as for other citizens, the Balkans, and the rest of Europe.

Epilogue

For well over a century and a half, virtually throughout the age of nationalism in southeastern Europe, the Macedonian question was the central issue dividing Balkan peoples and states. Neighboring Bulgaria, Greece, and Serbia struggled for possession of Macedonia. In order to justify their pretensions, each state claimed the Slav or ethnic Macedonians as its own (i.e., as Bulgarians, Greeks, or Serbs). Hence, from the very outset the territorial struggle was also a contest for the hearts and minds of the Macedonian majority in Ottoman Macedonia. Each state sought to win over or force to its own side all Macedonians, or at least those in the areas that it claimed and hoped to acquire and annex. These neighbors' imperialistic and annexationist policies and aims in turn necessitated that they deny any sort of distinct Macedonian identity—territorial, political, ethnic, national.

After they divided Macedonia by force of arms in the two Balkan Wars of 1912–13, they intensified and reinforced their denials because recognizing Macedonian identity would have threatened their past gains and/or future aspirations in the territory. Although the political left in each of them recognized the Macedonians as a distinct south Slav ethnic nation, their bourgeois ruling elites resorted to repression and violence to stamp out any signs or impulses of Macedonian separatism, patriotism, or nationalism.

During the push for national liberation in the Second World War, the Macedonians won the recognition of Communist Yugoslavia, and at the end of the war that of Fatherland Front Bulgaria. However, Yugoslavia's lasting—and Bulgaria's short-lived—recognition did not settle the Macedonian problem. It only focused the controversy. Greece, after the Civil War (1947–49), and Bulgaria, after the 1948 expulsion of Yugoslavia from the Cominform, had to come to terms with the Macedonian nation and republic in the Communist Yugoslav federation. The nationalist authoritarian regime in Athens, and the Stalinist in Sofia, adopted virtually the same position: deny the existence of a Macedonian nation or a Macedonian minority in its own country and call Tito's republic "artificial." These became and have remained the views of the two countries and of their official historians. They also "hoodwinked" (Captain P. H. Evans's term) many foreign observers, including scholars, into embracing their claims.

The Bulgarian ruling elite assumed and hoped that the multinational Yugoslav federation would soon collapse and that Tito's "artificial Macedonians" would reembrace their "natural and true" identity—the Bulgarian. Instead, after the bloody disintegration of Yugoslavia, the Macedonians chose to remain Macedonian. Greece regretted the collapse of its ally Yugoslavia, where the Serbs kept the "Skopjans" under control. However, even then the Greeks were determined to force the Macedonians there to remain under Serbian hegemony. It must have distressed them to see their small neighbor surmount their threats and embargoes, gain recognition, and survive as an independent state.

During the long struggle for Macedonia, some ethnic Macedonians adopted or had to adopt the national identity of one of the competing nations. This was not unusual or peculiar to Macedonians in the age of nationalism. Members of other dominated or oppressed ethnicities went through similar experiences, especially in the many regions in central and eastern Europe where the dominant nation or nations denied the existence of a people or peoples.

Under very trying circumstances, most ethnic Macedonians chose a Macedonian identity. That identity began to form with the Slav awakening in Macedonia in the first half of the nineteenth century. The process was continuous but complex and protracted. It was not complete until the struggle for national liberation in the Second World War and its aftermath. Yugoslav Macedonia, in an atmosphere of relative cultural freedom, standardized the Macedonian language, created a vibrant national culture, and facilitated national integration.

Bulgaria and Greece's denial of the Macedonian identity, nation, and minorities, and the same stance by some influential Serbian politicians and the Serbian Orthodox church, have kept alive the Macedonian problem: the "apple of discord" and the "stumbling block" to Balkan cooperation. It is difficult to comprehend, let alone rationalize, such denials in today's Europe. One may argue that in the past Macedonia's neighbors perceived recognition as a threat to their earlier gains or future aspirations there. Such thinking is now completely out of place. After the collapse of Communism in Europe, the end of the Cold War, and Yugoslavia's bloody wars of succession, it is inconceivable that any party would even consider using force to change frontiers.

By the same token, EU expansion into the Balkans should permit more enlightened and tolerant policies toward national minorities. Greece and Bulgaria are already EU members, Macedonia is a candidate, and Serbia, Albania, and possibly Kosovo are keen to join. In this European context, resolution of minority problems should emerge in accordance with the principles of the EU and UN charters: recognition of minorities and respect for their linguistic, cultural, and religious rights.

In any event, it seems that the time has come for a historic accommodation between the Macedonians and their neighbors. The precondition for that is the genuine acceptance by the latter of a Macedonian identity, nation, and state and of Macedonian national minorities. Indeed, by now this has become a Balkan necessity. There is no other acceptable solution to the Macedonian question.

Historians will continue to debate how the Macedonian identity formed, as they do with all others. However, there can be no doubt that a Macedonian nation exists. Denying the existence of the Macedonians in all parts of Macedonia did not help solve the Macedonian problem and did not contribute to Balkan stability in the past, and it will not do so in the future. Only a settlement that recognizes the Macedonians and respects their national rights would last and enhance stability and tranquility in the Balkans and in the united Europe.

Notes

Chapter 1: Land and People at the Crossroads

1. On the geography of Macedonia and its politicization in the age of nationalism, see H. R. Wilkinson, *Maps and Politics: A Review of the Ethnographic Cartography of Macedonia.* (Liverpool: University Press of Liverpool, 1951).

2. Memorandum of the Central Department of the Foreign Office, 26 Nov. 1925, cited in Andrew Rossos, "The British Foreign Office and Macedonian National Identity, 1918–1941," *Slavic Review* 53, no. 2 (summer 1994), 381 note 47.

3. On numbers, see Andrew Rossos, "The Macedonians of Aegean Macedonia: A British Officer's Report, 1944," *Slavonic and East European Review* 69, no. 2 (April 1991), 284–85.

4. Hugh Poulton, *Who Are the Macedonians?* (Bloomington and Indianapolis: Indiana University Press, 1995), 163–67.

5. Ibid., 148. See also V. Čašule, ed., *Od Priznavanie do negiranje. (Bugarski stavovi za makedonskoto prašanje). Stati, govori, dokumenti* (Skopje: Kultura, 1976), 18–20.

6. Poulton, *Who Are the Macedonians?* 145–46. See also D. K. Budinovski, *Makedoncite vo Albanija* (Skopje: Studentski zbor, 1983).

7. *Nova Makedonija* (Skopje), 13 Nov. 1994, 4; Sabrina P. Ramet, *Balkan Babel: The Disintegration of Yugoslavia from the Death of Tito to the War for Kosovo*, 3rd ed. (Boulder, Colo.: Westview Press, 1999), 188; Duncan M. Perry, "The Republic of Macedonia: Finding Its Way," in Karen Dawisha and Bruce Parrot, eds., *Politics, Power and the Struggle for Democracy in South-East Europe* (Cambridge: Cambridge University Press, 1997), 226.

8. On the situation of the Macedonians in Bulgaria and Greece, see Human Rights Watch/Helsinki, *Destroying Ethnic Identity: Selective Persecution of Macedonians in Bulgaria* (New York, 1991) and *Denying Ethnic Identity: The Macedonians of Greece* (New York, 1994).

Chapter 2: From Argeads to Huns (c. 600 BC—c. AD 600)

1. Eugene N. Borza, *In the Shadow of Olympus: The Emergence of Macedon* (Princeton, N.J.: Princeton University Press, 1990), 73.

2. Ibid., 73–6; A. S. Shofman, *Orherki po istorii Makedonii i makedonskogo naroda*, 2 vols. (Kazan: Kazanskii gosudarstvennyi universitet, 1960), I: 18.

3. Borza, *In the Shadow of Olympus*, 96. See also N. G. L. Hammond, *A History of Greece to 322 B.C.*, 3rd ed. (Oxford: Oxford University Press, 1986), 534–35.

4. N. G. L. Hammond and G. T. Griffith, *A History of Macedonia*, vol. II, *550–336 B.C.* (Oxford: Oxford University Press), 150.

5. Borza, *In the Shadow of Olympus*, 172.

6. Ibid., 96–7; see also R. M. Errington, *A History of Macedonia* (Berkeley: University of California Press), 3–4.

7. Borza, *In the Shadow of Olympus*, 30; Institut za nacionalna istorija, *Istorija na makedonskiot narod*, 3 vols. (Skopje: Nova Makedonija, 1969), I: 34.

8. Institut za nacionalna istorija, *Istorija na makedonskiot narod*, I: 35.

9. Borza, *In the Shadow of Olympus*, 231.

10. On the reign of Philip II, see J.R. Ellis, *Philip II and Macedonian Imperialism* (London, 1976); W. Lindsay Adams and Eugene N. Borza, eds., *Philip II, Alexander the Great and the Macedonian Heritage* (Lanham, Md.: University Press of America, 1982); N. G. L. Hammond, *Philip of Macedon* (Baltimore: Johns Hopkins University Press, 1994).

11. On Alexander the Great, see A. B. Bosworth, *Conquest and Empire: The Reign of Alexander the Great* (Cambridge: Cambridge University Press, 1988); and Peter Green, *Alexander of Macedon: 356–323 B.C. A Historical Biography* (Berkeley: University of California Press, 1991).

12. On the Hellenistic period, see Branko Panov, ed., *Istorija na makedonskiot narod*, vol. I, *Makedonija od praistoriskoto vreme do potpaǵaneto pod turska vlast (1371 godina)* (Skopje: Institut za nacionalna istorija, 2000), chaps. 7 and 8, 143–73.

13. On the three Macedonian wars, see ibid., 166–77; Shofman, *Ocherki po istorii*, I: 76–84.

14. On Macedonia under Roman rule, see Panov, ed., *Istorija na makedonskiot narod*, I: 178–201; Shofman, *Ocherki po istorii*, I: 85–106.

15. Panov, ed., *Istorija na makedonskiot narod*, I: 233–39, 273–84; Shofman, *Ocherki po istorii*, I: 105–6, 125–34.

Chapter 3: Medieval, Slavic Macedonia (c. 600–c. 1400)

1. D. Obolensky, *The Byzantine Commonwealth: Eastern Europe 500–1453* (New York: Praeger, 1971).

2. G. Ostrogorsky, *History of the Byzantine State* (New Brunswick, N.J.: Rutgers University Press, 1957), 301–2.

3. Blaže Ristovski, *Makedonskiot narod i makedonskata nacija*, 2 vol. (Skopje: Misla, 1983), I: 33.

4. Jean W. Sedlar, *East Central Europe in the Middle Ages, 1000–1500* (Seattle, Wash.: University of Washington Press, 1994), 258.

5. Barbara Jelavich, *History of the Balkans*, 2 vols. (Cambridge: Cambridge University Press, 1983), I: 27.

6. Sedlar, *East Central Europe*, 401.

7. Ibid., 402.

8. Ibid., 408. The scholarly literature on the formation of national identities and nations in the age of nationalism is vast. See especially E. J. Hobsbawm, *Nations and Nationalism since 1780: Programme, Myth, Reality*, 2nd ed. (Cambridge: Cambridge University Press, 1990); Miroslav Hroch, *Social Preconditions of National Revival in Europe: A Comparative Analysis of the Social Composition of Patriotic Groups among the Smaller European Nations* (Cambridge: Cambridge University Press, 1985); and *In the National Interest: Demands and Goals of European National Movements of the Nineteenth Century: A Comparative Perspective* (Prague: Faculty of Arts, Charles University, 2000).

9. On the early history of the Slavs, see Francis Dvornik, *The Slavs: Their Early History and Civilization* (Boston: American Academy of Arts and Sciences, 1956); A. P. Vlasto, *The Entry of the Slavs into Christendom. An Introduction to the Medieval History of the Slavs* (Cambridge: Cambridge University Press, 1970).

10. On the early history of the Macedonian Slavs, see Stjepan Antoljak, *Srednovekovna Makedonija*, vol. I (Skopje: Misla, 1985); Branko Panov, ed., *Istorija na makedonskiot narod*, vol. I, *Makedonija od praistoriskoto vreme do potpaǵaneto pod turska vlast (1371 godina)* (Skopje: Institut za nacionalna istorija, 2000), part 2: 261–308.

11. L. S. Stavrianos, *The Balkans since 1453* (New York: Holt, Rinehart and Winston, 1958), 26. See also Ostrogorsky, *History of the Byzantine State*, 263; Dvornik, *The Slavs*, 131. On the reign of Tsar Simeon, see Būlgarska akademiia na naukite, *Istoriia na Būlgariia*, vol. II, *Pūrva būlgarska dūrzhava* (Sofia: Būlgarska akademiia na naukite, 1981), part III: chap. 3, 278–322.

12. Institut za nacionalna istorija, *Istorija na makedonskiot narod*, 3 vols. (Skopje: Nova Makedonija, 1969), I: 107–8.

13. Obolensky, *The Byzantine Commonwealth*, 125; Stoyan Pribichevich, *Macedonia: Its People and History* (University Park: Pennsylvania State University Press, 1982), 73–5. See also D. Obolensky, *The Bogomils: A Study in Balkan Neo-Manichaeism* (Cambridge: Cambridge University Press, 1948); Makedonska akademija na naukite i umetnostite, *Bogomilstvoto na Balkanot vo svetloto na nainovite istražuvanja* (Skopje, 1982).

14. On Samuil and his state, see Stjepan Antoljak, *Samoilovata država* (Skopje: Misla, 1969).

15. For the latest scholarly research on Basil II, see Paul Stephenson, *The Legend of Basil the Bulgar-Slayer* (Cambridge: Cambridge University Press, 2003).

16. Ostrogorsky, *History of the Byzantine State*, 301.

17. Obolensky, *The Byzantine Commonwealth*, 131. See also Ostrogorsky, *History of the Byzantine State*, 131.

18. Antoljak, *Samoilovata država*; see also Obolensky, *The Byzantine Commonwealth*, 131; Pribichevich, *Macedonia*, 87–88.

19. Ostrogorsky, *History of the Byzantine State*, 302.

20. Ostrogorsky, *History of the Byzantine State*, 301–2. See also Obolensky, *The Byzantine Commonwealth*, 131; Pribichevich, *Macedonia*, 87–88.

21. Ostrogorsky, *History of the Byzantine State*, 310.

22. Ibid., 310; see also Pribichevich, *Macedonia*, 83.

23. Dvornik, *The Slavs*, 127.

24. Obolensky, *The Byzantine Commonwealth*, 138.

25. Dvornik, *The Slavs*, 84 note 2.

26. Obolensky, *The Byzantine Commonwealth*, 141.

27. Ibid., 141.

28. Ostrogorsky, *History of the Byzantine State*, 230. See also S. B. Bern-

shtein, *Konstantin i Mefodii* (Moscow, 1984); V. Sl. Kiselkov, *Slavianskite prosvetiteli Kiril i Metodii* (Sofia, 1946).

29. Obolensky, *The Byzantine Commonwealth*, 149.

30. Ibid., 325. On Kliment and Naum and the Ohrid Literary School, see Makedonska akademija na naukite i umetnostite, *Kliment Ohridski i ulogata na Ohridskata književna škola vo razvitokot na slovenskata prosveta* (Skopje, 1989) and *Svetite Kliment i Naum Ohridski i pridonesot na ohridskiot duhoven centar za slovenskata prosveta i kultura* (Skopje, 1995).

31. Ostrogorsky, *History of the Byzantine State*, 311.

32. Panov, ed., *Istorija na makedonskiot narod*, I, part 2: 429–37.

33. Ibid., 438–44.

34. On the Macedonian lands during the decline of the Byzantine empire, see ibid., 445–88; Ostrogorsky, *History of the Byzantine State*, 478–88.

35. On the Serbian conquest and rule of Macedonia, see Panov, ed., *Istorija na makedonskiot narod*, I, part 2: 499–550; Ostrogorsky, *History of the Byzantine State*, 499–533. On Tsar Dušan's reign, see Srpska knijževna zadruga, *Istorija sprskog naroda*, book I, *Od najstarijih vremena do maričke bitke (1371)*, ed. Sima Črković (Belgrade: Srpska knijževna zadruga, 1981), part 4: 511–65.

Chapter 4: Ottoman Rule (c. 1400–c. 1800)

1. For a good and concise treatment of the Ottoman conquest of Macedonia, see Aleksandar Stojanovski, ed., *Istorija na makedonskiot narod*, vol. II, *Makedonija pod turska vlast (od XIV do krajot na XVIII vek)* (Skopje: Institut za nacionalna istorija, 1998), 9–19.

2. The most balanced and interesting English-language discussion of the Ottoman administration and rule in the Balkans appears in L. S. Stavrianos, *The Balkans since 1453* (New York: Holt, Rinehart and Winston, 1958), parts 2 and 3: 33–213. See also Peter F. Sugar, *Southeastern Europe under Ottoman Rule, 1354–1804* (Seattle: University of Washington Press, 1977).

3. Stavrianos, *The Balkans since 1453*, 84, uses the term "Ruling Institution"; Barbara Jelavich, *History of the Balkans*, 2 vols. (Cambridge: Cambridge University Press, 1983), I: 41, refers to the "governing class."

4. Stavrianos, *The Balkans*, 83.

5. Ibid., 109. On the Orthodox church during the centuries of Ottoman rule, see Stephen Runciman, *The Great Church in Captivity* (Cambridge: Cambridge University Press, 1968); N. J. Pentzopoulos, *Church and Law in the Balkan Peninsula during the Ottoman Rule* (Salonika: Institute for Balkan Studies,

1967); Ivan Snegarov, *Istoriia na Okhridskata arkhiepiskopiia—patriarshiia ot padaneto i pod turtsite do neinoto unishtozhenie (1394–1767)* (Sofia, 1932).

6. M. S. Anderson, *The Eastern Question 1774–1923: A Study in International Relations* (New York: St. Martin's Press, 1966), xi–27; Albert Sorel, *The Eastern Question in the Eighteenth Century: The Partition of Poland and the Treaty of Kainardji* (New York: Fertig, 1969).

7. Stavrianos, *The Balkans*, 136.

8. On the decline of the Ottoman empire, see Sugar, *Southeastern Europe*, 187–95; Stavrianos, *The Balkans*, 117–36.

9. Sugar, *Southeastern Europe*, chap. 10, 209–32; Stavrianos, *The Balkans*, 137–53; Jelavich, *History of the Balkans*, I: 72–98.

10. Stavrianos, *The Balkans*, 150. On the Greek-dominated patriarchate of Constantinople, see also G. G. Arnakis, "The Greek Church in Constantinople and the Ottoman Empire," *Journal of Modern History* 24 (1952), 235–50.

11. Jelavich, *History of the Balkans*, I: 56. See also Sugar, *Southeastern Europe*, 252–4; Gale Stokes, "Church and Class in Early Balkan Nationalism," *East European Quarterly* 13, no. 2 (1979), 259–70.

12. Stojanovski, ed., *Istorija na makedonskiot narod*, II: 39–45.

13. Ibid., 79–118. On Islamization in Macedonia, see particularly Nijazi Limanoski, *Islamizacijata i etničkite promeni vo Makedonija* (Skopje: Makedonska kniga, 1993).

14. Institut za nacionalna istorija, *Istorija na makedonskiot narod*, 3 vols. (Skopje: Nova Makedonija, 1969), I: 235–36.

15. Stojanovski, ed., *Istorija na makedonskiot narod*, II: 94–101. See also Aleksandar Matkovski, *A History of the Jews in Macedonia* (Skopje: Macedonian Review Editions, 1982).

16. Aleksandar Matkovski examines and analyzes all forms of opposition to and resistance against Ottoman rule in Macedonia, from passive through spiritual to armed and revolutionary, in his *Otporot vo Makedonija vo vremeto na turskoto vladeenje*, 4 vols. (Skopje: Misla, 1983); the third volume deals with the ajdut movement. Matkovski summarizes his findings on the ajdutstvo in Stojanovski, ed., *Istorija na makedonskiot narod*, II: 165–88. On the ajduts, see also Bistra Tsvetkova, *Khaidutstvoto v Būlgarskite zemi prez 15–18 vek* (Sofia, 1971).

17. On the Karpoš uprising, see Matkovski, *Otporot vo Makedonija*, IV: 374–54; Stojanovski, ed., *Istorija na makedonskiot narod*, II: 218–37.

18. Stojanovski, ed., *Istorija na makedonskiot narod*, II: 142–47; Institut za nacionalna istorija, *Istorija na makedonskiot narod*, I: 287–96.

19. Stojanovski, ed., *Istorija na makedonskiot narod*, II:298–340; Institut za nacionalna istorija, *Istorija na makedonskiot narod*, I: 294–5.

20. Jelavich, *History of the Balkans*, I: 40. See also Hugh Poulton, *Who Are the Macedonians?* (Bloomington and Indianapolis: Indiana University Press, 1995), 37.

21. Stavrianos, *The Balkans*, 105.

22. Snegarov, *Istoriia na Okhridskata Arkhiepiskopiia—patriarshiia*. See also Stojanovski, ed., *Istorija na makedonskiot narod*, II: 343–70.

23. Stojanovski, ed., *Istorija na makedonskiot narod*, II: 432–61. See also Radmila Ugrinova-Skalovska, ed., *Damaskini* (Skopje: Makedonska kniga, 1975); Donka Petkova-Toteva, *Damaskinite v būlgarskata literatura* (Sofia, 1965).

24. Institut za nacionalna istorija, *Istorija na Makeedonskiot narod*, I: 298–9. See particularly the works of Risto Kantardžiev, *Makedonskoto prerodbensko učilište* (Skopje: Institut za nacionalna istorija, 1965) and *Naprednoto učilište vo Makedonija* (Skopje: Prosvetno delo, 1985).

Chapter 5: Ottoman Reform and Decline (c.1800–1908)

1. Institut za nacionalna istorija, *Istorija na makedonskiot narod*, 3 vols. (Skopje: Nova Makedonija, 1969), II: 8.

2. L. S. Stavrianos, *The Balkans since 1453* (New York: Holt, Rinehart and Winston, 1958), 301.

3. L. S. Stavrianos, *The Balkans 1815–1914* (New York: Holt, Rinehart and Winston, 1963), 31.

4. On the Ottoman reform movement in the nineteenth century, see F. E. Bailey, *British Policy and the Turkish Reform Movement: A Study in Anglo-Turkish Relations 1826–1853* (Cambridge, Mass.: Harvard University Press, 1942); Roderick H. Davison, *Reform in the Ottoman Empire, 1856–1876* (Princeton, N.J.: Princeton University Press, 1963); Robert Devereux, *The First Ottoman Constitutional Period: A Study of the Midhat Constitution and Parliament* (Baltimore: Johns Hopkins Press, 1963); Serif Mardin, *The Genesis of Young Ottoman Thought: A Study in the Modernization of Turkish Political Ideas* (Princeton, N.J.: Princeton University Press, 1962); Ernest E. Ramsaur, *The Young Turks: Prelude to the Revolution of 1908* (Princeton, N.J.: Princeton University Press, 1957).

5. Wayne S. Vucinich, *The Ottoman Empire: Its Record and Legacy* (Princeton, N.J.: D. Van Nostrand, 1965), 93, text of the Gulhané decree, 160–61; Stavrianos, *The Balkans since 1453,* 316–17. See also Bailey, *British Policy and the Turkish Reform Movement*, 193–205.

6. Stavrianos, *The Balkans since 1453*, 385.

7. Vucinich, *The Ottoman Empire*, 93–96, text of the Humayun decree, 161–64; Stavrianos, *The Balkans since 1453*, 385–88. See particularly Roderick Davison, *Reform in the Ottoman Empire*, chap. 2, 52–80.

8. Devereux, *The First Ottoman Constitutional Period*, particularly chap. 4, 80–97, and chap. 10, 235–50.

9. On the Balkan crisis of the 1870s, see B. H. Sumner, *Russia and the Balkans, 1870–1880* (Oxford: Clarendon Press, 1937); M. S. Anderson, *The Eastern Question 1774–1923: A Study in International Relations* (New York: St. Martin's Press), 178–210.

10. Stavrianos, *The Balkans since 1453*, 388.

11. Institut za nacionalna istorija, *Istorija na makedonskiot narod*, II: 15–16; Krste Bitovski, ed., *Istorija na makedonskiot narod*, vol. III, *Makedonija vo devetnaesetiot vek do balkanskite vojni (1912–1913)* (Skopje: Institut za nacionalna istorija, 2003), 17.

12. Institut za nacionalna istorija, *Istorija na makedonskiot narod*, II: 18.

13. Ibid., 20–23.

14. Ibid., 47–53.

15. For a clear and succinct definition of the Macedonian question, see Andrew Rossos, "The Macedonian Question and Instability in the Balkans," in Norman M. Naimark and Holly Case, eds., *Yugoslavia and Its Historians: Understanding the Balkan Wars of the 1990s* (Stanford, Calif.: Stanford University Press, 2003), 141–42.

16. On the historic Congress and Treaty of Berlin of 1878, see especially Sumner, *Russia and the Balkans*, 501–33; Anderson, *The Eastern Question*, 210–19.

17. Stavrianos, *The Balkans since 1453*, 517.

18. Ibid., 518. Bulgarian, Greek, and Serbian claims received extensive publicity. For a representative sampling of the divergent points of view, see on Serbian claims T. R. Georgevich, *Macedonia* (London, 1918); Jovan M. Jovanović, *Južna Serbija od kraja XVIII veka do oslobodjenja* (Belgrade, 1941). On Greek, see C. Nicolaides, *La Macédoine* (Berlin, 1899); G. Modes, *O makedonikon agon kai i neoteri makedoniki istoria* (Salonika, 1967). On Bulgarian, see I. Ivanov, *La question macédoine* (Paris, 1920); Institut za istoriia, Būlgarska akademiia na naukite, *Makedonskiot vūpros. Istoriko-politicheska spravka* (Sofia, 1963).

19. Institut za nacionalna istorija, *Istorija na makedonskiot narod*, II: 121–25. See also Risto Poplazarov, *Grčkata politika sprema Makedonija vo vtorata polovina na XIX i početokot na XX vek* (Skopje: Institut za nacionalna istorija, 1973).

20. Institut za nacionalna istorija, *Istorija na makedonskiot narod*, II:

121–25. See also Kliment Džambazovski, *Kulturno-opštestvenite vrski na makedoncite so Srbija vo tekot na XIX vek* (Skopje: Institut za nacionalna istorija, 1960).

21. Džambazovski, *Kulturno-opštestvenite vrski*, 164–80.

22. Institut za nacionalna istorija, *Istorija na makedonskiot narod*, II: 123–25; Džambazovski, *Kulturno-opštestvenite vrski*, 199–298.

23. Bitovski, ed., *Istorija na makedonskiot narod*, III: 40; Sumner, *Russia and the Balkans*, 112–17; Jelavich, *History of the Balkans*, I: 344; see also Thomas A. Meininger, *Ignatiev and the Establishment of the Bulgarian Exarchate: A Study in Personal Diplomacy* (Madison: State Historical Society of Wisconsin, 1970).

24. Stavrianos, *The Balkans since 1453*, 519.

25. Institut za nacionalna istorija, *Istorija na makedonskiot narod*, II: 125–28; Stavrianos, *The Balkans since 1453*, 518–19. See also Krste Bitovski, *Makedonija i Kneževstvo Bugarija (1893–1903)* (Skopje: Institut za nacionalna istorija, 1977).

26. For a brief account of the other propaganda in Macedonia in the second half of the nineteenth century, see Bitovski, ed., *Istorija na makedonskiot narod*, III: 46–49.

Chapter 6: National Awakening and National Identity (1814–1913)

1. The literature on the struggle in Macedonia is vast, but rather uneven and polemical. A good documentary survey in English of the activities of the neighboring Balkan states in Macedonia appears in George P. Gooch and Harold Temperley, eds., *British Documents on the Origins of the War, 1898–1914*, 11 vols. (London: HM Stationery Office, 1926–38), V: 100–23. For a balanced treatment in a Western language, see Fikret Adanir, *Die makedonische Frage: Ihre Entstehung und Entwicklung bis 1908* (Wiesbaden: Steiner, 1979); useful works in Western languages are Duncan M. Perry, *The Politics of Terror: The Macedonian Revolutionary Movement, 1893–1903* (Durham, N.C.: Duke University Press, 1988); Henry N. Brailsford, *Macedonia: Its Races and Their Future* (1906), reprint (New York: Arno Press, 1980); Elisabeth Barker, *Macedonia: Its Place in Balkan Power Politics* (1950), reprint (Westport, Conn.: Greenwood Press, 1980); Jacques Ancel, *La Macédoine* (Paris, 1930); Gustav Weigard, *Ethnographie von Makedonien* (Leipzig, 1924). For the Bulgarian, Greek, and Serbian points of view, see on Serbian T. R. Georgevich, *Macedonia* (London, 1918); Jovan M. Jovanović, *Južna Srbija od kraja XVIII veka do osvobodjenja* (Belgrade, 1941); on Greek C. Nicolaides, *La Macédoine* (Berlin,

1899); G. Modes, *O Makedonikon agon kai i neoteri makedoniki istoria* (Salonika, 1967); on Bulgarian I. Ivanov, *La question macédoine* (Paris, 1920); Institut za istoriia, Būlgarska akademiia na naukite, *Makedonskiat vūpros. Istoriko-politicheska spravka* (Sofia, 1963). Macedonian historians turned their attention to this problem more recently. See Kliment Džambazovski, *Kulturno-opštestvenite vrski na Makedoncite so Srbija vo tekot na XIX vek* (Skopje: Institut za nacionalna istorija, 1960); Risto Poplazarov, *Grčkata politika sprema Makedonija vo vtorata polorina na XIX i početokot va XX vek* (Skopje: Institut za nacionalna istorija, 1973); Krste Bitovski, *Makedonija i Kneżestvo Bugarija, 1893–1903* (Skopje: Institut za nacionalna istorija, 1977).

2. Karl Hron, *Das Volkstum der Slaven Makedoniens* (Vienna, 1890).

3. P. D. Draganov, *Makedonskoslavianskii sbornik s prilozheniem slovaria* (St. Petersburg, 1894).

4. Andrew Rossos, "Macedonianism and Macedonian Nationalism on the Left," in Ivo Banac and Katherine Vedery, eds., *National Character and National Ideology in Interwar Eastern Europe* (New Haven, Conn.: Yale Center for International and Area Studies, 1995), 236–39 and 251–54. See also Ivan Katardžiev, *Vreme na zreenje. Makedonskoto nacionalno prašanje meģu dvete svetski vojnie (1919–1930)*, 2 vols. (Skopje: Kultura, 1977), I, part 3: chaps. 1–4. Chapter 1 covers the Comintern, 2 the KPJ, 3 the KKE, and 4 the BKP.

5. Among the most significant pre-1939 scholarly studies of the Macedonians' national history were Krste P. Misirkov, *Za makedonskiite raboti* (Sofia: Liberalni klub, 1903), facsimile ed. (Skopje: Institut za makedonski jazik, 1974); Angel Dinev, *Makedonskite Slaviani* (Sofia, 1938); Kosta Veselinov, *Vūzrazhdaneto na Makedoniia i ilindeskoto vūstanie* (Sofia, 1939).

6. The most notable early works on the subject were Blaže Koneski's slender *Kon makedonskata prerodba. Makedonskite učebnici od 19 vek* (Skopje: Institut za nacionalna istorija, 1959); Blaže Ristovski's massive *Krste Misirkov (1874–1926). Prilog kon proučuvanjeto na razvitokot na makedonskata nacionalna misla* (Skopje: Kultura, 1966).

7. I requested permission to work on the Macedonian question in the archives in Bulgaria, Greece, and the Soviet Union several times in the late 1970s and throughout the 1980s. I had no luck in Greece or the Soviet Union. The chief administrator of the State Archives in Sofia granted me very restricted permission, but withdrew even that after two weeks.

8. Joakim Krčovski, *Sobrani tekstovi*, ed. Blaže Koneski (Skopje: Makedonska kniga, 1974), 5–19; also Blaže Ristovski, *Makedonskiot narod i makedonskata nacija*, 2 vols. (Skopje: Misla, 1983), I: 155–62.

9. On this early phase in the Macedonian awakening, see Koneski, *Kon makedonskata prerodba*, 5–14; Ristovski, *Makedonskiot narod*, I: 163–87,

194–96, 235–62, 263–80. See also Simeon Radev, *Makedoniia i būlgarskoto vūzrazhdane v XIX vek*, 3 vols. (Sofia: P. Slushkov, 1927–28), I.

10. Cited in Ljubiša Doklestić, *Srpsko-makedonskite odnosi vo XIX—ot vek* (Skopje: Nova Makedonija, 1973), 111; see also Džambazovski, *Kulturno-opštestvenite vrski*, 8–11, 55–57.

11. Cited in Ljubiša Doklestić, "Makedonskata osloboditelna borba i makedonskoto nacionalno prašanje," in Institut za nacionalna istorija, *Razvitok na državnosta na makedonskiot narod* (Skopje, 1966), 80. See also Dimitrija Miladinov and Konstantin Miladinov, *Zbornik na narodni pesni*, eds. Haralampie Polenaković and Todor Dimitrovski (Skopje: Makedonska kniga, 1983), xiii–xvi. The original title of the collection was *Būlgarski narodni pesni* (Zagreb: A. Jakić, 1861).

12. Misirkov, *Za makedonckite raboti*, 125.

13. See note 9 to this chapter; Misirkov, *Za makedonckite raboti*, 114, 122–26; Doklestić, *Srpsko-makedonskite odnosi*, 3–6; Džambazovski, *Kulturno-opštestvenite vrski*, 5–57. See also Horace G. Lunt, "Some Sociolinguistic Aspects of Macedonian and Bulgarian," in B. A. Stolz, I. R. Titunik, and L. Doležel, eds., *Language and Literary Theory* (Ann Arbor: University of Michigan Press, 1984), 97–102, 108; Victor A. Friedman, "Macedonian Language and Nationalism during the Nineteenth and Early Twentieth Centuries," *Balkanistica* 2 (1975), 84–86.

14. Ristovski, *Makedonskiot narod*, I: 132–34, 135.

15. Ibid., 133.

16. Ibid., 136–40; Slavko Dimevski, "Dve pisma na Petko Račov Slavejkov za makedonizmot," *Razgledi* (Skopje) 14, no. 3 (1973), 561–66.

17. Koneski, *Kon makedonskata prerodba*, 24–56; Friedman, "Macedonian Language and Nationalism," 86–7; Ristovski, *Makedonskiot narod*, I: 178–81.

18. See Rossos, "Macedonianism and Macedonian Nationalism on the Left," in Ivo Banac and Katherine Verdery, eds., *National Character and National Ideology in Interwar Eastern Europe* (New Haven, Conn.: Yale Center for Internatonal and Area Studies, 1995), 228–29.

19. Cited in V. I. Kosik, "Gordiev uzel Balkan," in R. P. Grishina, ed., *Makedoniia: Problemi istorii i kulturi* (Moscow: Institut Slavianovedeniia, Rossiiskaia akademiia nauk, 1999), 63. See also Simon Drakul, "Ruskite diplomatsko-strateški kontroverzi okolu makedonskoto prašanje vo ilindenskite decenii," in Makedonska akademija na naukite i umetnostite, *Sto godini od osnovanjeto na VMRO i 90 godini od ilindeskoto vostanie* (Skopje, 1994), 375.

20. Michael Seraphinoff, *The 19th Century Macedonian Awakening: A Study of the Life and Work of Kiril Pejchinovich* (Lanham, Md.: University Press of America, 1996), 133. See also Ristovski, *Makedonskiot narod*, I: 131.

In 1934, a Bulgarian official complained about a certain Macedonian activist who, while inspecting schools in Nevrokop, told pupils: "By next year we will be teaching *na našinski*" (in our language, in Macedonian). Quoted in Ristovski, *Makedonskiot narod*, II: 553. And, in 1936, in Zagreb, the Vardar Macedonian Student Society published the first and only issue of its *Naš vesnik*. The introductory article stating its aims could not and did not use the word "Macedonian." Instead, it declared that its aim was to acquaint the public with "the life of our region," "the life of our people," "the immense wealth of our popular folklore," "our countless melodic and warm folk songs," "the originality and beauty of our folk customs"; *Naš vesnik* (Zagreb), I (30 March 1937), 1.

21. Miladinov and Miladinov, *Zbornik na narodni pesni*, throughout the volume.

22. Evans's report appears verbatim in Andrew Rossos, "The Macedonians of Aegean Macedonia: A British Officer's Report, 1944," *Slavonic and East European Review* (London), 69, no. 2 (1991), 291–309.

23. Krste Bitovski, ed., *Istorija na makedonskiot narod*, vol. III, *Makedonija vo devetnaesettiot vek do balkanskite vojni (1912–1913)* (Skopje: Institut za nacionalna istorija, 2003), 171–83, 200–207, 244–62; Duncan M. Perry, *The Politics of Terror: The Macedonian Liberation Movements 1893–1903* (Durham, N.C.: Duke University Press, 1988), 31–106.

24. Koneski, *Kon makedonskata prerodba*, 24–25; Ristovski, *Makedonskiot narod*, I: 270–92; Lunt, "Some Sociolinguistic Aspects," 102–8; Friedman, "Macedonian Language and Nationalism," 88; Stojan Risteski, *Sozdavanjeto na sovremeniot makedonski literaturen jazik* (Skopje: Studentski zbor, 1988), 38–42.

25. Misirkov, *Za makedonckite raboti*, 1–2, 75–78.

26. Bitovski, ed., *Istorija na makedonskiot narod*, III: 101–34, 159–69, 184–219. However, see especially the writings of leaders and ideologists of Macedonian political nationalism such as Vardarski (P. Poparsov), *Stambolovshchinata v Makedoniia i neinite predstaviteli* (Vienna, 1894); Ǵ. Petrov, *Makedonskoto osvoboditelno delo na bŭlgarska pochva* (Sofia, 1902); G. Todorovski, ed., *Makedonskoto osvoboditelno delo* (Skopje: Misla, 1971), a Macedonian edition of Petrov's most important writings on the Macedonian question; D. Hadžidimov, *Makedonskoto osvoboditelno delo* (Lom, 1900), *Makedonskiia vŭpros* (Dupnitsa, 1901), and *Makedonskiia vŭpros i uchiteliat* (Kiustendil, 1902). For a Macedonian edition of his works on the Macedonian question, see G. Todorovski, ed., *Makedonskoto prašanje* (Skopje: Misla, 1974).

27. K. P. Misirkov, *Za makedonckite raboti* (Sofia: Liberalni klub, 1903), facsimile ed. (Skopje: Institut za makedonski jazik "Krste Misirkov," 1974).

28. On Macedonianism, see especially the works of B. Ristovski, *Makedonskiot narod i Makedonskaia nacija,* 2 vols. (Skopje: Misla, 1983); *Krste Petkov*

Misirkov, 1874–1926: Prilog kon proučuvanjeto na razvitokot na makedonskata nacionalna misla (Skopje: Kultura, 1966); "Vardar," *Naučno-literaturno i opštestveno-političko spisanie na K. P. Misirkov* (Skopje: Kultura, 1966); *Nace Dimov (1876–1916)* (Skopje: Makedonska akademija na naukite i umetnostite, 1973); *Dimitrija Čupovski, 1878–1940 i makedonskoto naučno-literaturno drugarstvo vo Petrograd*, 2 vols. (Skopje: Kultura, 1978); G. Todorovski, *Prethodnicite na Misirkov* (Skopje: Misla, 1968); S. Dimevski, *Za razvojot na makedonskata nacionalna misla do sozdavanjeto na TMORO* (Skopje: Kultura, 1980); M. Dogo, *Lingua e Nazionalità in Macedonia. Vicende e pensieri dei profeti disarmati, 1902–1903* (Milan: Jaca Book, 1985); Koneski, *Kon makedonskata prerodba*, 87–97.

Chapter 7: The VMRO and Ilinden (1893–1903)

1. The literature on the VMRO and the Ilinden Uprising (1893–1903) is extensive. For the various and at times differing interpretations of the events of this decade, see Makedonska akademija na naukite i umetnostite, *Sto godini od osnovanieto na VMRO i 90 godini od Ilindenskoto vostanie* (Skopje, 1994); Krste Bitovski, ed., *Istorija na makedonskiot narod*, vol. III, *Makedonija vo devetnaesettiot vek do balkanskite vojni (1912–1913)* (Skopje: Institut za nacionalna istorija, 2003), parts 4 and 5: 157–358; Manol Pandevski, *Nacionalnoto prašanje vo makedonskoto osloboditelno dviženje, 1893–1903* (Skopje: Kultura, 1974) and *Ilindenskoto vostanie vo Makedonija 1903* (Skopje: Institut za nacionalna istorija, 1978); Konstantin Pandev, *Natsionalosvoboditelnoto dvizhenie v Makedoniia i Odrinsko, 1878–1903* (Sofia: Nauka i izkustvo, 1978); Jutta de Jong, *Der nationale Kern des makedonischen Problems: Ansätze und Grundlagen einer makedonischen Nationalbewegung, 1890–1903* (Frankfurt: Lang, 1982); Duncan M. Perry, *The Politics of Terror: The Macedonian Liberation Movements 1893–1903* (Durham, N.C.: Duke University Press, 1988); Fikret Adanir, *Die makedonische Frage: Ihre Entstehung und Entwicklung bis 1909* (Wiesbaden: Steiner, 1979), chaps. 1, 2, and 3; Khristo Silianov, *Osvoboditelnite borbi na Makedoniia*, 2 vols. (Sofia: Izd. na Ilindenskata organizatsiia, 1933, 1943), I; Dino Kiosev, *Istoria na makedonskoto natsionalno revolutsionno dvizhenie* (Sofia: Otechestven front, 1954), parts 2 and 3 are still useful.

2. Perry, *The Politics of Terror*, 25.

3. Institut za nacionalna istorija, *Istorija na makedonskiot narod*, 3 vols. (Skopje: Nova Makedonija, 1969), II: 149–50.

4. Perry, *The Politics of Terror*, 26.

5. Institut za nacionalna istorija, *Istorija na makedonskiot narod*, II: 151–52.

6. L. S. Stavrianos, *The Balkans since 1453* (New York: Holt, Rinehart and Winston, 1958), 520.

7. This is the most common name in both scholarly and popular writing. Until 1905, its followers used, and it went by, various names—for example, Macedonian Revolutionary Committee, Macedonia Revolutionary Organization, or simply the Organization. Its 1897 statute referred to it as the Bulgarian-Macedonian-Adrianople Revolutionary Organization. In 1902, it became the Secret Macedonian-Adrianople Revolutionary Organization. Some sources referred to it as the 'Internal Organization.' Perry, *The Politics of Terror*, 221 note 10; Bitovski, ed., *Istorija na makedonskiot narod*, III, 161–62. VMRO became the official and accepted name after the Rila Congress in 1905; Ivan Katardžiev, "I.M.O.R.O.," *Macedonian Review* (Skopje), 20, no. 3 (1990), 151.

8. The average age of 13 of its leaders was 33 years in 1903. Ten of them had graduated from the gymnasium, and eight were teachers (Perry, *The Politics of Terror*, 182–83).

9. On the VMRO of the Ilinden period, its activities, and its aims, see Bitovski, ed., *Istorija na makedonskiot narod*, III, part 4: 159–286; Adanir, *Die makedonische Frage*, chaps. 2 and 3; de Jong, *Der nationale Kern des makedonischen Problems*; Perry, *The Politics of Terror*, chaps. 2 and 3, 31–106; Pandev, *Natsionalno osvaboditelnoto dvizhenie v Makedoniia*; Silianov, *Osvoboditelnite borbi*, I; Kiosev, *Istoriia na makedonskoto natsionalno*, part 3: 213–320.

10. H. R. Wilkinson, *Maps and Politics: A Review of the Ethnographic Cartography of Macedonia* (Liverpool: University Press of Liverpool, 1951), 1–3.

11. Cited in Perry, *The Politics of Terror*, 110; see also Bitovski, ed., *Istorija na makedonskiot narod*, III: 184–92.

12. Rossos, *Russia and the Balkans*, 4.

13. Perry, *The Politics of Terror*, 98. See also Bitovski, ed., *Istorija na makedonskiot narod*, III: 240–41.

14. Perry, *The Politics of Terror*, 125; Bitovski, *Istorija na makedonskiot narod*, III: 270–1. On Goce Delčev, see Hristo Andonov-Poljanski, *Goce Delčev i negovoto vreme*, 6 vols. (Skopje: Kultura, 1972); Dino Kiosev, *Gotse Delchev. Pisma i drugi materiali* (Sofia, 1967).

15. Four days later, on 6 August, a much smaller revolt began in the Adrianople vilayet, the so-called Preobrazhenski, or Resurrection Day Uprising. Bulgarian writing normally joins the two events as the Ilinden-Prebrazhenski Uprising. On the launch, course, and suppression of Ilinden, see Bitovski, ed., *Istorija na makedonskiot narod*, III, part 5: 289–358; Perry, *The Politics of Terror*, chap. 4; Adanir, *Die makedonische Frage*, chap. 3; Silianov, *Osvoboditelnite borbi*, I; Kiosev, *Istoriia na makedonskoto natsionalno*, part 3.

16. H. N. Brailsford, *Macedonia: Its Races and Their Future* (London: Methuen, 1906), 113; Perry, *The Politics of Terror*, 135.

17. *Makedoniia i Odrinsko (1893–1903). Memoar na vūtreshnata organizatsiia* (Sofia, 1904); cited in Perry, *The Politics of Terror*, 139.

18. Institut za nacionalna istorija, *Istorija na makedonskiot narod*, II: 245.

19. Bitovski, ed., *Istorija na makedonskiot narod*, III: 347.

20. Institut za nacionalna istorija, *Istorija na makedonskiot narod*, II: 248.

21. For Misirkov's critique of the revolutionary organization and the struggle against the Turks, see his *Za makedonckite raboti* (Sofia: Liberalnii klub, 1903), facsimile ed. (Skopje: Institut za makedonski jazik, 1974), chap. 1; Blaže Ristovski, *Makedonskiot narod i makedonskata nacija*, 2 vols. (Skopje: Misla, 1983), II: 256–74; Bitovski, ed., *Istorija na makedonskiot narod*, III: 410–18.

22. Bitovski, ed., *Istorija na makedonskiot narod*, III: 378–409; Adanir, *Die makedonische Frage*, chap. 4; Silianov, *Osvoboditelnite borbi*, II; Kiosev, *Istoriia na makedonskoto*, part 4.

23. See chapter 10.

Chapter 8: Decline and Partition (1903–1919)

1. For the partition of Macedonia in its Balkan and European contexts, see Andrew Rossos, *Russia and the Balkans: Inter-Balkan Rivalries and Russian Foreign Policy, 1908–1914* (Toronto: University of Toronto Press, 1981). See also Jovan Donev, *Golemite sili i Makedonija za vremeto na prvata balkanska vojna* (Skopje: Institut za nacionalna istorija, 1988); Petar Stojanov, *Makedonija vo vremeto na balkanskite i prvata svetska vojna (1912–1918)* (Skopje: Institut za nacionalna istorija, 1969); E. G. Helmreich, *The Diplomacy of the Balkan Wars 1912–1913* (Cambridge, Mass.: Harvard University Press, 1938).

2. Katardžiev, "I.M.O.R.O.," 153–61. On the post-Ilinden disintegration of the VMRO, see the works cited in note 22 of chapter 7.

3. Gligor Todorovski, *Makedonskoto prašanje i reformite vo Makedonija* (Skopje: Kultura, 1989), 131–59 and 233–55. See also Stavrianos, *The Balkans since 1453*, 523, 526; Barbara Jelavich, *History of the Balkans*, 2 vols. (Cambridge: Cambridge University Press, 1983), II: 94–95.

4. Bitovski, ed., *Istorija na makedonskiot narod*, III: 367–77; Institut za nacionalna istorija, *Istorija na makedonskiot narod*, II: 259–68.

5. For general information on the Young Turk Revolution, see Ernest E. Ramsaur, *The Young Turks: Prelude to the Revolution of 1908* (Princeton, N.J.: Princeton University Press, 1957); Feroz Ahmad, *The Young Turks: The Committee of Union and Progress and Turkish Politics, 1908–1914* (Oxford: Oxford University Press, 1969). On the revolution and Macedonia, see Bitovski, ed., *Istorija na makedonskiot narod*, III: 421–74.

6. Rossos, *Russia and the Balkans*, 5–7.

7. Ibid., chaps. 1 and 2, 8–69.

8. On the Balkan Wars and the partition of Macedonia, see works cited in note 1 to this chapter.

9. For general information on the situation in Macedonia during the Great War, see Ivan Katardžiev, *Istorija na makedonskiot narod*, vol. IV, *Makedonija meģu Balkanskite i Vtorate svetska vojna (1912–1941)* (Skopje: Institut za nacionalna istorija, 2000), 83–108.

10. Hristo Andonov-Poljanski, ed., *Dokumenti za borbata na makedonskiot narod za samostojnost i za nacionalna država*, 2 vols. (Skopje: Univerzitet Kiril i Metodij, 1981), I: no. 375, 578–82. See also *Makedonskii golos (Makedonski glas)* (St. Petersburg) 2, no. 10 (Aug. 1914) and no. 11 (20 Nov. 1914), facsimile ed. (Skopje: Institut za nacionalna istorija, 1968).

11. Andonov-Poljanski, ed., *Dokumenti*, no. 384, 593–95, no. 389, 602–3, no. 390, 603–4, no. 392, 605–6.

12. On the Macedonian question at the Paris Peace Conference, see Hristo Andonov-Poljanski, *Velika Britania i makedonskoto prašanje na parizkata mirovna konferencija vo 1919 godina* (Skopje: Arhiv na Makedonija, 1973). See also Ivan Katardžiev, *Vreme na zreenje: Makedonskoto nacionalno prašanje meģu dvete svetski vojni (1919–1930)*, 2 vols. (Skopje: Kultura, 1977), I: chap. 1, and *Istorija na makedonskiot narod*, IV: 109–27.

Chapter 9: Macedonia in Three Parts (1920s and 1930s)

1. Ivo Banac, *The National Question in Yugoslavia: Origins, History, Politics* (Ithaca, N.Y.: Cornell University Press, 1984), 49.

2. Ibid., 407. See also Wayne S. Vucinich, "Interwar Yugoslavia," in Vucinich, ed., *Contemporary Yugoslavia: Twenty Years of Socialist Experiment* (Berkeley and Los Angeles: University of California Press, 1969), 7–10.

3. L. S. Stavrianos, *The Balkans since 1453* (New York: Holt, Rinehart and Winston, 1958), 617.

4. Banac, *The National Question*, 407.

5. Stavrianos, *The Balkans since 1453*, 625.

6. On the situation in Vardar Macedonia, see Ivan Katardžiev, *Istorija na makedonskiot narod*, vol. IV, *Makedonija meģu Balkanskite i Vtorata svetska voja (1912–1941)* (Skopje, 2000), 135–85, and *Vreme na zreenje: makedonskoto prašanje meģu dvete svetski vojni, (1919–1930)*, 2 vols. (Skopje: Kultura, 1977), I: 23–85; Institut za nacionalna istorija, *Istorija na makedonskiot narod*, 3 vols. (Skopje: Nova Makedonija, 1969), III: 7–166; Aleksandar Apostolov,

Kolonizacijata na Makedonija vo stara Jugoslavija (Skopje: Kultura, 1966) and "Specifičnata položba na makedonskiot narod vo kralstvoto Jugoslavija," *Glasnik* (Skopje) 16, no. 1 (1972), 39–62.

7. Stavrianos, *The Balkans since 1453*, 620.

8. Banac, *The National Question*, 321; Katardžiev, *Istorija na makedonskiot narod*, IV: 148.

9. On the KPJ's influence in Macedonia, see Katardžiev, *Istorija na makedonskiot narod*, IV: 350–3, and *Vreme na zreenje*, I, part 3: chap. 3; Kiril Miljovski, *Makedonskoto prašanje vo nacionalnata programa na KPJ, 1919–1937* (Skopje: Kultura, 1962). See also next chapter of this book.

10. See Katardžiev, *Vreme na zreenje*, I: 171–83, and II: chap. 2; Dino Kiosev, *Istoriia na makedonskoto natsionalno revolutsionno dvizhenie* (Sofia: Otechestven front, 1954), 512–28. On the VMRO's activities in all three parts of Macedonia, see also the memoirs of its leader after 1924, Ivan Mikhailov, *Spomeni*, 4 vols. (Selci, Louvain, Indianapolis, 1952, 1965, 1967, 1973).

11. Cited in Andrew Rossos, "The British Foreign Office and Macedonian National Identity, 1918–1941," *Slavic Review* 53, no. 2 (summer 1994), 378 and note 36.

12. Cited in ibid., 378–79 and note 38.

13. See the works cited in note 10 to this chapter. See also Katardžiev, *Istorija na makedonskiot narod*, IV: 153–85, 450–60, 473–83.

14. Stavrianos, *The Balkans since 1453*, 663.

15. On economic conditions in Vardar Macedonia, see Institut za nacionalna istorija, *Istorija na makedonskiot narod*, III: 29–37, 56–58, 59–67; Katardžiev, *Istorija na makedonskiot narod*, IV: 162–74, 473–83; and Apostolov, *Kolonizacijata na Makedonija*.

16. Cited in Rossos, "The British Foreign Office," 378–79 and note 32.

17. Banac, *The National Question*, 320. See also Apostolov, *Kolonizacijata na Makedonija*.

18. Cited in Rossos, "The British Foreign Office," 372 and note 9.

19. See Andrew Rossos, "The Macedonians of Aegean Macedonia: A British Officer's Report, 1944," *Slavonic and East European Review* (London) 69, no. 2 (April 1991), 283 and notes 5 and 6.

20. Ibid., 284 and note 8.

21. Todor Simovski, "Balkanskite vojni i nivnite reprekusii vrz etničkata položba vo egejska Makedonija," *Glasnik* (Skopje) 16, no. 3 (1972), 61; also in Hugh Poulton, *Who Are the Macedonians?* (Bloomington and Indianapolis: Indiana University Press, 1995), 86.

22. Stojan Kiselinovski, *Grčkata kolonizacija vo egejska Makedonija (1913–*

1940) (Skopje: Institut za nacionalna istorija, 1981), 78–80, 90, and cited in Rossos, "The Macedonians of Aegean Macedonia," 283.

23. Kiselinovski, *Grčkata kolonizacija*, 108. Rossos, "The Macedonians of Aegean Macedonia," 285. See also Giorgi Abadžiev et al., *Egejska Makedonija vo našata nacionalna istorija* (Skopje: Institut za nacionalna istorija, 1951), 324–25; Dimitar Vlahov, *Makedonija. Momenti od istorijata na makedonskiot narod* (Skopje: Državno izdatelstvo, 1950), 345.

24. See Rossos, "The British Foreign Office," 379–80.

25. *Abecedar* (Athens: P. D. Sekellariu, 1925), facsimile ed. (Skopje: Makedonska revija, 1985).

26. Poulton, *Who Are the Macedonians?*, 88–9 and notes 30 and 31; Stojan Risteski, *Sozdavanjeto no sovremeniot makedonski literaturen jazik* (Skopje: Studentski zbor, 1988), 90–95.

27. For the valuable articles and commentaries that *Rizospastis* published on the Macedonians and the Macedonian question, see Josif Popovski, ed., *Makedonskoto prašanje na stranicite od "Rizospastis" meǵu dvete vojni* (Skopje: Kultura, 1982). On the KKE and the Macedonian question, see also Stojan Kiselinovski, *KPG i makedonskoto nacionalno prašanje, 1918–1940* (Skopje: Misla, 1985); Risto Kirjazovski, ed., *KPG i makedonskoto nacionalno prašanje, 1918–1974* (Skopje: Arhiv na Makedonija, 1982).

28. Cited in Rossos, "The British Foreign Office," 378 and note 35.

29. Cited in Rossos, "The Macedonians of Aegean Macedonia," 259 and complete text of the report 291–309.

30. On the situation of the Macedonians in Aegean Macedonia, see Katardžiev, *Istorija na makedonskiot narod*, IV: 208–12, and *Vreme na zreenje*, I: 85–106; Kiselinovski, *Grčkata kolonizacija*, 75–93; Lazar Mojsov, *Okolu prašanijeto na makedonskoto malcinstvo vo Grcija* (Skopje: Institut za nacionalna istorija, 1954), 207–87; Institut za nacionalna istorija, *Istorija na makedonskiot narod*, III: 261–76.

31. Ibid. However, see also Katardžiev, *Istorija na makedonskiot narod*, IV: 213–25 and 443–49; Poulton, *Who Are the Macedonians?* 85–89; Anastasia N. Karakasidou, "Politicizing Culture: Negating Ethnic Identity in Greek Macedonia," *Journal of Modern Greek Studies* 11 (1993), 1–28; Human Rights Watch/Helsinki, *Denying Ethnic Identity: The Macedonians of Greece* (New York: Human Rights Watch, 1994), 4–8.

32. Cited in Rossos, "The Macedonians of Aegean Macedonia," 293.

33. Institut za nacionalna istorija, *Istorija na makedonskiot narod*, III: 170.

34. Stavrianos, *The Balkans since 1453*, 651.

35. Katardžiev, *Istorija na makedonskiot narod*, IV: 226–52, 363–89, 461–7, and *Vreme na zreenje*, I: 107–19; Dimitar Mitrev, *Pirinska makedonija*

i drugi istoriografski ogledi (Skopje: Naša kniga, 1970), 126–202; Institut za nacionalna istorija, *Istorija na makedonskiot narod*, III: 169–244.

36. On the left after the Great War, see Katardžiev, *Istorija na makedonskiot narod*, IV: 225–66 and 317–19, and *Vreme na zreenje*, I, part 2: chap. 1; Dino Kiosev, *Istoriia na makedonskoto natisionalno revolutsionno dvizhenie* (Sofia: Otechestven front, 1954), 493–99.

37. Banac, *The National Question*, 321–2.

38. On the right and the VMRO after the Great War, see Katardžiev, *Istorija na makedonskiot narod*, IV: 266–87 and 308–17, and *Vreme na zreenje*, I: 171–83, and part 2: chap. 2; Kiosev, *Istoriia na makedonskoto natsionalno*, 512–28.

39. See next chapter of this book.

40. Stavrianos, *The Balkans since 1453*, 651.

41. On Mihailov's VMRO and its rule in Pirin Macedonia and over the Macedonians in Bulgaria, see works in note 35 to this chapter. However, see especially Zoran Todorovski, *VMRO 1924–1934* (Skopje: Robz, 1997).

42. Cited in Rossos, "The British Foreign Office," 393.

Chapter 10: Macedonian Nationalism: From Right to Left (1920s and 1930s)

1. Ivan Katardžiev, *Vreme na zreenje: makedonskoto nacionalno prašanje meǵu devete svetski vojni (1919–1930)*, 2 vols. (Skopje, 1977). The main title means "Time of Maturing."

2. On reestablishment of the Macedonian right after the Great War, see works in note 38 to chapter 9.

3. Dimo Hadžidimov, *Odbrani dela*, ed. Manol Pandevski, 2 vols. (Skopje: Kultura, 1984), II: 151–234. See also Ivan Katardžiev, "VMRO i makedonskoto osloboditelno dviženje od krajot na prvata svetska vojna do raspaǵanjeto na monizmot (1919–1990)," in Makedonska akademija na naukite i umetnostite, *Sto godini od osnovanjeto na VMRO i 90 godini od ilindenskoto vostanie* (Skopje: Makedonska akademija na naukite i umetnostite, 1994), 52; Institut za nacionalna istorija, *Istorija na makedonskiot narod*, 3 vols. (Skopje: Nova Makedonija, 1969), III: 171–72.

4. On reorganization of the Macedonian left after the Great War, see note 36 to chapter 9.

5. On the Vienna negotiations, including texts of the accords, see CK na VMRO (ob.), *Prednavnicite na makedonskoto delo*, ed. Ivan Katardžiev (Skopje: Kultura, 1983), 107–39. The original Bulgarian edition appeared in

Prague in 1926. See also Ivan Mikhailov, *Spomeni*, 4 vols. (Selci, Louvain, Indianapolis, 1952, 1965, 1967, 1973), II: 312–29; reminiscences of Mihailov's opponent on the left and founder and leader of the VMRO (ob.) Dimitar Vlahov, *Memoari* (Skopje: Nova Makedonija, 1970), 229–44; Katardžiev, *Vreme na zreenje*, I: 219–66; Kiosev, *Istoriia na makedonskoto natsionalno revolutsionno dvizhenie* (Sofia: Otechestven front, 1954), 500–504; Darinka Pačemska, *Vnatrešnata makedonska revolucionerna organizacija (obedineta)* (Skopje: Studentski zbor, 1985), 47–61.

6. On Aleksandrov and Protogerov's renunciation of their signatures, Aleksandrov's murder, and the final split in the VMRO, see CK na VMRO (ob.), *Prednavnicite*, ed. Katardžiev, 140–75; Mikhailov, *Spomeni*, 312–29; Vlahov, *Memoari*, 244–48; Katardžiev, *Vreme na zreenje*, 266–71; Kiosev, *Istoriia*, 500–4; Pačemska, *Vnatrešnata*, 64–68.

7. Ivan Katardžiev, "I.M.O.R.O.," *Macedonian Review* (Skopje) 20, no. 3 (1990), 161.

8. Zoran Todorovski, *VMRO 1924–1934* (Skopje: Robz, 1997), 244. This work provides the most interesting and balanced examination of Aleksandrov and Mihailov's VMRO.

9. Katardžiev, "VMRO i makedonskoto osloboditelno dviženje," 61; Todorovski, *VMRO 1924–1934*, 193–94.

10. Katardžiev, "I.M.O.R.O.," 158–59.

11. Ivo Banac, *The National Question in Yugoslavia: Origins, History, Politics* (Ithaca, N.Y.: Cornell University Press, 1984), 321–22.

12. Katardžiev, "VMRO i makedonskoto osloboditelno dviženje," 57; Todorovski, *VMRO 1924–1934*, 177–82, 243–50.

13. Todorovski, *VMRO 1924–1934*. See also Katardžiev, *Vreme na zreenje*, I: 271–96; S. Troebst, *Musolini, Makedonien und die Mächte, 1922–1930. Die "Innere makedonische revolutionare Organization" in der Südosteuropapolitik der faschistischen Italien* (Köln: Böhlau, 1987); S. Christowe, *Heroes and Assassins* (New York: R. M. McBride, 1935); and J. Swire, *Bulgarian Conspiracy* (London: Robert Hale, 1940).

14. I base the following discussion of the Macedonian left on a revised version of part of my study "Macedonianism and Macedonian Nationalism on the Left," in Ivo Banac and Katherine Verdery, eds., *National Character and National Ideology in Interwar Eastern Europe* (New Haven, Conn.: Yale Center for International Area Studies, 1995), 219–54.

15. Katardžiev, *Vreme na zreenje*, II, part 5; Stojan Kiselinovski, *KPG i makedonskoto nacionalno prašanje* (Skopje: Misla, 1985), 63–72; Dimitar Mitrev, *BKP i pirinska Makedonija* (Skopje: Kultura, 1960), 46–62; Kiril Miljovski, *Makedonskoto prašanje vo nacionalnato programa na KPJ, 1919–1937*, 109–40; Pačemska, *Vinatrešnata makedonska*, chap. 1.

16. Katardžiev in CK na VMRO (ob.), *Prednavnicite*, ed. Katardžiev, 44–46; Ivan Katardžiev, *Istorija na makedonskiot narod*, vol. IV, *Makedonija meģu Balkanskite i Vtorata svetska vojna (1912–1941)* (Skopje: Institut za nacionalna istorija, 2000), 343–48.

17. On the VMRO (ob.) and Communism and nationalism in divided Macedonia, see Katardžiev, *Istorija na makedonskiot narod*, IV: 473–511 (Vardar), 512–40 (Pirin), and 541–8 (Aegean). Institut za nacionalna istorija, *Istorija na makedonskiot narod*, 3 vols. (Skopje: Nova Makedonija, 1969), III: 47–56, 73–77, 84–89, 97–113, 137–53 (Vardar), 223–44 (Pirin), 261–73 (Aegean).

18. Josif Popovski, ed., *Makedonskoto prašanje na stranicite od "Rizospastis" meģu dvete vojni* (Skopje: Kultura, 1982), 5–11. On conditions in Aegean Macedonia, see also J. Papadopulos, "Od borbata na makedonskiot narod vo egejska Makedoniija," *Razgledi* (Skopje) 28, no. 9 (1976), 152–55, and "Od aktivnosta na VMRO (obedineta) vo egejskiot del na Makedonija," *Razgledi* (Skopje) 21, no. 1 (1979), 108–17; Risto Kirjazovski, "Aktivnosta na VMRO (obedineta) vo egejskiot del na Makedonija do 1936 godina," in Institut za nacionalna istorija, *70 godini VMRO (obedineta) 1925–1995)* (Skopje: Institut za nacionalna istorija, 1998), 109–19.

19. Andrew Rossos, "Macedonianism and Macedonian Nationalism on the Left," in Ivo Banac and Katherine Vedery, eds., *National Character and National Ideology in Interwar Eastern Europe* (New Haven, Conn.: Yale Center for International and Area Studies, 1995), 241–43.

20. Slavka Fidanova, "KPJ vo Makedonija vo vremeto od 1929 godina do aprilskata vojna," *Istorija* (Skopje) 16, no. 1 (1989), 57–101; Aleksandar Apostolov, "Od aktivnosta na naprednite studenti na belgradskiot universitet vo 1936 godina," *Istorija* (Skopje) 12, nos. 1–2 (1976), 28–63; L. Sokolov, "Prilog za makedonskoto studentsko dviženje vo Zagreb," *Istorija* (Skopje) 12, nos. 1–2 (1976), 1–27; Stojan Risteski, *Sozdavanjeto na sovremeniot makedonski literaturen jazik* (Skopje: Studentski zbor, 1988), 79–88.

21. Aleksandar Aleksiev, *Osnovopoložnicite na makedonskata dramska literatura* (Skopje: Kultura, 1976), 144–251; Miodrag Drugovac, *Makedonskata literatura* (*Od Misirkov do Racin*) (Skopje: Prosvetno delo, 1975), 69–145.

22. On Racin, see Blaže Ristovski, *Kačo Racin: Istorisko-literaturni istražuvanja* (Skopje: Makedonska kniga, 1983).

23. Risteski, *Sozdavanjeto na sovremeniot*, 106–8; Drugovac, *Makedonskata literatura*, 193–211; Blaže Ristovski, *Projavi i profili od makedonskata literaturna istorija*, 2 vols. (Skopje: Studentski zbor, 1982), I: 220.

24. Katardžiev, *Istorija na makedonskiot narod*, IV: 512–40.

25. Among them were *Makedonski studentski list* (1931–32), *Makedonska studentska tribuna* (1932–33), *Makedonsko zname* (1932–34), *Makedonska*

mladezh (1933–34), *Makedonska revolutsia* (1935), and *Makedonska zemia* (1936).

26. Ristovski, *Projavi i profili*, I: 230–46; Dimitar Mitrev, *Pirinska Makedonija i drugi istoriografski ogledi* (Skopje: Naša kniga, 1970), 217–20.

27. Its leading members included N. J. Vapcarov, A. Popov, M. Smatrakalev (A. Žarov), G. Abadžiev, D. Mitrev, and V. Aleksandrov. Joining later were V. Markovski, K. Nedelkovski, and M. Zafirovski, who had arrived more recently from Yugoslavia.

28. A good collection of writings on the MLK and of Vapcarov's poetry appears in Nikola J. Vapcarov, *Tvorbi*, ed. Gane Todorovski (Skopje: Misla, 1979). See especially the articles by Mitrev, 313–34, Ristovski, 256–90, and Todorovski, 429–47. See also M. Isaev, ed., *Sbornik Nikola Ionkov Vaptsarov* (Sofia, 1947), and Nikola Vapcarov, *Pesni za tatkovinata. Sobrani stihovi*, ed. Blaže Ristovski (Skopje: Misla, 1986).

29. According to A. Žarov (M. Smatrakalev) in Isaev, ed., *Sbornik Nikola Ionkov Vaptsarov*, 177.

30. Hristo Andonov-Poljanski, ed., *Dokumenti za borbata na makedonskiot narod za samostojnost i za nacionalna država*, 2 vols. (Skopje: Univerzitet Kiril i Metodij, 1981), II: no. 114, 220.

31. Cited in Rossos, "Macedonianism and Macedonian Nationalism on the Left," 248 and note 81.

32. Kosta Veselinov, *Vūzrazhdaneto na Makedoniia i Ilindenskoto vūstanie* (Sofia, 1939), 14.

33. Andonov-Poljanski, ed., *Dokumenti*, II: no. 186, 159–60.

34. Angel Dinev, *Makedonskite slaviani* (Sofia, 1938), 71–72.

35. I borrowed "the convenient barbarism 'Leftists'" from Captain P. H. Evans. See Andrew Rossos, "The Macedonians of Aegean Macedonia: A British Officer's Report, 1944," *Slavonic and East European Review* (London) 69, no. 2 (April 1991), 301.

36. Biblioteka "Makedonsko Zname", no. 1. *Ideite i zadachite na makedonskoto progresivno dvizhenie v Būlgaria* (Sofia, 1933), 6.

37. Cited in Rossos, "Macedonianism," 250 and note 91.

38. *Ideite i zadachite*, 7.

39. Ibid., 6.

40. For the citations from *Makedonska pravda*, see Rossos, "Macedonianism," 251–52 and notes 95, 96, and 97.

41. Katardžiev, *Istorija na makedonskiot narod*, IV: 480–511. See also Andonov-Poljanski, ed., *Dokumenti*, II: no. 74, 145; Ristovski, *Kočo Racin*, 141–44.

42. See Rossos, "Macedonianism," 252–53.

43. *Ideite i zadachite*, 9–10.

44. See two informative discussions: Kiril Miljovski, "Motivite na revolucijata, 1941–1944 godina vo Makedonija," *Istorija* (Skopje) 10, no. 1 (1974), 17–24; Cvetko Uzunovksi, "Vostanieto vo 1941 vo Makedonija," *Istorija* (Skopje) 10, no. 2 (1974), 83–123.

Chapter 11: War and Revolution (1940–1949)

1. Institut za nacionalna istorija, *Istorija na makedonskiot narod*, 3 vols. (Skopje: Nova Makedonija, 1969), III: 288.

2. Ibid., 293. On Bulgarian occupation policies, see Novica Veljanovski, ed., *Istorija na makedonskiot narod*, vol. V, *Makedonija vo Vtorata svetska vojna: narodno-osloboditelnata antifašistička vojna vo Makedonija (1941–1945)* (Skopje: Institut za nacionalna istorija, 2003), 56–69.

3. L. S. Stavrianos, *The Balkans since 1453* (New York: Holt, Rinehart and Winston, 1958), 768.

4. Hugh Poulton, *Who Are the Macedonians?* (Bloomington and Indianapolis: Indiana University Press, 1995), 109.

5. On Italian-Albanian occupation policies, see Veljanovski, ed., *Istorija na makedonskiot narod*, V: 70–75.

6. On the situation of German- and Italian-occupied Aegean Macedonia, see ibid., 419–25.

7. The full text of Captain Evans's lengthy report appears in Andrew Rossos, "The Macedonians of Aegean Macedonia: A British Officer's Report, 1944," *Slavonic and East European Review* 69, no. 2 (April 1991), 291–309, citation, 294.

8. Ibid., 297.

9. On attempts by occupation authorities to mobilize active collaboration, see Veljanovski, ed., *Istorija na makedonskiot narod*, V: 75–82 and 155–63 (Vardar Macedonia) and 427–46 (Aegean Macedonia).

10. Ibid., 305–9; Georgi Daskalov, *Uchasta na būlgarite v egeiska Makedoniia 1936–1946. Politichka i voenna istoriia* (Sofia, 1999), 549–55.

11. For clarity and convenience, I refer to the Bulgarian Communist Party, or the BKP, throughout this work. From 1927 to 1948, its official name was the Bulgarian Workers' Party.

12. See polemical writings by representatives of the KPJ and of the BKP. Works of the KPJ: Svetozar Vukmanović (Tempo), *Borba za Balkan* (Zagreb: Globus, 1981), English ed., *Struggle for the Balkans* (London: Merlin, 1990);

Slobodan Nešović, *Jugoslavija-Bugarska, ratno vreme, 1941–1945* (Belgrade: Narodna knijga, 1978). Works of the BKP: Tsola Dragoicheva, *Poveliia na dūlga (Spomeni i razmisli)*, 3 vols. (Sofia: Partizdat, 1972, 1975, 1979), III: especially 309–88. On the views of the KKE, see Stojan Kiselinovski, *Egejskiot del na Makedonija (1913–1989)* (Skopje: Kultura, 1990), 54–140, and Rossos, "The Macedonians of Aegean Macedonia," 286–88, and "Incompatible Allies: Greek Communism and Macedonian Nationalism in the Civil War in Greece, 1943–1949," *Journal of Modern History* 69, no. 1 (March 1997), 45–46.

13. Andrew Rossos, "Macedonianism and Macedonian Nationalism on the Left," in Ivo Banac and Katherine Verdery, eds., *National Character and National Ideology in Interwar Eastern Europe* (New Haven, Conn.: Yale Center for International and Area Studies, 1995), 239–40, 251–54. See also Ivan Katardžiev, ed., *Predavnicite na makedonskoto delo* (Skopje: Kultura, 1983), editor's introduction, 5–56; Darinka Pačemska, *Vnatrešnata makedonska revolucionerna organizacija (Obedineta)* (Skopje: Studentski zbor, 1985), 68ff; Dimitar Vlahov, *Memoari* (Skopje: Nova Makedonija, 1970), 251–366.

14. Stojan Kiselinovski, *Makedonski dejci (XX-ti vek)* (Skopje: Makavej, 2002), 245–48; Stojan Kiselinovski, ed., *Makedonski istoriski rečnik* (Skopje: Institut za nacionalna istorija, 2000), 512–13; Riste Bunteski-Bunte, "Aktivnosta na Metodija Šatorov vo VMRO (obedineta)," in Institut za nacionalna istorija, *Sedumdeset godini VMRO (obedineta) 1925–1995* (Skopje, 1998), 127–40, and *Metodija Šatorov-Šarlo (politički stavovi)* (Skopje: Društvo za nauka i umetnost-Prilep, 1996).

15. Kiselinovski, *Makedonski dejci*, 106–8; Kiselinovski, ed., *Makedonski istoriski rečnik*, 239–40. For more on Koliševski, see the next chapter.

16. Veljanovski, ed., *Istorija na makedonskiot narod*, V: 140–45; Makedonska akademija na naukite i umetnostite and Institut za nacionalna istorija, *Razvojot i karakteristikite na narodnoosloboditelnata vojna i revolucijata vo Makedonija* (Skopje, 1973), especially the contributions by K. Miljovski, 14–22, V. Brezoski, 175–92, and S. Fidanova, 193–216; Koce Solunski, *Kuzman Josifovski-Pitu (život-delo-vreme)*, 2 vols. (Skopje: Nova Makedonija, 1973), II: 7–123.

17. Rossos, "The Macedonians of Aegean Macedonia," 304 note 51; Veljanovski, ed., *Istorija na makedonskiot narod*, V: 209–301.

18. The text of the Manifesto appears in Hristo Andonov-Poljanski, ed., *Dokumenti za borbata na makedonskiot narod za samostojnost i nacionalna država*, 2 vols. (Skopje: Univerzitet Kiril i Metodij, 1981), II: no. 205, 406–11.

19. On the debate surrounding the Manifesto, see Veljanovski, ed., *Istorija na makedonskiot narod*, V: 182–93; Makedonska akademija na naukite i umetnostite and Institut za nacionalna istorija, *ASNOM. Pedeset godini makedonska*

država 1944–1994 (Skopje, 1995), especially the contributions by V. Ivanoski, 101–8, and S. Fidanova, 109–24; Solunski, *Kuzman Josifovski-Pitu*, II: 118–55.

20. Aleksandar T. Hristov, ed., *Zbornik na dokumenti od antifašitičkoto sobranie na narodnoto osloboduvanje na Makedonija (ASNOM)* (Skopje: Institut za nacionalna istorija, 1964); Makedonska akademija na naukite i umetnostite, *Ostvaruvanje na ideite za sozdavanje na makedonskata država i negoviot međunaruden odglas i odraz* (Skopje, 1977), especially the contributions by A. Hristov, 43–54, S. Gaber, 55–74, and N. Sotirovski, 75–82; Makedonska akademija na naukite i umetnostite and Institut za nacionalna istorija, *ASNOM*—a fine collection of articles about the first session of ASNOM.

21. Makedonska akademija na naukite i umetnostite and Institut za nacionalna istorija, *Čento i makedonskata državnost* (Skopje, 2004), especially the contributions by B. Ristovski, 5–22 (the introduction), B. Blagoev, 25–36, D. Petreska, 69–78, and V. Stojčev, 125–38; Riste Bunteski-Bunte, *Metodija Andonov-Čento-Makedonski naroden tribun* (Skopje: Institut za nacionalna istorija, 2002); Marjan Dimitrievski, Zoran Todorovski, and Riste Bunteski-Bunte, eds., *Metodija Andonov-Čento. Dokumenti i materiali* (Skopje: Državen arhiv na Makedonija, 2002).

22. See Andrew Rossos, "Incompatible Allies: Greek Communism and Macedonian Nationalism in the Civil War in Greece, 1943–1949," *Journal of Modern History* 69, no. 1 (March 1997), 47 and note 19.

23. The full text of Captain Evans's lengthy report appears in Rossos, "The Macedonians of Aegean Macedonia," 291–309.

24. Ibid., 305–7 and note 54, and Rossos, "Incompatible Allies," 49–51. See also Elisabeth Barker, *British Policy in South-East Europe in the Second World War* (London: Macmillan, 1976), 195–203; Risto Kirjazovski, *Makedonski nacionalni institucii vo egejskiot del na Makedonija (1941–1961)* (Skopje: Institut za nacionalna istorija, 1987), 21–33, 67–85.

25. Cited in Rossos, "Incompatible Allies," 51.

26. Ibid., 52.

27. L. S. Stavrianos, *The Balkans since 1453* (New York: Holt, Rinehart and Winston, 1958), 769.

28. On Pirin Macedonia during the Second World War, see Veljanovski, ed., *Istorija na makedonskiot narod*, V: 511–40; Dimitar Mitrev, *Pirinska Makedonija i drugi istoriografski ogledi* (Skopje: Naša kniga, 1970), 226–42.

29. Elisabeth Barker, "Problems of the Alliance: Misconceptions and Misunderstandings," in William Deakin, Elisabeth Barker, and Jonathan Chadwick, eds., *British Political and Military Strategy in Central, Eastern and Southern Europe in 1944* (London: Macmillan, 1988), 51. See also Andrew Rossos, "Great Britain and Macedonian Statehood and Unification 1940–49," *East European Politics and Societies* 14, no. 1 (winter 2000), 134–42.

30. Poulton, *Who Are the Macedonians?*, 107. However, see especially Novica Veljanovski, *Makedonija vo jugoslovensko—bugarskite odnosi 1944–1953* (Skopje: Matica makedonska, 1998); Slobodan Nešović, *Bledski sporazum. Tito—Dimitrov (1947)* (Zagreb: Globus, 1979).

31. Mitrev, *Pirinska Makedonija*, 255–56.

32. Ibid., 260–77; Vasil Jotevski, *Nacionalnata afirmacija na makedoncite vo pirinskiot del na Makedonija 1944–1948* (Skopje: Institut za nacionalna istorija, 1996).

33. Naum Pejov, *Makedoncite i graǵanskata vojna vo Grcija* (Skopje: Institut za nacionalna istorija, 1968), 111–30; Risto Kirjazovski, *Narodnoosloboditelniot front i drugite organizacii na makedoncite od egejska Makedonija, 1945–1949* (Skopje: Institut za nacionalna istorija, 1985), 77–93; William H. McNeill, *The Greek Dilemma: War and Aftermath* (Philadelphia: V. Gollancz, 1947), 158–81, 219–21; Heinz Richter, *British Intervention in Greece: From Varkiza to Civil War, February 1945 to August 1946* (London: Merlin, 1985), 151.

34. Rossos, "Incompatible Allies," 57–8. Kirjazovski, *Makedonski nacionalni institucii* and *Narodnooslobiditelniot front*.

35. Rossos, "Incompatible Allies," 59–61 and note 89; Kirjazovski, *Narodnooslobiditelniot front*, 164–66.

36. Pejov, *Makedoncite i graǵianskata vojna vo Grcija*, 167.

37. C. M. Woodhouse, *The Struggle for Greece, 1941–1949* (London: Hart-Davis, McGibbon, 1976), 262.

38. Cited in Rossos, "Incompatible Allies," 44.

39. Phyllis Auty, "Yugoslavia's International Relations (1945–1965)," in Wayne S. Vucinich, ed., *Contemporary Yugoslavia: Twenty Years of Socialist Experiment* (Berkeley and Los Angeles: University of California Press, 1969), 166.

40. See Rossos, "Incompatible Allies," 73–76.

Chapter 12: Yugoslav Macedonia: Politics and Government (1944–1991)

1. From 1944 to 1946, the official name of the state was the Democratic Federal Republic of Macedonia. The constitution of 1946 described it as the People's Republic of Macedonia. With the constitution of 1974, it became the Socialist Republic of Macedonia.

2. Milčo Balevski, *Makedonija včera i denes* (Skopje: Studentski zbor, 1980), 12–13.

3. On the KPJ's consolidation of power after the war, see Woodford McClellan, "Postwar Political Evolution," in Wayne S. Vucinich, ed., *Contemporary Yugoslavia: Twenty Years of Socialist Experiment* (Berkeley and Los Angeles: University of California Press, 1969), 119–26; Fred Singleton, *A Short History of the Yugoslav Peoples* (Cambridge: Cambridge University Press, 1985), 207–14; John R. Lampe, *Yugoslavia as History: Twice There Was a Country* (Cambridge: Cambridge University Press, 1996), 222–28.

4. Singleton, *A Short History,* 209–13; McClellan, "Postwar Political Evolution," 126–28; Lampe, *Yugoslavia as History,* 230–37.

5. R. J. Crompton, *The Balkans since the Second World War* (London: Longman, 2002), 22.

6. Singleton, *A Short History,* 211.

7. Ibid.

8. Ibid., 211–12.

9. On the economic transformation and the First Five-Year Plan, see ibid., 216–19; Lampe, *Yugoslavia as History,* 238–50; George Mecesich, "Major Trends in the Postwar Economy of Yugoslavia," in Wayne S. Vucinich, ed., *Contemporary Yugoslavia: Twenty Years of Socialist Experiment* (Berkeley and Los Angeles: University of California Press, 1969), 203–5, 207.

10. The history of the Macedonians in Communist Yugoslavia (1945–91) has not received adequate attention even in Macedonia. There is no comprehensive work on the period, and Western histories of Yugoslavia say little about the republic. Brief surveys appear in two publications: Evgeni Dimitrov, "Pedest godini sovremena makedonska država," in Makedonska akademija na naukite i umetnostite and Institut za nacionalna istorija, *ASNOM. Pedeset godini makedonska država 1944–1994* (Skopje, 1995), 17–36, and Novica Veljanovski, "Makedonija po vtorata svetska vojna," in Kosta Adžievski et al., *Zapoznajte ja Makedonija—Get Acquainted with Macedonia* (a bilingual publication) (Skopje: INA-Komerc, 2001), 122–37. On establishment of the Communist administration, see Novica Veljanovski, *Administrativno-centralističkiot period vo državnopravniot razvoj na Makedonija (1945–1953)* (Skopje: Institut za nacionalna istorija, 1992); Stephen E. Palmer, Jr, and Robert R. King, *Yugoslav Communism and the Macedonian Question* (Hamden, Conn.: Archon Books, 1971), 138–41; Stefan Troebst, "Yugoslav Macedonia, 1944–1953: Building the Party, the State and the Nation," *Berliner Jahrbuch für osteuropäische Geschichte*, no. 2 (1994), 103–39.

11. Palmer and King, *Yugoslav Communism and the Macedonian Question,* 137–8; Troebst, "Yugoslav Macedonia, 1944–1953," 132–34; Kosta Tsŭrnushanov, *Makedonizmŭt i sŭprotivata na Makedoniia sreshchu nego* (Sofia: Universitetsko izdatelstvo "Sv. Kliment Ohridski", 1992), 249–74.

12. Stojan Risteski, *Sudeni za Makedonija (1945–1985)*, 2 vols. (Ohrid: Macedonia Prima, 1995, 1996); Gligor Krsteski, ed., *Otpori i progoni, 1946–1950* (Skopje: Matica makedonska, 1994), especially the contributions by I. Katardžiev, 98–115, and Mihailo Minovski, 118–26; Ivan Katardžiev, "VMRO i makedonskoto osloboditelno dviženje od krajot na prvata svetska vojna do raspaǵanjeto na monizmot (1919–1990)," in Makedonska akademija na naukite i umetnostite, *Sto godini od osnovanjeto na VMRO i 90 godini od ilindenskoto vostanie* (Skopje, 1994), 69–73; Troebst, "Yugoslav Macedonia, 1944–1953," 134–35.

13. Although Lazar Koliševski dominated Macedonian political life for almost half a century, hardly anything scholarly has appeared about him even in Macedonia. There is no biography, and his lengthy, so-called memoir, which a Serbian journalist wrote on the basis of numerous meetings and interviews with him, reveals very little of substance: Dragan Kljakič, *Vremeto na Koliševski* (Skopje: Matica makedonska, 1994). The same holds for the collection of his speeches and articles in *Aspekti na makedonskoto prašanje* (Skopje: Kultura, 1962), expanded ed. (1980). For brief biographical sketches of Koliševski, see Stojan Kiselinovski, *Makedonski dejci (XX-ti vek)* (Skopje: Makavej, 2002), 106–8; Stojan Kiselinovski, ed., *Makedonski istoriski rečnik* (Skopje: Institut za nacionalna istorija, 2000), 239–40.

14. Elisabeth Barker, *Macedonia: Its Place in Balkan Power Politics* (1950), reprint (Westport, Conn.: Greenwood Press, 1980), 101.

15. On Metodija Andonov-Čento, see the valuable collection of articles in Makedonska akademija na naukite i umetnostite and Institut za nacionalna istorija, *Čento i makedonskata državnost* (Skopje, 2004), particularly B. Ristovski's introductory essay, "Čento i čentovizmot," 5–22, and the contributions by B. Blagoev, 25–37, D. Petrović, 179–82, M. Mihailov, 201–8, and K. Georgievski, 271–76. See also Risteski, *Sudeni za Makedonija*, I: 25–26; Troebst, "Yugoslav Macedonia, 1944–1953," 115–20; Marjan Dimitrijeski, Zoran Todorovski, and Riste Bunteski-Bunte, eds., *Metodija Andonov-Čento. Dokumenti i materiali* (Skopje: Državen arhiv na Republika Makedonija, 2002).

16. Ivo Banac, *With Stalin against Tito: Cominformist Splits in Yugoslav Communism* (Ithaca, N.Y.: Cornell University Press, 1988), 192–204; Troebst, "Yugoslav Macedonia, 1944–1953," 117, and note 31, 121–22, 135; Tsūrnushanov, *Makedonizmūt i sūprotivata*, 390–403.

17. Singleton, *A Short History*, 232.

18. On the debates of the 1960s, see Sabrina P. Ramet, *Nationalism and Federalism in Yugoslavia, 1962–1991*, 2nd ed. (Bloomington: Indiana University Press, 1992), 89–142; Lampe, *Yugoslavia as History*, 279–86; Singleton, *A Short History*, 244–50; Crompton, *The Balkans*, 122–31; Gale Stoakes, *The Walls Came Tumbling Down: The Collapse of Communism in Eastern Europe* (New York: Oxford University Press, 1993), 224–28.

19. Singleton, *A Short History*, 248.

20. Ramet, *Nationalism and Federalism*, 83–94; Lampe, *Yugoslavia as History*, 284–85.

21. Singleton, *A Short History*, 250.

22. Crompton, *The Balkans*, 132–33.

23. Bogdan Denitch, *Ethnic Nationalism: The Tragic Death of Yugoslavia* (Minneapolis: University of Minnesota Press, 1996), 61.

24. Lampe, *Yugoslavia as History*, 298–99.

25. Sabrina P. Ramet, *Balkan Babel: The Disintegration of Yugoslavia from the Death of Tito to the War for Kosovo* (Boulder, Colo.: Westview Press, 1999), 5.

26. Ibid., 17.

27. Lampe, *Yugoslavia as History*, 346–47.

28. Ramet, *Balkan Babel*, 18.

29. The literature on the decline and break-up of Yugoslavia is extensive. See particularly Ramet, *Balkan Babel*; Denitch, *Ethnic Nationalism*; Christopher Bennett, *Yugoslavia's Bloody Collapse: Causes, Course and Consequences* (New York: New York University Press, 1995); Tim Judah, *The Serbs: History, Myth and the Destruction of Yugoslavia* (New Haven, Conn.: Yale University Press, 1997); Aleksandar Pavkovič, *The Fragmentation of Yugoslavia: Nationalism in a Multinational State* (New York: St. Martin's Press, 1997); Susan L. Woodward, *Balkan Tragedy: Chaos and Dissolution after the Cold War* (Washington, D.C.: Brookings Institution, 1995); Lenard J. Cohen, *Broken Bonds: The Disintegration of Yugoslavia* (Boulder, Colo.: Westview Press, 1993); Branka Megaš, *The Destruction of Yugoslavia: Tracking the Break-up* (London: Verso, 1993).

30. Jan Richlìk and Miroslav Kouba, *Dějiny Makedonie* (Prague: Lidové noviny, 2003), 230–32; Ramet, *Nationalism and Federalism*, 94–100, 142. See also the writings of the two leading Macedonian reformers: Krste Crvenkovski, *Sojuzot na komunistite na Makedonija i demokratizacijata na opštestvoto* (Skopje: Kultura, 1971) and *Vo odbrana na makedonskata kauza* (Ohrid: Nezavisni izdanija, 1989); and Slavko Milosavlevski, *Strav od promeni. Krizata na političkiot sistem na Jugoslavija vo sedumdesettite godini* (Skopje: Komunist, 1991) and *Dvete lica na sobitijata* (Skopje: Zumpres, 1996).

31. On Metodija Andonov-Čento, see the works in note 15 to this chapter.

32. See the brief biographical sketches of Vlahov in Kiselinovski, *Makedonski dejci*, 47–48, and Kiselinovski, ed., *Makedonski istoriski rečnik*, 107–8; but especially Vlahov's reminiscences, *Memoari* (Skopje: Nova Makedonija, 1970).

33. On Lazar Kolievski, see note 13 to this chapter.

34. As a Serbian official of the Yugoslav Ministry of Foreign Affairs observed

in 1980: "It was more important for Belgrade to sell 'Fičos' [Yugoslav Fiats] in Greece than to concern itself with the human and national dimensions of the Macedonian question." See Palmer and King, *Yugoslav Communism and the Macedonian Question*, 189–98; Katardžiev, "VMRO i makedonskoto osloboditelno dviženie," 70–71.

35. Hugh Poulton, *Who Are the Macedonians?* (Bloomington and Indianapolis: Indiana University Press, 1995), 148–62 and 162–71; Human Rights Watch/Helsinki, *Denying Ethnic Identity: The Macedonians of Greece* (New York: Human Rights Watch, 1994), and *Destroying Ethnic Identity: Selected Persecution of Macedonians in Bulgaria* (New York: Human Rights Watch, 1991).

36. Slavko Dimevski, *Istorija na makedonskata pravoslavna crkva* (Skopje: Makedonska kniga, 1989), chaps. 6–9, 981–1134. See also Palmer and King, *Yugoslav Communism and the Macedonian Question*, 165–73; Poulton, *Who Are the Macedonians?* 180–82; Ramet, *Balkan Babel*, 108–9.

Chapter 13: Economics, Culture, Minorities (1994–1991)

1. On conditions of life in pre-1939 Yugoslav Macedonia, see Ivan Katardžiev, *Istorija na makedonskiot narod*, vol. IV, *Makedonija* meģu *Balkanskite i Vtorata svetska vojna (1912–1944)* (Skopje: Institut za nacionalna istorija, 2000), 167–75; Aleksandar Apostolov, *Kolonizacijata na Makedonija vo stara Jugoslavija* (Skopje: Kultura, 1966), 43–77; Violeta Ačkoska, *Agrarno-sopstveničkite odnosi, promeni i procesi vo Makedonija 1944–1953* (Skopje: Institut za nacionalna istorija, 1998), 39–51.

2. Nikola Uzunov, "Stopanskiot razvoj vo Republika Makedonija vo periodot 1945–1994 godina," in Makedonska akademija na naukite i umetnostite and Institut za nacionalna istorija, *ASNOM. Pedeset godini makedonska država 1944–1994* (Skopje, 1995), 366.

3. This periodization derives from Nikola Uzunov's excellent study: ibid., 355–73.

4. Ibid., 356–59.

5. Ibid., 361–66.

6. On the agrarian reforms (1945–48) and the failure of collectivization (1949–53), see Ačkoska,, *Agrarno-sopstveničkite odnosi*, particularly chap. 5, 162–215, and chap. 7, 258–84.

7. Uzunov, "Stopanskiot razvoj vo Republika Makedonija," 370.

8. Ibid., 370.

9. Ibid., 371.

10. Stojan Risteski, *Sozdavanjeto na sovremeniot makedonski literaturen jazik* (Skopje: Studentski zbor, 1988), 138–66; Stojan Kiselinovski, *Statusot na makedonskiot jazik vo Makedonija (1913–1987)* (Skopje: Misla, 1987), 112–19; Risto Kirjazovski, *Makedonski nacionalni institucii vo egejskiot del na Makedonija (1941–1961)* (Skopje: Institut za nacionalna istorija, 1987), 263–73.

11. Risteski, *Sozdavanjeto na sovremeniot makedonski literaturen jazik,* 131–90; Horace G. Lunt, "The Creation of Standard Macedonian: Some Facts and Attitudes," *Anthropological Linguistics* 1, no. 5 (June 1959), 19–26, and "Time and the Macedonian Language," *Indiana Slavic Studies,* 10 (1999), 3–15; Victor A. Friedman, "The Socio-linguistics of Literary Macedonian," *International Journal of Sociology of Language* 52 (1985), 31–57.

12. Petre Georgievski, "Asnomskoto konstituiranje na državnosta i promenite vo obrazovanieto," in Makedonska akademija na naukite i umetnostite and Institut za nacionalna istorija, *ASNOM. Pedeset godini makedonska država 1944–1994* (Skopje, 1995), 403.

13. Nada Jurukova, "Prosvetnata politika na ASNOM," in Makedonska akademija na naukite i umetnostite and Institut za nacionalna istorija, *ASNOM. Pedeset godini makedonska država 1944–1994* (Skopje, 1995), 413.

14. Ibid., 413–14.

15. Ibid., 413.

16. Ibid., 417–20.

17. Georgievski, "Asnomskoto konstituiranje na državnosta," 402.

18. Ibid., 404.

19. In 1980, the director of the Institute for Balkan Studies in Salonika denied the existence of the Macedonian language and nation. When a listener pointed out that there were writers using Macedonian, he argued that that was not possible, since there was no medieval literary tradition in a so-called Macedonian language. And when a listener suggested that the medieval south Slav literature was largely in Church Slavonic and was the common literary heritage of all Orthodox south Slavs, he ended the meeting.

20. Milan Ǵurčinov, "Podemot na makedonskata umetnička literatura vo godinite po ASNOM," in Makedonska akademija na naukite i umetnostite and Institut za nacionalna istorija, *ASNOM. Pedeset godini makedonska država 1944–1994* (Skopje, 1995), 425. On the flowering of Macedonian poetry, see Milan Ǵurčinov, *Nova makedonska književnost (1945–1980)*, 2 vols. (Skopje: Studentski zbor, 1996), I: 31–87; Duško Nanevski, *Makedonskata poetska škola* (Skopje: Misla, 1977), part 2; Milne Hilton and Graham W. Reid, eds., *Reading the Ashes: An Anthology of the Poetry of Modern Macedonia* (Pittsburgh: University of Pittsburgh Press, 1977).

21. Cited in Ǵurčinov, "Podemot na makedonskata umetnička literatura." 426.

22. Ibid., 425–26, 429–30. See also Ǵurčinov, *Nova makedonska književnost*, I: 91–156; Hristo Georgievski, *Makedonskiot roman 1952–1982* (Skopje: Misla, 1983) and *Makedonskiot roman 1952–2000* (Skopje: Matica makedonska, 2001).

23. Ǵurčinov, "Podemot na makedonskata umetnička literatura," 426. See also Ǵurčinov, *Nova makedonska književnost*, I: 157–73; Aleksandar Aleksiev, *Osnovopoložnicite na makedonskata dramska literatura* (Skopje: Kultura, 1976); Jelena Lužina, *Istorija na makedonskata drama. Makedonskata bitova drama* (Skopje: Kultura, 1995).

24. Georgi Stradelov, "Asnomskite načela na makedonskata kultura vo poslednovo polovina stoletie (1944–1994)," in Makedonska akademija na naukite i umetnostite and Institut za nacionalna istorija, *ASNOM. Pedeset godini makedonska država 1944–1994* (Skopje, 995), 393.

25. Stephen E. Palmer Jr and Robert King, *Yugoslav Communism and the Macedonian Question* (Hamden, Conn.: Archon Books, 1971), 178; Jan Rychlìk and Miroslav Kouba, *Dějiny Makedonie* (Prague: Lidové noviny, 2003), 240.

26. Hugh Poulton, *Who Are the Macedonians?* (Bloomington and Indianapolis: Indiana University Press, 1995), 121. For the 1961 census, see Milčo Balevski, *Makedonija včera i denes* (Skopje: Studentski zbor, 1980), 13; for the 1991 and 1994 censuses, Sabrina Ramet, *Balkan Babel: The Disintegration of Yugoslavia from the Death of Tito to the War for Kosovo* (Boulder, Colo.: Westview Press, 1999), 188.

27. Georgievski, "Asnomskoto konstituiranje na državnosta," 406; Poulton, *Who Are the Macedonians?* 125–26, 139.

28. Palmer and King, *Yugoslav Communism and the Macedonian Question*, 177.

29. Poulton, *Who Are the Macedonians?* 122.

30. Ibid., 126–27. On the Albanians in Macedonia, see also Slavko Milosavlevski and Mirče Tomovski, *Albancite vo Republika Makedonija 1945–1995. Legislativa, politička dokumentacija, statistika* (Skopje: Studentski zbor, 1997).

Chapter 14: Independent Republic (1991–2004)

1. Duncan M. Perry, "The Republic of Macedonia: Finding Its Way," in Karen Dawisha and Bruce Parrot, eds., *Politics, Power and the Struggle for Democracy in South-East Europe* (Cambridge: Cambridge University Press, 1997),

233; Hugh Poulton, *Who Are the Macedonians?* (Bloomington and Indianapolis: Indiana University Press, 1995), 175.

2. Sabrina P. Ramet, "The Macedonian Enigma," in Sabrina P. Ramet and Ljubiša S. Adamovich, eds., *Beyond Yugoslavia: Politics, Economics, and Culture in a Shattered Community* (Boulder, Colo.: Westview Press, 1995), 214, note 15.

3. Gligorov speaking in Ohrid in late August 1991, from notes in author's possession.

4. Ibid. On Gligorov, see his memoirs, *Makedonija e sè što imame* (Skopje: TRI, 2001); see also the brief biographies of him in Perry, "The Republic of Macedonia," 246–47; Henryk J. Sokalski, *An Ounce of Prevention: Macedonia and the UN Experience in Preventive Diplomacy* (Washington, D.C.: United States Institute of Peace Press, 2003), 44–45; Tom Gallagher, *The Balkans in the New Millennium: In the Shadow of War and Peace* (London and New York: Routledge, 2005), 81–82.

5. Gligorov in Ohrid in late August 1991. He continued to leave the door open to Macedonia's participation in some future loose confederation of sovereign, independent, democratic Yugoslav states, even though he doubted that it would ever come about.

6. Republic of Macedonia, *Ustav na Republika Makedonija* (Skopje: NIP, 1991), 3; Perry, "The Republic of Macedonia," 252.

7. Sabrina P. Ramet, *Balkan Babel: The Disintegration of Yugoslavia from the Death of Tito to the War for Kosovo* (Boulder, Colo.: Westview Press, 1999), 192. See also Loring M. Danforth, *The Macedonian Conflict: Ethnic Nationalism in a Transnational World* (Princeton, N.J.: Princeton University Press, 1995), 144–45.

8. Poulton, *Who Are the Macedonians?*, 177. See also Gligorov, *Makedonija e sè što imame*, 170–90; Alice Ackermann, *Making Peace Prevail: Preventing Violent Conflict in Macedonia* (Syracuse, N.Y.: Syracuse University Press, 1999), 81–83.

9. Ramet, "The Macedonian Enigma," 218.

10. Ramet, *Balkan Babel*, 184. On the Greek-Macedonian conflict, see especially Danforth, *The Macedonian Conflict*, 28–55; John Shea, *Macedonia and Greece: The Struggle to Define a New Balkan Nation* (Jefferson, N.C., and London: McFarland and Company, 1997), 211–374; Gligorov, *Makedonija e sè što imame*, especially chap. 18, 335–92. Makedonska akademija na naukite i umetnostite, *Macedonia and Its Relations with Greece* (Skopje, 1993).

11. Cited in Ramet, "The Macedonian Enigma," 220. See also Republic of Macedonia, *Independence through Peaceful Self-determination: Documents* (Skopje: Balkan Forum, 1992).

12. Remarks by consul general of Greece, Faculty Club, University of Toronto, March 1992, notes in author's possession.

13. Takis Michas, *Unholy Alliance: Greece and Milošević's Serbia* (College Station: Texas A&M University Press, 2002),

14. Ramet, *Balkan Babel*, 191.

15. Michas, *Unholy Alliance*, 48.

16. On the search for international recognition, see Gligorov, *Makedonija e sè što imame*, especially chaps. 16–19, 262–443; Ramet, *Balkan Babel*, 183–87; Perry, "The Republic of Macedonia," 267–72. See also Ackermann, *Making Peace Prevail*; Sokalski, *An Ounce of Prevention*.

17. On domestic politics, see Gligorov, *Makedonija e sè što imame*, chaps. 11–15, 155–261; Ramet, *Balkan Babel*, 191–93; Perry, "The Republic of Macedonia," 233–44.

18. Ramet, "The Macedonian Enigma," 225.

19. U.S. Department of State, Bureau of European and Eurasian Affairs, Nov. 2004, *Background Note: Macedonia*. www.state.gov/r/pa/ei/bgn/26759.htm, 5.

20. Ibid., 5.

21. Ibid.

22. John Phillips, *Macedonia: Warlords and Rebels in the Balkans* (New York: I. B. Tauris, 2004), 75.

23. U.S. Department of State, *Background Note: Macedonia*, 6.

24. Ibid.

25. On the Albanian question, see Gligorov, *Makedonija e sè što imame*, 427–43; Poulton, *Who Are the Macedonians?* 125–37; Perry, "The Republic of Macedonia," 251–54; Ramet, *Balkan Babel*, 187–91; Tom Gallagher, *The Balkans in the New Millennium: In the Shadow of War and Peace* (London and New York: Routledge, 2005), 82–96.

26. Mitko Arsovski, Risto Damjanovski, and Stojan Kuzev, *Vojnata vo Makedonija vo 2001 godina* (Skopje: Matica makedonska, 2006). See also Gallagher, *The Balkans in the New Millennium*, 96–100, and Phillips, *Macedonia: Warlords and Rebels in the Balkans*.

27. Gallagher, *The Balkans in the New Millennium*, 101–8; see also International Crisis Group, reports and briefing papers: *Macedonia: War on Hold*, Balkan Briefing, 15 Aug. 2001, *Macedonia: Filling the Security Vacuum*, Balkan Briefing, 8 Sept. 2001, and *Macedonia: No Room for Complacency*, Europe Report No. 149, Brussels, 23 Oct. 2003; Vasko Popetrevski and Veton Latifi, "The Ohrid Framework Agreement Negotiations," in Keith S. Brown, Paulette Farisides, Saso Ordanoski, and Agim Fetahu, eds., *Ohrid and Beyond: A Cross-*

ethnic Investigation into the Macedonian Crisis (London: Institute for War and Peace Reporting, 2002), 49–57.

28. Ibid. Vladimir Jovanovski and Lirin Dulovi, "A New Battleground: The Struggle to Ratify the Ohrid Agreement," in Brown et al., eds., *Ohrid and Beyond*, 59–72.

29. Phillips, *Macedonia*, 136–37.

30. See International Crisis Group, *Macedonia: No Room for Complacency*; Zoran Bojarovski and Nazim Rashidi, "The Art of Compromise: Reconciliation and the Implementation of the Framework Agreement," in Brown et al., eds., *Ohrid and Beyond*, 95–104.

Bibliography

Aarbake, Vemand. *Ethnic Rivalry and the Quest for Macedonia, 1870–1913*. Boulder, Colo.: East European Monographs, 2003.

Abadžiev, Giorgi, et al. *Egejska Makedonija vo našata istorija*. Skopje, 1957.

Abecedar. Athens: P. D. Sakellariou, 1925. Facsimile ed., Skopje: Makedonska revija, 1985.

Ackermann, Alice. *Making Peace Prevail: Preventing Violent Conflict in Macedonia*. Syracuse, NY: Syracuse University Press, 1999.

Ačkoska, Violeta. *Agrarno-sopstveničkite odnosi, promeni i procesi vo Makedonija, 1944–1953*. Skopje: Institut za nacionalna istorija, 1998.

——— *Zadrugarstvoto: agrarnata politika, 1945–1955*. Skopje: Institut za nacionalna istorija, 1994.

Adams, W. L., and E. N. Borza, eds. *Philip II, Alexander the Great and the Macedonian Heritage*. Lanham, Md.: University Press of America, 1982.

Adanir, Fikret. *Die makedonische Frage: Ihre Entstehung und Entwicklung bis 1908*. Wiesbaden: Steiner, 1979.

——— "The Macedonians in the Ottoman Empire, 1878–1912." In Andreas Kappeler, Fikret Adanir, and Alan O'Day, eds., *The Formation of National Elites*. Vol. VI in Comparative Studies on Governments and Non-Dominant

Groups in Europe, 1850–1940. New York: Dartmouth/New York University Press, 1992, 161–91.

——— "The Socio-political Environment of Balkan Nationalism: The Case of Ottoman Macedonia 1856–1912." In H-G. Houpt, M. G. Müller, and S. Woolf, eds., *Regional and National Identities in Europe in the XIXth and XXth Centuries*. The Hague and Boston: Kluver Law International, 1998, 221–54.

Ahmad, Feroz. *The Young Turks: The Committee of Union and Progress in Turkish Politics 1908–1914*. Oxford: Oxford University Press, 1969.

Ajanovski, Vangel. *Egejski buri*. Skopje: Institut za nacionalna istorija, 1975.

Akademiia nauk SSSR. Institut istorii. *Istoriia Vizantii*. 3 vols. Moscow, 1967.

Aleksiev, Aleksandar. *Osnovopoložnicite na makedonskata dramska literatura*. Skopje: Kultura, 1976.

Alexander, Stella. *Church and State in Yugoslavia since 1945*. Cambridge: Cambridge University Press, 1979.

Ancel, Jacques. *La Macédoine*. Paris: Delagrave, 1930.

Anderson, M. S. *The Eastern Question, 1774–1923*. London: St. Martin's Press, 1966.

Andonov-Poljanski, Hristo. *Goce Delčev i negovoto vreme*. 6 vols. Skopje: Kultura, 1972.

——— *Velika Britanija i makedonskoto prašanje na pariskata mirovna konferencija vo 1919 godina*. Skopje: Arhiv na Makedonija, 1973.

Andonov-Poljanski, Hristo, ed. *Documents on the Struggle of the Macedonian People for Independence and a Nation-state*. 2 vols. Skopje: University of Cyril and Methodius, 1985.

Andonovki, Hristo. *Makedoncite pod Grcija vo borbata protiv fašizmot, 1940–1944*. Skopje: Goce Delčev, 1968.

Angelov, D. *Bogomilstvoto v Būlgariia*. Sofia, 1969.

——— *Istoriia na Vizantiia*. 3 vols. Sofia, 1963, 1965, 1976.

——— *Vizantiia. Politicheska istoriia*. Sofia, 1994.

Antić, Vera, *Od srednokekovnata književnost*. Skopje: Makedonska kniga, 1976.

Antoljak, Stjepan. *Samoilovata država*. Skopje: Institut za nacionalna istorija, 1969.

——— *Srednovekovna Makedonija*. Vol. I. Skopje: Misla, 1985.

Apostolov, Aleksandar. *Kolonizacijata na Makedonija vo stara Jugoslavija*. Skopje: Kultura, 1966.

——— "Od aktivnosta na naprednite studenti na belgradskiot univerzitet vo 1936 godina." *Istorija* (Skopje) 12, nos. 1–2 (1976), 28–63.

——— "Specifičnata položba na makedonskiot narod vo kralstvoto Jugoslavija." *Glasnik* (Skopje) 16, no. 1 (1972), 39–62.

Apostolski, Mihailo. *Osloboditelnata vojna na makedonskiot narod, 1941–1945*. Skopje: Goce Delčev, 1965.

Apostolski, Mihailo, and Haralampie Plolenakovich, eds. *The Socialist Republic of Macedonia*. Skopje: Macedonian Review Editions, 1974.

Argiropoulos, Periklis. *O makedonikos agon*. Salonika, 1957.

Arnakis, G. G. "The Greek Church in Constantinople and the Ottoman Empire." *Journal of Modern History* 24 (1952), 235–50.

Arsov, Lupčo. *Svedoštva (Memoari)*. Skopje: Komunist, 1983.

Arsovski, Mitko, Risto Damjanovski, and Stojan Kuzev. *Vojnata vo Makedonija vo 2001 godina*. Skopje: Matica makedonska, 2006.

Austin, M. M. *The Hellenistic World from Alexander to the Roman Conquest*. Cambridge: Cambridge University Press, 1981.

Auty, Phyllis. "Yugoslavia's International Relations (1945–1965)." In Wayne S. Vucinich, ed., *Contemporary Yugoslavia: Twenty Years of Socialist Experiment*. Berkeley and Los Angeles: University of California Press, 1969.

Auty, Phyllis, and Richard Clogg, eds. *British Policy toward Wartime Yugoslavia and Greece*. London: Macmillan, 1975.

Avramovski, Živko. *Balkanska antanta, 1934–1940*. Belgrade, 1986.

Badian, E. "Greeks and Macedonians." In Beryl Barr-Sharrar and Eugene N. Borza, eds., *Macedonia and Greece in Late Classical and Early Hellenistic Times*. Washington, D.C.: National Gallery of Art, 1982, 33–51.

Bailey, F. E. *British Policy and the Turkish Reform Movement: A Study in Anglo-Turkish Relations 1826–1853*. Cambridge, Mass.: Harvard University Press, 1942.

Balevski, Milčo. *Makedonija včera i denes*. Skopje: Studentski zbor, 1980.

Banac, Ivo. *The National Question in Yugoslavia: Origins, History, Politics*. Ithaca, N.Y.: Cornell University Press, 1984.

——— *With Stalin against Tito: Cominformist Splits in Yugoslav Communism*. Ithaca, N.Y.: Cornell University Press, 1988.

Barker, Elisabeth. *British Policy in South-East Europe in the Second World War*. London: Macmillan, 1976.

——— *Macedonia: Its Place in Balkan Power Politics*. 1950. Reprint, Westport, Conn.: Greenwood Press, 1980.

——— "Problems of the Alliance: Misconceptions and Misunderstandings." In William Deakin, Elisabeth Barker, and Jonathan Chadwick, eds., *British Political and Military Strategy in Central, Eastern and Southern Europe in 1944*. London: Macmillan, 1988.

Belčevski, Jovan. *Aftokefalnosta na makedonskata pravoslavna crkva*. Skopje: Studentski zbor, 1986.

——— *Ohridskata arhiepiskopija od osnovanjeto do pagjanieto na Makedonija pod turska vlast*. Skopje, 1997.

Berkes, Niazi. *The Development of Secularism in Turkey*. Montreal: McGill University Press, 1964.

Bernshtein, S. *Konstantin i Mefodii*. Moscow, 1984.

Birnbaum, Henrik. *Aspects of the Slavic Middle Ages and Slavic Renaissance Culture*. New York: Peter Lang, 1991.

Bitovski, Krste. *Makedonija i kneževstvo Bugarija (1893–1903)*. Skopje: Institut za nacionalna istorija, 1977.

——— *Makedonija vo golemata istočna kriza (1875–1881)*. Skopje: Studentski zbor, 1982.

——— *Solunskite atentati*. Skopje: Institut za nacionalna istorija, 1985.

Bitovski, Krste, ed. *Istorija na makedonskiot narod*. Vol. III, *Makedonija vo devetnaesettiot vek do balkanskite vojni (1912–1913)*. Skopje: Institut za nacionalna istorija, 2003.

Blinkhorn, Martin, and Thanos Veremis, eds. *Modern Greece: Nationalism and Nationality*. Athens: Sage-Eliamep, 1990.

Bogoev, Ksente. "The Macedonian Liberation Organization (VMRO) in the Past Hundred Years." *Macedonian Review* (Skopje) 23, nos. 2–3 (1993), 118–28.

Borza, Eugene N. *In the Shadow of Olympus: The Emergence of Macedon*. Princeton, N.J.: Princeton University Press, 1990.

——— *Makedonika. Essays* (English-language book). Ed. Carol G. Thomas. Claremont, Calif., 1995.

Bosworth, A. B. *Conquest and Empire: The Reign of Alexander the Great*. Cambridge: Cambridge University Press, 1988.

——— *From Arian to Alexander: Studies in Historical Interpretation*. Oxford: Oxford University Press, 1988.

Brailsford, Henri Noel. *Macedonia: Its Races and Their Future*. 1906. Reprint New York: Arno Press, 1980.

Brezoski, Velimir. "Prilog kon periodizacijata na osloboditelnata vojna vo Makedonija." In Makedonska akademija na naukite i umetnostite and Institut za nacionalna istorija, *Razvojot i karakteristikite na narodnoosloboditelnata vojna i na revolucjata vo Makedonija*. Skopje, 1973, 175–92.

Brown, Keith. *The Past in Question: Modern Macedonia and the Uncertainties of Nation*. Princeton, N.J.: Princeton University Press, 2003.

Brown, Keith S., Paulette Farisides, Saso Ordanoski, and Agim Fetahu, eds.,

Ohrid and Beyond: A Cross-ethnic Investigation into the Macedonian Crisis. London: Institute for War and Peace Reporting, 2002.

Buckova-Martinova, Fana. *I nie sme deca na majkata zemja . . .* Skopje: Združenie na decata begalci od Egenskiot del na Makedonija, 1998.

Budimovski, D. K. *Makedoncite vo Albanija.* Skopje: Studentski zbor, 1983.

Būlgarska akademiia na naukite (BAN). *Istoriia na Būlgariia.* 8 vols. (14 vols. planned). Sofia: Būlgarska akademiia na naukite, 1979, 1981, 1982, 1983, 1985, 1987, 1991; Sofia: Gal-Iko, 1999.

Buntevski-Bunte, Riste. *Metodija Andonov-Čento: Makedonski naroden tribun.* Skopje: Institut za nacionalna istorija, 2002.

——— *Metodija Šatorov-Šarlo (Politički stavovi).* Skopje: Društvo za nauka i umetnost-Prilep, 1996.

Čakarjanovski, Ǵorgi. *Glavniot štab i državnosta na Makedonija (1941–1945).* Skopje, 2001.

Čašule, Vanga, ed. *Od priznavanje do negiranje. (Bugarski stavovi za makedonskoto prašanje). Stati, govori, dokumenti.* Skopje: Kultura, 1976.

Čepreganov, Todor. *Britanskite voeni misii vo Makedonija, 1942–1945.* Skopje: Institut za nacionalna istorija, 2000.

Chrisowe, Stojan. *Heroes and Assassins.* New York: R. M. McBride, 1935.

CK na VMRO (Ob.). *Predavnicite na makedonskoto delo.* Ed. Ivan Katardžiev. Skopje: Kultura, 1983.

Clucas, Lowell. *The Byzantine Legacy in Eastern Europe.* New York: Columbia University Press, 1998.

Cohen, Lenard J. *Broken Bonds: The Disintegration of Yugoslavia.* Boulder, Colo.: Westview Press, 1993.

Cowan, Jane K., ed. *Macedonia: The Politics of Identity and Difference.* London: Pluto Press, 2000.

Crampton, R. J. *The Balkans since the Second World War.* London: Longman, 2002.

——— *Eastern Europe in the Twentieth Century.* London: Routledge, 1994.

Crvenkovski, Krste. *Na branikot na makedonskata samobitnost.* Skopje: Institut za nacionalna istorija, 1998.

——— *Sojuzot na komunistite na Makedonija i demokratizacijata na opštestvoto.* Skopje: Kultura, 1971.

——— *Vo odbrana na makedonskata kauza.* Ohrid: Nezavisni izdanija, 1989.

Dakin, Douglas. *The Greek Struggle in Macedonia.* Salonika: Institute for Balkan Studies, 1966.

Danforth, Loring M. *The Macedonian Conflict: Ethnic Nationalism in a Transnational World.* Princeton, N.J.: Princeton University Press, 1995.

Daskalakis, A. *The Hellenism of the Ancient Macedonians*. Salonika: Institute for Balkan Studies, 1965.

Daskalov, Georgi. *Uchastta na būlgarite v egeiska Makedonija, 1936–1946*. Sofia, 1999.

Davison, Roderick H. *Reform in the Ottoman Empire, 1856–1876*. Princeton, N.J.: Princeton University Press, 1963.

Dawisha, Karen, and Bruce Parrot, eds. *Politics, Power and the Struggle for Democracy in South-east Europe*. Cambridge: Cambridge University Press, 1997.

Dedijer, Vladimir. *The Battle Stalin Lost: Memoirs of Yugoslavia, 1948–53*. New York: Gosset, 1972.

Dedijer, Vladimir, et al. *History of Yugoslavia*. New York: McGraw-Hill, 1974.

de Jong, Jutta. *Der nationale Kern des makedonischen Problems. Ansätze und Grundlagen einer makedonischen Nationalbewegung (1890–1903)*. Frankfurt: Peter Lang, 1982.

Devereux, Robert. *The First Ottoman Constitutional Period: A Study of the Midhat Constitution and Parliament*. Baltimore: Johns Hopkins Press, 1963.

Dimevski, Slavko. "Dve pisma na Petko Račov Slavejkov za makedonizmot." *Razgledi* (Skopje) 14, no. 3 (1973), 561–6.

——— *Istorija na makedonskata pravoslavna crkva*. Skopje: Makedonska kniga, 1989.

——— *Makedonskoto nacionalno osloboditelno dviženje i egzarhijata (1893–1912)*. Skopje: Kultura, 1963.

——— *Mitropolitot skopski Teodosij-život i dejnost (1846–1926)*. Skopje: Kultura, 1965.

——— *Za razvojot na makedonskata nacionalna misla do sozdavanjeto na TMORO*. Skopje: Kultura, 1980.

Dimevski, Slavko, V. Popovski, S. Skarić, and M. Apostolski. *Makedonskata liga i ustavot za državno ureduvanje na Makedonija od 1880*. Skopje: Misla, 1985.

Dimitrievski, Marjan, Zoran Todorovski, and Riste Buntevski-Bunte. *Metodija Andonov-Ćento. Dokumenti i materiali*. Skopje: Državen arhiv na Republika Makedonija, 2002.

Dinev, Angel. *Makedonskite slaviani*. Sofia, 1938.

——— *Odbrani dela*. 3 vols. Ed. Vladimir Kartov. Skopje: Kultura, 1983.

Dobrinov, Decho. *VMRO (obedineta)*. Sofia, 1993.

Dogo, Marco. *La dinamite e la mezzaluna. La questione macedone nella pubblicistica Italiana 1903–1908*. Udine: Del Bianco Editore, 1983.

——— *Lingua e nazionalità in Macedonia. Vicende e pensieri di profeti disarmati 1902–1903*. Milan: Jaca Book, 1985.

Doklestić, Ljubiša. "Makedonskata osloboditelna borba i makedonskoto nacionalno prašanje." In Institut za nacionalna istorija, *Razvitok na državnosta na makedonskiot narod*. Skopje, 1966, 70–86.

——— *Srpsko-makedonskite odnosi vo XIX-ot vek*. Skopje: Nova Makedonija, 1973.

Donev, Jovan. *Golemite sili i Makedonija za vremeto na prvata balkanska vojna*. Skopje: Institut za nacionalna istorija, 1988.

Draganov, Petar D. *Makedonskoslavianskii sbornik s prilozheniem slovaria*. St. Petersburg, 1894.

Dragoicheva, Tsola. *Poveliia na dŭlga (spomeni i razmisli)*. 3 vols. Sofia: Partizdat, 1972, 1975, 1979.

Drakul, Simon. *Arhimandrit Anatolij Zografski*. Skopje: Institut za nacionalna istorija, 1988.

——— "Ruskite diplomatsko-strateški kontroverzi okolu makedonskoto prašanje vo ilindenskite decenii." In Makedonska akademija na naukite i umetnostite, *Sto godini od osnavanjeto na VMRO i 90 godini od ilindenskoto vostanie*. Skopje, 1994, 361–96.

Drugovac, Miodrag. *Makedonskata literatura. (Od Misirkov do Racin)*. Skopje: Prosvetno delo, 1975.

Dvornik, Francis. *The Slavs in European History and Civilization*. New Brunswick, N.J.: Rutgers University Press, 1962.

——— *The Slavs: Their Early History and Civilization*. Boston: American Academy of Arts and Sciences, 1956.

Džambazovki, Kliment. *Kulturno-opštestvenite vrski na makedoncite so Srbija vo tekot na XIX vek*. Skopje: Institut za nacionalna istorija, 1960.

Edin Makedonets. *Bŭlgarskata propaganda v Makedoniia i Odrinsko*. Sofia, 1902.

Ellis, J. *Philip II and Macedonian Imperialism*. London: Thames and Hudson, 1976.

Errington, R. M. *A History of Macedonia*. Berkeley: University of California Press, 1990.

Fidanova, Slavka. "KPJ vo Makedonija vo vremeto od 1929 godina do aprilskata vojna." *Istorija* (Skopje) 16, no. 1 (1980), 57–101.

——— "Nacionalniot moment—faktor vo krevanje na masite vo Makedonija vo tekot na osloboditelnata borba (1941–1944)." In Makedonska akademija na naukite i umetnostite and Institut za nacionalna istorija, *Razvojot i karakteristikite na narodnoosloboditelnata vojna i revolucijata vo Makedonija*. Skopje, 1973, 193–216.

Fine, John V. A. *The Early Medieval Balkans*. Ann Arbor: University of Michigan Press, 1983.

——— *The Late Medieval Balkans*. Ann Arbor: University of Michigan Press, 1987.

Frankel, Eran, and Christina Kramer, eds. *Language Contact—Language Conflict*. New York: Peter Lang, 1993.

Friedman, Victor A. "Macedonian Language and Nationalism during the Nineteenth and Early Twentieth Century." *Balkanistica* 2 (1975), 83–98.

——— "The Socio-linguistics of Literary Macedonian." *International Journal of Sociology of Language* 52 (1985), 31–57.

Gaber, Stevan. "ASNOM i nekoi teoretski problemi na makedonskata državnost." In Makedonska akademija na naukite i umetnostite, *ASNOM. Ostvaruvanje na ideite za sozdavanje na makedonskata država i negoviot meǵunaroden odglas i odraz*. Skopje, 1977, 55–73.

Gallagher, Tom. *The Balkans in the New Millennium: In the Shadow of War and Peace*. New York: Routledge, 2005.

Gellner, E. *Nations and Nationalism*. Oxford: Basil Blackwell, 1988.

Genov, G. P. *Iztochniat vūpros*. 2 vols. Sofia, 1925–26.

Georgiev, E. *Istinata za sozdatelite na būlgarskata i slavianskata pismenost*. Sofia, 1969.

Georgievich, T. R. *Macedonia*. London, 1918.

Georgievski, M. *Prilozi od starata makedonska kniževnost i kultura*. Skopje, 1997.

Georgievski, Risto. *Makedonskiot roman 1952–1982*. Skopje: Misla, 1983.

——— *Makedonskiot roman 1952–2000*. Skopje: Matica makedonska, 2001.

Gigov, Strahil. *Sek'avanja (Memoari)*. Skopje: Naša kniga, 1970.

Glenny, Misha. *The Balkans 1804–1999: Nationalism, War and the Great Powers*. London: Granta Books, 1999.

——— *The Fall of Yugoslavia*. 2nd ed. New York: Penguin Books, 1993.

Gligorov, Kiro. *Makedonija e sè što imame*. Skopje: Izdavački centar TRI, 2001.

Gligorov, Vladimir. *Why Do Countries Break Up? The Case of Yugoslavia*. Uppsala: Acta Universitatis Upsaliensis, 1994.

Golabovski, S. *Istorija na makedonskata muzika*. Skopje, 1999.

Green, P. *Alexander of Macedon: 356–323 B.C.: A Historical Biography*. Berkeley: University of California Press, 1991.

Grigorovich, Viktor. *Ocherk puteshestviia po europeiskoi Turcii*. Moscow, 1877.

Grishina, R. P., ed. *Makedoniia. Problemi istorii i kulturi*. Moscow: Rossiiskaia akademiia nauk, Institut slavianovedeniia, 1999.

Grozdanov, C. *Portreti na svetitelite od Makedonija od IX–XVIII vek*. Skopje, 1983.

Ǵurčinov, Milan. *Nova makedonska književnost(1945–1980)*. 2 vols. Skopje: Studentski zbor, 1996.

——— "Podemot na makedonskata umetnička literatura vo godinite po ASNOM." In Makedonska akademija naukite i umetnostite, *Pedeset godini makedonska država 1944–1994*. Skopje, 1995. 423–31.

——— *Sovremena makedonska književnost*. Skopje: Misla, 1983.

Hadžidimov, Dimo. *Makedonskoto prašanje*. Ed. Gane Todorovski. Skopje: Misla, 1974.

——— *Odbrani dela*. 2 vols. Ed. Manol Pandevski. Skopje: Kultura, 1984.

Hammond, N. G. L. *A History of Greece to 322 B.C.* 3rd ed. Oxford: Oxford University Press, 1986.

——— *A History of Macedonia*. Vol. I, *Historical Geography and Prehistory*. Oxford: Oxford University Press, 1972.

——— *The Macedonian State: Origins, Institutions, and History*. Oxford: Oxford University Press, 1989.

——— *Philip of Macedon*. Baltimore: Johns Hopkins University Press, 1994.

Hammond, N. G. L., and G. T. Griffith. *A History of Macedonia*. Vol. II, *550–336 B.C.* Oxford: Oxford University Press, 1979.

Hammond, N. G. L., and F. W. Walbank. *A History of Macedonia*. Vol. III, *336–167 B.C.* Oxford: Oxford University Press, 1988.

Hobsbawm, Eric J. *Nations and Nationalism since 1780: Programme, Myth, Reality*. 2nd ed. Cambridge: Cambridge University Press, 1990.

Holton, Milne, and Graham W. Reid, eds. *Reading the Ashes: An Anthology of the Poetry of Modern Macedonia*. Pittsburgh: University of Pittsburgh Press, 1977.

Hristov, Aleksandar. "Konstitutivni elementi vo sozdavanjeto na makedonskata država vo jugoslavenskata federacija." In Makedonska akademija na naukite i umetnostite, *ASNOM. Ostvaruvanje na ideite za sozdavanje na makedonskata država i negoviot meǵunaroden odglas i odraz*. Skopje, 1977, 45–53.

——— *Sozdavanje na makedonskata država, 1878–1978*. 4 vols. Skopje: Misla, 1985.

Hroch, Miroslav. *In the National Interest: Demands and Goals of European National Movements of the Nineteenth Century: A Comparative Perspective*. Prague: Faculty of Arts, Charles University, 2000.

——— *Social Preconditions of National Revival in Europe: A Comparative Analysis of the Social Composition of Patriotic Groups among Smaller European Nations*. Cambridge: Cambridge University Press, 1985.

Hron, Karl. *Das Volkstum der Slaven Makedoniens. Ein Beitrag zur Klärung der Orientfrage*. Vienna, 1890.

Human Rights Watch/Helsinki. *Denying Ethnic Identity: The Macedonians of Greece*. New York, 1994.

——— *Destroying Ethnic Identity: Selective Persecution of Macedonians in Bulgaria*. New York, 1991.

Hussey, J. M. *The Byzantine World*. New York: Harper and Row, 1961.

Iaranoff, D. *La Macédoine économique*. Sofia, 1931.

Institute for Balkan Studies. *Ancient Macedonia*. 5 vols. Salonika, 1970, 1977, 1983, 1986, 1993.

Institute for War and Peace Reporting. *Ohrid and Beyond: A Cross-ethnic Investigation into the Macedonian Crisis*. London, 2002.

Institute of National History (Institut za nacionalna istorija). *A History of the Macedonian People*. Skopje: Macedonian Review Editions, 1979.

Institut za Istoriia, Būlgarska akademiia na naukite. *Makedonskiat vūpros. Istoriko-politicheska spravka*. Sofia, 1963.

Institut za makedonski jazik "Krste Misirkov." *Krste P. Misirkov i nacionalno-kulturniot razvoj na makedonskiot narod do oslobudvanjeto*. Skopje, 1976.

Institut za nacionalna istorija (INI). *Istorija na makedonskiot narod*. 3 vols. Skopje: Nova Makedonija, 1969.

——— *Istorija na makedonskiot narod*. 5 vols. Skopje: Institut za nacionalna istorija, 2000, 1998, 2003, 2000, 2003.

——— *Kniga za Ilinden*. Skopje, 1969.

——— *Makedonija kako prirodna i ekonomska celina*. Skopje, 1978.

——— *Razvitok na državnosta na makedonskiot narod*. Skopje, 1966.

——— *70 godini VMRO (obedineta) 1925–1995*. Skopje, 1998.

Isaev, M., ed. *Sbornik Nikola Ionkov Vaptsarov*. Sofia, 1947.

Ivanov, Iordan. *Būlgarite v Makedoniia*. Sofia, 1945.

——— *Būlgarski starini v Makedoniia*. Sofia: Nauka i izkustvo, 1970.

——— *La question macédoine*. Paris, 1920.

Ivanovski, Orde. *Dimo Hadži Dimov—život i delo*. Skopje, 1996.

Ivanovski, Vasil. *Zašto nie makedoncite sme oddelna nacija*. Ed. Ivan Katardžiev. Skopje: Arhiv na Makedonija, 1995.

Jelavich, Barbara. *History of the Balkans*. 2 vols. Cambridge: Cambridge University Press, 1983.

——— *Russia's Balkan Entanglements, 1806–1914*. Cambridge: Cambridge University Press, 1991.

Jotevski, Vasil. *Nacionalnata afirmacija na makedoncite vo pirinskiot del na Makedonija 1944–1948*. Skopje: Institut za nacionalna istorija, 1996.

Jovanović, Jovan M. *Južna Srbija od kraja XVIII veka do osvobodjenija*. Belgrade, 1941.

Kantardžiev, Risto. *Makedonskoto prerodbensko učilište*. Skopje: Kultura, 1965.

Karakachanov, Krasimir. *VMRO—100 godini borba za Makedoniia*. Sofia: Izd. na VMRO-SMD, 1996.

Karakasidou, Anastasia N. *Fields of Wheat, Hills of Blood: Passages to Nationhood in Greek Macedonia, 1870–1990*. Chicago: University of Chicago Press, 1997.

——— "Politicizing Culture: Negating Ethnic Identity in Greek Macedonia." *Journal of Modern Greek Studies* 11 (1993), 1–28.

Kartov, Vladimir. *Borbata na KPJ za rešavanje na nacionalnoto prašanje vo Jugoslavija, 1919–1954*. Skopje: Prosvetno delo, 1983.

Katardžiev, Ivan. "IMORO." *Macedonian Review* (Skopje) 20 (1990), no. 1–2, 31–42, and no. 3, 139–61.

——— *Istorija na makedonskiot narod*. Vol. IV, *Makedonija meģu Balkanskite i Vtorata svetska vojna (1912–1941)*. Skopje: Institut za nacionalna istorija, 2000.

——— *KPJ vo Makedonija do obznanata*. Skopje: Kultura, 1961.

——— *The Macedonian Uprising in Kresna 1878*. Skopje: Macedonian Review Editions, 1980.

——— *Makedonija sproti vtorata svetska vojna*. Skopje: Menora, 1999.

——— *Po krvicite na makedonskata istorija*. Skopje: Kultura, 1986.

——— *Sto godini od formiranjeto na VMRO*. Skopje: Misla, 1993.

——— *Susedite na Makedonija—včera, denes, utre*. Skopje: Menora, 1988.

——— "VMRO i makedonskoto osloboditelno dviženje od krajot na prvata svetska vojna do raspaģanjeto na monizmot." In Makedonska akademija na naukite i umetnostite, *Sto godini od osnovanjeto na VMRO i 90 godini od ilindenskoto vostanie* (Skopje, 1994), 45–73.

——— *Vreme na zreenje. Makedonskoto nacionalno prašanje meģu dvete svetski vojni 1919–1930*. 2 vols. Skopje: Kultura, 1977.

Katardžiev, Ivan, ed. *VMRO (obedineta). Dokumenti i materiali*. Skopje: Institut za nacionalna istorija, 1991.

Khristov, Khristo. *Agrarnite otnosheniia v Makedoniia prez XIX i nachaloto na XX vek*. Sofia, 1964.

——— *Būlgarskite obshchini prez vūzrazhdaneto*. Sofia, 1973.

Kiosev, Dino. *Gotse Delchev. Pisma i drugi materiali*. Sofia, 1967.

——— *Istoriia na makedonskoto natsionalno revolutsionno dvizhenie*. Sofia: Otechestven front, 1954.

Kirjazovski, Risto. *Makedonski nacionalni institucii vo egejskiot del na Makedonija (1941–1961)*. Skopje: Institut za nacionalna istorija, 1987.

——— *Makedonskoto nacionalno prašanje i graǵanskata vojna vo Grcija*. Skopje: Institut za nacionalna istorija, 1998.

Kirjazovski, Risto, ed. *KPG i makedonskoto nacionalno prašanje 1918–1974*. Skopje: Arhiv na Makedonija, 1982.

Kiselinovski, Stojan. *Grčkata kolonizacija vo egejska Makedonija (1913–1940)*. Skopje: Institut za nacionalna istorija, 1981.

——— *Egejskiot del na Makedonija (1913–1989)*. Skopje: Kultura, 1990.

——— *Etničkite promeni vo Makedonija (1913–1995)*. Skopje: Institut za nacionalna istorija, 2000.

——— *KPG i makedonskoto nacionalno prašanje, 1918–1940*. Skopje: Misla, 1985.

——— *Makedonski dejci (XX-ti vek)*. Skopje: Makavej, 2002.

——— *Statusot na makedonskiot jazik vo Makedonija*. Skopje: Misla, 1987.

Kiselinovski, Stojan, ed. *Makedonski istoriski rečnik*. Skopje: Institut za nacionalna istorija, 2000.

Klincharov, I. G. *Pop Bogomil i negovoto vreme*. Sofia, 1947.

Kljakić, Dragan. *Vremeto na Koliševski*. Skopje: Matica makedonska, 1994.

Kočov, Stojan. *Ideološkiot aktivizam nad makedoncite pod Grcija*. Skopje: Matica makedonska, 2000.

Kofos, Evangelos. *Nationalism and Communism in Macedonia*. Salonika: Institute for Balkan Studies, 1964.

Koledarov, P. *Imeto Makedoniia vo istorichneskata geografiia*. Sofia, 1985.

Koliopoulos, John S. *Plundered Loyalties: World War II and Civil War in Greek West Macedonia*. New York: New York University Press, 1999.

Koliševski, Lazar. *Aspekti na makedonskoto prašanje*. 2nd, expanded ed. Skopje: Kultura, 1980.

Koneski, Blaže. *Istorija na makedonskiot jazik*. Skopje: Kočo Racin, 1965.

——— *Kon makedonskata prerodba. Makedonskite učebnici od 19 vek*. Skopje: Institut za nacionalna istorija, 1959.

——— *Za makedonskata literatura*. Skopje: Kultura, 1967.

Kosik, V. I.. "Gordiev uzel Balkan." In R. P. Grishina, ed., *Makedoniia: problemi istorii i kulturi*. Moscow: Institut slavianovedeniia, Rossiiskaia akademiia nauk, 1999, 59–71.

Kosik, V. I., ed. *Makedoniia. Put'k samostoiatelnosti. Dokumenti*. Moscow: Raduga, 1997.

Kousoulas, Dimitrios G. *Revolution and Defeat: The Story of the Communist Party of Greece*. London: Oxford University Press, 1965.

Kramer, Christina. "Language in Exile: The Macedonians of Toronto." In Eran Frankel and Christina Kramer, eds., *Language Contact—Language Conflict*. New York: Peter Lang, 1993, 154–83.

Krsteski, Gligor. *Otpori i progoni, 1946–1950*. Skopje: Matica makedonska, 1994.

Kūnchov, Vasil. *Izbrani proizvedeniia*. 2 vols. Sofia: Nauka i izkustvo, 1970.

Labon, Joanna, ed. *Balkan Blues: Writings out of Yugoslavia*. Evanston, Ill.: Northwestern University Press, 1994.

Lampe, John R. *Yugoslavia as History: Twice There Was a Country*. Cambridge: Cambridge University Press, 1996.

Lampe, John R., and Mark Mazower. *Ideologies and National Identities: The Case of Twentieth Century Southeastern Europe*. New York: Central European University Press, 2003.

Lape, L'uben. *Makedonija vo XVIII, XIX i XX vek. Odbrani trudovi*. Skopje: Kultura, 1992.

Lape, L'uben, ed. *Odbrani tekstovi za istorijata na makedonskiot narod*. 2 vols. 3rd ed. Skopje: Univerzitet Kiril i Metodij, 1975.

Laskaris, M. *To anatolikon zitima, 1800–1923*. 2 vols. Salonika, 1948, 1954.

Lazarov, Lazar. *Opštestveno-ekonomskiot razvoj na N. R. Makedonija vo periodot na obnovata i industrializacijata (1944–1957)*. Skopje: Institut za nacionalna istorija, 1988.

——— *Opštestveno-političkite organizacii vo obnovata i izgradbata na N. R. Makedonija, 1944–1948*. Skopje: Institut za nacionalna istorija, 1979.

Limanoski, Nijazi. *Islamizacijata i etničkite promeni vo Makedonija*. Skopje: Makedonska kniga, 1993.

Litavrin, G. G. *Vizantija i slaviane*. St. Petersburg, 1999.

Lunt, Horace G. "The Creation of Standard Macedonian: Some Facts and Attitudes." *Anthropological Linguistics* 1, no. 5 (June 1959), 19–26.

——— *A Grammar of the Macedonian Literary Language*. Skopje: Dravno, 1952.

——— "On Macedonian Nationality." *Slavic Review* 45, no. 4 (winter 1986), 729–34.

——— "Some Socio-linguistic Aspects of Macedonian and Bulgarian." In B. A. Stolz, I. R. Titunik, and L. Doležel, eds., *Language and Literary Theory*. Ann Arbor: University of Michigan Press, 1984, 83–132.

Lužina, Jelena. *Istorija na makedonskata drama. Makedonskata bitova drama*. Skopje: Kultura, 1995.

"Macedonia." *Journal of Modern Greek Studies* 14, no. 2 (Oct. 1996).

Mackridge, Peter A., and Eleni Yannakakis. *Ourselves and Others: The Development of a Greek Macedonian Identity since 1912*. Oxford: Berg Publishers, 1997.

Madolev, Georgi T. *Vŭorŭzhenata borba v Pirinskiia krai*. Sofia: BKP, 1966.

Magaš, Branka. *The Destruction of Yugoslavia: Tracking the Break-up, 1980–92*. London: Verso, 1993.

Makedonskii golos (Makedonski glas). Organ storonikov nezavisimoi makedonii (St. Petersburg, 1913–14). Facsimile ed. Skopje: Institut za nacionalna istorija, 1968.

Makedonska akademija na naukite i umetnostite (MANU). *ASNOM. Ostvaruvanje na ideite za sozdavanje na makedonskata država i negoviot meǵunaroden odglas i odraz*. Skopje, 1977.

——— *Čento i makedonskata državnost*. Skopje, 2004.

——— *Kliment Ohridski i ulogata na ohridskata književna škola vo razvojot na slovenskata prosveta*. Skopje, 1989.

——— *Kresenskoto vostanie vo Makedonija 1878–1881*. Skopje, 1982.

——— *Makedonija vo istočnata kriza 1875–1881*. Skopje, 1978.

——— *Razvojot i karakteristikite na narodnooslobóditelnata vojna i na revolucijata vo Makedonija*. Skopje, 1973.

——— *Školstvoto, prosvetata i kulturata vo Makedonia vo vremeto na preródbata*. Skopje, 1979.

——— *Sto godini od osnovanjeto na VMRO i 90 godini od Ilindenskoto vostanie*. Skopje, 1994.

Makedonska akademija na naukite i umetnostite (MANU) and Institut za nacionalna istorija (INI). *ASNOM. Pedeset godini makedonska država 1944–1994*. Skopje, 1995.

Makedonski Nauchen Institut. *Makedoniia kato prirodno i stopansko tsialo*. Sofia, 1945.

Malkovski, Džordži. *Profašističkite i kolaboracionističkite organizacii i grupi vo Makedonija, 1941–1944*. Skopje, 1989.

Mamurovski, Taško. *Bugarskata propaganda vo jugozapadna i centralna egejska Makedonija (1941–1944)*. Skopje: Institut za nacionalna istorija, 1989.

Matkovski, Aleksandar. *A History of the Jews in Macedonia*. Skopje: Macedonian Review Editions, 1982.

——— *Kreposništvoto vo Makedonija vo vreme na turskoto vladeenje*. Skopje, 1978.

——— *Makedonija vo delata na stranskite patopisci, 1371–1864*. 4 vols. Skopje: Misla, 1991–92.

——— *Otporot vo Makedonija vo vremeto na turskoto vladeenje*. 4 vols. Skopje: Misla, 1983.

McNeill, William H. *The Greek Dilemma: War and Aftermath*. Philadelphia: V. Gollancz, 1947.

Meininger, Thomas A. *Ignatiev and the Establishment of the Bulgarian Exarchate: A Study in Personal Diplomacy*. Madison: State Historical Society of Wisconsin, 1970.

Michas, Takis. *Unholy Alliance: Greece and Milošević's Serbia*. Austin, Tex.: A&M University Press, 2002.

Mihailov, Mile. *Prašanjeto za obedinuvanjeto na Makedonija vo Vtorate svetska vojna*. Skopje, 2000.

Mikhailov, Ivan. *Macedonia: A Switzerland of the Balkans*. St. Louis, Mo.: Liberator Press, 1949.

——— *Spomeni*. 4 vols. Selci, Louvain, Indianapolis, 1952, 1965, 1967, 1973.

Miladinov, Dimitrija, and Konstantin Miladinov. *Zbornik na narodni pesni*. Eds. Haralampie Polenaković and Todor Dimitrovski. Skopje: Makedonska kniga, 1983. Originally published as *Būlgarski narodni pesni*. Zagreb: A. Jakić, 1861.

Miljovski, Kiril. *Makedonskoto prašanje vo nacionalnata programa na KPJ (1919–1937)*. Skopje: Kultura, 1962.

——— "Motivite na revolucijata 1941–1944 godina vo Makedonija." *Istorija* (Skopje) 10, no. 1 (1974), 17–24.

——— "Nekoj osobenosti na revolucijata od 1941 do 1944 godina vo Makedonija." In Makedonska akademija na naukite i umetnostite and Institut za nacionalna istorija, *Razvojot i karakteristikite na narodnoosloboditelnata vojna i na revolucijata vo Makedonija*. Skopje, 1973, 14–22.

Milosavlevski, Slavko. *Dvete lica na sobitijata*. Skopje: Zumpres, 1996.

——— *Jugoslovenskite socialisti-komunisti i makedonskoto prašanje (1918–1945)*. Skopje: Studentski zbor, 1992.

——— *Sociologija na makedonskata nacionalna svest*. Skopje: Kultura, 1992.

——— *Strav od promeni. Krizata na političkiot sistem na Jugoslavija vo sedumdesettite godini*. Skopje: Komunist, 1991.

Milosavlevski, Slavko, and Mirče Tomovski. *Albanicite vo Republika Makedonija, 1945–1995. Legislativa, politička dokumentacija, statistika*. Skopje: Studentski zbor, 1997.

Minoski, Mihailo. *Avnojska Jugoslavija i makedonskoto nacionalno prašanje (1943–1946)*. Skopje, 2000.

——— *Federativnata ideja vo makedonskata politička misla (1887–1919)*. Skopje: Studentski zbor, 1985.

Misirkov, Krste P. *Odbrani stranici*. Ed. Blaže Ristovski: Skopje: Misla, 1991.

——— *Za makedonckite raboti*. Sofia: Liberalen klub, 1903. Facsimile ed. Skopje: Institut za makedonski jazik, 1974.

Mitrev, Dimitar. *BKP i pirinska Makedonija*. Skopje: Kultura, 1960.

——— *Pirinska Makedonija i drugi istoriografski ogledi*. Skopje: Naša kniga, 1970.

Modes, G. *O makedonikon agon kai i neoteri makedoniki istoria*. Salonika, 1967.

Mojsov, L. *Okolu prašanjeto na makedonskoto nacionalno malcinstvo vo Grcija*. Skopje: Institut za nacionalna istorija, 1954.

Mokrov, Boro. *Makedonskiot revolucioneren pečat*. Skopje: Misla, 1979.

Mpramos, K. *Slavokommounistikaì organoseis en Makedonia. Propaganda kai epanastatiki drasi*. Salonika: Institute for Balkan Studies, 1994.

Naimark, Norman A., and Holly Case, eds. *Yugoslavia and Its Historians: Understanding the Balkan Wars of the 1990s*. Stanford, Calif.: Stanford University Press, 2003.

Nanevski, Duško. *Makedonskata poetska škola*. Skopje: Misla, 1977.

Nešović, Slobodan. *Bledski sporazumi. Tito–Dimitrov (1947)*. Zagreb: Globus, 1979.

——— *Jugoslavija—Bugarska, ratno vreme, 1941–1945*. Belgrade: Narodna knjiga, 1978.

Nicolaides, C. *La Macédoine*. Berlin, 1899.

Obolensky, D. *The Bogomils: A Study in Balkan Neomanichaeism*. Cambridge: Cambridge University Press, 1948.

——— *The Byzantine Commonwealth: Eastern Europe, 500–1453*. New York: Praeger, 1971.

Oliva, P. *Řecko mezi Makedonii a Římem*. Prague, 1995.

Ostrogorsky, G. *History of the Byzantine State*. New Brunswick, N.J.: Rutgers University Press, 1957.

Pačemska, Darinka. *Vnatrešnata makedonska revolucionerna organizacija (obedineta)*. Skopje: Studentski zbor, 1985.

Paleshutski, Kostadin. *Iugoslavskata komunistichka partia i makedonskiat vūpros, 1919–1945*. Sofia: Būlgarska akademia na naukite, 1985.

——— *Makedonsko osvoboditelno dvizhenie sled pūrvata svetovna voina (1918–1924)*. Sofia: Būlgarska akademia na naukite, 1993.

——— *Makedonsko osvoboditelno dvizhenie 1924–1934*. Sofia: Akademichko izd-vo "Prof. Marin Drinov," 1998.

Palmer, Stephen E., and Robert R. King. *Yugoslav Communism and the Macedonian Question*. Hamden, Conn.: Archon Books, 1971.

Pandev, Konstantin. *Natsionalnoosvoboditelnoto dvizhenie v Makedoniia i Odrinsko 1878–1903*. Sofia: Nauka i izkustvo, 1979.

Pandevski, Manol. *Ilindenskoto vostanie vo Makedonija 1903*. Skopje: Institut za nacionalna istorija, 1978.

——— *Nacionalnoto prašane vo makedonskoto osloboditelno dviženje (1893–1903)*. Skopje: Kultura, 1974.

——— *Vnatrešnata makedonski revolucionerna organizacija i neovrhovizmot*. Skopje, 1983.

Panov, Branko. *Srednovekovna Makedonija*. 2 vols. Skopje: Misla, 1985.

Panov, Branko, ed. *Istorija na makedonskiot narod*. Vol. I, *Madekonija od praistoriskoto vreme do potpaǵanjeto pod turska vlast (1371 godina)*. Skopje: Institut za nacionalna istorija, 2000.

Panovska, Liljana. *Terorot vo egejskiot del na Makedonija, 1941–1944*. Skopje: Institut za nacionalna istorija, 1995.

Pantazopoulos, N. J. *Church and Law in the Balkan Peninsula during the Ottoman Rule*. Salonika: Institute for Balkan Studies, 1967.

Penušliski, Kiril. *Narodnata kultura na egejska Makedonija*. Skopje, 1992.

Perica, Vjekoslav. *Balkan Idols: Religion and Nationalism in Yugoslavia*. New York: Oxford University Press, 2004.

Perry, Duncan M. "Destiny on Hold: Macedonia and the Dangers of Ethnic Discord." *Current History* 83, nos. 1–2 (March 1992), 119–26.

——— *The Politics of Terror: The Macedonian Revolutionary Movements, 1893–1903*. Durham, N.C.: Duke University Press, 1988.

——— "The Republic of Macedonia: Finding Its Way." In Karen Dawisha and Bruce Parrot, eds., *Politics, Power, and the Struggle for Democracy in Southeast Europe*. Cambridge: Cambridge University Press, 1997, 226–81.

Petrov, Ǵorče. *Makedonskoto osloboditelno delo*. Ed. Gane Todorovski. Skopje: Misla, 1971.

Petruševski, I. *Makedonija na karti*. Skopje, 1987.

Pettifier, James, ed. *The New Macedonian Question*. New York: St. Martin's Press, 1999.

Phillips, John. *Macedonia: Warlords and Rebels in the Balkans*. New York: I. B. Tauris, 2004.

Pirivatrić, Srdjan. *Samuilova država. Obim i karakter*. Belgrade, 1997.

Polenaković, Haralampie. *Studii za Miladinovci*. Skopje: Misla, 1973.

Poplazarov, Risto. *Grčkata politika sprema Makedonija vo vtorata polovina na XIX i početokot na XX vek*. Skopje: Institut za nacionalna istorija, 1973.

Popović, V. *Iztočno pitanje*. Belgrade, 1928.

Popovski, Josif, ed. *Makedonskoto prašanje na stranicite na "Rizospastis" meǵu dvete vojni*. Skopje: Kultura, 1982.

Popovski, Tošo. *Makedonskoto nacionalno malcinstvo vo Bugarija, Grcija i Albanija*. Skopje: Makedonska kniga, 1981.

Popovski, Vlado. *Makedonskoto nacionalno-osloboditelno diviženje do-TMORO*. Skopje, 1989.

Popovski, Vlado, and L. I. Zhila, eds. *Makedonskii vopros v dokumentakh kominterna*. Vol. I, part 1: *1923–1925 gg*. Skopje: Gurga, 1999.

Poulton, Hugh. *Who Are the Macedonians?* Bloomington and Indianapolis: Indiana University Press, 1995.

Pribichevich, Stoyan. *Macedonia: Its People and History*. University Park: Pennsylvania State University Press, 1982.

Proeva, N. *Studii za antičkite Makedonci*. Skopje, 1997.

Pulevski, Ǵorǵija M. *Odbrani stranici*. Ed. Blaže Ristovski. Skopje: Makedonska kniga, 1974.

——— *Slavjansko–makedonska opšta istorija*. Eds. Blaže Ristovski and Biljana Ristovska-Josifovska. Skopje: Makedonska akademija na naukite i umetnostite, 2003.

Radev, Simeon. *Makedoniia i būlgarskoto vūzrazhdane v XIX vek*. 3 vols. Sofia: P. Glushkov, 1927–28.

Rakovski, Pavle. *KP na Grcija i Makedoncite*. Skopje: Institut za nacionalna istorija, 1990.

Ramet, Sabrina P. *Balkan Babel: The Disintegration of Yugoslavia from the Death of Tito to the War for Kosovo*. 3rd ed. Boulder, Colo.: Westview Press, 1999.

——— "The Macedonian Enigma." In Sabrina P. Ramet and Ljubiša S. Adamovich, eds., *Beyond Yugoslavia: Politics, Economics, and Culture in a Shattered Community*. Boulder, Colo.: Westview Press, 1995.

Ramet, [Sabrina P.] Pedro. *Nationalism and Federalism in Yugoslavia, 1963–1983*. Bloomington: Indiana University Press, 1984.

Ramsaur, Ernest E. *The Young Turks: Prelude to the Revolution of 1908*. Princeton, N.J.: Princeton University Press, 1957.

Republic of Macedonia. *Independence through Peaceful Self-determination: Documents*. Skopje, 1992.

Richter, Heinz. *British Intervention in Greece: From Varkiza to Civil War, February 1945 to August 1946*. London: Merlin, 1985.

Risteski, Stojan. *Sozdavanjeto na sovremeniot makedonski literaturen jazik*. Skopje: Studentski zbor, 1988.

——— *Sudeni za Makedonija (1945–1985)*. 2 vols. Ohrid: Macedonia prima, 1995.

Ristović, Milan. *Dug povratak kući. Deca izbeglice iz Grčke u Jugoslaviji, 1948–1960*. Belgrade: Čiboja štampa, 1998.

Ristovski, Blaže. *Dimitrija Čupovski 1878–1940 i makedonskoto naučno-literaturno drugarstvo vo Petrograd*. 2 vols. Skopje: Kultura, 1978.

——— *Istorija na makedonskata nacija*. Skopje: Makedonska akademija na naukite i umetnostite, 1999.

——— *Kočo Racin. Istorisko-literaturni istražuvanja*. Skopje: Makedonska kniga, 1983.

——— *Krste P. Misirkov (1878–1926)*. Skopje: Kultura, 1966.

——— *Macedonia and the Macedonian People*. Vienna-Skopje: Simag Holding, 1999.

——— *Makedonskiot folkor i nacionalnata svest. Istražuvanja i zapisi*. 2 vols. Skopje: Studentski zbor, 1987.

——— *Makedonskiot narod i makedonskata nacija*. 2 vols. Skopje: Misla, 1983.

——— *Makedonskiot stih, 1900–1944. Istražuvanja i materiali*. 2 vols. Skopje: Misla, 1980.

——— *Nace P. Dimov (1876–1916)*. Skopje: Makedonska akademija na naukite i umetnostite, 1973.

——— *Vasil Ikonomov (1848–1934)*. Skopje: Institut za nacionalna istorija, 1985.

Rossos, Andrew. "The British Foreign Office and Macedonian National Identity." *Slavic Review* 53, no. 2 (summer 1994), 369–94.

——— "The Disintegration of Yugoslavia, Macedonia's Independence and Stability in the Balkans." In Brad K. Blitz, ed., *War and Change in the Balkans: Nationalism, Conflict and Cooperation*. Cambridge: Cambridge University Press, 2006, 110–17.

——— "Great Britain and Macedonian Statehood and Unification, 1940–1949." *East European Politics and Societies* 14, no. 1 (winter 2000), 119–42.

——— "Incompatible Allies: Greek Communism and Macedonian Nationalism in the Civil War in Greece, 1943–1949." *Journal of Modern History* 69, no. 1 (March 1997), 42–76.

——— "Macedonianism and Macedonian Nationalism on the Left." In Ivo Banac and Katherine Verdery, eds., *National Character and National Ideology in Interwar Eastern Europe*. New Haven, Conn.: Yale Center for International and Area Studies, 1995, 219–54.

——— "The Macedonian Question and Instability in the Balkans." In Norman

M. Naimark and Holly Case, eds., *Yugoslavia and Its Historians: Understanding the Balkan Wars of the 1990s*. Stanford, Calif.: Stanford University Press, 140–59 and 245–54.

——— "The Macedonians of Aegean Macedonia: A British Officer's Report, 1944." *Slavonic and East European Review* 69, no. 2 (April 1991), 282–309.

——— *Russia and the Balkans: Inter-Balkan Rivalries and Russian Foreign Policy 1908–1914*. Toronto: University of Toronto Press, 1981.

——— "Serbian–Bulgarian Relations, 1903–1914." *Canadian Slavonic Papers* 23, no. 4 (Dec. 1981), 394–408.

Roudometof, Victor. *Collective Memory, National Identity, and Ethnic Conflict: Greece, Bulgaria and the Macedonian Question*. Westport, Conn.: Praeger, 2002.

Roudometof, Victor, ed. *The Macedonian Question: Culture, Historiography, Politics*. Boulder, Colo.: East European Monographs, 2000.

Runciman, Steven. *Byzantine Civilization*. 1933. Reprint London: Methuen, 1961.

——— *The Great Church in Captivity*. Cambridge: Cambridge University Press, 1968.

Russinow, Dennison. *The Yugoslav Experiment, 1948–1974*. Berkeley: University of California Press, 1977.

Rychlík, Jan. *Dějiny Bulharska*. Prague: Nakladatelství Lidové Novini, 2002.

Rychlík, Jan, and Miroslav Kouba. *Dějiny Makedonie*. Prague: Nakladatelství Lidové Novini, 2003.

Sazdov, Tome. *Makedonskata narodna poezija*. Skopje, 1966.

Sazdov, Tome, and Vera Stojčevska-Antić. *Makedonska knijževnost*. Zagreb, 1988.

Sedlar, Jean W. *East Central Europe in the Middle Ages, 1000–1500*. Seattle and London: University of Washington Press, 1994.

Sedov, V. V. *Proiskhozhdenie i rannaia istoriia slavian*. Moscow, 1979.

Seraphinoff, Michael. *The 19th Century Macedonian Awakening: A Study of the Works of Kiril Pejčinovich*. Lanham, Md.: University Press of America, 1996.

Shatev, Pavel. *Vo Makedoniia pod robstvo. Solunskoto sŭzakliatie*. Sofia, 1943.

Shea, John. *Macedonia and Greece: The Struggle to Define a New Balkan Nation*. Jefferson, N.C., and London: McFarland and Co., 1997.

Shofman, A. S. *Ocherki po istorii Makedonii i makedonskogo naroda*. 2 vols. Kazan: Kazanskii gosudarstvenyi universitet, 1960.

Siliianov, Khristo. *Osvoboditelnite borbi na Makedoniia*. 2 vols. Sofia: Iz. na ilindenskata organizatsia, 1933, 1943.

Siljan, Rade, ed. *Prilozi na nastavata po lietratura. Makedonski dramski pisateli, razkažuvači i romansieri*. Skopje: Matica makedonska, 2001.

——— *Prilozi za nastavata po literatura. Makedonskata poezija*. Skopje: Matica makedonska, 2001.

Simovski, Todor. "Balkanskite vojni i nivnite reprekusii vrz etničkata položba na egejska Makedonija." *Glasnik* (Skopje) 16, no. 3 (1972), 61–75.

Smith, A. D. *The Ethnic Origins of Nations*. Oxford: Oxford University Press, 1986.

Snegarov, Ivan. *Istoria na okhridskata arkhiepiskopiia*. 2 vols. Sofia, 1924, 1932.

Sokolov, L. "Prilog za makedonskoto studentsko dviženje vo Zagreb." *Istorija* (Skopje) 12, nos. 1–2 (1976), 1–27.

Solunski, Koce. *Kuzman Josifovski-Pitu. (Život-delo-vreme)*. 2 vols. Skopje: Nova Makedonija, 1973.

Sotirovski, Nikola. "ASNOM—sinteza na nacionalniot i državnopravniot faktor vo istorijata na makedonskiot narod." In Makedonska akademija na naukite i umetnostite, *ASNOM. Ostvaruvanje na ideite za sazdavanje na makedonskata država i negoviot meǵunaroden odglas i odraz*. Skopje, 1977, 75–82.

Srpska književna zadruga (SKZ). *Istorija srpskog naroda*. 6 books in 10 vols. Belgrade: Srpska književna zadruga, 1981–83.

Stalev, Georgi. *Pregled na makedonskata literatura od XIX vek*. Skopje, 1963.

Stamatoski, Trajko. "Misli za makedonskiot literaturen jazik." In Makedonska akademija na naukite i umetnostite, *ASNOM. Pedeset godini makedonska država 1944–1994*. Skopje, 1995, 375–86.

Stanovčić, Vojislav. "History and Status of Ethnic Conflicts." In Dennison Russinow, ed., *Yugoslavia: A Fractured Federalism*. Washington, D.C.: Wilson Center Press, 1998, 32–40.

Statelova, E., R. Popov, and V. Tamkova. *Istoriia na bŭlgarskata diplomatiia 1878–1913*. Sofia, 1994.

Stavrakis, Peter J. *Moscow and Greek Communism, 1944–1949*. Ithaca, N.Y.: Cornell University Press, 1989.

Stavrianos, L. S. *Balkan Federation: A History of the Movement toward Balkan Unity in Modern Times*. 1944, reprint Hamden: Anchor Books, 1964.

——— *The Balkans since 1453*. New York: Holt, Rinehart and Winston, 1958.

Stawowy-Kawka, Irena. *Historia Macedonii*. Wroclaw: Ossolineum, 2002.

Stephenson, Paul. *The Legend of Basil the Bulgar-Slayer*. Cambridge: Cambridge University Press, 2003.

Steppan, Hans-Lothar. *Der mazedonische Knoten. Die Identität der Mazedo-*

nier Dargstellt am beispiel des Balkanbundes (1878–1914). Frankfurt: Peter Lang, 2004.

Stojanov, Petar. *Makedonija vo vremeto na balkanskite i prvata svetska vojna (1912–1918)*. Skopje: Institut za nacionalna istorija, 1969.

——— *Petar Pop Arsov vo nacionalno-revolucionernoto dviženje na makedonskiot narod (1868–1919)*. Skopje: Kultura, 1963.

Stojanovski, Aleksandar. *Makedonija vo turskoto srednovekovie (od krajot na XIV do početokot na XVIII vek)*. Skopje: Kultura, 1989.

——— *Raja so specialni zadolženija vo Makedonija*. Skopje: Institut za nacionalna istorija, 1990.

Stojanovski, Aleksandar, ed. *Istorija na makedonskiot narod*. Vol. II, *Makedonija pod turska vlast (od XIV do krajot na XVIII vek)*. Skopje, Institut za nacionalna istorija, 1998.

Stojčevska-Antić, Vera. *Kliment i Naum Ohridski vo narodnata tradicija*. Skopje: Naša kniga, 1982.

Stokes, Gale. "Church and Class in Early Balkan Nationalism." *East European Quarterly* 13, no. 2 (1979), 259–70.

——— *The Walls Came Tumbling Down: The Collapse of Communism in Eastern Europe*. New York: Oxford University Press, 1993.

Stolz, Benjamin A., ed. *Studies in Macedonian Language, Literature, and Culture: Proceedings of the First North American–Macedonian Conference*. Ann Arbor: Michigan Slavic Publications, 1995.

Sugar, Peter F. *Southeastern Europe under Ottoman Rule*. Seattle: University of Washington Press, 1977.

Sujecka, Jolanta, ed. *The National Idea as a Research Problem*. Warsaw: Institute of Slavonic Studies, Polish Academy of Sciences, 2002.

Sumner, B. H. *Russia and the Balkans, 1870–1880*. Oxford: Clarendon Press, 1937.

Swire, J. *Bulgarian Conspiracy*. London: Robert Hale, 1940.

Szobries, Torsten. *Sprachliche Aspekte des Nation-Bildung in Mazedonien: Die kommunistische Presse in Vardar-Mazedonien (1940–1943)*. Stuttgart: Franz Steiner, 1999.

Taškovski, Dragan. *Kon etnogenezata na makedonskiot narod*. Skopje: Naša kniga, 1974.

Terziovski, Rastislav. *Denacionalizatorskata dejnost na bugarskite kulturno-prosvetni institucii vo Makedonija*. Skopje, 1974.

Todorovski, Gane. *Istoriografski temi*. Skopje: Naša kniga, 1990.

——— *Prethodnicite na Misirkov*. Skopje: Misla, 1974.

——— *Traktati za soncel'ubivite*. Skopje: Kultura, 1974.

Todorovski, Gligor. *Makedonskoto prašanje. Reformite vo Makedonija.* Skopje: Kultura, 1989.

——— *Reformite na golemite evropski sili vo Makedonija (1829–1905).* 3 vols. Skopje: Studentski zbor, 1984.

——— *Srbija i reformite vo Makedonija.* Skopje: Institut za nacionalna istorija, 1987.

——— *Srpski izvori za istorijata na makedonskiot narod (1890–1912).* Skopje: Studentski zbor, 1985.

Todorovski, Mile. *Partizanskite odredi i narodnoosloboditelnata vojska na Makedonija vo oslobiditelnata vojna i revolucijata od 1941–1944.* Skopje: Institut za nacionalna istorija, 1972.

Todorovski, Zoran. *VMRO 1924–1934.* Skopje: Robz, 1997.

Trajanovski, Aleksandar. *Crkovno-učilišnite opštini vo Makedonija.* Skopje: Institut za nacionalna istorija, 1988.

Troebst, Stefan. *Die bulgarisch–jugoslawischen Kontroverse um Makedonien, 1967–1982.* Munich: Oldenburg, 1983.

——— "Yugoslav Macedonia, 1944–1953: Building the Party, the State and the Nation." *Berliner Jahrbuch für osteuropäische Geschichte*, 1994, part 2, 103–39.

Tsūrnushanov, Kosta. *Makedonizmūt i sūprotivata na Makedoniia sreshchu nego.* Sofia: Univerzitetsko izdatelstvo "Sv. Kliment Okhridski", 1992.

Tsvetkova, Bistra. *Khaidutstvo v būlgarskite zemi prez 15–18 vek.* Sofia, 1971.

Tupurkovski, V. *Filip II.* Skopje: Titan, 1995.

——— *Istorija na Makedonija. Od drevnina do smrta na Aleksandar Makedonski.* Skopje: Titan, 1993.

——— *Istorija na Makedonija. Od smrta na Aleksandar Makedonski do makedonsko-rimskata vojna.* Skopje: Titan, 1994.

Urginova-Skalovska, R., ed. *Damaskini.* Skopje: Makedonska kniga, 1975.

Uzunovski, Cvetko. "Vostanijeto vo 1941 vo Makedonija." *Istorija* (Skopje) 10, no. 2 (1974), 83–123.

Vacalopoulos, A. E. *History of Macedonia 1354–1833.* Trans. Peter Megann. Salonika: Institute for Balkan Studies, 1973.

Vakalopoulos, Konstantinos A. *Modern History of Macedonia 1830–1912. (From the Birth of the Greek State until Liberation.)* Athens: Barbounakis, 1988.

Vanchev, I. *Novo-būlgarskata prosveta v Makedonija prez vūzrazhdaneto (do 1878 godina).* Sofia, 1982.

Vapcarov, Nikola. *Pesni za tatkovinata.* Ed. Blaže Ristovski. Skopje: Misla, 1986.

——— *Tvorbi*. Ed. Gane Todorovski. Skopje: Misla, 1979.

Vardarski [Petar Pop Arsov]. *Stambulovshchinata v Makedoniia i neizinite predstaviteli*. Vienna, 1894.

Vasilev, Alexander A. *History of the Byzantine Empire*. 2 vols. Madison: University of Wisconsin Press, 1960.

Veljanovski, Novica. *Makedonija vo jugoslovensko—bugarskite odnosi, 1944–1953*. Skopje: Institut za nacionalna istorija, 1998.

——— *Narodnata vlast vo Makedonija, 1941–1944*. Skopje: Misla, 1983.

Veljanovski, Novica, ed. *Istorija na makedonskiot narod*. Vol. V, *Makedonija vo Vtorata svetska vojna. Narodnooslobiditelnata antifašistička vojna vo Makedonija (1941–1945)*. Skopje: Institut za nacionalna istorija, 2003.

Veremi, Pietro. *Vite di Confine: Etnicità e Nazionalismo nella Macedonia Occidentale Greca*. Rome: Meltimi, 2004.

Veselinov, Kosta. *Vūzrazhdaneto na Makedoniia i ilindenskoto vūstanie*. Sofia, 1939.

Vlahos, Nik. *To Makedonikon os fasis tu anatoliku zitimatos (1878–1908)*. Athens, 1935.

Vlahov, Dimitar. *Memoari*. Skopje: Nova Makedonija, 1970.

Vlasto, A. P. *The Entry of the Slavs into Christendom: An Introduction to the Medieval History of the Slavs*. Cambridge: Cambridge University Press, 1970.

Vražinovski, T. *Narodna mitologija na Makedoncite*. Skopje, 1998.

Vucinich, Wayne S. *The Ottoman Empire: Its Record and Legacy*. Princeton, N.J.: D. Van Nostrand, 1965.

——— *Serbia between East and West: The Events of 1903–08*. Stanford, Calif.: Stanford University Press, 1954.

Vucinich, Wayne S., ed. *Contemporary Yugoslavia: Twenty Years of Socialist Experiment*. Berkeley and Los Angeles: University of California Press, 1969.

Vukmanović, Svetozar [Tempo]. *Borba za Balkan*. Zagreb: Globus, 1981. English ed. *Struggle for the Balkans*. London: Merlin, 1990.

Weigand, Gustav. *Ethnographie von Makedonien*. Leipzig: F. Brandstetter, 1924.

Wilkinson, H. R. *Maps and Politics: A Review of the Ethnographic Cartography of Macedonia*. Liverpool: University Press of Liverpool, 1951.

Winnfirth, Tom J. *The Vlachs: The History of a Balkan People*. New York: St. Martin's, 1987.

Wolf, Robert Lee. *The Balkans in Our Time*. Rev. ed. New York: W. W. Norton & Company, 1978.

Woodward, Susan L. *Balkan Tragedy: Chaos and Dissolution after the Cold War*. Washington, D.C.: Brookings Institution, 1995.

——— *Socialist Unemployment: The Political Economy of Yugoslavia, 1945–1990*. Princeton, N.J.: Princeton University Press, 1995.

Žaček, V., and V. Starčević, eds. *Dějiny Jugoslavie*. Prague: Svoboda, 1970.

Zdraveva, Milka. *Makedonija vo meǵunarodniot soobrak'aj i trgovija*. Skopje, 1986.

Zografski, Dančo. *Razvitokot na kapitalističkite elementi vo Makedonija vo vreme na turskoto vladeenje*. Skopje, 1967.

Zografski, Todor G., and Dimče A. Zografski. *KPJ i VMRO (obedineta) vo vardarska Makedonija vo periodot 1920–1930*. Skopje: Institut za nacionalna istorija, 1974.

Zotiades, George B. *The Macedonian Controversy*. Salonika: Institute for Balkan Studies, 1961.

Index